D0212685

FLORIDA STATE
UNIVERSITY LIBRARIES

JUL 24 2000

TALLAHASSEE, FLORIDA

The History of Crime and Criminal Justice Series

RETHINKING SOUTHERN VIOLENCE:

Homicides in Post–Civil War Louisiana, 1866–1884

Gilles Vandal

Ohio State University Press
Columbus

HV
6533
.L8
V35
2000

Copyright © 2000 by The Ohio State University.
All rights reserved.

Library of Congress Cataloging-in-Publication Data

Vandal, Gilles.
    Rethinking Southern violence : homicides in post–Civil War Louisiana,
1866–1884 / Gilles Vandal.
        p. cm. — (The history of crime and criminal justice series)
    Includes bibliographical references and index.
    ISBN 0-8142-0838-X (cloth : alk. paper).—ISBN 0-8142-5041-6 (pbk. :
alk. paper)
    1. Homicide—Louisiana—History—19th century.   2. Violence—
Louisiana—History—19th century.   3. Whites—Louisiana—Mortality.
4. Blacks—Louisiana—Mortality.   5. Louisiana—History—19th century.
6. Louisiana—Race relations.   7. Louisiana—Social conditions.   I. Title.
II. Series.

HV6533.L8 V35 2000
364.15′23′0976309034—dc21   99-054309

Text design by Nighthawk Design.
Type set in Sabon by Graphic Composition, Inc.
Printed by Thomson-Shore, Inc.

The paper used in this publication meets the minimum requirements of the
American National Standard for Information Sciences—Permanence of Paper
for Printed Library Materials. ANSI Z39.48–1992.

9 8 7 6 5 4 3 2 1

To my wife, Diane, and my two children, Roxane and Jérémie,
for their support and love

Contents

Acknowledgments

This study is the result of a continuing interest in Southern violence that began during my doctoral studies at the College of William and Mary, Virginia. I first became acquainted with the significance of post–Civil War violence in the South during a seminar with the late Professor Herbert Gutman. Following Professor Gutman's suggestion, my research on the New Orleans riot evolved into a dissertation under the direction of Professor Ludwell H. Johnson.

The New Orleans riot, following the Memphis riot, is most revealing about the post–Civil War white Southern psyche. It clearly demonstrates the unwillingness of most Southern whites in the years following the Confederate defeat to accept the political, economic, and social transformation brought about by emancipation. Even more the New Orleans riot unveils how most Southern whites remained defiant in their determination to maintain the South as a "white man's country." In the course of my investigation, I became keenly aware of the complexity of post–Civil War violence, both in Louisiana and in the South more generally. I then saw the need to push my inquiry further into Southern violent behavior with a systematic analysis of the various patterns it assumed in Louisiana during these troubled years.

From the outset the present work seeks to revisit Southern violence from a new analytical perspective. The main challenge of the present study, and perhaps its most important innovation, is that it relies on a delicate balance between the analysis of quantitative data and of information gleaned from various traditional sources. Using this approach it is possible to discern various patterns of violence and to verify how these patterns relate to contemporary perceptions.

I have accumulated debts to many people and institutions since undertaking the research for this book in the early 1980s, and it is impossible to mention all who helped. I wish first to acknowledge the generous financial support of the Fonds FCAR of the Quebec government and of the Social Sciences and Humanities Research Council of Canada without which the present study could never have been undertaken.

This systematic study on Louisiana violence between 1866 and 1884 required long, detailed, and tedious operations related not only to collecting cases but also to checking names through census reports and making sure that cases were not repeated before they were computerized. I am particularly grateful to several graduate students whose collaboration was important in collecting information on each case and preparing the data for processing. A special mention must be made of two students, Marc Dugas and Mario Lambert, who lent their skill as research assistants. The personnel of computer services at the Université de Sherbrooke have always been available for solving technical problems related to the preparation and processing of the data.

I want also to express my deepest gratitude to two of my English-speaking colleagues, Peter Gossage and Peter Southam, for their courteous efforts in reading and editing the manuscript. Their contribution went beyond seeing to matters of grammar and style—no small task considering that I am French-speaking—for they also furnished many insights.

Needless to say this work would have been impossible without the kind assistance and collaboration of the staffs of numerous libraries and archives in Louisiana and Washington, D.C. Particularly important were the Center for Louisiana Studies and the Louisiana Room of the Dupré Library at the University of Southwestern Louisiana, the Department of Archives and the Louisiana Room of the Troy H. Middleton Library at Louisiana State University, the Department of Archives at Tulane University Library, the Department of Archives at the New Orleans Municipal Library, and the National Archives and the Library of Congress.

Finally I want to thank the *Journal of Interdisciplinary History* for graciously permitting me to print a revised version of my article "Black Violence in Louisiana: A Forgotten Aspect of Post–Civil War History," 25, Summer 1994, 45–64. Although I have previously dealt with different aspects of Louisiana violence in several articles published in *Louisiana History* and in the *Journal of Social History*, the seven other chapters of this book consist essentially of new materials.

Introduction

Southern history and culture has long been associated with violence. Even before the Civil War, Southern society was infamous for its vigilance committees, frequent feuds, street fights, duels, and whisky brawls.[1] During the years immediately after the Civil War, violence in the South reached new heights, taking on racial and political overtones. Throughout the twentieth century, the South maintained a distinct character as the most violent area of the United States.[2] This cultural particularity has long puzzled historians, social scientists, and other observers of Southern society, and various interpretations have been developed to explain why violence was more prevalent in the South than in any other region of the country.

Southern Violence as a Cultural Phenomenon

Horace V. Redfield, a nineteenth-century journalist who specialized in covering homicide, was the first to undertake and publish a rigorous quantitative study on the particular propensity of Southern people to resort to lethal violence. His investigation of the causes and patterns of homicidal behavior in the United States led him to develop a comprehensive explanation of Southern violence. Redfield described the South as a frontier society where a high sense of honor, individualistic values, a habit of carrying concealed weapons, high liquor consumption, and an overall failure of the administration of justice were the ingredients that made violent behavior an integral part of day-to-day life. According to Redfield, these particular social conditions generated an acceptance of violence and explained a tendency to resort to violence and murder when solving personal disputes. In his view, the

1

Civil War did not constitute in itself an important cause of homicidal behavior, because the tradition of violence was already deeply rooted within Southern society before the war.[3]

In the same vein, Wilbur Cash showed in his master work *The Mind of the South,* published more than fifty years ago, that Southern violence was an integral part of a style of life that could be explained only culturally. For Cash as for Redfield, the conditions of the frontier lasted longer in the South than in other regions, and this left an important legacy that forged the Southern mentality and played a major role in making violence a distinct characteristic of Southern society.[4] Moreover, Cash added a new explanation in pointing out that Southern violence was also rooted in slavery. The need for plantation society to resort to violence to control slaves had a deep effect on racial relations, forging both the white and the black personality and establishing a paradox of mutual dependency, racial opposition, and black submission.[5]

Research over the last forty years has added new elements and put emphasis on particular aspects of the Southern tradition of violence. Some authors link the higher rates of homicide in the region to its particular socioeconomic structure. These authors tend to explain the South's higher levels of homicide and crime by the fact that the region was more rural and poorer or suffered greater from economic inequality than the rest of the nation.[6] Meanwhile other authors continue to emphasize the predominance of cultural factors. Higher crime rates for both races confirm, they argue, the cultural particularity of Southern society. In all these writings, the South is described as having developed a subculture of violence unique in the United States.[7]

The comparative studies of Sheldon Hackney (1969) and Raymond Gastill (1971) have given new impetus to the interpretation that the high levels of violence and homicide in the South are rooted in the region's cultural experience. Building on a comparative sociohistorical and cultural approach, these authors point out that variations in homicide rates among the regions of the United States are explained by differences in cultural heritage and subcultural traditions that reinforce or diminish human tendency toward violent behavior. In particular they reinforce the view that higher rates of homicide in the South are deeply rooted in a regional subculture of violence underlined by a frontier spirit, a lack of laws, a weakness of public institutions, and a particular code of honor.[8]

This framework is not without ambiguity. If the persistence of higher rates of personal violence appeared to be a characteristic of Southern society, the concept of a subculture of violence raises major methodological problems. The latter is explicitly based on a vision of culture whose norms and values are difficult to evaluate. It is therefore almost impossible to quantify the impact of such a culture on nineteenth-century homicide rates.[9] Nevertheless the effect of these studies has been to raise new issues and to develop an analytical framework that permits a better understanding of Southern violence. The pertinence of this historiographical tradition for social historians is well illustrated by the studies of Edward L. Ayers, Dickson D. Bruce Jr., David Grimsted, Samuel C. Hyde Jr., Grady McWhiney, and Bertram Wyatt-Brown.[10]

Violence in Post–Civil War Louisiana

The present study will focus on violence in the state of Louisiana during the post–Civil War period. In the wake of the breakup of the old plantation order, the emancipation and recognition of the civil and political rights of former slaves, and the economic disruption brought by the war, the South underwent a deep social and political upheaval. The social demoralization that affected the white community after the war, the conflicts over the rights and status of freedmen, the racial animosity raised by black political assertiveness, the new labor relations developing within a context of economic change, and the retreat of the Federal government from its earlier commitment to a policy of civil rights were factors that contributed to a rise in violence in the South. Not surprisingly this troubled period of Southern history has attracted much attention in recent historical literature, giving rise to a new comprehensive approach that seeks to show how both races struggled to adjust to the new economic, social, and political changes brought by the war.[11]

Historians of the Dunning school explain the high level of violence during this period by the fact that white people found it difficult to obtain a fair hearing before the courts since the latter had become dominated by white Republicans and blacks. This interpretation no longer stands.[12] Studies of post–Civil War violence published during the last forty years usually cover specific race riots or give a general overview of political violence and race relations in a particular state or for the entire South.[13] They also pay special attention to the social context of atrocities committed by informal and secret organizations such as the Ku Klux Klan, the Knights of the White Camelia, and other paramilitary bands.[14] In their search to explain the tensions and conflicts that characterized the period, historians since 1960 have paid particular attention to white violence against blacks, showing how this violence was frequent, mostly unprovoked, and arbitrary.[15] And yet in spite of the generally high quality of their work, most historians who have examined post–Civil War violence present a limited analysis. Their investigations have rarely brought them to conduct a thorough examination of individual cases, to place these within their social and political context, or to explain why levels of violence were high in some areas or among certain groups and not in other areas or among other groups.

Studying violence, and more particularly homicide, in post–Civil War Louisiana is of particular interest because of special conditions pertaining to the Pelican State during this period. Louisiana was at the center of Federal Reconstruction policy from the time of the New Orleans riot of 1866, which played a major role in bringing to the South the so-called Radical Reconstruction. After the war the state continued to receive special attention under President Ulysses S. Grant's administration. James F. Casey, the brother-in-law of President Grant's wife, played a major role in Louisiana politics from the time he was appointed collector of the customs of the port of New Orleans. New Orleans was also the command center of the Gulf Department after the Civil War. Furthermore, Reconstruction lasted the longest in Louisiana, which was also the center of the controversial election of 1876 when the contested vote put President Rutherford Hayes into the White House.[16] On another level, Louisiana suffered more than any other Southern state from the effects of the Civil War described above. These circumstances may explain why Louisiana emerged after the war as the most violent Southern state, with the sole exception of Texas.[17]

Louisiana was also the only Southern state, with the exception of South Carolina, where blacks formed a clear majority of the eligible voters after the war. Blacks became, by their sheer numbers, the masters of the political situation. This was particularly true in rural areas where blacks comprised 60 percent of the population. By forming a solid bloc of voters for the Republican party, blacks left white conservatives with no hope of carrying the state elections without controlling black voters.[18] Louisiana also had several cultural, economic, and religious characteristics that gave the state a distinct character. For all these reasons, Louisiana represents an ideal case for the study of the motivations of violence in the post–Civil War South.

As pointed out earlier, most of the studies of post–Civil War violence treat the South as a whole and draw general conclusions, ignoring the fact that violence varies from one state to another and even among regions within a single state. There are several advantages in undertaking a detailed study of one state. First, the social, political, and historical factors that influence violence and affect the homicide rates are generally similar for the different social groups within a particular state. Second, blacks and whites living within the same state are subject to the same legislation; they are confronted by the same judicial apparatus and by the same tradition of law enforcement. Third, the data can be drawn from the same set of sources, thereby avoiding the discrepancy that might arise from different approaches to recording homicides. Finally, by covering various regions of the state, it is possible to compare the influence of various factors such as population density, concentration of blacks, difference in crop production, and rural versus urban characteristics, to the regional distribution and intensity of homicide during these years.

The Methodological Approach

A thorough examination of the patterns of violence and the various factors underlying that violence is important if we are to reach a better understanding of social changes affecting Louisiana during the troubled post–Civil War era. However, such a study is not without difficulty. How is one to be sure that the results obtained in analyzing the various factors underlying violence and criminality will not be determined by the way violence and criminality are defined or by the way the data is collected? The obvious danger is that the main conclusions of a study will simply reflect the premises. This question is fundamental since too often crime rates, and more particularly rates of personal violence, do not necessarily reflect a real increase in the number of incidents or the emergence of new patterns of criminal activity, but can be simply the result of the development of new methods of collecting information, apprehending criminals, or defining criminal behavior.[19] As such, crime rates often fluctuate with change of public policies as the police authorities respond either to demands for greater tolerance or for more law and order.[20] Consequently it has often been stated that the general problem of underreporting makes it difficult to go beyond a very impressionistic portrayal of most forms of violence and criminality.[21]

Not surprisingly, social historians have traditionally been very cautious in studying criminality and violence because of their distrust of criminal statistics. Those who have attempted to investigate the subject noted the unreliable character of official data, particularly regarding petty crimes, which went largely underreported. Such data provide only limited and sketchy results and do not indicate the real degree of crime and violence. Yet, it is widely acknowledged that students of criminality and violence are on safer ground when dealing with homicide. Although homicide is but one among a variety of forms of violence and cannot consequently be a synonym for violence, this particular type of crime is not only the most serious but it is also the most immune to the problem of definition or changes in the level of tolerance as reflected in the public control of crime.[22]

Therefore an analysis centered on homicide rates gives a more reliable measure of the extent of violence. Murders, homicides, manslaughters, and all other forms of violent death have always represented the highest expression of violence and attracted the greatest attention. This explains why homicides are widely reported. Homicide rates also represent a generally accurate indication of the actual number of offenses, since there is always a body to account for.[23] Consequently homicide is the kind of crime that is the most likely to be discovered, prosecuted, or at least recorded. Homicide is a good indicator of the actual level of violence and can furnish an index for the analysis of how violence reflected social change and the influence of social transformation on homicidal behavior.[24] It follows that homicide records and accounts of killings are important sources for social history.[25]

It remains that, for political or other reasons, too many cases of homicide in post–Civil War Louisiana were simply dismissed. Judicial authorities often did not record the killing of blacks and often failed to prosecute whites for such crimes. Therefore indictment records, when they have survived, do not represent a reliable source for building a comprehensive picture of homicidal behavior. For example, indictment figures for antebellum South Carolina were inferior to 50 percent of the homicide activity.[26]

The limits of indictment records could have been supplemented by health officer or coroner reports, but both these types of records were not completed and could not be relied on—as was the case in the Northern states—for several reasons: Louisiana had no health official outside of New Orleans before the 1880s; coroners were not required to have medical training until the adoption of the 1879 constitution came into effect; coroner juries had the liberty to decide whether there was a good cause for the killing and that therefore no trial was needed; in many instances when a man was to shot death, no physician was called to the scene and, as a result, no official record was made.[27] The limited nature of the information contained in official data explains why in a parish such as Caddo, there were more than 500 people killed between 1868 and 1875, but only 46 charges of homicide either as murder or manslaughter were brought to court.[28] Therefore a study on homicides based on data collected by public officials would contain loopholes and would probably be less reliable than other criminal studies based on official statistics. Police records or judicial archives are even less useful for establishing a general overview of the level of violence for the state of Louisiana, since these sources are often missing for certain regions for a period of several years.[29]

In summary, official homicide statistics represent only a general and fragile indication of what is happening. As they largely depend on the way data are collected by local officials, a great many cases remain unreported. Consequently official homicide rates give only an aggregate view of homicidal behavior and generally represent a rather poor tool to analyze the general patterns of personal violence in a particular society.[30]

New trends in social science show a shift from the analysis of the characteristics of violence and crime within the same group of offenders to an analysis of the different criminal behavior of various groups charged with the same offense. Such analysis requires the use of charts for each category in order to establish the various criminal tendencies and to indicate the different patterns of victim-offender relations between groups. Clearly, official data too often does not allow one to make such cross-relations.[31]

Finally, official statistics on homicide do not say anything about changes in the basic characteristics of homicide during a given period. While we can assume that homicide rates are an indication of social changes, by relying solely on such rates there is a danger of losing sight of the social characteristics that lie behind these rates or burying the particular dynamic of homicidal behavior under demographic analysis or simple statistical correlation.[32]

One must not forget that homicide rates in themselves do not say anything about the factors that cause homicide or are at the root of homicidal behavior. Homicide statistics take on meaning only when it is possible to put homicidal patterns in relation to one with the other. Consequently any study on homicide needs to develop a methodological approach that integrates both an analysis based on homicide rates and an examination of the various characteristics that underlie the homicides in question.[33] Any analysis of violence needs to include not only an analysis of collective data, but also a study of individual cases. The latter makes it possible to develop a collective biography of both victims and perpetrators of homicide. It is therefore necessary and even essential to link homicide rates to individual data since both series are complementary.[34]

As official data are often unreliable and do not reflect the true level of homicide, it is first necessary to develop a more exact measure of the real number of offenses. Second, in order to get a full understanding of homicidal patterns, it is necessary to analyze the basic characteristics of each individual case—to base the study as closely as possible on the individuals involved. Only then is it possible to deal with homicidal behavior not simply as collective data but as the basis for studying thoroughly the various factors underlying violence among various groups or regions within a particular state.[35]

Since homicide is fundamentally a relationship—albeit a violent one—between two or more individuals, homicidal behavior can say much about the dynamics of social relationships in a particular society. But if it is to do so we must have a knowledge of the persons involved. Consequently collecting information on each and every incident becomes paramount for the establishment of the various personal patterns of homicidal behavior. A detailed examination of homicide gives an overview of the social tensions within a particular society and makes it possible to evaluate more exactly the nature of violence in that society. Although many homicides are not premeditated acts, and are instead the result of sudden angry impulse, socially significant patterns nevertheless emerge.

It is possible to avoid the weaknesses of official data by identifying individual cases of homicide and collecting data from alternative sources. It is nevertheless important to proceed with caution in establishing a repertoire of individual cases of homicide in nineteenth-century Louisiana or any other society.[36] Homicide is arbitrary as a category, since it depends on whether or not the victim of an assault died. Any investigation of it is further influenced by the way contemporaries or students of criminality define it, and by the biases, limitations, and omissions of the sources that report it.[37]

In the present study, the term "homicide" is used in its broadest possible sense as applied in nineteenth-century Louisiana.[38] It includes not only homicide cases brought before the courts, but also murders committed by terrorist groups reported to investigating committees and all violent deaths reported by local newspapers. Therefore our definition of homicide is similar to the one of Professors Martin Daly and Margo Wilson who include all cases of "interpersonal assaults and other acts directed against another person that occur outside the context of warfare, and that prove fatal."[39] Moreover, in our definition of homicide a "case" must equal one body. And yet, the creation of a reliable index that approaches as closely as possible the real number of offenses depends largely on the reliability of available sources.

The Sources

The diversity, quantity, and quality of available sources make a study of homicidal behavior in post–Civil War Louisiana not only possible but also easier than in most other Southern states. Indeed, violence was more regularly reported and better documented in Louisiana than in any other Southern state. The National Archives in Washington contain the general correspondence and documents of both the Gulf Department and the Freedmen's Bureau as well as four miscellaneous reports on the subject of murders and outrages occurring in Louisiana after the war.[40] Violence was also investigated by joint committees of the Louisiana State Assembly.[41] The annual reports of the State Attorney General[42] and the annual State Penitentiary Reports[43] are two other major sources for the investigation of individual cases of homicide.

The congressional reports and executive documents of the post–Civil War period constitute the most far-reaching and best sources of information. Never before or since has violence in a state attracted such national attention. No less than ten congressional committees made the journey to Louisiana to investigate the conditions in the state. The congressional committees made extensive reports on the various riots that struck the Pelican State in 1866 (New Orleans riot), in 1868 (the New Orleans, Caddo, Bossier, St. Bernard, and St. Landry riots), in 1873 (Colfax riot), in 1874 (Coushatta affair and the White League uprising), in 1876 (Mount Pleasant riot and troubles in East Baton Rouge, and in the two Felicianas), in 1878 (troubles in the parishes of Tensas, Natchitoches, St. Mary, and Pointe Coupée, and the Caledonia riot in Caddo parish), and finally the causes of the Great Exodus of 1879. Each of these committees compiled in its reports hundreds and sometimes thousands of pages of testimony. Furthermore, both houses of Congress received no less than eight major executive documents during this period from the federal administration concerning the state of affairs in Louisiana. The House Executive Document no. 30 of 1875 was particularly important as it furnished 150 pages of tables and lists of victims of homicide and violence.[44]

The above mentioned sources have been complemented by a thorough examination of the numerous New Orleans and parish newspapers published in Louisiana between 1865 and 1884. If congressional reports and executive documents mainly dealt with major incidents of violence, Louisiana newspapers regularly reported the violent incidents occurring locally. Consequently newspapers, particularly the countryside newspapers, represented an essential source of information on isolated cases of homicide.[45]

More than a century ago Redfield noted that in the absence of reliable official sources on the number of homicides in the South, newspapers constituted the most promising source for a systematic and detailed database on the subject.[46] Indeed, nineteenth-century newspapers contain information of inestimable value for the understanding of the mental world of that period. Use of this material, however, as the use of any historical source, raises a number of problems of interpretation. First of all, it is possible to object that newspapers give a deformed picture of crime since they reflect the prejudices of the period and offer essentially qualitative information. Second, newspapers have a tendency to report only the most sensational cases of homicide. Moreover, the understanding of violence and brutal murders in any society cannot be based simply on journalistic taste for the most sensational murders. Therefore, they cannot say much about the risk for any person to die from violence and even less about the rate of violent death in any particular society.[47]

Used with caution, newspapers can nevertheless furnish important information on the circumstances surrounding homicide and can substantially increase our knowledge and comprehension of contemporary attitudes toward homicide. Therefore newspapers represent an excellent source for completing this study's data set, for analyzing the different aspects of homicidal behavior, and for furnishing valuable information on nineteenth-century Louisianian attitudes toward both violence and offenders.[48] As well as qualitative description, newspapers are a source of information on origins of specific cases of homicide not otherwise available.

Only by confronting collected data on homicide with detailed examples reported by newspapers and other sources is it possible to reach a clear understanding of contemporary attitudes, the underlying causes, and the nature and the real level of violence.

The Nature and Limits of the Data

Studying homicide in post–Civil War Louisiana remains nevertheless a difficult and hazardous task. Many murders committed after the war were not recorded by military authorities, and for their part civil officials frequently made no special record of cases where a black man was killed. Nor was an effort made to solve such crimes, particularly if the murderer was a white man. Too often the men who committed such atrocities successfully concealed their identity. The assault was often made in the absence of witnesses, and when the body of a black man was found and the evidence of his murder conclusive, the doer of the deed generally disappeared. Local newspapers and the congressional reports contained countless notices such as: "Last Saturday night a colored man named Bryant Offort, who lived on Samuel McLean's plantation in this parish was taken from his home by some unknown persons and killed in the most brutal and atrocious manner." In 1874 the number of people killed in Caddo parish by unknown parties became so alarming that the parish coroner, afraid for his life, preferred to resign rather than carry out his duties. The coroner of West Feliciana parish reported in 1876 that twenty-one murders had been committed in the previous twelve months, six of which were cold-blooded assassinations by unknown parties.[49]

A data set of this nature obviously contains many flaws, biases, limitations, and omissions and as a result can only be used with caution. The information is limited by the fact that it often relies on distorted information: articles in Democratic-oriented or Republican-inspired newspapers based on hearsay; contradictory testimonies by sworn witnesses of varied political allegiances contained in Congressional reports, documents, and general correspondence of the Gulf Department or the Freedmen's Bureau. Moreover the data for the years 1879 to 1884 are essentially based on a single source: reports of local newspapers. One may argue here that this study's data set suffers from a major flaw as it relies only on newspaper accounts and that the decrease of the number of blacks killed by whites could be largely explained by the absence of federal investigation. Nevertheless it may also be argued more correctly that if there were no such inquiry, it was because the years 1879 to 1884 did not suffer from any major riot, as did the years of 1866 to 1878. If Congressional reports and executive documents mainly dealt with major incidents of violence, Louisiana newspapers regularly reported the violent incidents occurring locally. Consequently, newspapers, particularly in the countryside, represented an essential source of information on isolated cases of homicide.

Fundamental questions arise regarding the reliability of such a data set. For instance how can we be sure that many cases do not remain unreported while others may be counted twice? Nevertheless, the sources available, in spite of their biases and limitations, are sufficiently numerous and varied to allow the creation of a reliable index of homicides.

Information for this study has been collected on each and every reported violent act that ended in a death, with the exception of accidents, suicides, and infanticides.[50] In order to avoid duplication or repetition of cases, only cases for which clear information on the name of the victim or the murderer, as well as the date and place where the homicide was committed, were included in the data set. Although a military investigation and several congressional reports ascertained that at least 68 blacks died during the St. Bernard riot of 1868, the names of only 23 blacks who died in the riot were reported, and therefore, only 23 names were entered in the data set. The same approach was used in entering data on each violent incident that ended with one or several deaths. It is important to remember that the actual level of homicide in Louisiana was considerably higher than the number of incidents contained in the data set.

Although data drawn from the above mentioned sources is influenced by contemporary prejudices and contemporary ways of defining criminal behavior, it nevertheless allows us to establish patterns of deadly violence. While it is possible that some homicides may have never been reported or may have been wrongly classified in official reports, it is impossible to envisage a systematic error over a long period in the compilation of the data. Therefore variations in the distribution of homicide over the years and on a geographical basis among the regions of Louisiana can not be attributed simply to error. In other words, the data accurately reflect the patterns of homicidal behavior that this investigation wishes to analyze.

It has been possible, by cross-checking each individual case in a variety of sources, to diminish the deficiencies of the lists of cases and to establish a relatively accurate data set that provides comprehensive information on the frequency of homicides in Louisiana after the Civil War.[51] Data was compiled on 4,986 homicides that occurred in Louisiana between 1866 and 1884. The numbers appear rather high with an annual average of 262 and an annual rate of 32 per 100,000 inhabitants. And yet these numbers are supported by many contemporary sources.

Redfield, in his study of homicides in the United States, found similar numbers for Louisiana for the years 1868 to 1878. By conducting a thorough investigation through local newspapers of fourteen parishes and then extrapolating for the rest of Louisiana, he reached an annual average of 203 homicides, which translates to an annual rate of 28 per 100,000 inhabitants. From his investigation, he concluded that at least 3,000 homicides had been committed in Louisiana between 1868 and 1878.[52] General Philip H. Sheridan, for many years commander of the Gulf Department and the Fifth Military District (which included Louisiana), provided similar numbers. In January 1875 he telegraphed Secretary of War W. W. Belknap that "since the year 1866, nearly thirty-five hundred persons, a great majority of whom were colored, have been killed in this state."[53] The census office reported that 178 homicides were committed in Louisiana in 1880, compared to the 167 found that same year in the present data.[54]

The data for this study is supported not only by contemporary testimonies but by the generally accepted view that the South and Louisiana, in particular, were a particularly violent region during the years following the Civil War. It confirms that Louisiana had a homicide rate that went beyond the common standard for the period.[55]

The Scope of the Study

The database serving as the basis for the present study represents a rich source of information dealing with the victims and the perpetrators of homicide as well as on the place, date, and circumstances surrounding such incidents. One may confidently argue that the database is sufficiently large to provide for a systematic analysis of the patterns of violence during this particularly troubled period of Louisiana's history. The data establishes the general patterns of homicide in space and time, the differences in the homicidal behavior of various social and racial groups, and the reasons that motivated these violent acts.

Furthermore, by extending the years covered in the study from 1866 to 1884, it is possible to analyze how the patterns of homicidal behavior changed with the end of Reconstruction. This allows us to understand how various groups adjusted not only to the immediate post–Civil War period but also to the new political and social context of the early Redemption years.[56] In doing this, the study covers two distinct periods, the years of Reconstruction from 1866 to 1876 and the early Redemption period from 1877 to 1884.

This book will attempt to answer a series of questions: What were the patterns of violence and their geographical distribution? Did these patterns vary between New Orleans and the rural areas? What was the social and political context within which collective violence tended to occur? How much violence was political and directed against blacks? Did the emergence of lynching reflect white inability to adjust to social and political changes? How much violence originated from blacks and what was the blacks' response to white violence?

My analysis attempts to go beyond the general interpretation according to which Southern violence was rooted in a particular cultural tradition even though it does not deny this basic premise. Raising new questions and examining the issues from various perspectives reveals patterns of violence that have remained hidden until now. In the process the present study will demonstrate that Southern politics and violence were more complex phenomena than hitherto thought.

PART I

Homicides in a Geographic Perspective

1

Rural versus Urban Patterns of Homicides

In New Orleans on April 12, 1874, Edward L. Coleman and Charles Behrens, both of whom were under the influence of alcohol, engaged in a dispute about a billiard game and came to blows. Behrens drew a knife and attempted to stab Coleman, but he was prevented by onlookers. The dispute seemed to have come to an end without any bloodletting. A few hours later, however, when Behrens met Coleman on the street, the latter drew a handgun and fired three shots. As Behrens fell down mortally wounded, Coleman rushed to his victim and fired a fourth shot. Then putting his gun to the head of his former friend, Coleman fired a fifth and a sixth shot. A police officer, attracted by the sound of the gunshots, arrived on the scene and arrested Coleman. However colorful it may appear, this case was not unusual; a similar murder occurred in New Orleans the very same night.[1] Although the above case occurred in an urban context, local newspapers frequently reported cases of the same sort in rural areas.

American historians have rarely examined differences in patterns of crime between urban and rural areas. This gap in the literature is particularly surprising in light of recent historical research in other parts of the world, most notably in Europe. Scholars there have increasingly focused on the way differing patterns of social disorganization and social demoralization in both rural and urban areas create specific patterns of criminal behavior.[2] The dichotomy between rural and urban behavior was not new in America,[3] but it reached a climax in the South during the second half of the nineteenth century, taking on new significance in light of the radical changes that occurred in that region during and after the Civil War.

Urban and Rural Settings

Of all Southern states Louisiana provides the most promising setting for a case study of violence—and more particularly homicide—from an urban-rural perspective. Not only does the Pelican State include New Orleans, the largest city of the South, but the remaining parts of Louisiana, which during the period 1866–84 contained roughly three quarters of the state's population, can be considered essentially rural.

With a population of 168,000 inhabitants in 1860, New Orleans ranked sixth in size among American urban centers. Prior to the Civil War, successive waves of old American, Irish, and German immigrants had been added to the early Creole community, giving New Orleans a cosmopolitan character unique in the South. In the years following the Civil War, the flow of European immigration ceased, and the Crescent City suffered an economic stagnation. By 1880, when its population stood at 216,000, New Orleans had fallen to the fourteenth rank among American cities.[4] Its growth in population during this period was essentially attributed to two factors: consolidation of the city with its suburban areas and an increase in black population.

Before the war, New Orleans already possessed one of the largest urban black populations in the Union. With the Civil War and emancipation, freedmen in their hundreds abandoned the countryside and flocked to the Crescent City in search of work. Within only ten years the influx of freedmen more than doubled the city's black population, increasing it from 24,500 in 1860 to 50,450 in 1870.[5] During this period the proportion of blacks in the city's population rose from 15 to 26 percent.

Economic factors explain the slowing of the city's growth and the changing composition of its population. In 1860, New Orleans was known as the second largest commercial center of the United States and the most important cotton market in the world. The Crescent City's prosperity at this time did not rest solely on its status as a commercial entrepôt. It was also a major center of industrial production for the southern United States.[6] However, the economic situation of New Orleans changed radically during the Civil War and Reconstruction.

The years immediately following the Civil War were a trying time for the New Orleans economy. In fact the most significant economic trend affecting New Orleans in the aftermath of the Civil War was the advent of large-scale unemployment. Even in periods of relative prosperity, unemployment had been a problem in the Crescent City. Cyclical unemployment linked to the fluctuation in the demand for labor was particularly apparent in New Orleans as the business and trading season lasted only four months.[7] This endemic problem reached new heights after the war, as the city was struck by a crippling economic depression. During this period, the press regularly reported instances of distress. Gatherings of the hungry unemployed, publicly clamoring for work, became an almost daily occurrence. Starving, poverty-stricken men loitered in town squares during the day and slept on street benches at night.[8]

During this time the Louisiana countryside underwent an even deeper economic and social transformation. The social fabric of rural Louisiana differed greatly from that of New Orleans. While blacks formed more than 60 percent of the rural population as a whole, they were unevenly distributed among the various rural areas. The black population was mainly concentrated in the parishes situated along the main waterways, where the large cotton and sugar plantations were found. While they formed 60 to 90 percent of the population in these particular parishes, they represented only 20 percent in the western parts of the state. Thus the freeing of the blacks after the war had a particularly strong effect in the parts of the state whose economy depended on the plantation system.

The plantation system only survived in Louisiana because of major changes in farming methods and the credit system. Partly ruined by the war and threatened with foreclosure and bankruptcy during Reconstruction, planters were forced to bow to pressures from freedmen for better wages and also depend on local merchants for credit instead of brokers as they had in the past.[9]

The war and emancipation did not only force radical changes in methods of farming, traditional trading arrangements were also transformed. During the early years of Reconstruction, planters at first attempted to continue providing their freedmen with rations, clothing, and other necessary goods. But lack of credit and high interest rates made the operation of a plantation store a greater risk than most small planters were able or willing to undertake.[10] As a consequence the rural stores, which had maintained a precarious existence at the periphery of the plantation world before the war, were suddenly propelled into the center of the new farming system.[11]

As merchants began to give credit to cotton farmers and field hands for the purchase of household and farm supplies on a yearly basis with

Table 1.1
Cities, Towns, and Villages in Louisiana

Population	1860	1870	1880
Less than 100	0	2	25
100 to 199	2	9	29
200 to 499	11	15	36
500 to 999	6	16	19
1,000 to 1,999	10	12	12
2,000 or more	7	5	10
Total	36	59	131

Sources: Federal Census Reports of 1860, 1870, and 1880.

settlement due at harvesttime, merchants and store owners replaced planters as the principal villains of the period in the minds of the black population. Many blacks blamed local merchants and store owners for their troubles. These allegations were not without foundation: in 1878 U.S. District Attorney Albert H. Leonard charged white conservatives of northern Louisiana with systematically cheating blacks by demanding exorbitant prices for goods. For example, store owners often sold bacon at a price of 20 to 25 cents per pound when they had paid only 13 cents or less.[12]

The consequences of the emergence of local merchants and store owners were not limited to the economic sphere. The local stores, which appeared at almost every crossroads, achieved considerable importance as places of social interaction. They served as post offices, news emporiums, everyday meeting places for the community, and places where men gathered to play checkers, swap yarns, and discuss politics.[13] In the process the isolated country stores gave birth to villages and small towns (table 1.1), as social and economic activities consolidated around them.[14]

While commerce and industry were the main activities in towns and villages, these centers also spawned public service institutions: academies for boys, convents for girls, and churches of various denominations. Most towns and many villages had a newspaper transmitting information to the surrounding countryside.[15] Towns served as the main places of amusement for adjacent rural areas with their taverns, billiard parlors, ballrooms, and racetracks. Towns attracted large crowds from the surrounding countryside, particularly on weekends and holidays. As people from the countryside flocked into towns on Saturday night, they often drank to excess and got involved in personal quarrels.[16]

Southern towns were notorious during the post–Civil War period for disturbances. Besides being places where the rural population congregated for trading, drinking, and socializing, towns also lacked policing, and as a consequence fights and streets brawls were frequent. The main reason for disturbances, though, was their emergence as places for political activity. The most significant riots taking places in small towns and villages were political: Opelousas in 1868, Baton Rouge and Donaldsonville in 1870, Colfax in 1873, Caledonia in 1878, and Loreauville in 1884.

To understand differences of levels of violence and homicide in New Orleans compared to the rural areas during Reconstruction, it is necessary to take into account differences in economic organization, social structure, the relative size of the black populations as well as immigrant populations, police organization, and the presence of Federal troops. It is important to compare New Orleans with the rest of Louisiana and to see how homicidal behavior in rural areas differed from that in New Orleans.

The Nature of Homicide

Data was compiled on 4,986 homicides that occurred in Louisiana between 1865 and 1884, 771 of which were committed in New Orleans and 4,215 in rural areas (fig. 1.1). This record presents a vivid picture of the level of physical violence that occurred in Louisiana after the Civil War. The cumulative evidence is overwhelming. New Orleans had an annual homicide rate of 23 persons per 100,000 during Reconstruction and 16.5 during the early Redemption era. With such homicide rates, the Crescent City maintained the reputation for violent crime that it had earned before the war. Police reports and statistics on police arrests, which were regularly published in New Orleans newspapers, show that after the war the city maintained an average of four homicides per month.[17]

One must not lose sight of the fact that New Orleans had been a "paradise" for murderers during the 1850s. Then, the city had an average of five homicides per month. Information was filed on 95

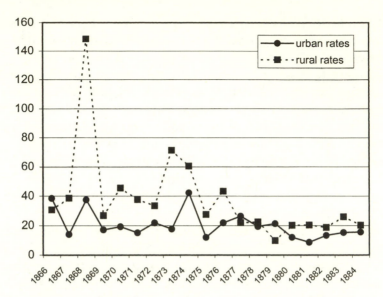

Figure 1.1 Annual Homicide Rate per 100,000 Inhabitants

murders, 15 manslaughters, and 97 attempted murders between December 1853 and November 1854. Thirty-three murders were committed in New Orleans between May 1 and October 31, 1855, but the peak was reached in November 1859 with 13 homicides.[18] At that time anti-Irish and Know-Nothing riots had given New Orleans the unenviable reputation of being the most violent city in the Union. In May 1860, for example, the mayor of Cincinnati reported that during the preceding year, only 16 murders were committed in his city; by 1860, New Orleans had a homicide rate three times higher than Cincinnati.[19]

In spite of the high levels of violence and the numerous riots that troubled New Orleans during Reconstruction, the Crescent City's criminal record showed a marked, long-term decline after the Civil War, eventually falling below that of many Northern cities. New Orleans had different homicide patterns than most Northern cities. Cities such as Boston, Buffalo, Cincinnati, and Chicago underwent a rapid increase of crime after the war. For example, 92 murders and cases of manslaughter were committed in 1883 in Cincinnati. This gave that city an annual rate for that year of 34 per 100,000 persons compared to 16.5 in post–Reconstruction New Orleans.[20] By the 1890s, New Orleans homicide rates had decreased to an annual level of less than 10. While New Orleans had a population of less than

300,000 people during the 1890s, the superintendent of the city police reported that 22 murders were committed in the city in 1892, 34 in 1894, 35 in 1895, 37 in 1896, and 25 in 1897.[21]

Meanwhile in Louisiana's rural areas, the changes in the homicide rates were even more dramatic. During the 1850s the country parishes were considered to be rather "peaceful places."[22] It was quite another story after the war. With an annual rate of 51 homicides per 100,000 persons during Reconstruction, rural Louisiana became one of the most violent regions of the South. The data show nevertheless that the end of Reconstruction brought an important decline in the homicide rates here also. With annual levels below 20, the rural parishes displayed similar rates after 1876 to those found in New Orleans.

The distribution of homicides over time suggests that in both rural and urban Louisiana political violence contributed in an important way to the variation in homicide rates. The years 1866, 1868, and 1874, which were marked by important political riots and upheavals in both New Orleans and the country parishes, all had above-average levels of homicide. Further confirmation is provided by the example of the year 1879, which had the lowest number of homicides. During that year white authorities and newspapers repeatedly called on whites to show self-restraint in order to limit the migration of blacks to Kansas on the one hand and on the other hand to insure support for the adoption of the new state constitution.[23]

Significantly, blacks were victims of 68 percent of all homicides that occurred in Louisiana between 1866 and 1884, while whites were the presumed perpetrators of 74 percent of all homicides, with 82 percent when the victims were whites and 72 percent when the victims were blacks (table 1.2). When these numbers are put in a rural-urban perspective, they do not yield the same result at all.

The social dislocation brought about by the war and the political tension generated by emancipation of the slaves is clearly reflected in the homicide patterns in the rural parishes. Although whites composed less than 40 percent of the rural population, they committed more than 80 percent of all attributed homicides during Reconstruction and 46 percent in the early Redemption era. Clearly black lives were not secure in the rural parishes after the war. Blacks represented 71 percent of the homicide victims for the years 1866 to 1876 and 61 percent for the years 1877 to 1884. However, the percentage of blacks killed by whites dropped from 81 percent to 38 percent between the periods 1866–1876 and 1877–1884, while the percentage of whites

Table 1.2
Racial Distribution of Homicides, 1866–1884

	1866–1876				1877–1884			
	Urban	%	Rural	%	Urban	%	Rural	%
Unknown by unknown	74	15.3	280	9	64	22.4	318	28.5
Unknown by whites	48	9.9	138	4.5	22	7.7	62	5.5
Unknown by blacks	16	3.3	71	2.3	12	4.1	44	3.9
Blacks by unknown	9	1.8	265	8.6	14	4.9	54	4.8
Whites by unknown	46	9.7	133	4.3	19	6.6	38	3.4
Whites by blacks	18	3.7	99	3.2	9	3.1	52	4.6
Whites by whites	160	32.9	394	12.7	71	24.8	178	16.0
Blacks by whites	86	17.7	1,393	45	14	4.9	139	12.4
Blacks by blacks	28	5.7	326	10.5	61	21.3	231	20.7
Total	485	100.0	3,099	100.0	286	100.0	1,116	99.6

killed by whites remained almost the same, declining slightly from 80 to 77 percent. The political and racial tension that characterized the Reconstruction period is further demonstrated by an annual ratio of 81 white homicides that dramatically declined to 17 during the early Redemption period. At the same time, the black annual ratio declined from 14 to 9 homicides per 100,000 persons.[24]

The data also reveal that New Orleans did not suffer as much as the country parishes from racial tension. Although the New Orleans black population doubled immediately after the war, its percentage remained constant at 26 percent of the city's population. As a consequence blacks never posed the same political threat that they did in the rural parishes where they represented 60 percent of the population. Blacks were victims of only 29 percent of the New Orleans homicides and committed during Reconstruction only 17 percent of urban murders. The end of Reconstruction shows a dramatic change, however, since 47 percent of the victims and 42 percent of the perpetrators of murders in New Orleans were blacks during this later period. By the early 1880s the New Orleans black population had clearly become more violent than the city's white population.

Homicide statistics are particularly revealing about the nature of race relationships in both urban and rural areas. When fatal disputes occurred between whites and blacks, blacks were the most frequent victims. This was particularly true in rural parishes during Reconstruction, where for each white killed by a black there were at least fourteen blacks killed by whites. In New Orleans the latter ratio was three to one. It therefore appears that the danger of aggression on the

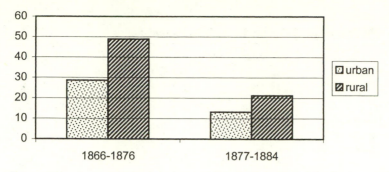

Figure 1.2   Collective Homicides in Rural and Urban Louisiana (percentages)

part of blacks either in New Orleans or in the country parishes was minimal. Whenever a black struck a white, such action seems to have been a desperate act committed as a last resort. In the relatively rare cases when such an act occurred it was invariably reported by the press in full detail.[25]

The instances of collective homicides differed from urban to rural areas (fig. 1.2). New Orleans, which possessed a large police force and served as the regional headquarters of the Federal army, was a much less auspicious setting for collective violence than the rural areas of Louisiana where state law enforcement officers were generally absent.

Forty-one percent of the killings in rural areas involved more than one perpetrator, compared to less than 20 percent in New Orleans. Moreover, the data reveal that collective violence was particularly frequent in rural areas during the Reconstruction period and that it was directed mostly against blacks. Indeed most of the murders of whites by whites (87%), blacks by blacks (83%), and whites by blacks (62%) were committed by a single individual, while the killing of blacks by whites usually involved at least two perpetrators (71%). This adds further backing to this study's contention that whites killed blacks not simply through personal quarrels between individuals but as members of a group and as a means of social control. As we shall see further on, the data also reveal an absence of justice for Louisiana blacks on the one hand and on the other hand reveal the racial tensions and the failure of the white community to adjust to a new reality. With the end of Reconstruction, homicides in rural areas tended to revert to the previously more common one-to-one confrontation.[26]

No less significant is the fact that 31 people (5%) in New Orleans

Table 1.3
Number of Times People Committed Homicide

	1866–1876				1877–1884			
	Urban	%	Rural	%	Urban	%	Rural	%
At least one	386	94.8	1,258	78.4	277	96.5	808	94.5
Two	18	4.4	217	13.5	9	3.1	40	4.7
Three to five	3	0.7	93	5.8	1	0.3	6	0.7
Six to ten			29	1.8			1	0.1
More than ten			6	0.3				
Total	407	99.9	1,603	99.8	287	99.9	855	100.0

and 402 (19%) in rural areas were involved as perpetrators of more than one homicide (table 1.3). The numbers were particularly high for whites in the countryside during Reconstruction.[27] Indeed the data show that white violence against blacks in the country parishes was well organized. By the mid-1870s, it had increasingly become the specialty of paramilitary organizations under the tighter control of their leaders.[28]

Data also indicate, both with regard to New Orleans and to the country parishes, that younger members of the population had a greater propensity to commit homicides than did their elders.[29] This is particularly true for young blacks who seemed less afraid then their white contemporaries to resort to violence in order to solve disputes. Fifty-five percent of blacks who committed homicides in rural areas and 52 percent of those who did so in New Orleans were less than 30 years old, compared to 38 percent and 35 percent of the same age group for whites. The greater tendency of whites in their thirties in both New Orleans (35%) and rural parishes (26%) to be involved, compared to only 10 percent and 20 percent respectively for blacks, is an indication of the impact of the war on young whites who had fought for the Confederacy and who had thus become accustomed to violence.

There were also important differences between the urban and rural worlds with regard to the social status of persons involved in homicide. We found information on the occupations[30] of 327 people who committed homicide in New Orleans and 1,231 in the rural parishes. Most people in New Orleans who committed homicides came from the lower social strata of the community (60%), while data in the rural parishes show that people who committed homicides were spread more evenly throughout the different levels of society (fig. 1.3).

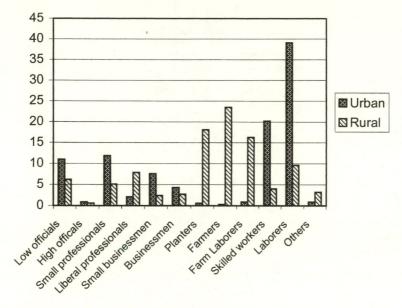

Figure 1.3 Occupation of People Involved in Homicides (percentages)

In fact the involvement of a large number (29%) of members of the social and economic elites is one of the most striking characteristics of homicidal behavior in rural Louisiana. Finally the presence among those involved in rural homicide of large numbers of skilled workers, day laborers, businessmen, professionals, and public officials seems to support the hypothesis that homicides tended to take place in rapidly growing towns and villages or were at least committed by people who lived in such places.[31]

The Causes of Homicide

To determine why people in both New Orleans and the country parishes committed murder is not an easy task, because local newspapers and other contemporary sources are often silent on the origins or circumstances surrounding such incidents.[32] Indeed many homicides, particularly in the cases where blacks were killed by whites, were reported as having mysterious or unknown causes.[33] This is why in both New Orleans and the rural areas 56 percent of the cases had no apparent cause. The difficulty of fixing the exact motive in a homicide is

Table 1.4
Motives Underlying Homicides in Louisiana, 1866–1884

Motives	Urban Homicides	%	% by Whites	Rural Homicides	%	% by Whites
Political	102	30.4	93.8	748	40.6	95.3
Election	16			278		
Riot	82			412		
Other	4			58		
Economic	19	5.7	68.5	136	7.4	74.3
Labor	12			61		
Business	7			49		
Other				26		
Social	46	13.7	54.0	113	6.1	61.0
Gambling	4			22		
Drunkenness	30			44		
Social party				28		
Being sick				2		
Other	12			82		
Racial	11	3.3	100.0	55	3.0	89.1
Familial	62	18.4	67.3	144	7.8	48.2
Family	8			55		
Marital	30			32		
Jealousy	24			57		
Personal	62	18.4	62.3	350	19.0	67.3
Honor	11			74		
Self-defense	9			58		
Anger	29			115		
Other	13			103		
Criminal	34	10.1	59.1	297	16.1	78.1
Robbery	17			132		
Rape & sexual assault	3			45		
Resisting arrest	9			51		
Arson				4		
Murder				65		
Unknown	435			2372		
Total	336	100.0	72.3	1843	99.9	79.0

further complicated by the fact that we often need to determine among various motives the main cause. Nevertheless a thorough examination of each case, drawing on a variety of sources, gives a fair idea of the motives or causes behind homicides in post–Civil War Louisiana (table 1.4).

As we have seen previously, people living in the rural areas of Louisiana had a greater propensity to commit murder than those living in New Orleans. Although the origins and causes of homicide were relatively similar in both areas, a greater percentage of homicides in

New Orleans originated from familial and social causes, while political and social control of blacks was at the basis of a greater proportion of killing in the country parishes.

With regard to New Orleans, the data also demonstrate that for each major category of causes, except politics, blacks had a greater propensity to commit murder than their 25 percent proportion in the population would indicate. This is particularly true after Reconstruction. However, a completely different story emerges with regard to the countryside. Particularly during Reconstruction, white representation in each category of causes for homicide far exceeds their relative proportion (40%) in the rural population.

Although sketchy, information on the underlying causes of murder shows that politics was the main root of violence in Reconstructed Louisiana. By their sheer numbers, black voters became the potential masters of the political situation; by forming a solid bloc of voters for the Republican party, blacks left white conservatives with no hope of carrying state elections without exercising some form of control over black voters. Consequently much of the white anger was directed against blacks who began to engage in political activities, joined Republican clubs, and asserted their right to vote or to hold office. Without minimizing other factors, politics was truly at the root of most violence in Louisiana.[34]

Family conflicts, marital quarrels, and disputes over women were also important factors leading people to kill one another, particularly in New Orleans. For example, Thomas E. Mercer, a merchant and planter of Bossier parish, was killed in August 1875 by two of his brothers-in-law, J. M. Sledge and W. McKinney.[35] Overall the relative scarcity of intrafamilial homicides is striking when compared to modern industrial societies.[36] Domestic conflicts and family quarrels represented a major cause of homicidal behavior in New Orleans, but they were much less significant in the country parishes particularly when compared to political violence.

The countryside was often the scene, both before and after the Civil War, of deadly family feuds. The most famous family feud of nineteenth-century Louisiana was between the families of General St. John Liddell and Colonel Charles Jones, two prominent planters of Catahoula parish. The feud, which took a tragic turn in 1870, was rooted in an old quarrel over a question of honor, the origins of which went back to the early 1850s. The dispute began in 1852 when a Mississippi lady who had felt insulted by something reported to have been said by Jones, asked the help of Liddell for reparation. Liddell agreed to accompany the lady to Jones's plantation, where the lady fired shots at Jones, wounding him severely in the face and body. Jones held Liddell responsible. Jones's vendetta resulted in the death of several persons over the years, among them the father of General Liddell. Finally, in February 1870, Colonel Jones and his two sons ambushed and killed General Liddell. After the Joneses surrendered to the local sheriff, they were attacked by a group of whites. Only one of the sons escaped, while the father and the other son were killed.[37]

The Liddell-Jones feud was not unique. Rapides parish was shaken by a similar vendetta between the family of Captain Hooe and Dr. Luckett that also had a tragic conclusion in 1870 with the assassination of Captain Hooe on the steamer *Kate Kinney*.[38] Livingston parish was similarly troubled for years by the Lanier-Kirby feud that only ended after several members of both families had been killed.[39] These various feuds clearly reflected the profound sense of honor that permeated social relations in nineteenth-century Louisiana.

Although nineteenth-century Louisianians considered that family affairs did not belong in court, family feuds reveal the difficulty of peacefully settling conflicts in matters of family or personal honor. Therefore family feuds not only disrupted community life by challenging loyalties among families and friends, but also demonstrated the unstable character of rural life of nineteenth-century Louisiana and Southern society in general.[40]

Nineteenth-century Louisianians had an acute sense of personal honor, and leading members of both rural and urban communities regularly resorted to duels and deadly fights to settle quarrels. The New Orleans police were unable to prevent the killing of Colonel J. J. Bryant in January 1867 by Judge Frederick Tate of Texas. Police had more success in 1878 in stopping a duel in progress between former congressman J. Hale Sypher and a prominent lawyer named A. C. Allen.[41]

Similar deadly fights between leading members of local communities disturbed many rural parishes. For example, in September 1868 an old feud between John W. Hudson and Charles P. Thompson, both of St. Landry parish, came to an end when Thompson and his two sons killed Hudson. In May 1874, P. Fontelieu, a member of the State Legislature from Vermilion parish, was shot and wounded by Sheriff Shaw. Both were Democrats. In May 1875, Judge Sherburne of Terrebonne parish was arrested and brought to trial for killing ex-judge James Belden. In February 1876, Dr. Robert D. Phelps, mayor of Bastrop, was ambushed and murdered in the town's street by W. C. Lyons, the parish sheriff of Morehouse since 1873. In 1878 Dr. Jos Bosee was killed by Absolom W. Ford and accomplices in Calcasieu as part of an old feud.[42]

At the same time, New Orleans was frequently the scene of conflicts within particular ethnic groups. This was particularly the case after the war when fights sporadically broke out between groups of Sicilian and other Italian immigrants. For these groups who had strongly integrated social values based on a code of honor, a killing often degenerated into mob fights. For example, twenty Sicilians were arrested in the vegetable market for disturbing the peace and resisting arrest in May 1869. During that fight, one person was killed and two others were wounded. Two months later, a new fight broke out as some Sicilians tried to avenge the victim of the May outbreak. The city newspapers reported numerous murders that were linked to Sicilian quarrels.[43]

Homicide committed in relation to other forms of criminal activities was particularly prevalent in rural parishes where criminal behavior was the third major cause of homicides. Most murders linked to criminal activities originated in robberies (44%), avenging a murder (22%), resisting arrest (17%), and rape and sexual assault (15%). Most of these homicides were committed by whites and were directed against blacks. The fact that relatively few homicides related to criminal activities occurred in New Orleans is most revealing with regard to the capacity of the police to maintain order in the city.[44]

If we are to believe the press, the most common cause of homicide in New Orleans was a drunken brawl in bars followed by bloody fights in the street. Whisky was perceived as the main ingredient of violence as in most other cities. When people drank it took only "a spilled drink, a careless remark, or an argument about a game of poker," to give a sudden dispute a tragic proportion. Drunkenness opened the door to all kinds of crimes.[45] City police reports show that a large part of police work in New Orleans was related to alcohol. Not surprisingly a large proportion of cases of police officers who were killed while on duty occurred when they became involved in drunken brawls. For 1869 alone, three police officers were killed in such street brawls.[46]

Although both the city press and the rural conservative press in its coverage of homicide tended to emphasize heavy consumption of whisky on the part of blacks, evidence shows that heavy drinking was just as much a characteristic of the white community. Nineteen out of twenty crimes committed against persons in New Orleans were reported as having grown out of whisky consumption. Furthermore, local newspapers asserted that one-half to two-thirds of all homicides in rural Louisiana were directly or indirectly linked to heavy drinking.[47] Although most observers linked the frequency of homicides in rural areas to the general custom of carrying concealed weapons and the practice of gambling in public places where intoxicating drinks were freely sold, data show a rather small number of homicides in either New Orleans (9%) or the rural parishes (2.5%) in which alcohol is listed as the primary cause. Neither did poker games and other forms of gambling appear to have been a major cause of homicides, in spite of what was said in the conservative press.[48]

Although there existed a considerable degree of public consciousness about the danger of carrying arms, Louisiana law tolerated the bearing of arms as long as they were visible. Bearing concealed weapons, on the other hand, was a crime. The presence of pistols and other concealed weapons seems to have been a major contributing factor, easily turning trivial disputes into deadly encounters.[49] State Attorney General Simon Belden asserted in his 1870 report that half of the homicides committed in the state were directly linked to the widespread practice of carrying concealed weapons.[50] Carrying a concealed weapon was first of all a measure of self-defense, but it also often led to tragic consequences when quarrels led to physical violence. The regular recourse to pistols and knives during personal disputes created a particularly alarming situation in New Orleans in the post–Civil War decades. In New Orleans, as in other cities, the very presence of guns was a leading cause of homicide. In other words, the carrying of concealed weapons had a direct effect on the city's homicide rates.[51]

After nine murders were committed during a single week in March 1879, the New Orleans authorities felt compelled to adopt a stringent new ordinance limiting people's right to carry concealed weapons.[52] Yet uprooting this habit proved to be a major problem, because violence was so deeply rooted in the public conscience and the bad habit of bearing arms came from the top levels of society. In January 1869, John Nixon Jr., a well-known editor and former member of the city council, was killed by C. W. Cammack, who carried a concealed weapon. Both gentlemen were members of the select Boston Club.[53] In February 1880, Speaker Ogden did not hesitate to carry a concealed weapon even on the floor of the State House.[54]

The Failure of Social and Political Control

It was fashionable for contemporaries to blame the state administration and its law enforcement officers for the high level of violence in Louisiana. Country newspapers regularly protested that criminals, robbers, rapists, and murderers were too often acquitted: escaping due punishment by resorting to legal technicalities or by pleading insanity. When criminals were not liberated by bad or ignorant jurors, so argued the press, they were too often set free by governors abusing their power to pardon.[55] Such views are born out by the condition of affairs in New Orleans. Twenty-four people arrested for homicide during the summer of 1871 were set free after pleading intoxication or insanity. Out of 303 killings committed in New Orleans between 1870 and 1880, 46 were found guilty of murder without capital punishment, 44 were found guilty of manslaughter, 116 were found not guilty, and 59 cases ended with *nolle prosequi* (being unwilling to pursue). Only eleven persons (4%) were sentenced to death, and more than half were granted executive pardons. In the end only five persons, two blacks and three white foreigners, were punished according to law. This means in the final analysis that only 2 percent of the people charged with homicide were finally executed.[56]

The situation was similar in the country parishes where corruption and gerrymandering were resorted to in the selection of jurors at criminal trials. Social and pecuniary influences were brought to bear on jurors by influential, well-to-do offenders. Finally, the fear of revenge from criminals had an important influence on jurors. The detention, trial, and punishment of offenders became more and more farcical and uncertain. Although murders were regularly committed, most people doubted that the perpetrators would be brought to justice.[57] The situation was further complicated in the rural areas by the unwillingness of whites to sit with blacks on the same jury.[58]

The inefficiency of the legal process does not on its own furnish an adequate explanation as to why so many blacks were killed in the country parishes during Reconstruction. White commentators were rather quick to blame white radicals and black politicians of manipulating black votes, and by such means installing "corrupt" government. Whites in Louisiana did not really accept postwar changes and particularly objected to the political implications of such changes, realizing that in the long run political equality meant social equality. Furthermore the rumors of black insurrection that spread through post–Civil War Louisiana provided the rationale for killing blacks and preserving the state as a "white man's country." As the political climate worsened in 1868 and again in 1874, the state became deeply divided between Republicans and Democrats. The local Democratic leadership called for white solidarity and expressed its determination to resort to summary means, if necessary, to correct the wrongs brought about by radical policies.[59]

Although the New Orleans press complained about the inability of the city police to control serious crimes such as homicides after the war,[60] the statistics tell a different story. The Republican administration made an effort to furnish the city with better police protection by shifting administrative control from city council to the newly created board of metropolitan police, modernizing police operations in the process and doubling the size of the force.[61] As a consequence the city's homicide rate declined sharply during the post–Civil War period, compared to the peak it reached during the 1850s.

Conditions were quite different in the rural areas. In many parishes the general atmosphere of lawlessness that prevailed after the war explains why no official had either the authority or the inclination to bring criminals to justice after the war. Moreover the existing force was not adequately prepared to act against armed revolt in a significant way.[62] The work of local sheriffs became more and more difficult during these troubled years because of the tendency of many whites and blacks to harbor criminals and fugitives.[63] The work of a sheriff was not without danger. Nine sheriffs were killed and several others wounded while executing their official duties. Among the most notable cases were the killing of Sheriff Henry H. Pope during the political trouble of St. Mary parish in October 1868; the assassination of Sheriff George Stubinger by a black who resisted arrest in Iberia parish in December 1869; the brutal murder of Sheriff John H. Wisner in Ouachita parish on March 31, 1870, by the notorious Beaver's gang who struck the parish jail to free some of their members; and the assassination of Sheriff F. S. Edgerton in Red River parish on August 30, 1874.[64]

This led to numerous complaints about the failure of sheriffs and their deputies to arrest offenders. Apprehending a criminal could take a long time. For example, Charles and Eugene Simon of Lafayette parish were charged with the murder of Robert Dickerson in January 1867, but they were not arrested until August 1874.[65] Given these particular conditions, many sheriffs, finding it almost impossible to enforce the law, chose to resign,[66] while others became the accomplices of criminals or adopted a passive stance offering no resistance to mobs who broke into jails to kill prisoners.[67]

In 1867, Congress temporarily forbade the organization of militia units in the Southern states. As a consequence the Louisiana state government found itself seriously hampered in its control over civil society. As it did not possess a professional state police, the government was forced to depend either on local authorities or on Federal troops for the maintenance of peace and order in the remote districts where its authority was often nonexistent. The *New Orleans Tribune* had already proposed in December 1866 the organization of a loyal militia as the only means to insure on a long-term basis the enforcement of all United States laws and the protection of loyal citizens, particularly in the country parishes where Federal soldiers were few. The *Tribune* renewed its demand for such a militia in 1867, but to no avail. As a consequence in May 1868, whites of Bossier parish refused to acknowledge the authority of the newly elected Republican officials and allowed former Democratic officials to retain their offices.[68] This inability to maintain order had tragic consequences in 1868 when political turmoil and violence swept the state.

As a temporary measure the state legislature authorized Governor Warmoth to use the New Orleans Metropolitan Police as a militia, and in June 1870 a state militia was established on a racially mixed basis under the command of former Confederate General James Longstreet. The immediate objective of the new force was to prevent the recurrence of endemic violence, which in the two preceding years had led to such disastrous results, and to furnish the governor with a means of intervening in parishes where discontent and resistance to the Republican authorities appeared deeply rooted.[69] The existence of black militia was important for the survival of blacks' voting rights and the rights of blacks to hold office. But nothing incited whites to violence as much as the sight of black soldiers and black armed civilians. The very presence of armed black men annoyed and scared the white community as whites saw the "demoralizing effects" that black soldiers had on freedmen. After Governor Warmoth chose to station a black militia regiment in Shreveport in June 1870, a number of parishes held meetings to protest against the organization of black militia.[70] As a result the new militia was almost exclusively used in New Orleans. It proved to be no match for the white paramilitary organizations of 1873 and the White League of 1874. As a consequence, in rural areas, blacks had to depend largely on Federal troops for protection.[71]

Democrats and the Democratic press repeatedly protested against undue military interference and the presence of troops,[72] but Republican officials and the military agreed that the appearance of troops usually had a salutary effect on the level of unrest in the more volatile parishes or regions of Louisiana. General W. H. Emory, who commanded the district of Louisiana in 1873, wrote to General W. T. Sherman that he believed it proper that "a force should always be kept within call," ready to intervene "on the least threat or sign of riot." This view was shared by U.S. Marshal S. P. Packard and by Governor W. P. Kellogg who repeatedly told President Grant and Attorney General Williams during the summer of 1874 that they were "unable to enforce the laws of Congress without a posse of troops."[73]

Governor Kellogg and other Republican officials had good reason to wish to perpetuate the presence of Federal troops in Louisiana. Confronted by an increasing resistance on the part of the white population, the Republican government could not survive without the assistance and support of the troops. The Federals were called upon to quell disturbances no less than thirty-eight times in Reconstructed Louisiana.

The ability of Federal troops to restore or maintain order was particularly apparent in New Orleans. Nearly half of all military interventions (18 out of 38) occurred in that city. This was not only due to the fact that New Orleans was the capital and the political center of Reconstructed Louisiana; New Orleans was also the military headquarters for the South, and a large number of troops were constantly stationed close to the city. Consequently, swift military intervention easily prevented outbreaks of violence in that city from degenerating into massacres of the type that occurred on July 30, 1866, when 48 people were killed and more than 150 wounded.[74]

The situation was quite different in the country parishes where there was no permanent military presence capable of rapidly restoring peace and order. Military authorities did not have enough troops for a thorough occupation of rural Louisiana,[75] and authorities in Washington became increasingly reluctant after 1868 to authorize the use of soldiers as policemen.[76] Although the white population did fear army interference, they hardly accepted it as legitimate. Further, any military intervention outside of New Orleans was always delayed by the fact that an officer had to be sent to investigate the conditions in any disturbed parish before a decision to send troops could be taken. This meant that troops were not generally able to prevent violence but were mainly used to restore order after violence had already broken out.[77] As a result blacks living in rural areas were left with no military protection after 1867 and were forced to look out for themselves.

Conclusion

The analysis of homicidal behavior, particularly when it is undertaken from an urban-rural perspective, is most revealing with regard to the racial, social, and political tensions that troubled Louisiana after the Civil War. One major conclusion of the present study is that homicides in New Orleans differed significantly from the rural pattern.

Compared to the 1850s, Reconstruction brought a marked improvement in the control of violence in New Orleans. The annual homicide rate underwent a sharp decline as the city police became better organized, more numerous, and more professional. Moreover local authorities could count now on the presence of Federal troops in the vicinity of the city in case of disturbance. In addition, since whites formed an overwhelming majority of the voters in the city, racial and political tensions were less apparent than in rural areas. As a consequence more urban homicides resulted from personal or familial quarrels and fewer were racially or politically oriented than in the country parishes. The post–Reconstruction years saw a dramatic shift in homicides, however, characterized by a sharp rise in black intraracial rates. As we shall see in the following chapters, this increase in black homicide rates brought New Orleans closer to the patterns of homicide characteristic of twentieth-century American cities.

Meanwhile the data reveal how violence in rural areas, particularly during Reconstruction, was mostly committed by whites against blacks. As will be shown, white violence in country parishes did not occur by accident or at random; it was well-organized and politically oriented, occurring in situations where the race issue held center stage. Much of the violence in country parishes was rooted in white fear of black unrest and generated by white determination to reassert and reinforce the color line; its patterns varied greatly depending on the prevailing local conditions.

Homicides in Rural Areas:
A Regional Perspective

Caddo parish had a reputation for violence that can be traced as early as July 1870, when the *Jefferson State Register* declared that disorderly ruffians had given the parish an unenviable reputation. This view was amplified by the *Donaldsonville Chief,* which asserted in March 1875 that Caddo was living up to its infamous name and rightly deserved to be called "Bloody Caddo." The newspaper went on to say that human life was held so cheaply there that scarcely a week passed without bringing news from Caddo and surrounding parishes of some horrible new crime. During the same period three congressional committees concluded that Bloody Caddo merited its epithet, since the worst men known to any civilized country lived within its limits. Caddo parish was not unique, though; most of the other parishes of the Red River region, situated in the northwestern corner of Louisiana, were subject to the same atmosphere of terror.[1]

By commenting on the particularly violent character of the Red River parishes, and more particularly of Caddo, contemporary witnesses were suggesting that patterns of violence differed in Louisiana from parish to parish, and from region to region. This perception found its way into Horace V. Redfield's 1880 study that demonstrated the existence of a variety of patterns of violence among the different Southern states.[2] In recent decades social scientists have taken up this same line of enquiry pointing out that in both Europe and America local factors affected the regional distribution of rates of violence within any particular region or country.[3]

This analysis of homicides from a regional perspective will demonstrate how the nature and level of post–Civil War violence varied widely within Louisiana depending on the social and geographic context. In revealing the differing interplay of cultural, demographic, economic, political, and social factors in the various regions of the state, these collected data indicate underlying causes that affected violence and how these causes varied from one region to another.

As much as any other state in the Union, Louisiana, with its diverse old stock American, Black, Catholic, French, and immigrant communities, contained a level of structural and cultural heterogeneity capable of influencing local and regional patterns of violence. Consequently a look at homicides from a local perspective promises to be particularly revealing about the general trend of violence and the influence that various cultural traditions might have on such patterns.[4]

A Regional Analysis

The creation of a homogeneous statistical series measuring trends and variations in homicidal behavior and including socioeconomic and political variables offers the possibility of developing a general model for a fixed period of time. Such a model can help to deepen our understanding of the main characteristics of Louisiana society as they relate to homicide at both a global and regional level. However, as certain historians have pointed out, the creation of indexes of this sort raises methodological problems. Although such historians as Roger Lane and Eric H. Monkkonen have acknowledged that homicide indexes can provide the most precise possible record of serious violence, they have also pointed out that such indexes are often virtually worthless because of the minimal numbers involved when dealing with data at the local or even the regional level. In many instances when counties or parishes with a small population are studied over a short period of time, this constitutes a base too small to be statistically significant.[5] The data on post–Civil War Louisiana however are broadly based and cover a sufficiently large period to overcome the potential deficiencies inherent to local or regional studies.

This study examines the data not from a parish, but a regional perspective for two important reasons. First of all, it is not the absolute number of homicides in a given area that is important, but the relative measure of the difference of homicide rates between areas. Any increase in the number of homicides, from the slightest to the most acute, has a disproportionate effect on the parish rates depending on whether or not the population of a given period is large or small. For this reason, an analysis based on regions rather than parishes, although sensitive to local variations, will be less representative of the local variations, but it will give a more accurate description of the regional situation.[6]

Second, the parish as the analytical basis was not retained for a more fundamental reason. The number of parishes, the political subunits of Louisiana, varied between 48 to 58 during the course of the post–Civil War period. Dividing the study area into such a large number of entities was both cumbersome and irrelevant from a comparative methodology point of view. Indeed such factors as demographic composition, distance from the state capital, percentage of blacks, nature of the economy, social structure, and political tradition varied more at the regional than at the parish level. Therefore one must not look at Louisiana as an amorphous whole, but as a melding of shifting interest groups and various social and political behaviors. Each separate region of the state possessed its particular economic and demographic characteristics, its particular history, and its particular cultural tradition, while parishes within each region tended to share such characteristics. These, of course, are the factors that underlay the particular social and homicidal behavior in the regions and consequently affect its patterns of violence.[7]

Several attempts have been made at defining the regional composition of Louisiana. Because of its French cultural past, several historians and social scientists have put a particular emphasis on the difference between the French and Anglo Saxon regions. This division of the state into two great ethnicity-based sections seemed justified because Louisiana political factions often aligned themselves on this basis.[8] Various other commentators have pointed to a greater cultural diversity in Louisiana. For example, in 1865 Secretary of State Stanislas Wrotnoski claimed that the state was divided into four distinct sections.[9] For his part, Samuel E. Lockett, in his geographical and topographical survey of 1873, divided Louisiana into six regions.[10] In his report to the Federal Census Bureau in 1884, Eugene W. Hilgard used data on population, tilled land, and agricultural production to prove the existence of no less than seven different regions.[11] Finally, in 1955 Alvin L. Bertrand defined ten social and cultural regions within the state of Louisiana.[12]

Therefore this analysis creates an intermediary level of social and cultural areas between the parish and state levels. This approach

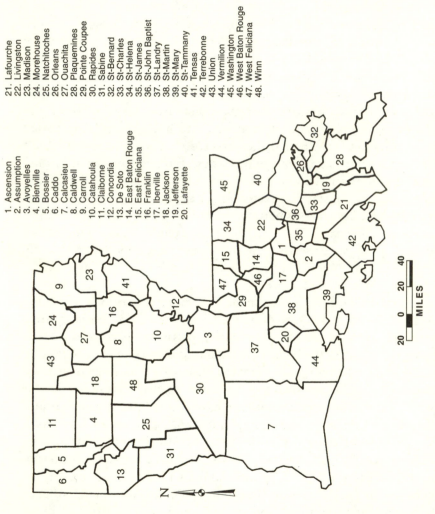

1. Ascension
2. Assumption
3. Avoyelles
4. Bienville
5. Bossier
6. Caddo
7. Calcasieu
8. Caldwell
9. Carroll
10. Catahoula
11. Claiborne
12. Concordia
13. De Soto
14. East Baton Rouge
15. East Feliciana
16. Franklin
17. Iberville
18. Jackson
19. Jefferson
20. Lafayette

21. Lafourche
22. Livingston
23. Madison
24. Morehouse
25. Natchitoches
26. Orleans
27. Ouachita
28. Plaquemines
29. Pointe Coupee
30. Rapides
31. Sabine
32. St-Bernard
33. St-Charles
34. St-Helena
35. St-James
36. St-John Baptist
37. St-Landry
38. St-Martin
39. St-Mary
40. St-Tammany
41. Tensas
42. Terrebonne
43. Union
44. Vermillion
45. Washington
46. West Baton Rouge
47. West Feliciana
48. Winn

Louisiana Parishes, 1868. *Source:* Historical Records Survey WPA, New Orleans Public Library

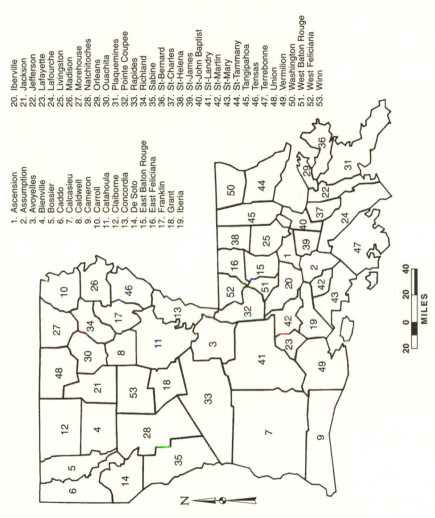

1. Ascension
2. Assumption
3. Avoyelles
4. Bienville
5. Bossier
6. Caddo
7. Calcasieu
8. Caldwell
9. Cameron
10. Carroll
11. Catahoula
12. Claiborne
13. Concordia
14. De Soto
15. East Baton Rouge
16. East Feliciana
17. Franklin
18. Grant
19. Iberia

20. Iberville
21. Jackson
22. Jefferson
23. Lafayette
24. Lafourche
25. Livingston
26. Madison
27. Morehouse
28. Natchitoches
29. Orleans
30. Ouachita
31. Plaquemines
32. Pointe Coupee
33. Rapides
34. Richland
35. Sabine
36. St-Bernard
37. St-Charles
38. St-Helena
39. St-James
40. St-John Baptist
41. St-Landry
42. St-Martin
43. St-Mary
44. St-Tammany
45. Tangipahoa
46. Tensas
47. Terrebonne
48. Union
49. Vermilion
50. Washington
51. West Baton Rouge
52. West Feliciana
53. Winn

Louisiana Parishes, 1870. *Source:* Historical Records Survey WPA, New Orleans
Public Library

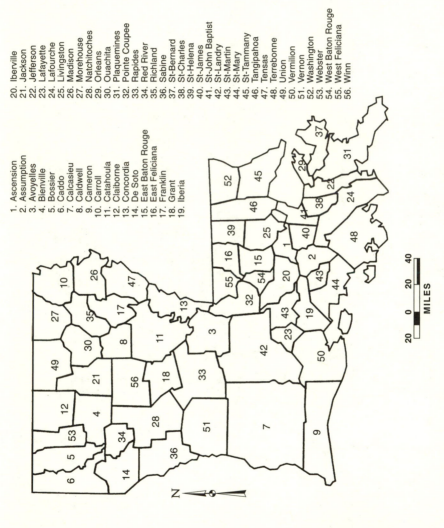

1. Ascension
2. Assumption
3. Avoyelles
4. Bienville
5. Bossier
6. Caddo
7. Calcasieu
8. Caldwell
9. Cameron
10. Carroll
11. Catahoula
12. Claiborne
13. Concordia
14. De Soto
15. East Baton Rouge
16. East Feliciana
17. Franklin
18. Grant
19. Iberia
20. Iberville
21. Jackson
22. Jefferson
23. Lafayette
24. Lafourche
25. Livingston
26. Madison
27. Morehouse
28. Natchitoches
29. Orleans
30. Ouachita
31. Plaquemines
32. Pointe Coupee
33. Rapides
34. Red River
35. Richland
36. Sabine
37. St-Bernard
38. St-Charles
39. St-Helena
40. St-James
41. St-John Baptist
42. St-Landry
43. St-Martin
44. St-Mary
45. St-Tammany
46. Tangipahoa
47. Tensas
48. Terrebonne
49. Union
50. Vermilion
51. Vernon
52. Washington
53. Webster
54. West Baton Rouge
55. West Feliciana
56. Winn

MILES
20 0 20 40

Louisiana Parishes, 1872. *Source:* Historical Records Survey WPA, New Orleans Public Library

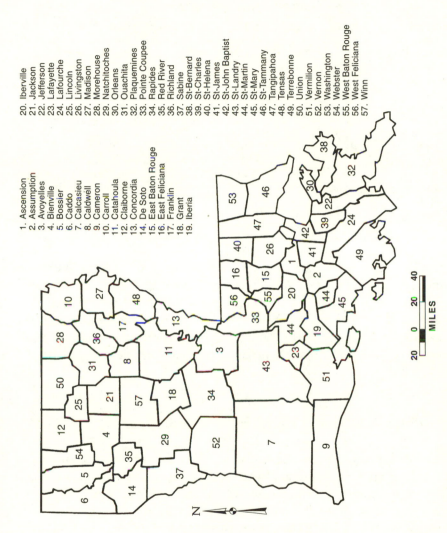

1. Ascension
2. Assumption
3. Avoyelles
4. Bienville
5. Bossier
6. Caddo
7. Calcasieu
8. Caldwell
9. Cameron
10. Carroll
11. Catahoula
12. Claiborne
13. Concordia
14. De Soto
15. East Baton Rouge
16. East Feliciana
17. Franklin
18. Grant
19. Iberia

20. Iberville
21. Jackson
22. Jefferson
23. Lafayette
24. Lafourche
25. Lincoln
26. Livingston
27. Madison
28. Morehouse
29. Natchitoches
30. Orleans
31. Ouachita
32. Plaquemines
33. Pointe Coupee
34. Rapides
35. Red River
36. Richland
37. Sabine
38. St-Bernard
39. St-Charles
40. St-Helena
41. St-James
42. St-John Baptist
43. St-Landry
44. St-Martin
45. St-Mary
46. St-Tammany
47. Tangipahoa
48. Tensas
49. Terrebonne
50. Union
51. Vermilion
52. Vernon
53. Washington
54. Webster
55. West Baton Rouge
56. West Feliciana
57. Winn

MILES

20   0   20   40

Louisiana Parishes, 1876. *Source:* Historical Records Survey WPA, New Orleans Public Library

Table 2.1
Major Characteristics of Each Rural Region of Louisiana

Regions	% Rural Pop.	% Black Pop.	% Pop. Density/ Sq. Mile	Ethnicity	Economy
Red River	13.5	72.9	11.4	Anglo Saxon	cotton plantations
Western	1.9	19.5	4.0	Anglo Saxon	farms, timber
Southwestern	2.4	22.3	2.1	French Catho.	rice, beef, timber
Northern	9.4	47.0	18.2	Anglo Saxon	timber, family farms
North. Central Hill	5.6	41.1	7.2	Anglo Saxon	family farms, timber
Northern Bluff Land	5.8	63.3	8.7	Anglo Saxon	cotton plantations
Mississippi Delta	10.1	83.0	16.2	Anglo Saxon	cotton plantations
South Central prairies	9.1	46.5	14.3	French Catho.	beef, farms
Sugar Bowl	23.2	59.3	18.5	French Catho.	sugar plantations
Bluff Land	7.8	70.9	32.0	diverse	cotton plantations
Florida parishes	4.9	37.9	7.7	Anglo Saxon	small farms
Bayou	5.9	62.0	15.9	diverse, French	seafood, sugar, farms

provides comparable data for each area for the entire period. The delineation of this study's subregions was done on the basis of the geographical, economic, demographic, and cultural characteristics of each region.[13] For the purpose of this study, various local characteristics are used to define thirteen different cultural and social areas, twelve of which are located in rural Louisiana (table 2.1 and figs. 2.1, 2.2).

Patterns of Regional Homicidal Behavior

The breakdown of homicide statistics, either by number, percentage, or annual rates, shows that violence varied significantly from one region to another within Louisiana after the Civil War. However, the data also show quite different patterns whether we consider Reconstruction or the early Redemption years (table 2.2). A close look at each region unveils the influence of regional particularities on local patterns of violence.

The Red River area, composed of the seven parishes of Bossier, Caddo, De Soto, Red River, Natchitoches, Grant, and Rapides, had two particular social characteristics that fostered violence and made

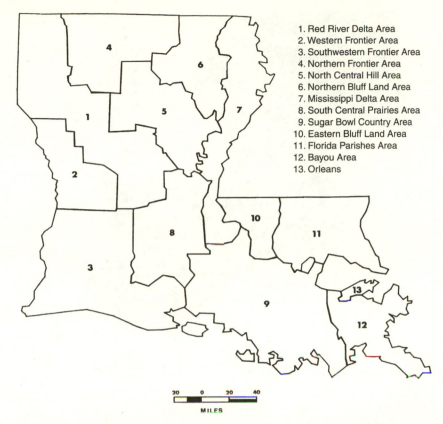

1. Red River Delta Area
2. Western Frontier Area
3. Southwestern Frontier Area
4. Northern Frontier Area
5. North Central Hill Area
6. Northern Bluff Land Area
7. Mississippi Delta Area
8. South Central Prairies Area
9. Sugar Bowl Country Area
10. Eastern Bluff Land Area
11. Florida Parishes Area
12. Bayou Area
13. Orleans

20   0   20   40
MILES

Figure 2.1 Geographic and Cultural Regions of Louisiana, 1865–1884

it unique among the regions of Louisiana after the war. First, the Red River area, located in the northwestern corner of the state and bordered by Texas and Arkansas, was the most remote region in Louisiana. Evidence suggests that the Red River parishes were at the time a part of a larger frontier area covering most of northern and western Louisiana that had only been recently settled.[14] While the Red River region had only 13 percent of the state's rural population, more than 50 percent of the homicides that occurred outside of New Orleans took place within its borders. No matter how we look at the figures, the Red River parishes emerge as the most violent area in Louisiana after the Civil War. During Reconstruction the annual homicide rate of this region was almost 200 per 100,000 inhabitants.[15]

The frontier mentality alone can not explain why violence was so much higher in Red River parishes than elsewhere in Louisiana, as

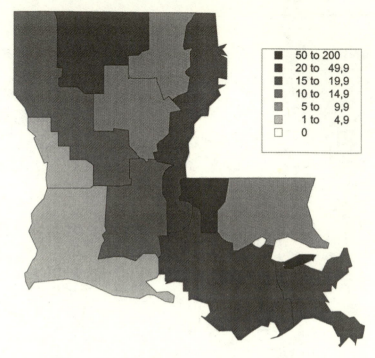

Figure 2.2 Population Density per Square Mile

	50 to 200
	20 to 49,9
	15 to 19,9
	10 to 14,9
	5 to 9,9
	1 to 4,9
	0

Table 2.2
Regional Distribution of Rural Homicides

| Regions | Reconstruction | | | Early Redemption | | |
	N	%	Annual Rates	N	%	Annual Rates
Red River	1,558	51.4	196.3	238	21.4	24.6
Western	42	1.3	36.5	20	1.8	19.9
Southwestern	34	1.1	24.0	31	2.8	16.4
Northern	142	4.7	25.7	49	4.4	9.5
North. Central Hill	128	4.2	37.9	24	2.2	11.1
Northern Bluff Land	188	6.2	54.7	93	8.3	25.4
Mississippi Delta	106	3.5	17.8	123	11.1	18.1
South Central prairies	203	6.7	37.6	81	7.3	14.5
Sugar Bowl	315	10.4	23.3	291	26.2	20.5
Bluff Land	196	6.5	42.6	54	4.8	14.5
Florida parishes	50	1.6	17.3	60	5.4	21.7
Bayou	67	2.2	19.1	48	4.3	21.3
Total	3,029	99.8	51.6	1,112	100.0	19.2

Note: Annual rates were calculated on the basis of 100,000 inhabitants drawn from the 1870 federal census for the Reconstruction period and the 1880 federal census for the early Redemption period.

other regions share the same characteristics and were far from having comparable rates of homicide. One must therefore look at a second factor in order to understand the intensity of violence in this part of the state.[16] The white population of the Red River region was made of Americans of Scotch-Irish descent from such Southern states as Georgia, the two Carolinas, Tennessee, and Kentucky. The subculture of violence that this white population had inherited from the Highlands of Scotland was enhanced by the frontier mentality of the region and the psychological effects that two centuries of slavery had on race relations.[17] The white population in that region was, however, outnumbered three to one by blacks whose presence was essential to the maintenance and development of the large cotton plantations gathered along the fertile banks of the Red River.[18] The need to keep the black majority under control became paramount in the eyes of the white population during the post–Civil War period. It was this major factor that made the region particularly violent.[19]

The Red River parishes constituted the only region in Louisiana that was spared by the Civil War. The region did not live through the terror, famine, and other sufferings brought by the war; there was no rebuilding, no repair, or reconstruction that needed to be done there. Furthermore the war brought prosperity to the region, as Shreveport became the capital of Confederate Louisiana after the fall of New Orleans. As the region escaped invasion and was occupied only after the surrender of the Southern armies, white people there did not feel they had been vanquished.[20] As a result the white community of the Red River region was periodically dominated by a class of daring, brave, and utterly reckless men who stubbornly opposed the Federal government and its Reconstruction policy and who strongly resented the presence of Federal troops, particularly when those occupying forces were composed of black regiments.[21] These men firmly resisted the changes brought by the war and did not shrink from anything, even from murder.[22] Violence, consequently, became the ultimate instrument in coercing blacks into submissiveness and maintaining the area as a "white man's country."

Politics emerges as the main reason why this particular region was so violent. Indeed, the Red River parishes, where 58 percent of all homicides originated from political causes, was the only region of Louisiana where this factor scored more than 50 percent. Fifty-five percent of homicides in the Red River parishes took place during only three years: 28 percent in 1868, 15 percent in 1873, and 12 percent in 1874. It was during these years that the Bossier and Caddo riots of 1868, the Colfax massacre of 1873, and the Coushatta affair of 1874 took place. On each of these occasions whites became determined to overthrow Republican rule, and as a consequence blacks suffered campaigns of terror. During these campaigns it became almost impossible even for whites to maintain allegiance to the Republican party and to remain alive.[23] Except for the Caledonia and Natchitoches riots of 1878, the Red River parishes suffered less from political violence after 1876.[24]

The patterns of homicides were dissimilar in the western area of Louisiana, a region that had quite different cultural, social, and economic characteristics than the Red River parishes. Covering Sabine parish and the newly created parish of Vernon, bordered to the west by Texas and to the east by the Red River area, the western region formed a sparsely populated frontier area. With its variety of soils and its forests, the region was made up of hill country unsuitable to large plantations. The economy of the region rested mainly on small farming and timber. These factors explain why, among all the regions of Louisiana, the western region had the lowest percentage of blacks, and its population was mainly formed of old Anglo Saxon stock.[25]

These particular conditions did influence the pattern of homicides in that region. As in other regions, most murders were concentrated in 1867 and 1868, which together account for 35 percent of cases. And yet the frontier spirit of the western region was reflected by the fact that crime outranked politics 36 to 23 percent as the main factors of homicidal behavior. Since 90 percent of homicides occurred in Sabine, a parish bordering the Red River region, geographical proximity may have had a contagious effect. A most notable politically motivated homicide occurred in 1883 when Alfred Lout, a Democrat who had held the office of sheriff since 1872, was assassinated by other Democrats in a street of Many, the parish seat of Sabine.[26]

The dominant characteristics of the southwestern region, which covered the parishes of Calcasieu, Cameron, and Vermilion, were its prairies, its coast of marsh, and its extensive forests. The economy of the region had traditionally depended on the herds of cattle that roamed the prairies. After the war, with the growth in importance of cotton and sugar, the introduction of rice and crawfish, and the development of the lumber industries, the region underwent an economic boom.[27]

Southwestern Louisiana had particular demographic and cultural features. The local population was made up largely of French and Catholics of Acadian ancestry. Stereotyped as being "nonchalant and boisterous," the local population was then also described by contemporary observers as taking life one day at a time, enjoying a gregarious social life, and remaining unperturbed by the political turmoil of the period.[28] The region had, along with the western area, the lowest percentage of blacks among its population. But the economic transformation that followed the war affected the demographic composition of the region, particularly in the lumber industry in Calcasieu, where, during the 1870s, a large number of immigrants settled.[29] These cultural and social factors influenced the patterns of violence in the region.

During more than a quarter century, southwestern Louisiana was disturbed by outlaws who claimed that the cattle that fed upon the prairies were the property not of ranchers but of anyone capable of catching them. These men made Abbeville their center of operations.[30] As a consequence vigilance committees became a feature of southwestern Louisiana. The most notable incident involving vigilance violence occurred in September 1873 in Vermilion, which had for years been plagued by cattle and horse thieves. A committee of vigilantes was formed in the parish in the late summer of 1873, as "thieves are getting more numerous and bolder than was ever known before in the parish." On September 5 and 10, 1873, twelve members of a band of cattle thieves were lynched.[31] Through such actions, the vigilance committees created a climate of terror in the southwest region that was vigorously denounced by the press. The committees were described by some members of the press as groups of banditti and outlaws, no better than the ones against whom they acted.[32] Other vigilance committees were formed in Vermilion parish in 1875, 1876, and 1879.[33]

During Reconstruction, homicides were mainly concentrated in Vermilion parish and were largely due to vigilantes and to personal feuds. Still, southwestern Louisiana had, despite its vigilance violence, homicide rates 50 percent below average. But by the early Redemption period, although the region's homicide rate had fallen, it now became equivalent to the Louisiana average. Most violence now occurred in Calcasieu parish and was related to labor troubles in the lumber industry.[34]

Not surprisingly, politics played a marginal role (15%) among the causes of homicide. On the other hand, homicidal behavior was deeply rooted in the social conditions of the region as shown by the fact that criminal activities and personal affrays each contributed to 28 percent of homicides, while family feuds were the causes for 21 percent.

Northern Louisiana mainly consisted of a hilly region bordered by Arkansas, the Red River parishes, the Central Hill, and the Northern Bluff Land regions. The hill country was not amenable to large plantations. Consequently the local economy centered on the growing of cotton, corn, and sweet potatoes on small farms and plantations by hardworking farmers. The lack of fertile land in the area was partly compensated for by a rich variety of timber. The years after the Civil War were marked by the development of many thriving villages that arose all over the region, many of them along the new railroad lines that linked the region to the outside world. Forty-seven percent of the population of the region was of African American descent, while the white population was mainly, as was the case in the Red River parishes, of old American stock and affiliated with the Baptist Church.[35]

While gangs of horse thieves and other outlaws were found in every region of the state, the geographical characteristics of northern Louisiana and the inefficiency of local authorities made that region an ideal place for thieves. As a consequence many bands of outlaws operated in that area in the years following the Civil War. The sheriff of Claiborne found it so dangerous to carry out his duties that he refused to go to some parts of the parish under his jurisdiction. On several occasions it was necessary for local authorities to ask the military to send troops into the area.[36]

In spite of these particular conditions, the northern area had a homicide rate half of its 10 percent share of the rural population. The presence of a significant black population explains why politics was the major cause of homicide, accounting for 33 percent of all cases. Although the years 1868 with 20 percent and 1873 with 13 percent of homicides counted during the period were the two most violent years, the region suffered from no major riots or disturbances.

The Northern Central Hill region was composed of a variety of soils and types of timber. Although blacks formed 41 percent of the population, it was mainly inhabited, as in other northern regions, by a white population of Scotch-Irish descent. The local economy was diversified and subsisted on timber, cattle, and the growing of cotton, corn, and sweet potatoes. The region had few plantations, and small farms were the rule.[37]

The percentage of homicides were proportionate to the region's share of population, which was relatively well spread over the years. This was largely due to the fact that the Northern Central Hill region did not suffer as much as surrounding areas from racial and political tension. Having a lower percentage of black people than many other areas, politics were at the roots of only 23 percent of homicides. Meanwhile 25 percent of homicides were related to criminal activities, most of which were committed by the Guillory and the West and Kimball gangs, two notorious groups of outlaws that disturbed the region between 1865 and 1873.[38]

The Northern Bluff Lands, located on the southern border of Arkansas, was composed of a mixture of alluvial lands, hill country, and forest. As a consequence the region developed an economy divided between large plantations and small farms, and timber and other small industries. The construction of the Vickburg, Shreveport, and Pacific Railroad, which crossed the region, had a major economic impact. Here, as in the northern region, railway construction contributed to the development of thriving small towns. The population of blacks (63.3%) was the fourth highest among the twelve rural regions.[39]

The region became particularly violent during the years after the war. A group of former Confederate guerrilla jayhawkers, known as the "Black Horse Cavalry," terrorized the region and more particularly Franklin parish, for years transforming that parish into a den of murderers and robbers. This and other former semi-guerrilla bands became closely connected with the "Knights of the White Camelia," an organization dedicated to the restoration of the Pelican State as a "white man's country," that terrorized the region during the summer and fall of 1868.[40]

Although vigilance committees were organized in Franklin and Richland parishes to maintain order and to arrest the lawless, under such conditions parish sheriffs found it almost impossible to enforce the law. Many, such as A. W. Moore, the sheriff of Franklin parish, chose to resign, while others were brutally murdered in the course of duty. On March 31, 1870, Sheriff John H. Wisner of Ouachita was murdered by the notorious Beaver's gang during a jail break. Six years later, in August 1876, B. H. Dinkgrave, another sheriff of Ouachita, was murdered. The region also suffered in September 1873 the assassinations of District Judge Thomas Crawford and District Attorney A. H. Harris.[41]

As a consequence the region had the second highest homicide rate during Reconstruction and the highest rate during the early Redemption period. Thirty-five percent of homicides in the Northern Bluff Lands occurred in the years 1867 and 1868, during which the Knights of the White Camelia were particularly active.[42] The situation in the region was closely related to the high percentage of blacks. As a consequence of racial tension being particularly high, politics was the most important cause of homicide, accounting for 39 percent of cases.

The Mississippi Delta region ranks among the most fertile lands in the world with its many rivers and bayous contributing yearly to its alluvial soil. As a result the region possessed the richest cotton plantations of the state and the highest proportion of blacks, representing no less than 83 percent of the population. After the war the Mississippi Delta area remained essentially a plantation world without towns or villages.[43] The high concentration of blacks, early military occupation during the war, and the ease with which troops could intervene were all important factors in producing a particularly low level of violence in this region.[44]

Although the Mississippi Delta area had 10 percent of the state rural population, the region's homicide share was only 3.5 percent during Reconstruction, the lowest level of homicide in the state during that period. The willingness of the planters to cooperate with Republican officials and to accept black political predominance were contributing factors at this stage.[45] The situation changed dramatically after 1876, for in 1878 the Mississippi Delta area became one of the most violent regions of the state as white conservatives sought to overthrow local Republican officials.[46] In several parishes the number of people killed during the early Redemption period doubled the number killed during Reconstruction. Personal disputes nevertheless remained the major cause of homicide with 30 percent throughout this period, while politics rank second with 28 percent.

The South Central prairies, which included the parishes of Lafayette, St. Landry, and Avoyelles, were largely inhabited by a French population of Acadian origin who had lived for almost a century as squatters in the prairies. As was the case in southwestern Louisiana, their living was closely linked to the raising of cattle, poultry, and mules. Nevertheless, cotton and sugar plantations increasingly became an important feature of the region. This latter factor explained why blacks represented 47 percent of the population of the region.[47]

The region offered a propitious environment for gangs of outlaws, as in northern Louisiana. Bands of outlaws, such as the Fontenot and the Guillory gangs, terrorized blacks and committed numerous atrocities in the parish of St. Landry between 1865 and 1873.[48] Even so, local authorities showed determination in reducing criminal activities in the region. At considerable risk to his life, C. C. Duson, who was sheriff in St. Landry between 1872 and 1886, worked closely with District Judge Huspeth and District Attorney Perrodin to insure that criminals were not only arrested but convicted.[49]

Although criminal activities and social frays were important causes of deadly violence in the region, politics remained the major cause, accounting for 30 percent of homicide in the South Central prairies. This was largely due to the Opelousas riot of 1868, one of the worst political disturbances of the period, during which more than one hundred blacks were massacred.[50]

The 1868 Opelousas riot had a major effect on the subsequent decision by the black population in this region to remain aloof from politics, allowing leading whites to dominate the Republican ticket. John Simmes was the only black to hold an office of any consequence in St. Landry between 1868 and 1874.[51] Although St. Landry parish was the birthplace of the White League movement in 1874, politics remained a secondary factor of homicidal behavior after 1868. By the early Redemption era, the South Central prairies had become one of the least violent regions in Louisiana.

The Sugar Bowl area, located in the lower part of Louisiana, was the largest region of the state with its nineteen parishes. It possessed some of the finest plantations in the state and had developed a distinctive regional subculture based on the plantation life.[52] This subculture was affected by the many problems that plagued the sugar industry after the war, as major changes affected the areas of labor relations, techniques of production, ownership of the plantations, and methods of sugar refining.[53] While most whites were French Catholics, blacks formed a clear majority with 60 percent of the region's population.

The Sugar Bowl area with 23 percent of the state's rural population, had only 10 percent of rural homicides during Reconstruction. This percentage climbed to 26 percent by the early Redemption period. Politics represented the first cause of homicides, with 26 percent, ahead of personal disputes (24%), criminal activities (18%), and family feuds (14%). Despite the numerous strikes and labor troubles that affected the region, only 5 percent of the homicides were economically related. It is also interesting to note that homicides in the Sugar Bowl region were not concentrated in any particular parish or any particular year; no year exceeded 8 percent of the total.

Politics remained the major cause of homicides during the early Bourbon period due in great extent to the Loreauville riot of 1884, the last major political riot of the period.[54] Nevertheless, fighting among blacks appears to have been the major cause of the increase in the homicide rates during the early Redemption period. By the early 1880s, local newspapers repeatedly reported mortal combat among blacks, which reflected increasing tensions within the black community. For example, the coroner of St. Mary parish held fifteen inquests for homicides between October 1882 and March 1883, and five blacks were killed by other blacks in Assumption parish in July 1882.[55]

The Bluff Land area, which includes the parishes of East Baton Rouge, East Feliciana, and West Feliciana, consists of largely alluvial lands suited for growing corn, cotton, and sugar. There were few towns, but the most important center outside of New Orleans, Baton Rouge, a city of 8,000 people, was located in the area. The white population, a mixture of people of British descent, Creoles, and more recent European immigrants, was one of the smallest percentages in any region of the state with only 30 percent.[56] Moreover, the Bluff Land area had with 70 percent one of the highest concentrations of black people in the state.

During both periods the Bluff Land area had a percentage of homicides lower than its percentage of population. Nevertheless politics with 35 percent was the main cause of violence, while personal conflicts (15%), criminal activities (14%), and social disputes (15%) represent the other major causes of deadly violence. The violence in the region climaxed in the year 1876 when 36 percent of all murders committed in that region occurred. That was the year of the Mount Pleasant riot.[57]

The stealing and illegal traffic of cottonseed and corn was mainly responsible for the turmoil that affected the parishes of East Baton Rouge, East Feliciana, and West Feliciana during the mid-1870s. The planters organized committees to find both the freedmen they presumed were responsible for the thefts and the merchants who were buying the stolen property. The planting classes considered that the store owners involved in this illegal trade were bringing the merchant class into disrepute and ought to be hanged. With the aim of compelling black laborers and white local merchants to quit the seed-cotton traffic, groups of white "regulators" conducted a campaign of terror: roving about the parishes killing and burning stores and gin-houses.[58]

The end of Reconstruction marked a major shift in the patterns of violence in the Bluff Land area, with a substantial drop in the number of killings in all parishes: from 48 to 6 in East Feliciana, from 50 to 9 in West Feliciana, and from 98 to 39 in East Baton Rouge. As a consequence the homicide rates in the region dropped from one of the highest rates in the state during Reconstruction (42 per 100,000 inhabitants) to one of the lowest by the early Redemption years (14 per 100,000 inhabitants).

The Florida parishes were largely inhabited by small Anglo Saxon and Protestant farmers with a reputation as an honest, intelligent, and hardworking people. The presence of a few large plantations explains the 38 percent black population in the area. The region experienced the growth of small towns and villages after the war due to development of the timber industry and various manufacturing products.[59]

With 5 percent of the state's rural population, the Florida parishes had a share of only 1.5 percent of homicides during Reconstruction. But the early Redemption period became more tense and violent as the percentage of homicides climbed to 5.4 percent. The year 1883, which accounted for 15 percent of homicides, was particularly violent. Looking at causes, only 17 percent originated from politics, while personal affrays (27%), family feuds (18%), and criminal activities (18%) were the most important factors contributing to homicidal behavior. By the early Redemption period, lynching became an increasing feature of the violence in the Florida parishes. The Amite lynching of four blacks on December 31, 1879, was the most notorious case.[60]

The Bayou area was a low, flat, sea marshland cut up by many bayous, lakes, swamps, inlets, and bays. These geographical characteristics brought the development of dispersed small communities remote from each other and from the rest of the state. The local population was composed of a mixture of African Americans and people of Spanish, Acadian, German, and Italian descent who mainly lived from hunting, fishing, growing vegetables, and raising cattle for domestic purposes.[61]

Although the Bayou area had a large black population (62%), it proved to be one of the least violent regions of rural Louisiana with only 2 percent of rural homicide during Reconstruction and 4 percent during the early Redemption period. Politics was nevertheless the major cause of homicide, accounting for 39 percent of cases, while personal disputes (17%) and family conflicts (16%) rank respectively second and third. This situation was largely due to the St. Bernard riot of 1868 and the fact that political violence in New Orleans often extended to the neighboring parish of Jefferson.[62] Still, the isolated nature of the communities in this region, their proximity to New Orleans, and the ability of the Federal troops to intervene largely explained the lower homicide rates.

The Significance of Regional Distribution

A look at the general regional distribution of homicides in rural Louisiana after the Civil War shows that violence did not follow the same pattern over time. The point to be emphasized here is that violence was deeply affected by local factors. We have also seen that it varied depending on the social and cultural areas in which the violence occurred.

A first major conclusion is that the concentration of blacks in a region had a direct impact on its homicide rates, because most murders were politically motivated and most political murders were directed against blacks (figs. 2.3 and 2.4). In all rural areas the majority of the victims of white homicides were blacks, even in regions where whites formed a large majority of the population. Only in three regions, the Sugar Bowl, Mississippi Delta, and the Bayou area, did we find a situation where close to half of the black victims of homicide were killed by blacks (fig. 2.5). These three were also among the regions with the highest proportion of black individuals. Meanwhile, an overwhelming proportion of white victims were killed by whites with the exception of the Bayou area where almost half of the white victims were killed by blacks. In almost every region there was little danger of whites being killed by blacks despite the rumors of black insurrection and black intentions of killing whites (figs. 2.6 and 2.7).

The percentage of homicide committed by either blacks or whites is particularly revealing. In every region blacks have a homicide rate far below their proportion of the population. In some regions, such as the Red River parishes, the white homicide rates were more than four times higher than those of blacks. Meanwhile in every region the percentage of black victims of homicide was far above the percentage

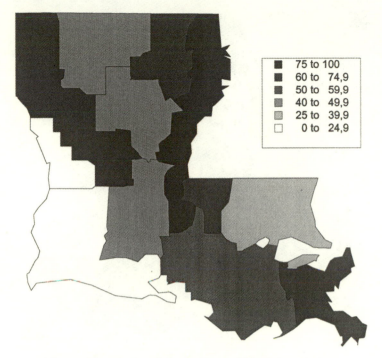

Figure 2.3   Regional Percentage of Black Population

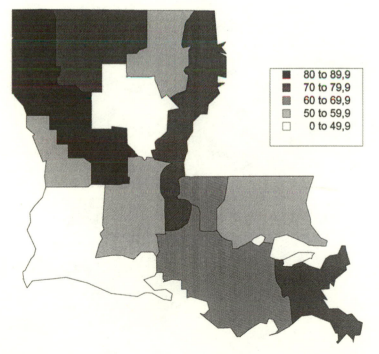

Figure 2.4   Regional Percentage of Black Victims of Homicide

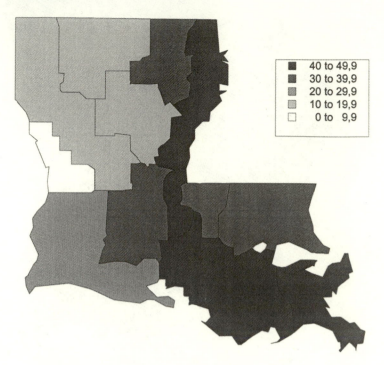

Figure 2.5   Regional Percentage of Blacks Killed by Blacks

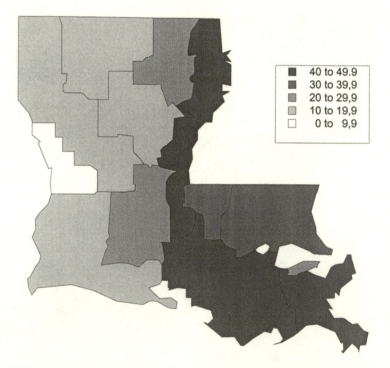

Figure 2.6   Regional Percentage of Homicides Committed by Blacks

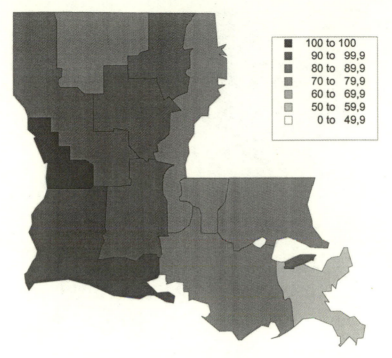

■	100 to 100
■	90 to 99,9
■	80 to 89,9
■	70 to 79,9
■	60 to 69,9
■	50 to 59,9
□	0 to 49,9

Figure 2.7 Regional Percentage of Whites Killed by Whites

of blacks in the population. Although blacks had a lower propensity than whites to commit murder, they were in greater danger than whites of being the victims of such crimes.

The rates of violence tended to drop suddenly in the parishes of the Mississippi Delta where the percentage of blacks was over 80 percent. Furthermore, homicide rates were particularly high in the parishes with a black population of between 50 and 75 percent. This seems to indicate that violence was used as a means of social control and as a way of scaring blacks from the polls in the parishes where blacks formed a majority below 75 percent. Such action could not have been effective where black population was over 75 percent. This hypothesis is further substantiated by the fact that violence was much lower in the parishes with a black population below 40 percent, where whites did not have to resort to violence in order to control the political process and gain offices.

The determination of the white community to maintain a "white man's country" is further shown by the circumstances surrounding

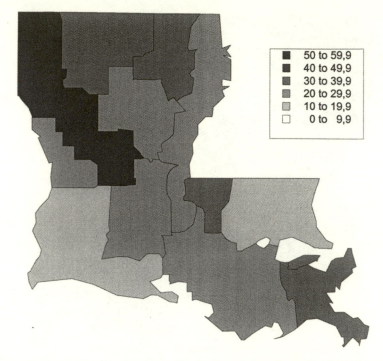

Figure 2.8 Regional Percentage of Politics as a Major Factor of Homicide

homicides. Politics were at the root of most violent deaths, and the highest instances of homicide occurred in areas where blacks were beginning to engage in political activities, joining Republican clubs and asserting their right to vote. Since this was the case in many regions of Louisiana, the object of political control over blacks can not by itself explain the situation in the Red River where whites were so much more violent than anywhere else in Louisiana. In the Red River region some unique factors must have come into play for it to have become the place in Louisiana where human life was least respected. As we have seen above, the Red River parishes was the only region spared by the war, and as a consequence the white population there not only did not feel vanquished but became dominated by a reckless class of people (fig. 2.8).

The regional distribution of homicides changed over the years. In 1868, although violence covered most of the state and only a handful of parishes were left untouched, it was nevertheless concentrated mainly in five parishes (Bossier, Caddo, Jefferson, St. Bernard, and

St. Landry), where major riots occurred in September and October 1868. In those two months whites attempted to establish their control throughout the state by a systematic campaign of terror, and as a result it was estimated that more than a thousand blacks lost their lives during riots or the "negro hunts" that followed.[63]

The years 1868 to 1872 were relatively quiet as political violence subsided, except for two riots that occurred on the night of the 1870 election in Donaldsonville, Ascension parish, and in Baton Rouge,[64] two parishes that had been practically untouched by the general outburst of 1868. Nevertheless these riots represented minor incidents when compared to the 1868 troubles.

The election of 1872 and more particularly the accession to power of the Kellogg government in the spring of 1873 sparked a new wave of violence. The state authorities were compelled to send metropolitan detachments to Livingston and St. Martin parishes. The violence climaxed with the Colfax riot on Easter day of 1873 as white conservatives attempted to prevent Republican elected officials from taking office. During that single day more than a hundred blacks were savagely murdered.[65] By the summer of 1874 political violence spread all over the state. Unlike 1868 the violence took more the form of a general campaign of intimidation than a generalized campaign of murder.[66]

The mid-1870s brought a significant change in the regional distribution of violence as the Bluff Land area, which had been left relatively untouched by the 1868 wave of violence, took fire. By 1876, this area had suffered two years of repeated outbursts of sociopolitical and socioeconomic violence occasionally degenerating into small riots.[67] The same phenomenon occurred in the Northern Bluff Land area, a region that had been quiet since 1868.

The last wave of political violence occurred in 1878 when major disturbances occurred in the parishes of Natchitoches and Caddo, both located in the Red River area, which, as we have seen, had already more than its share of homicide. The 1878 violence was more widespread than that of earlier years since it also struck the parishes of Concordia, Madison, Pointe Coupée, and Tensas located in the Mississippi Delta area, a region that had until then been relatively untouched by political violence.

Taken as a whole, the evidence suggests that a remote region with a high proportion of blacks within its population was more susceptible to violence than a region that had a high proportion of blacks but was closer to New Orleans. Most of rural Louisiana was remote from the control of civil or military authorities. And it was particularly difficult for Federal troops or state militia to intervene quickly in the most remote of all regions of the state, the Red River parishes. The ability of the army to perform its duty and to protect blacks depended largely on the nature of territory. Further complicating matters, the withdrawal of Federal troops from Shreveport in early 1869 made the desperadoes of northwest Louisiana all the more defiant.

The only parishes where blacks and white Republicans were generally protected from intimidation were the ones situated along the main river system. These parishes possessed not only the best lands and the finest plantations of the state, but also the largest concentrations of black population. In these areas, white conservatives were reluctant to resort to intimidation because violence would inevitably have the effect of disrupting crop production. The river parishes were also easily accessible to Federal troops whose mission was to maintain order. As a general rule, more intimidation and violence during Reconstruction took place in parishes that could be reached only by overland transportation.[68]

Conclusion

The present analysis reveals not only that rural Louisiana was more heterogeneous than one may at first thought but also that levels of homicide do vary greatly even within a single state depending on the particular local, political, social, economic, and cultural conditions. This study presents an analysis of the differential impact of these factors on homicide rates in the various regions of the state. The analysis further shows that each region had its own dynamic and that people in various regions did not react in the same way to similar problems because the condition was different.

This distribution of homicides among the various regions stressed all the more the contrast between the lawless and law-abiding regions of the state. Thus the regions with extremely high or extremely low white homicide rates also had extremely high or extremely low black homicide rates. These patterns of homicide did not however hold throughout the years. By the early Redemption era, the distribution of homicide rates became more homogeneous among the various regions of the state.

PART II

The Collective Nature of Homicides

A Most Troubled State: Lawlessness and Popular Disturbance

In late September 1868 an intoxicated trader from Arkansas stopped at the Shady Grove plantation in Bossier parish and asked if there were any radical Republicans. When a young boy pointed out an old black man, the trader pulled out his pistol and fired twice at the aged freedman, missing him both times. This event was followed by the organization of a black posse that proceeded to arrest the trader. A skirmish later took place between the black posse and a group of whites who tried to free the trader. After a bloody fight, the white man was finally released. Whites became so enraged over this matter that they launched a general "negro hunt." In the process, some 185 blacks were killed in Bossier and Caddo parishes.[1]

Political and racial riots, street and tavern brawls, labor and ethnic disturbances, and the actions of criminal bands and lynch mobs, are all forms of collective violence that, taken together, constitute a rough barometer of social and political unrest. These various forms of popular disturbance are important to study not only because they show the willingness of people to act outside the law, but also because they reveal much about the radical social disorganization that affected Louisiana after the Civil War.[2]

The South achieved notoriety during the nineteenth century for its frequent outbursts of violence. In post–Civil War Louisiana violence had become so common, particularly during election periods, that the state legislature was forced to vote no less than three election laws and a riot act in order to cope with the problem.[3] The numerous riots and acts of violence committed during the weeks preceding the presidential election of 1868 and during the summer and fall of 1874, show the readiness of Louisiana whites to resort to extreme violence in order to restore their social and political dominance over the black masses.[4]

The goal of the present chapter is threefold: first, to analyze the various patterns of collective violence and to examine the social and political context that brought people to get involved in riots, disturbances, and other acts of lawlessness; second, to investigate the roots of collective violence and to determine the proportion originating in labor disputes, criminal bands, political and racial antagonisms, or personal and social conflicts; and third, to examine the role of paramilitary organizations such as the Knights of the White Camelia and the White League and to determine how collective acts of violence, particularly political violence, originated from concerted action by whites. In the process we shall be able to determine how paramilitary violence represented a desperate attempt by whites to regain the rights they had once enjoyed over the land and the black population. Finally, in order to get a better understanding of the issue of collective violence, we will compare individual and collective patterns of homicide.[5]

Patterns of Collective Violence

Social scientists and historians have long noted the important distinction between individual and collective forms of violence. While individual or personal violence is commonly considered simply as a crime, collective violence evokes more complex connotations, being often perceived as a form of community protest or popular resistance to intolerable pressure. Students of the phenomenon have nevertheless generally distinguished between violence committed by criminal bands on the one hand and violence committed by people resisting state or local authorities on the other hand. The nature and composition of the violent crowd, their strategies, targets, and grievances are all essential ingredients in analyzing collective violence with a view to understanding its significance.[6]

While collective violence can be generally defined as a radical interruption of social order within a community, it remains a particularly difficult phenomenon to understand when one attempts to become more specific. As Charles Tilly has asserted, collective violence often grows out of actions "which are not intrinsically violent, and which are basically similar to a much larger number of collective actions occurring without violence in the same period and setting."[7] Not surprisingly, the definition of collective violence largely depends on the way the observer looks at it.

One can apply the legal definition of a riot as any disturbance involving the participation of three or more people. Contemporaries generally see popular disturbances differently depending on classes or races involved. In recent years, social scientists have contributed to refine the perception we may have of crowd behavior. They have shown first of all that collective violence or "popular disturbance" differs from individual violence due to its mass character. Their analysis further shows that people involved in collective violence do not necessarily share the same values, and their participation is not always based on the same motivations. Social scientists tend to limit the definition of collective violence to disturbances resulting from a rudimentary and temporarily organized crowd or group. This definition excludes all forms of institutionalized actions.[8] Certain historians such as Hobsbawm, Rudé, and Thompson have enlarged the definition of collective violence to include all forms of popular disturbances whether or not they are institutionally related.[9] It is this last approach that this present study adopts.

Among the many obstacles that face the student of popular disturbance, the first is methodological and arises from the paucity of firsthand accounts by people involved in such events. Too often information is limited to press accounts reflecting the prevalent prejudices and values of reporters. As a consequence it is difficult to get a clear view not only of the motives and feelings of the people involved, but also of the nature of the crowd, its composition, and its way of acting. It is important to keep in mind that the social or political importance of a popular disturbance is not always related to the type of information generally included in press reports such as the number of participants or the number of people killed or arrested. For example, the slaughter of six white Republican officials in the parish of Red River in August 1874 did more to demoralize both white Republicans and blacks than the massacre of more than 100 blacks during the Opelousas riot of 1868. Despite such limitations most social scientists and historians believe that information of this type provides a good basis for analyzing popular disturbances.[10]

For this study, information has been collected from various sources regarding all major incidents of collective violence perpetrated in

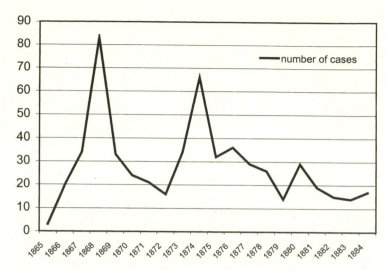

Figure 3.1 Annual Distribution of Major Incidents of Collective Violence

Louisiana during the post–Civil War period. For the purpose of this analysis, a major incident of collective violence is defined as any reported political, labor, social, or racial disturbance or any act of lawlessness that involved ten or more people. Furthermore, different acts of collective violence that occurred during a single riot were not included separately in the data as they had already been counted as part of the said riot.[11] Finally, an incident did not need to be deadly to be included in the present data. While political riots that ended with many deaths were counted, so were cases of destruction of property by white mobs and labor disturbances that caused no violent deaths. Based on these criteria, no less than 565 major incidents of collective violence occurred in Louisiana after the Civil War (fig. 3.1).

These data confirm the accepted view that post–Civil War Louisiana was a very troubled region, particularly during the Reconstruction years. With 402 reported cases, the Reconstruction era suffered 71 percent of the major incidents of collective violence and lawlessness during the entire period. The years 1868 and 1874 were particularly troubled with 83 and 66 incidents respectively, reflecting the political climate of the period. The early Redemption era, in contrast, was comparatively quiet with only 163 incidents, or 29 percent of the total for the period. The annual average shows a substantial drop from 33 violent episodes a year for the first period, to only 20 per year for the latter period as political riots, disturbances, and skirmishes fell dramatically.

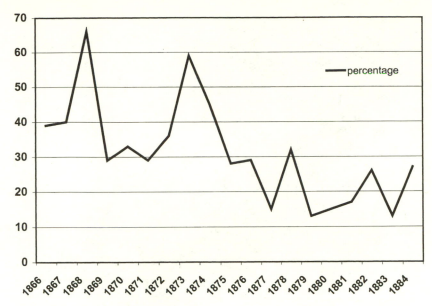

Figure 3.2 Annual Percentage of Homicides Resulting from Collective Violence

One can establish a close correlation between the number of incidents of collective violence and the annual variation in the number of people who died from such violence. Indeed, collective violence had a direct impact on the percentage of people killed. Almost half of the homicides that occurred during Reconstruction were committed by more than one person. The years 1868, 1873, and 1874, which saw major political disturbances, were the only three years with a percentage above 40 percent. These statistics are even more striking when one compares them with the less than 20 percent of homicides committed during the early Redemption period that involved more than one person (fig. 3.2).

The regional distribution of major incidents of collective violence and lawlessness is most revealing. These incidents were largely concentrated in two regions, the Red River area and the Sugar Bowl parishes, which accounted for 22 percent and 19 percent respectively (fig. 3.3). As we have seen, the Red River area was particularly troubled, suffering some of the worst political riots of the period: the Bossier and Caddo riots of 1868, the Colfax massacre of 1873, the Coushatta affair of 1874, the Caledonia riot and the Natchitoches trouble of 1878. On the other hand, the Sugar Bowl area was more the prey of bands of outlaws and robbers. For its part, New Orleans, which was

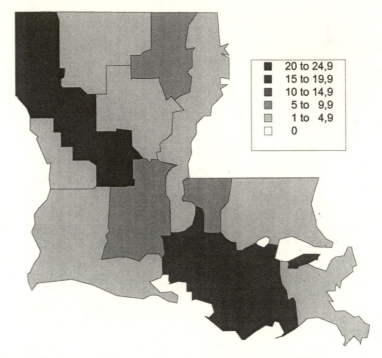

Figure 3.3   Regional Percentage of Major Incidents of Collective Violence

better policed and benefitted from the constant presence of Federal troops, had in proportion to its population the smallest ratio of disturbances. Although New Orleans did suffer a few major riots, such as the riots of 1866 and 1868 and the battle of Liberty Place in 1874, more than 60 percent of the Crescent City's disturbances were not political but labor related.

The correlation between the number of major disturbances and the number of people killed in a particular region yielded further interesting results (fig. 3.4). The data show that three regions, the Red River area, the Northern area, and the Northern Central Hill country, had more than 50 percent of their homicides committed by more than one person. In addition, almost half of the state homicides committed by more than one person occurred in the Red River area alone, which was also the most disturbed region in Louisiana. In contrast, the Sugar Bowl area, despite its high number of disturbances, had a rather low percentage of homicides committed by more than one person. The absence of major political disturbances and riots in that region ex-

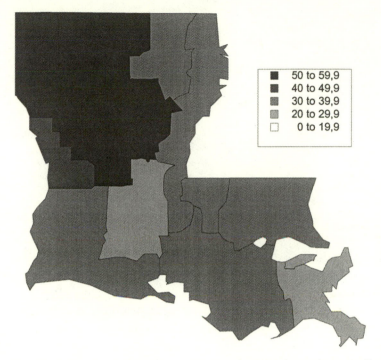

Figure 3.4 Regional Percentage of Homicides Resulting from Collective Violence

plains this particular situation. In all other regions, most people killed died in one-to-one encounters.

The Racial Nature of Collective Violence

A significant tendency revealed by the data is the high incidence of collective violence originating from whites. While whites were responsible for 85 percent of cases of collective violence, blacks were responsible for only 15 percent of such cases. Although the number of cases decreased significantly between the Reconstruction and the early Redemption periods, the racial proportional shares remained almost the same. Whites were largely responsible for lynch mobs and were also the instigators of the great majority of the riots and acts of lawlessness. Black involvement in such disturbances was mainly limited to labor conflicts, attempts at rescuing blacks arrested for alleged crimes, and participation in outlaw and robber bands.

Table 3.1
Collective Nature of Homicidal Behavior, 1866–1884

	Individual		Collective		% Collective
	N	%	N	%	
Unknown by unknown	451	16.4	33	1.9	6.8
Unknown by whites	218	7.9	59	3.5	21.3
Unknown by blacks	118	4.3	11	0.6	8.5
Blacks by unknown	81	2.9	29	1.7	26.4
Whites by unknown	69	2.5	19	1.1	21.6
Whites by whites	612	22.5	257	15.3	29.6
Blacks by whites	514	18.7	1,126	67.0	68.7
Whites by blacks	125	4.5	58	3.4	31.7
Blacks by blacks	564	20.5	88	5.2	13.5
Total	2,752	100.0	1,680	99.7	37.9

The fact that most incidents of collective violence and lawlessness were committed by whites emphasizes the racial nature of collective homicide in post–Civil War Louisiana (table 3.1). In 69 percent of cases where whites killed blacks, the incident involved more than one person, while only 30 percent of the cases when the victim was white, involved more than one white. The statistics are even more striking when one considers black homicidal behavior. No matter the race of the victim, when blacks killed other people, they usually acted alone. Yet the tendency of blacks being involved in mortal personal encounters was higher when the victim was black (86%) than when he was white (68%). This aggregate data clearly shows that blacks were more in danger of falling victim of collective killing than whites; 52 percent of blacks killed were murdered by more than one person, compared to 30 percent in the case of whites. Meanwhile, 52 percent of the times when whites committed a murder they acted in groups, compared to only 16 percent for blacks. Furthermore, blacks were victims in 81 percent of instances of white collective killings. Overall the evidence clearly points to the conclusion that white violence was of an organized nature while this was not the case with black violence.

The nature of collective violence is better understood when one examines the occupations of the perpetrators. The data show that violence against blacks, both individual (50%) and collective (65%), was largely committed by two particular groups: planters and farmers. The need felt by these particular groups to control blacks emerges as a paramount factor leading to collective violence (fig. 3.5). This is made even more obvious when one looks at occupation variables in white

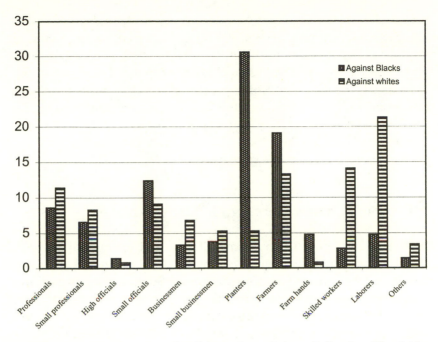

Figure 3.5 Occupations of Whites Committing Collective Homicide: Percentages

violence against whites. Here, only 18 percent of individual violence and 24 percent of the collective violence originated from planters and farmers, both forms of white violence being well spread among the different occupational categories. Local planters and farmers thus assumed the leadership of the Redemption campaign that was nevertheless supported by white conservatives of differing social and economic groups.

While whites who worked small farms had no love for the large planters, they had even less love for blacks. They were fiercely opposed to universal suffrage and to equal rights before the law for blacks. The opposition between poor whites and blacks became sharper after the war, as economic depression accentuated the effect of black competition, increasing racial antagonism.[12] Meanwhile, planters faced with economic ruin were anxious to maintain their control over black labor. Consequently both small farmers and large planters, particularly those who were concentrated in large cotton areas, became advocates of white supremacy, although their motives differed.[13]

But lawlessness and acts of collective violence were not the sole prerogative of whites. In March 1866, Lieutenant M. F. Daugherty, an agent of the Freedmen's Bureau in Gretna, Jefferson parish, reported that street fights and other disturbances between blacks and poor whites were frequent. Daugherty blamed this racial animosity on the inability of "the negroes to conduct themselves in a polite manner and in keeping with their true condition." He particularly criticized blacks for their habit of coming into town heavily armed and for using their weapons without provocation.[14] Disturbances of this sort were reported regularly all over the state by local newspapers.[15]

A Favorable Atmosphere for Collective Violence

Although street brawls, disturbances, riots, and various acts of lawlessness are social phenomena common to all traditional societies, they were particularly characteristic of the South during the second half of the nineteenth century. The war not only emancipated the slaves and produced social dislocation, it also helped to develop within the white community a greater tolerance for violence. One of the bloodiest wars in history had contributed to making bloodshed more acceptable. To the extent that fighting men had come to learn that killing fellow citizens was not so grave a matter, the war weakened moral principles and encouraged men to take justice into their own hands, creating an atmosphere of lawlessness.

The war had an influence on both blacks and whites. Blacks ran away from the plantations; white deserters hid in the countryside; and returning soldiers encountered difficulties in readapting to civilian life. Bands of guerrillas, known as jayhawkers, who had roamed the region in the later stages of the war transformed themselves during Reconstruction into gangs of marauders and robbers. The Lawson Kimball and John West band was typical of Louisiana post–Civil War gangs of outlaws and robbers. These two notorious criminals had led separate guerrilla bands during and after the war and later joined forces. They operated during the late 1860s in Winn parish and made incursions into the adjoining parishes. They were involved in the 1866 murder of Lieutenant Butts of the U.S. Army. They rode and robbed throughout the countryside, killing blacks and stealing horses. The band was finally dismantled in April 1870 when its members were either killed or arrested by a vigilance committee.[16] The Kimball and West gang, the Beaver, the Black Horse Cavalry, the Fontenot, and the Guillory gangs were indeed the most notorious of such bands plundering rural Louisiana with total impunity for a number of years.[17]

The presence of criminal bands was not limited to the years immediately after the war. During the middle and late 1870s and early 1880s, many bands of outlaws continued to prey on several regions of Louisiana. The Cicero gang emerged as one of the worst bands of outlaws. In 1874 and 1875, in a locality commonly called "Hog Thief Point" about 12 miles south of Shreveport, that gang committed a number of atrocious murders, several of them extremely brutal. A similar well-organized gang operated during the early 1880s in the lower part of St. Landry in the neighborhood of Grand Coteau, killing blacks during the night and creating a reign of terror.[18]

As Federal authorities did not have enough troops in Louisiana to maintain law and order in rural areas, these gangs contributed to the general atmosphere of anarchy that prevailed in the Pelican State after the war. Gangs rode around the countryside, whipping and robbing freedmen, and defying the military and civil authorities before retreating to the swamps that offered secure hiding places.[19]

Nevertheless criminal activity was not limited to former guerrillas and jayhawkers. Blacks were also involved in acts of lawlessness as they regularly attempted to rescue other blacks who had been arrested for robberies or other crimes. In December 1867, blacks in Franklin, St. Mary parish, attempted to rescue a band of black horse thieves from St. Landry who had been put in jail.[20] In the same month intense excitement prevailed at St. Martinville after a mulatto who had shot at O. Delahousaye Jr., a white constable, was arrested. When blacks tried to rescue the prisoner from the hands of a sheriff, the latter was promptly reinforced by whites, and only the swift intervention of the Freedmen's Bureau agent prevented a riot from breaking out.[21] In 1868 a group of black outlaws committed a series of assassinations close to the town of Tigerville. Parties lay in ambush along the Opelousas railroad and fired on passing trains. In the ordeal, four railroad employees were murdered. The band was acting without any ostensible motive or reason. Robbery could hardly be the supposed motive, since the band took no measures to throw the car off the road.[22] In 1872, William Smith, a black arraigned on a charge of hog stealing, was rescued from the guard of a constable by a band of thirteen armed blacks while on his way to Monroe to appear before the district judge.[23] In

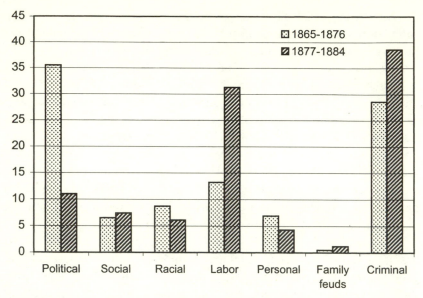

Figure 3.6 Motives Underlying Major Incidents of Collective Violence (percentages)

June 1874 some fifty blacks attempted to rescue the supposed murderer of "Old Eastin" from jail in Napoléonville, but they were stopped by some four or five whites who had been posted there to prevent a rescue.[24]

Criminal activities were the underlying causes of 32 percent of the incidents of collective violence during the entire period: 29 percent during Reconstruction and 39 percent for the early Redemption era (fig. 3.6). Data on the more primary reasons for which people were killed yields further interesting information (fig. 3.7). While depredations committed by criminal bands represent, in terms of numbers, the major cause of collective violence, they remain a rather secondary factor in explaining homicides. Contrary to the assertion made by contemporaries, criminal bands usually only resorted to homicide as a last recourse. As shown in figure 3.7, the number of homicides committed by outlaw bands in the process of committing a crime were quite limited.

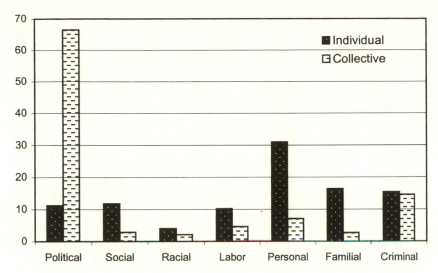

Figure 3.7   Motives Underlying Collective Homicide (percentages)

Popular Disturbances as a Means of Social Control

It is an unquestionable fact that the general atmosphere of violence and anarchy that prevailed in the South after the Civil War influenced all aspects of social interaction during that troubled period as political riots, social and labor disturbances, murders and other personal disputes reached unprecedented levels. In many parishes after the war, no one had the authority or was willing to bring criminals to justice.[25]

Consequently sheriffs increasingly resorted the posse and other forms of citizen police to maintain law and order. It was such a posse, composed of 150 whites and led by Sheriff Hill, that arrested 48 blacks in August 1868 in Bossier parish when rumors of a black insurrection began to circulate. The whole affair began when the sheriff attempted to arrest several blacks on the charge of stealing cattle.[26] It eventually led to a riot that struck the parish in late September of the same year.

Often whites did not wait for the official formation of a posse before getting together to regulate the countryside. Bands of masked men regularly took to the road, committing various atrocities and not hesitating to stain their hands with blood upon the slightest provocation. In 1867 eight freedmen who had been arrested on the charge of having killed a planter, were met, while being taken to prison, by a party of masked men. Two of the prisoners were shot dead, and the six others were also probably murdered since no trace of them was ever found.[27] Incidents of this sort were not uncommon in post–Civil War Louisiana.

The simple rumor of a black insurrection was enough to generate an upheaval of all whites of the surrounding areas. For example, a rumor was spread in the parish of West Feliciana in September 1874 that blacks were gathering to attack the town of Bayou Sara. The rumor created a wild excitement among the town population. As a black crowd was coming to town, the black sheriff of the parish called a posse of thirteen whites and chose to stop the black crowd at the entry of the town. After a few shots were fired, the black crowd ran in all directions. Meanwhile fifty whites from the surrounding country gathered in Bayou Sara to give assistance to the posse. The incident ended only after 400 blacks, who had gathered at Kellertown to define an appropriate course, chose to disperse in order to avoid a riot.[28]

This periodic and exaggerated fear of black insurrections brought frightful and bloody retribution on the black community. With each new rumor of an impending black uprising, the parishes were then transformed into a hunting ground, as whites all over the region rallied, feeling it their duty to crush the insurrection at its beginning. Posses were organized and whites scouted the rural areas in paramilitary groups in search of rebellious freedmen. During these "negro hunts," countless numbers of freedmen were taken from their homes and either killed or forced to leave their homes, crops, and all they possessed.[29]

Whenever a black man had a dispute with a white man, the fact that he should be sustained by another black would instantly rally the entire white community, convinced that it was facing a riot.[30] In July 1874 a black man named Sam Wallis had a quarrel in Shreveport with a white merchant named Demetz. When Demetz wounded Wallis, a row involving some 40 blacks versus a group of whites developed. The blacks retired only after a swift intervention on the part of the city police prevented the conflict from reaching tragic proportions.[31]

A similar incident occurred in Ascension parish in June 1881. An old white man named William J. Dowling was travelling along the coast peddling fishing lines and was going from Uncle Sam plantation to Jacobs's sawmill, when he was arrested by a gang of fifteen black men from Uncle Sam's place, who charged Dowling with robbing Alexis Lagroue, a black man, of his money. As the crowd was going back to the plantation with their prisoner, proclaiming their intention of punishing him in their own way, their noise attracted the notice of a party of young white men in L. N. Landry's store, who went out and rescued the old man from the blacks. After many threats the blacks agreed to surrender their prisoner in order to avoid an open confrontation.[32]

White interference in black quarrels often deteriorated into racial violence, as if it was the duty of whites to regulate black behavior. In Pointe Coupée in March 1880, a white attempted to suppress a row between a black man and his wife. As the black man resisted the interference, the white shot and killed the black.[33] A similar incident occurred in the same parish in August 1881 when a black dance degenerated into a row on a Saturday night. Lieutenant Chenevert, a planter and former Confederate officer but not a member of the U.S. army, was killed while he tried, with the assistance of a few other whites, to reestablish order. Furthermore, another white and a few blacks were wounded during the brawls. As the news spread, a large crowd of whites gathered on Sunday morning at the site of the incident and proceeded to arrest fifteen blacks. Both black and white communities were extremely agitated. As a consequence the stores of the town remained closed and business was suspended for a few days.[34]

All in all, family feuds, parties, and social conflicts of various types rarely worsened into collective violence. Social causes represent only 21 percent of all collective incidents of violence. These causes did not vary much between Reconstruction and the early Redemption period. Moreover, in comparative terms, relatively few people died in such disturbances. This shows a willingness among people to solve their personal disputes on a one-to-one basis rather than through mobilizing community action.

Labor Disturbances as a Cause of Collective Violence

Labor represented the fundamental issue for Southern planters after the war due to the abolition of slavery. The survival of the plantation system necessitated a bitter and prolonged process involving major changes in farming methods and in the credit system. Partly ruined by the war and threatened with foreclosure and bankruptcy during Reconstruction because of crop failures and overtaxation, planters were also faced with pressures on the part of freedmen for better wages and long contracts. Planters gradually found in the annual contract system, developed by the Freedmen's Bureau, the best method for preserving the old plantation organization. But freedmen were often reluctant to work under the wage system, since it implied gang labor reminiscent of the old servile system. Since planters refused to sell or even to rent lands to freedmen, sharecropping emerged as the system most acceptable to both sides.[35]

The transformation of farming methods did not prevent blacks from striking or protesting against their labor condition. There were rare instances of black laborers assaulting and even killing their employers. Labor disturbances in rural Louisiana were often described by whites as a black uprising, riot, or insurrection, raising the worst white pre-antebellum fears.[36] In fact disturbances on plantations were not limited to blacks, as they also originated from Chinese laborers discontented with their conditions.[37] For example, Chinese working on the plantation of William Shaffer and M. J. Williams in Terrebonne parish made an uprising in September 1871 and seized the overseer of the plantation.[38] Fights between planters that competed for labor were also an important cause of labor disturbances. As James Payne hired laborers from Virginia, some whites tried to entice the laborers away from him. The fight that ensued took a tragic turn, as one night a group of whites came to Payne's plantation and set fire to the gin-house. Payne was killed while trying to defend his property.[39]

Furthermore, labor disturbances in rural Louisiana originated also from fields of economic activities other than agricultural: out of fifty major labor disturbances that occurred in the Louisiana countryside, eight were of this type. The most notable strikes involved the hod carriers in Shreveport in 1869, black coal heavers in Brashear city in 1875, lumbermen in 1877 and 1879 in Calcasieu, draymen in Shreveport in 1880, and finally railroad workers on the Vicksburg, Shreveport, and Pacific Railroad in April 1882 and March 1883.[40]

The Brashear strike is a good example of the nature of labor disturbance in a small town. In late August 1875, a large gang of black coal heavers employed by Charles Morgan began to protest for higher wages. Rumors spread that the blacks were threatening to burn the town and kill all those who opposed them. Apprehending a riot, Mayor St. Claire, Town Attorney Winchester, and Councilman Mac-Cready took decisive steps to control the so-called black strike.[41] But in fact, the crisis had been blown out of proportion. No strike had

Table 3.2
Labor Disturbances in Louisiana, 1866–1884

Regions	1866–1876		1877–1884		Total	
	N	%	N	%	N	%
Rural parishes	30	56.7	20	39.2	50	48.1
New Orleans	23	43.3	31	60.8	54	51.9
Total	53	100.0	51	100.0	104	100.0

taken place; blacks had only demanded to be paid in money rather than in goods at the Ehrman's store, because they felt cheated by Ehrman. During the fight that followed a dozen shots were fired, all by whites. The only wounded person was black. The whole disturbance, which ended with the arrest of several black workers, showed that the control of black labor remained paramount even for white Republican officials.[42]

Labor disturbances in particular were not limited to rural areas as more than half occurred in New Orleans (table 3.2). Both white and black workers of the Crescent City developed a class consciousness after the war, not hesitating to strike together in order to maintain or improve their wages and working conditions. On many occasions they opted for class solidarity that went beyond racial division.[43]

While strikes and other forms of labor disturbances had already been part of the social features of antebellum New Orleans, the economic depression that struck the city during Reconstruction led to an increase of such disturbances. Indeed labor disturbances emerged after the war as the most significant form of popular conflict, most incidents of collective violence being labor related. While strikes in New Orleans affected almost every trade, they were still mainly concentrated at the port: longshoremen on the levees were responsible for 27 strikes, a proportion of 50 percent of all city strikes between 1865 and 1884.[44] Strikes by longshoremen predominated during Reconstruction,[45] while strikes in other trades were more frequent during the early Redemption period.[46]

Labor disturbances, described regularly as labor riots, work stoppages, disputes over crop settlements, and other forms of labor disruptions, represented 18 percent of all incidents of collective violence in Louisiana, but only 10 percent of homicides and only 5 percent of collective homicides. Labor conflict was not directly a major cause of violence in Louisiana.

The Political Motives for Collective Violence

Post–Civil War violence in Louisiana has to be considered in relation to Southern thought and values at the time. Whites in Louisiana, as elsewhere in the South, were afraid of losing their sense of identity, and they were not ready to accept the changes that threatened the images they had of themselves and of blacks. Consequently white violence has to be understood from a racist and white supremacist perspective, as a reactionary fear by a large segment of the white population and as a desperate attempt to regain the rights they had once enjoyed over the lands and the black population.[47]

In 1866 and 1867, but more particularly during the spring and summer of 1868, activities of bands of whites working as paramilitary organizations, such as the Knights of the White Camelia, were reported in various parishes. These bands roamed the countryside in the night, terrorizing blacks and preventing them from joining Republican clubs.[48] State government reports demonstrate that violence in 1868 resulted from a concerted action aimed at forcing blacks to abstain from voting and at driving white Republican leaders out of the state.[49] By the summer and fall of 1868, violence in Louisiana clearly took a political overtone and started with rumors that a victory for Horatio Seymour and Frank Blair at the presidential election would mean the overthrow of Reconstruction. Blacks could avoid intimidation and violence by joining Democratic clubs that gave them "protection papers."[50] As white passions reached a paroxysm of rage, violence degenerated into mass murder during the 1868 presidential election when Louisiana was struck by numerous major riots.[51]

A second wave of violence began in 1873 on the part of white conservatives, fiercely opposed to the new Republican administration led by Governor W. P. Kellogg, attempting to prevent the installation of local Republican officials in several parishes. The state authorities were compelled to send detachments of the New Orleans Metropolitan Police into several rural areas to reestablish order. The crisis culminated on Easter day, April 13, 1873, when hundreds of whites from Grant, Rapides, and Catahoula parishes rallied at Colfax where they slaughtered more than one hundred blacks in cold blood. Blacks with their throats cut were left in the field for later burial by the military authorities.[52]

The year 1874 was marked by an uprising of the White League, a loosely structured, paramilitary and antiradical organization, which took temporary control of the whole state. The strategy of the White

League was aimed not only at intimidating blacks but also at expelling white Republicans from local parishes.[53] During the summer and fall of 1874, the *Shreveport Times* and other rural papers repeatedly called on whites to rally for concerted action, and if necessary to resort to political assassination of the radical white leaders throughout northwest Louisiana. The *Times*'s "extreme and blood-thirsty utterances" were so widely quoted that they attracted national attention to the dangerous conditions prevailing in Louisiana.[54]

Blacks in rural Louisiana were made to feel the wrath of the white community as whites began roaming rural areas in paramilitary groups. Frightful stories began to circulate about the violent conditions prevailing in many parishes. The *Shreveport Times* acknowledged that blacks in Caddo and throughout the adjoining parishes were uneasy, "in doubt as to the intention of the white people," frightened, and in a "frame of mind to be led by bad men into action that will bring upon them a fearful retribution." Blacks became terrorized and apprehensive for their lives. As they suffered numerous acts of violence from the White Leaguers, many chose to sleep out in the woods to escape the white fury. Numerous bodies of unknown blacks were later found.[55]

Calls for violence issued by the *Shreveport Times* prompted large numbers of whites to leave Shreveport in Caddo parish on August 30, 1874, for Coushatta in Red River parish to participate in the murder of six white Republican officials. The brutal slaughter of these white officials had a devastating effect on the Republican leadership. The *Times* asserted that it was the duty of the white community to kill the members of the returning board and proposed to dispose of all radical legislators by lynching them. Not surprisingly, all Republican officials in northern Louisiana felt forced to resign in order to avoid a reenactment of the Coushatta tragedy.[56] The White League uprising culminated with the victory of the battle of Liberty Place in New Orleans in September 1874.

The victory was short-lived, however, as the Federal army quickly reestablished Republican officials in New Orleans and other parts of the state. Among ways subsequently employed to compel blacks to abstain from voting or to vote for the White League ticket, calls were issued to planters to discharge all workers who would vote Republican.[57] This campaign of intimidation continued in 1875 and 1876 as white conservatives bulldozed Republicans officials and compelled them to resign.

The election of 1876 marked a shift in strategy as white conservatives resorted to violence, not so much to prevent blacks from voting, but in order to force them to vote for the Democratic ticket.[58] Several political murders were committed in various parishes, the most notable being the killing of Sheriff Dinkgrave in Ouachita parish. Yet as a rule, conservatives devised a strategy that avoided open confrontation with Republican authorities. As a consequence the only major riot of 1876 occurred on June 20th in the parish of East Baton Rouge when some twenty blacks were killed in what became known as the Mount Pleasant massacre.[59]

In 1878 white conservatives pursued their strategy of influencing the vote of the parishes of north Louisiana, which had a large black population, in order to create a Democratic majority. The situation quickly got out of control as a riot broke out on the night of the election at Caledonia, a village twenty-five miles below Shreveport on the Red River. The riot broke out as a group of whites led by Deputy Sheriff McNeil, following rumors that blacks had gathered arms in the vicinity of the polls, attempted to search a house owned by a black.[60] At first the fight involved seventy-five blacks and about twenty whites, but as only a few blacks were armed, they were rapidly driven into the swamps and other hiding places by the whites.[61]

Then a "negro hunt" began as white reinforcements gathered from diverse places and parishes. The unrest lasted several days. It is difficult to ascertain the exact number of blacks who were killed during the riot and the "hunt" that followed. The whites took no prisoners and did not take care of the wounded. United States District Attorney Leonard fixed the number of blacks killed between fifty to seventy-five, while the Democratic press put at first the number at fifteen. Meanwhile the U.S. Senatorial Committee that investigated the riot fixed the number of blacks killed at twenty. Only two whites were reported wounded. Thus ended radical rule in Caddo parish as the Democratic party carried the election by 1,500 votes.[62]

Riots broke out in Natchitoches and Caddo, while bulldozing and general intimidation became the rule in Madison, Concordia, and Tensas. Whites also organized themselves into paramilitary groups and terrorized blacks in other parts of the state.[63] The level of violence shocked Governor F. T. Nicholls, a moderate Democrat who was opposed to the use of violence. Meanwhile, in many parishes Democrats succeeded in carrying the election by fraud and ballot-stuffing. In Natchitoches, the Democratic party carried the parish by a vote of 2,811 to 0, while in Caddo, Concordia, Madison, and Tensas the large Republican majorities of 1876 simply evaporated.[64]

While politics was not a major factor in individual homicides (11%), it represented the single most important cause in collective killing (67%). Indeed, 85 percent of people killed for political reasons died during major disturbances. As Leon Litwack has asserted, white violence was well-organized.[65] Evidence shows that whites did not assault or kill blacks at random but followed a deliberate and selective policy aimed at intimidating white Republicans, eliminating black leadership, and terrorizing the black population. Congressional committees reported numerous instances in which black males were taken out of their cabins and shot by unknown white parties, while the victims' wives and children remained unmolested. During the St. Landry riot of 1868, which deteriorated into mass-murder, only blacks wearing a red string tied around their arms were exempted from white violence.[66]

White conservative leaders publicly promoted the killing of blacks and scalawags as a solution for Louisiana's political ills. In 1868 local White Camelia leaders selected targets in their respective parishes among prominent or politically active blacks and among white Republicans.[67] Even more effective was the White League, whose strategy was simple and direct. It consisted of intimidating not only blacks and white Republicans, but also any moderate white not afraid of speaking his mind. The White League strategy consisted of a mixture of social ostracism and physical violence. Political murders were only a part of this exercise of intimidation.[68]

Consequently much of the white anger was directed against blacks who began to engage in political activities, join Republican clubs, and assert their right to vote. Blacks who wished to play a political role were systematically singled out. Out of 1,450 blacks who fell victim to white violence during Reconstruction, 24.6 percent were local or state officeholders or held an office within the Republican party.

During the riot that struck the St. Bernard parish in October 1868, all black constables, justices of the peace, and police jury members were killed. Even being a member of the state legislature did not ensure immunity from violence, as several black senators and house members became special targets of the white fury. William R. Meadows, an ex-slave and former member of the 1867 constitutional convention was killed in May 1868 in Claiborne parish. Senator Alexander François from St. Martin parish was beaten to death in May 1869 by Colonel Fournet after the former published a letter on the abuses practiced on blacks in his parish. John Gair and John Wiggins, two members of the House of Representatives, were respectively poisoned and shot in 1873 and 1875. Joseph Lofficial was killed after being elected to the legislature in November 1870. Joseph Antoine, son of Ceasar C. Antoine, was killed during the presidential campaign of 1868. Finally, Franklin St. Clair, a candidate for the state house in 1868, was killed while returning from a speaking engagement in Morehouse parish.[69]

Many charges of larceny, robbery, and other property offenses against white Republicans were politically motivated. In many instances the charge of stealing chickens was used to justify the killing of white Republicans. Many eminent black politicians also met with the same fate on trumped-up charges of stealing hogs, chickens, and cattle.[70] By regularly accusing white radicals of inciting blacks to murder and robbery, Democratic newspapers all over the state justified attacks against white Republicans and Republican newspapers. Consequently the presses and offices of the following Republican newspapers were destroyed by white mobs: the *St. Landry Progress* on September 28, 1868; the *Attakapas Register* on October 19, 1868; the *Claiborne Republican* on November 17, 1868; the *Marksville Weekly Register* on December 30, 1868; and the *Shreveport Southwestern Telegram* on December 23, 1874.[71]

Conclusion

The post–Civil War years were without doubt the most tumultuous period in Louisiana history. The numerous incidents of collective violence that struck the Pelican State after the Civil War reveal the brutal character of nineteenth-century Louisiana society. The evidence is devastating; it confirms the frightful stories of murder, intimidation, rowdyism, and lawlessness reported in the correspondence of both the Freedmen's Bureau and Gulf Department, and the numerous testimonies contained in the reports and executive documents submitted to Congress. It shows that in Louisiana, human life was of little value in what became a war of race during Reconstruction.

Several factors were linked in bringing about the general atmosphere of anarchy that prevailed in Louisiana after the war: the demoralization of the white population following a bitter defeat; the racial and political animosity produced by emancipation; the social disorganization generated by the emergence of lawless groups; and the unsteady economic condition brought by depression and the transformation of the plantation economy.

Above all the turmoil of the period may be seen as the expression of the frustration of the white community in general as it found itself unable to cope with the new political situation. With emancipation, Louisiana—along with the rest of the South—saw the emergence of a new political order that introduced blacks into local, state, and national politics. The numerous political riots that struck Louisiana during Reconstruction reflect the white resistance to this major transformation brought about by the integration of blacks into the political process. The development of lynching and vigilantism in post–Civil War Louisiana demonstrate unequivocally the nature of white response to the changes generated by emancipation.

Toward a Reign of Terror: Vigilantism and Lynch Law

I n August 1877, Baptiste Celestin, a black resident of St. Mary parish, was arrested by thirty armed men and brought before the local justice of the peace on the charge of larceny. Due proceedings were held and witnesses summoned, a majority of whom were members of the local vigilance committee. After a full investigation of the case, the accused man was discharged for lack of evidence. The members of the vigilance committee took charge of the case themselves and sentenced the man to exile beyond the borders of Louisiana for twenty years.[1] Such cases were not unusual in rural Louisiana before and after the war. Celestin was in fact quite lucky since lynching became increasingly the punishment reserved for those caught stealing in post–Civil War Louisiana.

By the late nineteenth century, vigilantism became both the preferred response of Louisiana's established classes when confronted by a threat to their predominance and a method used by these same classes for dealing with social turmoil. They increasingly chose to use violence against other individuals or classes as a way to "preserve status quo at times when the formal system of rule enforcement is viewed as ineffective or irrelevant."[2] In this sense vigilantism and lynching were the products of a rupture in the judicial system. Such practices rested on the belief in the ultimate right of local citizens to enforce order: a belief fostered by a society in which violence had become a regular part of daily life. Believing that they could not obtain justice from the legally constituted authorities, people taking justice into their own hands was the only remedy for an intolerable situation.[3]

The historical study of vigilantism and lynching in North America has recently received a new impetus.[4] Although historians have for a long time acknowledged that vigilantism and, more particularly, lynching were widespread in the South after the Civil War, most historians have until recently doubted that a "credible history of the phenomenon could be made for lack of sufficient information."[5] As a consequence the only systematic analysis of lynching and vigilantism has come almost exclusively from other social scientists, mainly sociologists who have relied on data collected either by the *Chicago Tribune* or the National Association for the Advancement of Colored People on lynching in the late nineteenth and early twentieth centuries.[6] No systematic quantitative analysis has so far been done for Louisiana on this subject covering the years 1866 to 1884.[7]

Drawing upon but not limiting itself to statistical data, this chapter examines the emergence and the salient patterns of vigilantism and lynching in post–Civil War Louisiana. By paying particular attention to the nature and the causes of vigilantism and lynching, this study seeks to determine to what extent these two phenomena were interconnected and examine how they evolved over the period. In the process, their relation to the contradictions inherent in the white society's fundamental values shall be determined.

Lynching versus Vigilantism

Before looking at the data, we must first define what is meant by vigilantism and lynching. During the second half of the nineteenth century in Louisiana, vigilantism and lynching became a part of the established pattern of violence used by dominant groups of citizens to ensure the maintenance of public order, the protection of social mores, and as a means of countering social change. Organized secretly or carried out openly, such violence was given different epithets such as mob law, lynch law, or vigilantism. The groups involved were, over the period, called regulators, citizens' protective associations, committees of safety, bulldozers, lynching mobs, vigilantes, vigilance movements, or vigilance committees.[8] All these groups had the following characteristics in common: they operated under what they considered extraordinary emergency conditions, and since they were not ready to wait for the slow and uncertain action of the legal system, they operated outside of the law.[9]

Vigilance committees can be defined as groups of citizens organized to preserve the community from crimes or to deal "popular justice"[10] in regions where courts and constitutional authorities seemed power-less to enforce the law. Springing from what was seen as inadequacies in protective law, these committees represented a popular response to depredations committed by alleged criminals in a particular region or state. Although they took the law into their own hands and dealt out punishment without any pretense of legality or due process of law, vigilance committees in Louisiana differed from lynch mobs by the fact that they were well organized and better disciplined.[11]

Vigilance committees could operate for weeks and even months be-fore disbanding. The duties and organization of each committee were clearly specified in its statutes. Not only were most committees di-rected by an executive, many had written constitutions, maintained a list of members, held regular monthly meetings, kept minutes of their proceedings, and received regular reports from surrounding wards and precincts. Membership was conditional on unanimous vote of the reg-ular members and involved payment of a membership fee. Some vigi-lance committees even published advertisements in local newspapers inviting all people interested in justice to attend their meetings.[12]

Lynching differed from vigilantism by its more spontaneous and less organized nature. Rather than offering society protection against bands of criminals, as vigilance committees did, lynching was a means of punishing particular alleged criminals. Lynching has been defined as a popular and extralegal punishment administered by an excited mob resulting in the death or maiming of one or more victims.[13] Such a definition is too general, however, to be applicable for this study covering the years 1866 to 1884.

It is also important to differentiate lynchings from riots. Lynching is habitually the killing of one or more persons who is/are seized and illegally executed for an alleged crime, while a riot usually involves the haphazard killing of people at random by a mob under strong excitement. Therefore the latter type of violent death is excluded from consideration. Furthermore, all cases of murders committed by bands of outlaws were also rejected. If including in the definition of lynching all cases in which an individual was killed in a riot or was victim of a brutal murder committed by more than one person, the number of people lynched in post–Civil War Louisiana would have run to more than a thousand.[14] For the purposes of the present study, a lynching incident is defined as an act of violence in which one or more victims were seized and summarily tried before being maimed or put to death for having allegedly committed a crime or violated established social mores.[15]

The Distribution of Lynching and Vigilantism

With this criteria information was collected on 33 vigilance committees and 239 incidents of lynching[16] that occurred between 1866 and 1884 (figs. 4.1 and 4.2). The statistical breakdown of the data gives an overall panorama of the evolution of lynching and vigilantism in Louisiana. Although the number of lynchings may appear rather high, they are nevertheless similar to the well-documented figures for the 1890s.[17] The collected data represent a significant record of the structure of community control in the context of the important social change affecting Louisiana during the post–Civil War decades. It is particularly significant that the peak year for vigilantism was 1876, a year that preceded important social and political change, and that lynching was also particularly high in 1868 and 1874, two years that saw attempts by conservative white Democrats to overthrow Republicans from power. The data furthermore suggest that it was over a long period of time that public opinion in Louisiana gradually grew

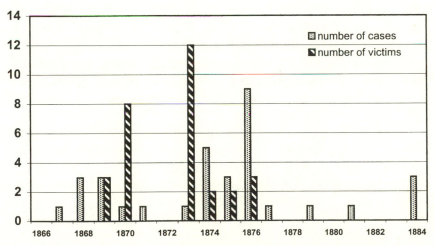

Figure 4.1 Annual Distribution of Vigilance Committees

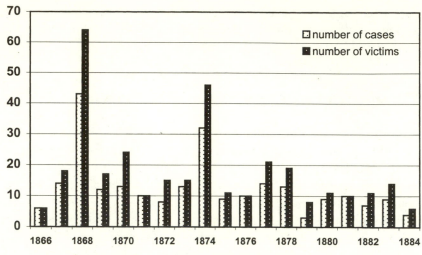

Figure 4.2 Annual Distribution of Lynchings

comfortable with the idea that vigilantism and lynching were accept-able—an attitude we know existed at the end of the century.

Evidence supports James Cutler's assertion that there was a ten-dency "for vigilance societies organized in the interest of the law and order" to fall under the control of the more vicious and lawless ele-ments of society, in the process losing any restraint they may have had in using violence. Indeed, the data show that vigilantism preceded lynching and set the tone for popular justice in Louisiana. While vigi-lance committees were an important feature of the late antebellum period, lynching remained exceptional.[18] While both forms of popular justice remained prevalent throughout Reconstruction, their paths di-verged with the end of radical rule. Vigilance violence almost disap-peared during the early Redemption period, while lynching remained an important feature of the time.[19]

Protected by their market value under slavery, blacks were rarely victims of lynching prior to the Civil War.[20] This was no longer the case after the war. With emancipation, extralegal killing of blacks by whites became a disturbing feature of race relations in Louisiana and in the South in general.[21] Blacks were victims of 73 percent of the lynching incidents occurring during Reconstruction and 68 percent of those occurring during the early Redemption years (table 4.1). These percentages are similar to the ones presented by other historians or social scientists regarding the same period.[22] The average number of

Table 4.1
Racial Distribution of Lynching in Louisiana

	Whites	Blacks	% of Blacks	Total
1866–76	46 (67)	124 (168)	73.0	170 (235)
1877–84	22 (31)	47 (69)	68.0	69 (100)
Total	68 (98)	171 (237)	71.7	239 (335)

Note: Numbers in parentheses are the number of people killed.

victims per incident, however, is a little higher during Reconstruction (1.38) and early Redemption (1.45) than during the period of 1882 to 1930 (1.24).[23]

The racial nature of lynching is further shown by the direct implication of whites in 238 out of 239 lynching incidents of the period. For their part, black people were rarely influenced by the lawless spirit of the period as far as lynching was concerned. Indeed lynching paradoxically furnished occasions for biracial cooperation, as shown by seven instances of blacks being killed by integrated mobs.[24] For example, George Stubinger, the sheriff of Iberia parish was murdered in December 1869 by a black while attempting to maintain order. A group composed of whites and blacks immediately caught and lynched the black without any form of trial.[25] Moreover, civil authorities in Caddo intervened in 1875 against a group of blacks, preventing them from lynching a member of their own race.[26]

The breakdown of statistics on a regional basis shows that vigilantism and lynching varied greatly in total frequency and in rates among the various regions of the state. Indeed more than 50 percent of the vigilance committees were located in the Sugar Bowl area. Twenty-four out of 33 vigilance committees originated in the 19 Cajun and Creole parishes of southern Louisiana: four of those parishes—Lafayette, Iberia, St. Mary, and Vermilion—had 19 vigilance committees (fig. 4.3). Vigilantism in southern Louisiana seems to have been a local response to a local problem: what to do with the cattle thieves of the region.[27] Meanwhile, a third of Louisiana lynchings were concentrated in the seven parishes of the Red River Delta, a region that had less than 10 percent of the state population (fig. 4.4). Vigilantism and lynching were thus concentrated in two distinct regions of Louisiana.[28]

The data do not support the "power-threat" theory developed by sociologists that argues that whites would be more likely to use collective violence, such as lynching, when they formed a small minority in

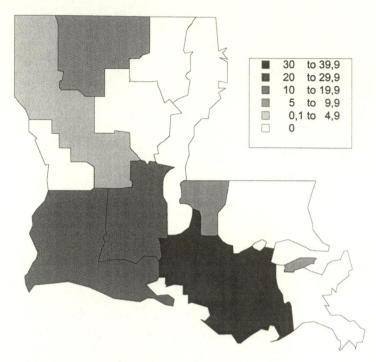

Figure 4.3   Regional Percentage of Vigilance Committees, 1866–1884

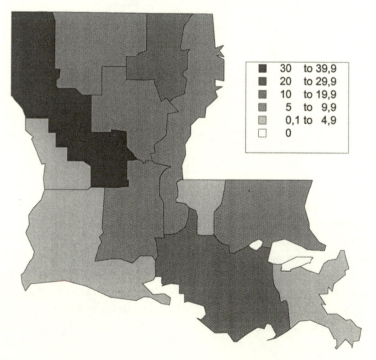

Figure 4.4   Regional Percentage of Lynching, 1866–1884

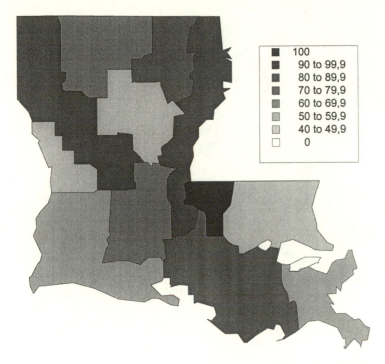

■	100
■	90 to 99,9
■	80 to 89,9
■	70 to 79,9
■	60 to 69,9
■	50 to 59,9
■	40 to 49,9
□	0

Figure 4.5   Regional Percentage of Lynching with Black Victims, 1866–1884

an area.[29] Indeed several areas with a large black population had a comparatively small rate of lynching of blacks, while other districts with a small black population had a much higher rate (figs. 4.5, 4.6, 4.7).[30] However, the data do support Cutler's view that regional sub-cultural factors played an important role, as we can see from the different ways in which southern and northern Louisiana resorted to lynching.[31]

The Nature of Lynching and Vigilantism

The way that both vigilance committees and lynching mobs exercised punishment reveals much about the evolution of popular justice in Louisiana. Vigilance committees issued sharp warnings in the local press to all criminals, ordering them to leave the state. The usual punishment of vigilance committees consisted of banishment for a first offence, lashing if resistance was encountered, and hanging for a

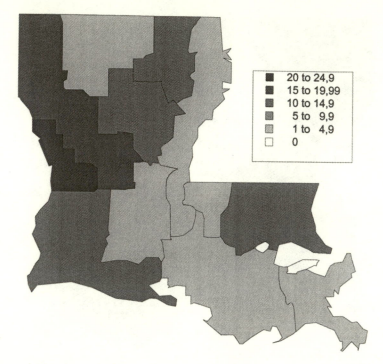

Figure 4.6 Annual Rate of Blacks Lynched per 10,000 Inhabitants, 1866–1884

second offense. Punishments were pronounced during informal meetings. Although they resorted on a few occasions to summary executions, the practice of banishment remained the main tool of popular justice after the war. For example, in 1868 four blacks in Lafayette parish were given twenty-four hours to leave the state by a committee of thirty men. Similar advice was also given to four blacks in Iberia parish in July 1874.[32]

Vigilance committees became particularly violent on two occasions. The first incident occurred in April 1870, when a vigilance committee put an end to the ravages of the West and Kimball gang, a notorious band of criminals in Winn parish, by killing eight members and capturing several others.[33] The second incident involved the September 1873 lynching of twelve members of a band of cattle thieves in Vermilion parish. They had been previously advised by the local vigilance committee to leave the parish, but instead of doing so, 150 "cattle thieves" armed themselves and threatened to destroy the town of Abbeville. Three hundred members of the local vigilance committee

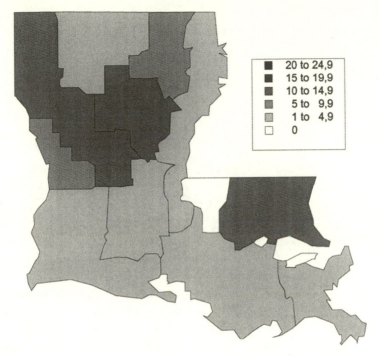

Figure 4.7 Annual Rate of Whites Lynched per 10,000 Inhabitants, 1866–1884

then seized and lynched twelve members of the band.[34] Still, when compared to lynch mobs, Louisiana vigilance committees showed much greater restraint in the use of violence. Indeed, 82 percent of vigilance committees had no reported victims (table 4.2).

Lynching was completely absent in New Orleans throughout the period, but in the countryside, lynching was regularly used by white conservatives as a policy of terror, representing a dramatic warning to all blacks who dared to challenge white supremacy.[35] Furthermore, vigilance committees never resorted to sadism or torture as was the case with lynch mobs after the Civil War. Although some historians have argued that lynching in its most dreadful forms did not appear until the 1880s,[36] mutilating bodies of victims was already a part of the ritual of lynching in the early Reconstruction years. There were no less than twenty-seven instances (or 16% of the cases of lynching) during that period in which blacks were shot, had body parts amputated, or were slowly tortured, mutilated, or burned at the stake.[37]

Table 4.2
Number of Victims per Incident

Number	Lynchings	Vigilantism	Total
0	14 (0)	27 (0)	41 (0)
1	179 (179)	1 (1)	180 (180)
2	18 (36)	1 (2)	19 (38)
3	12 (36)	1 (3)	13 (39)
4	7 (28)	1 (4)	8 (32)
5	3 (15)	0 (0)	3 (15)
6	4 (24)	0 (0)	4 (24)
8	1 (8)	1 (8)	2 (16)
9	1 (9)	0 (0)	1 (9)
12	0 (0)	1 (12)	1 (12)
Total	239 (335)	33 (30)	272 (365)

Note: Numbers in parentheses are the number of people killed. As shown by the data, in 14 lynching incidents, the victims did not die.

There were also several instances of blacks being seized and brought to the woods to be chained together, shot, set on fire and eventually thrown into lakes, bayous, or rivers.[38] Bryant Offort, a black who was killed in De Soto parish on September 6, 1868, was stabbed thirty-seven times.[39] Whites could become brutal and sadistic in lynching blacks: in three particular instances blacks were horribly burned. In one such case in 1868, the hands and feet of Lloyd Shorter were chopped off, coal-oil was poured upon him, and he was set on fire before being thrown into the Red River. Jake McReady, a black who had allegedly killed a white named George Simpson, met the same gruesome fate in 1874 when he was taken during the night from his cabin by a group of armed white men led by the son of the victim. McReady's hands and feet were tied, and turpentine was poured on him. The whites then shot him several times and cut his throat before setting him on fire. Henry Jones was luckier. Having been shot by a group of whites, he feigned death. He was then thrown between two logs. After piling some rotten wood on him, the whites set fire to the pile and left. He was severely burned, but escaped with his life.[40]

Mutilation of victims was not limited to blacks, as shown by the brutal execution of six officials of Red River parish in August 1874, whose bodies were afterward mutilated during the so-called Coushatta affair.[41] As a consequence white moderates became so intimidated that they were afraid to speak their minds, choosing instead to detach themselves from politics.[42]

In a period of political and racial stress such as Reconstruction, sadism and slow torture became an expression of hatred, rage, and anarchy, as well as serving as a dramatic warning to all blacks who dared to challenge white supremacy.[43] By the late 1870s and early 1880s, new modes of increasingly sadistic punishment were devised as part of the ritual of lynching, such as putting the victims in the carcass of a cow and letting them slowly die.[44]

The taking of prisoners forcibly from jail and killing them was another practice that distinguished lynching from vigilantism. While vigilantism was aimed at restoring peace and order by bringing possible criminals to court, lynching was the ultimate expression of community will. Lynch mobs broke into jails on a regular basis, taking out alleged criminals in order to kill them. There were also many instances of prisoners being taken out of the hands of sheriffs during transit and lynched.[45] The failure to protect prisoners from mobs was not limited to white conservative sheriffs. For example, George Essex, a black sheriff of St. John the Baptist, was charged with failing to oppose a mob that had seized and hung Valcour St. Martin and did not attempt afterward to arrest the perpetrators of this unlawful murder. As a consequence, District Attorney F. B. Earhardt asked the judge of the Fourth Judicial District that Essex be suspended from office.[46]

The evidence confirms that vigilantism was essentially related to the protection of society against crimes and disorder. Seventy percent of Louisiana vigilance committees were organized as a means of putting an end to thievery in the countryside. Before any specific crimes had been committed, rumors that bands of robbers were operating in a particular region were often enough to generate the formation of preventive vigilance committees.[47] Even cities did not escape vigilantism. The determination of citizens in New Orleans to put an end to hoodlumism resulted in the formation of three such committees.[48] The citizens of the city of Baton Rouge set up a similar committee in June 1868 as a means of capturing criminals and protecting lives and property.[49] Illegal traffic and contraband activities were problems that persisted after the war and periodically led to the formation of vigilance committees in the parishes of East Baton Rouge, East Feliciana, and West Feliciana in 1874–1876, in the parishes of Richland and St. Tammany in 1878, and in Grant parish in 1880.[50]

In contrast lynching displayed a quite different pattern of justification between Reconstruction and the early Redemption periods (figs. 4.8 and 4.9). Data shows that only 15 percent of lynching incidents

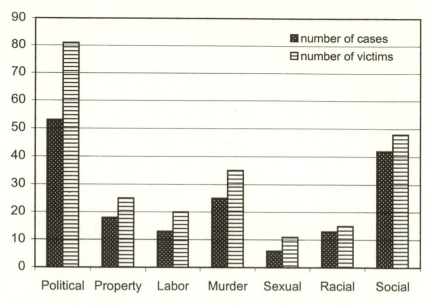

Figure 4.8   Assigned Motives for Lynching, 1866–1876

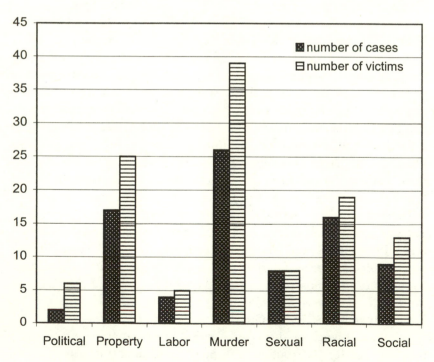

Figure 4.9   Assigned Motives for Lynching, 1877–1884

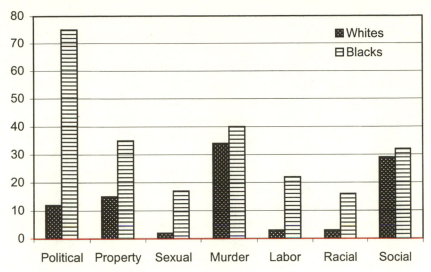

Figure 4.10 Motives for Lynching by Race of Victims, 1866–1884

originated with a view to protecting property or maintaining law and order, while political motives (23%),[51] murders or attempted murders (22%),[52] and social and personal conflicts (28%) were at the root of more than 70 percent of all lynchings. The comparison between Reconstruction and the early Redemption period yields some interesting differences. While 31 percent of lynchings during Reconstruction were politically motivated, only 3 percent originated from politics during the early Redemption period. Socially motivated lynchings also decreased—although not as markedly—dropping from 32 percent to only 13 percent. Meanwhile, the percentage of lynchings motivated by murder rose from 14 to 37 percent, while those rooted in property crimes increased from 15 to 23 percent.

To be fully understood, the causes surrounding lynching must be analyzed in relation to their racial dimension as shown by fig. 4.10. Although the causes surrounding the lynching of whites and blacks followed similar patterns, they differed somewhat. Indeed, either politics, white racial prejudice, or black insubordination were at the root of more than 50 percent of black lynchings, while two-thirds of the white lynchings originated from murders or antisocial behaviors. Moreover, very few whites were lynched for having personal relations with a black of the opposite gender.[53] However, the high proportion of lynchings where blacks were victims set a trend for the future when, by the turn of the century, lynching and lynching of blacks became virtually synonymous.

Evidence shows that alleged murders and other criminal behaviors were the cause of more than a third of the incidents in which blacks were lynched. Still, many more blacks were lynched during Reconstruction for breaking of contract, concealment of arms, boasting, using offensive language, or simply racial prejudice. These offenses seem trivial, but in fact they represented for many whites a serious challenge to white supremacy and to the preservation of social order. Florrind Johnson, a black, was burned to death for being too intimate with a white woman, while William Jones was lynched in April 1872 for simply laughing about a white woman. Black workers were also killed for trying to rent land as happened on January 9, 1869, when three blacks were shot and their throats cut in Caddo parish because they did not want to live under white protection.[54] The black population learned the hard way that the white community would tolerate no break in the established social order.

Nevertheless political motives remained the single most important cause of black lynching, as lynching and threats of lynching represented an important political instrument in insuring that Louisiana remained a "white-man's country."[55] As the political climate worsened in 1868 and again in 1874, the state became deeply divided between Republicans and Democrats. Local Democratic leadership called for white solidarity and was determined to resort to summary means, if necessary, to correct the wrongs brought on by radical policies.[56]

Since black clergymen played a major role in the black community and black churches served as sites for political meetings, they both became special targets of white fury. Black clergymen were regularly assaulted, beaten, and even murdered. The murders of black clergyman were often very brutal. For example, Willis Johnson was savagely murdered while visiting a friend in St. Landry parish in June 1872. The band of white men surrounded the house, breaking in and seizing Johnson, who, while begging for time to say a prayer, was immediately shot and killed by a volley.[57] Another black clergyman named Julius Steward was killed in Bossier parish in October 1874. He was tied up and killed on horseback.[58] The disruption of black church services and the burning of black churches were regular occurrences as well. Two black churches were burned in May and September 1874 in Iberia parish because the local black community refused to endorse the

White League platform. Afterward the White League went so far as to offer to help rebuild the churches conditional on the political support of the black community. The local black community steadfastly refused.[59]

The Justification for Lynching and Vigilantism

It was fashionable for commentators to blame the state administration and its law enforcement officers for this unfortunate state of affairs. The country newspapers protested that too many criminals, robbers, rapists, and murderers were acquitted and escaped due punishment by resorting to legal technicalities.[60] Local newspapers played a major role in the rationalization of lynching as a justifiable activity. As a consequence vigilantism and lynching came to be seen as a remedy to an intolerable situation.[61]

Although mob law was not officially approved, many whites felt it was the only solution because the law and courts seemed powerless. This apparent mockery of justice and the inability of the public prosecutors to secure convictions alarmed property holders and concerned citizens who then resorted to extreme means to put an end to crime. The problem was aggravated by the fact that white people, as a rule, displayed too much sympathy for fellow whites who were charged with criminal offenses. This made the task of mustering aid in apprehending alleged criminals more difficult and helped to develop the general belief that there was no public sentiment for justice in Louisiana.[62]

The inefficiency of law enforcement can not by itself furnish the explanation of why so many blacks were lynched during Reconstruction. Whites were quick to blame white radicals and black politicians of manipulating black votes and in the process installing "corrupt" government. The majority of whites in Louisiana were opposed to postwar changes and particularly objected to the political implications of such changes. In this context, the rumors of black insurrection that troubled post–Civil War Louisiana provided the rationale for the lynching of many blacks. When blacks did not conform to traditional white racist conceptions, the hidden fear of black revolt and insurrection intensified within the white community. In a society where communication was still primarily verbal, the most trivial incident could give way to the wildest rumors about the organization of black secret societies whose members were fully armed and plotting to kill every white man, child, and woman and to divide up their property.[63] As a consequence whites repeatedly organized posses, paramilitary groups, and lynch mobs as a means of nipping black insurrection in the bud.

As a black spread the rumor that white people in the Atchafalaya area were getting ready to make a descent on blacks, blacks left their fields, procured arms, and organized themselves as well as possible, throwing out pickets to give the alarm. All blacks deserted their homes for several days, apprehending an eminent attack that never materialized. A committee composed of leaders of the black and white communities was formed to reduce the tension and find the origins of the rumor.[64]

Such forms of lynch mobs did not end with Reconstruction as rumors of black insurrectionary plots were still used to justify violence during the 1878 congressional election in the troubled parishes of Tensas, Madison, Natchitoches, and Caddo. Furthermore, five blacks were lynched in Pointe Coupée parish in 1878 following rumors of a negro plot to kill the leading white men of the region.[65]

Political tension in one parish had often an influence on surrounding parishes. Such was the case following the killing of Captain John Peck who had led the assault on the house of Alfred Fairfax in Tensas parish in October 1878. As whites from surrounding parishes rushed into Tensas to support the local white population, similar troubles broke out in Concordia, Madison, and Ouachita. All over the region tension ran high between blacks and whites. This was particularly obvious in Ouachita parish, which bordered Tensas, where a conflict seemed impending. As a consequence of the spread of racial tension, four blacks were killed in one single day in Monroe by a group of whites on horseback.[66]

While the regular use of violence such as lynching had been justified in the face of extraordinary circumstances under the rule of radicalism, after 1876 many whites thought that there was no longer any necessity for mob law and that no excuse could be offered to justify it.[67] With the end of radical rule, the fear of rape became the new rationale on the part of whites to justify lynching.[68] No black had been lynched for rape during the decade before the war, and alleged sexual assaults of blacks on white women were rare during Reconstruction. The most notorious cases were the lynching of six blacks in Grant parish in November 1873 for the alleged rape and murder of Mrs. Lacour, and that of a black in April 1875 in St. Landry for the alleged rape and murder of the wife of George Lanthier.[69] Due to the low number of reported cases, the alleged rape of white women by blacks did not excite public opinion during Reconstruction. This situation changed dramatically during the early Redemption era.

Toward the end of radical rule, the Louisiana country press began to report an alarming increase in the number of rapes committed by blacks upon white women since the abolition of slavery. These papers reported that since blacks were no longer under control, or restrained by fear, rape was becoming the single most important cause for the increase of lynchings in Louisiana. Local newspapers even advocated the rule of "Judge Lynch" in all unquestionable cases of rape, and acknowledged that as long as law was not enforced, the "wild justice of revenge" would not be "wholly unjustifiable." This rationalization of lynching as a way of punishing blacks for atrocious crimes played a major role in the transformation of the image of blacks into a sub-human species.[70] Although Professor Joel Williamson asserted that it was not until 1889 that rape became used as a justification for the lynching of blacks, evidence shows that this was already the case in Louisiana during the late 1870s and early 1880s.[71]

Despite the assertion of the Louisiana press that rape committed by blacks upon white women was, by 1880, at the root of most lynching, evidence shows that, in fact, alleged rape formed less than 7 percent of the assigned causes for lynching blacks. Furthermore, the charges of alleged rape were often pitifully fraudulent. They remain an important expression of the manipulation of white racial and sexual fears and beliefs regarding blacks.[72]

Although few people overtly denounced lynching, many whites were troubled by its evolution. They acknowledged that mob rule was the most hideous, pernicious, and merciless form of disturbance, and they disapproved of the way mobs usurped the function of the law, becoming judge, jury, and executioner.[73] Protests arose in many parishes and regions of Louisiana after 1876. Following the successive lynchings of Charles McLean and John C. Vance, both charged with arson, meetings attended by the most influential citizens and the wealthiest bankers and entrepreneurs of the region were held in Shreveport, Caddo parish, to condemn the high-handed outrages committed by the lawless mobs.[74] Even the lynching of blacks was denounced, as shown by a petition of citizens of Carroll parish in 1877. A similar protest was also issued in 1877 by a committee of citizens in Rayville, Richland parish.[75] Blacks in St. Tammany parish held a meeting in June 1882 to protest the brutal and summary execution of Mealy Howard who was charged with raping a white woman.[76]

In Louisiana, as elsewhere, the emergence of a strong opposition to vigilantes often took the form of antivigilance committees and reflected deep social and economic conflicts.[77] This opposition was particularly manifest after the lynching of the twelve alleged outlaws who had resisted the vigilance committee in Vermilion parish in September 1873. The proceedings of the committee created a climate of terror in the lower parishes and met with stiff opposition from the press. The committees were described by the press as groups of banditti and outlaws, no better than the ones against whom they acted.[78]

Yet in spite of the fact that many people came to deplore lynching and vigilantism, others continued to consider these practices necessary evils. Even though some law officers occasionally tried to resist a lynch mob, the plain truth was that lynching was usually endorsed by local community leaders and occurred with the connivance of local officers. On several occasions, the "best classes" in Shreveport openly advocated the capture and hanging without trial of men accused of being desperadoes.[79] While moderate whites often condemned lynching, fearful of reprisal, their inaction was mainly motivated by self-preservation. As a consequence they did nothing to stop it, and since officials did not attempt to arrest lynchers, the latter not surprisingly felt they had public support for their actions. In the final analysis lynching was made possible largely because it was for the most part "tolerated" by the local community.[80]

Conclusion

The point to be emphasized here is that the emergence of popular justice in Louisiana must be put in its historical context. Post–Civil War lynching was particularly influenced by the redefinition of the black status and race relations and the determination of a large majority of whites to maintain their land as a "white man's country." In that process new rationales for lynching were developed reflecting new social and political conditions.

Mid-nineteenth-century America saw a period of tremendous change and upheaval as Southern society had to adjust itself not only to the destruction left by the Civil War and the abolition of slavery, but also to the "radical" Reconstruction policy of the federal government. Moreover, the traditional mechanisms of social control were disrupted as the South passed from a plantation society, used to solving its tensions and conflicts internally, to a society administered by Republican and black officials who depended more heavily on the federal government. Both vigilantism and lynching were obviously forms of social control used as a response to a dramatic situation. As such they were clear manifestations of the social tension that underlay white attempts to assert their supremacy over the black masses.

Vigilantism and lynching reveal much about the values of the white Louisiana society and what this society considered as acceptable standards of behavior. Not only did whites in Louisiana feel that justice was not adequately administered, the determination of these whites to enforce their own interpretation of social values on all groups that lived within the limits of their parishes and even beyond is apparent. Indeed blacks were lynched because they had aroused the white ire, although they may or may not have committed some criminal or other offense.

Such a siege mentality created the psychological conditions that made lynching generally acceptable, and this had tragic consequences on the future of both white and black communities. Lynching with all its ritual represented not only the response of the white community to imaginary threats, it also reminded blacks that violence could always be used as a policy for enforcing white supremacy. However, lynching was directed not only toward blacks but also against whites who did not conform to social mores. As such, lynching also played an important and powerful role in forging public opinion and in forcing whites to accept and join the ranks of a white supremacist point of view. Thus, the white community found in lynching a way of diminishing its frustration, suppressing dissent, and correcting the course of history. In the process lynching played a fundamental role in making what became known by the late nineteenth and first half of the twentieth centuries as the solid South.

PART III

Homicidal Behavior among Particular Groups

Homicides in a Gender Perspective

The parish of Rapides was struck on March 28, 1870, by another of those family tragedies that seemed so common in nineteenth-century Louisiana. On that day, E. J. Barrett killed Edward Rowe, his father-in-law. Rowe had been previously arrested on charges of having assaulted his wife. Learning that her husband was to be released from jail, Mrs. Rowe called on her son-in-law for protection. Following his release, Rowe went immediately home. As he entered his house in a threatening manner, he was killed by his son-in-law who prevented him from assaulting his mother-in-law.[1] Although it was the man, not the woman, who was killed, this case of domestic violence reflects the particular condition of many women in post–Civil War Louisiana and is symptomatic of the kind of violence to which they were subjected.

One of the most interesting dichotomies to emerge in mid-nineteenth-century America was that between gender values. This dichotomy was not new, but it reached a climax in the South in the second half of the nineteenth century, taking on greater significance in light of the radical disjunction that occurred in the region during and after the Civil War.[2] From this perspective, it is possible to retrace the gender patterns of violence in Louisiana after the Civil War, to achieve a better understanding of both men's and women's homicidal behavior, and also to examine what these patterns reveal about gender relationships in nineteenth-century Louisiana.

With this in mind, the present chapter is less concerned with building a general theory about gender and homicidal behavior than with presenting the general patterns. It attempts to retrace the main trends by identifying the victims and the offenders, by examining their age and social setting, and by establishing regional distributions and more especially variations in the rural versus urban patterns. Moreover, it asserts the need to look at the role of women both as victim and perpetrators. Finally, it explains how women's homicidal behavior was distinct from that of men in terms of its nature, frequency, and organization. This gendered analysis of homicidal behavior can tell us much about the role and status of women in Southern society. It should also help to clarify the Southern perception of acceptable behavior for both men and women in nineteenth-century Louisiana.

Traditionally students of criminality have not given much importance to female criminality, but recent studies have shown the need to understand the basic problems concerning female criminality and to establish an analytical framework for such criminal behavior. Indeed interpreting female criminality and the place of women in the world of criminality is not easy and provides a number of pitfalls for the unwary student.[3]

Females as Victims

Historians, criminologists, and other social scientists have noted the considerable difference that has divided male and female criminal behavior.[4] The present study of homicide in Louisiana largely confirms the conclusion of previous studies. Modern evidence shows that fewer women are killed than their share of the population would indicate, but the number of female victims in Louisiana after the war was unusually low.[5] Although they formed more than 50 percent of the population, women represented only 5.6 percent of the victims of homicide in the Pelican State during that troubled period. Indeed the small numbers of women who were victims of homicide is a striking feature of the present analysis.

For both periods, Reconstruction and early Redemption, an average of 13 women per year were killed in Louisiana, while the annual average of men killed dropped from 286 to 120. Official statistics usually reveal a ratio of ten to one in the number of crimes and violent acts committed by men and women.[6] But the ratio between men and women is much larger than one would expect, particularly during Reconstruction.

Overall women represented 4.4 percent of the victims of homicide

Table 5.1
Racial Distribution of Homicides by Gender

Race of Victims and Offenders	Male Victims	%	Female Victims	%	Total	%
Unknown by unknown	343	8.0	35	13.9	378	8.3
Whites by unknown	214	5.0	11	4.3	225	5.0
Blacks by unknown	328	7.7	5	2.0	333	7.4
Unknown by whites	169	3.9	6	2.4	175	3.9
Whites by whites	825	19.3	50	20.0	875	19.3
Blacks by whites	1,587	37.2	58	23.1	1,645	36.4
Unknown by blacks	63	1.4	1	0.3	64	1.4
Whites by blacks	176	4.1	7	2.7	183	4.0
Blacks by blacks	515	13.2	78	31.1	593	13.1
Total	4,270	99.8	251	99.8	4,521	99.5

Note: 465 cases for which we had no information on the gender of the victim are not included in this table.

in Louisiana during Reconstruction and 8.6 percent during the early Redemption period. As we have seen previously, the difference in homicidal behavior is even greater between the rural areas and New Orleans. The data clearly show that women in New Orleans were at greater risk of becoming victims of a homicide than rural women. Women represented 10.5 percent of the victims of homicide in New Orleans during Reconstruction, compared to only 3.8 percent in rural areas. This difference continued during the early Redemption era, when women represented 13.1 percent of the victims of homicide in New Orleans compared to 7.6 percent in the country parishes.

A close look at the racial patterns is even more revealing. Although black men and women each represented 67 percent of the victims of their respective gender (table 5.1), the percentage varied over the period and between rural and urban areas. During Reconstruction, both black men and black women were respectively victims of 27.2 and 27.5 percent of the homicides that occurred in New Orleans, or the same proportion as their ratio in the city population (26%). But during the early Redemption period, the percentage of black women killed increased faster than that of black men, reaching respectively 37.1 and 33.7 percent of all homicides committed in New Orleans. These numbers contrasted even more with those observed in the rural areas. Although blacks formed 60 percent of the population in country parishes, black men represented 75 percent of all male victims of homicide, while the percentage was 80 percent for black women. The percentage of black men killed in the countryside during the early Redemption era dropped to 59 percent, a percentage lower than their proportion in the rural population. It went otherwise for black women, for whom the percentage decreased only slightly to 76 percent. Black women in both New Orleans and in the country parishes were at greater risk than their white counterparts to be victims of homicide.

Although 42 percent of black female murder victims were killed by whites, they represented a rather small percentage (3.5%) of the total number of black victims. This discrepancy is partly explained by the political situation; after all, black men represented a special target for white political violence. In many instances whites took black men from their cabins and killed them, leaving the victims' wives and children unmolested. Congressional reports contain countless testimonies such as the following:

> On last Tuesday night, several, say ten or twelve men armed with gun and pistols went to Hon. T. C. Anderson's plantation, managed by Mr. John O. Richard, near Grand Coteau and took an old colored man named Glaston out of his cabin and shot and killed him. The wife and son of the deceased and others were in the cabin, but were not molested. The armed party seemed to be particularly in search of another colored man named Colas or Nicholas. It is not known what the object, or reason was for killing him. The men of the armed party were not known by the witnesses to the killing.[7]

Collective violence was an integral part of post–Civil War social and political conditions. While 43 percent of the male victims were killed by more than one person, this was the case for only 19 percent of the female victims of homicide. The gender difference is even greater when analyzed from a racial perspective: 52 percent of black men and 24 percent of black women were victims of collective violence, compared to 30 percent for white men and 11 percent for white women.

The fact that 65 percent of the women who were killed were below thirty years old is most revealing. Male attraction toward young women made them more subject and vulnerable to violence. But the data also show that young women were less submissive and therefore more likely to attract the ire of men. Finally, married women who benefited from the protection of a husband were less in danger than single women.

Overall, violence against women was largely a white male phenomenon. Almost three-fifths (57%) of all women killed in Louisiana after the Civil War were murdered by white men. The number of white women killed was small, but nine-tenths (87.7%) of them died at the hands of white men. In comparison, 42 percent of black women killed were by white men, the percentage being much higher (63%) during Reconstruction. Finally black women were the victims in only 13 percent of black homicides.

Paradoxically, the apparent frailty of women, considered as the weaker sex, was what gave white women a special protection in Southern society.[8] These sexual stereotypes were also the basis on which rested the social control of female behavior. In the process family life and motherhood were sources of meaning in women's lives.[9] As the culture of honor in the South was a basic characteristic of masculinity, the Southern culture, whose roots went back to the Cavalier era, encouraged women to be submissive and cast them into idealized roles as wives and mothers. Victorian morality, which reinforced the tendency of the Southern culture to limit the role of the women to the home sphere, left little place for women's independence and subjected them to men for livelihood and leadership. The fate of most women was to leave the father's home to search for security in marriage.[10]

As a result of their own alleged vulnerability, women needed male protection. The man's role was also defined by the culture of honor and afterward by the Victorian moral code. As a consequence, any husband or father ought to protect his wife or daughter not only from physical assault but also against charges against her virtue or slanders against her reputation. In the process, not only women's lives centered around the family, but the defense of womanly virtue became a prime motive for community action.[11] Ultimately this culture of honor, reinforced by the Victorian code, had great consequences on women's psyches, reducing them, as it did, to the role of victim.

Black women also enjoyed, albeit to a lesser degree, male protection as members of the "weaker" gender. But as fewer black women stayed at home as housewives or mothers than did white women, they were more subject to violence. Yet the number of black women who fell victim to violence, as we have seen, was rather small compared to black men. This phenomenon largely derived from strong pressure within the black community to adopt the culture of honor. Indeed, black husbands saw in the withdrawal of black women from the fields an indispensable aspect of their newly won freedom, a sign of their own manhood, a proof of their authority over the black family, a way to break with the plantation tradition, and a guarantee of protection against whites. Furthermore, the emergence of a patriarchal society among the black community was further strengthened by the access of black men to the right to vote and hold office. As a result the black male role was defined around the public world, while black women saw their role reduced to the private sphere of family life.[12]

Still white violence against blacks could be most brutal and sadistic, no matter whether the victim was male or female. This much is shown by the horrible mutilation and murder of Lucy Smith, who was killed in 1868 by a group of white men who cut off her breast, then disembowelled and decapitated her. Grisly as it was, the case of Lucy Smith was not unique. Several other black women suffered the same fate. One of them was literally ripped open in Bossier parish in September 1868.[13] Whites, furthermore, had no monopoly on brutality against black women. For example, Randall Thompson, a black man, savagely killed Susan Brown, an old black woman, with a stick in New Orleans in February 1873.[14]

The period of Civil War and Reconstruction ushered in with emancipation engendered a tremendous change and upheaval that saw the arrival of blacks into politics and the transformation of the plantation system. Any analysis of the motives behind homicide in this context must therefore account for the social tensions of the period, not only from a racial but also from a gender perspective. The results of such an analysis, presented in fig. 5.1, yield some further interesting information on the prevailing condition of women.

As politics was a man's affair and as Reconstruction was the most violent period in American history, the prominence of political motives largely explains why men and women were not subjected to the same level of violence. Indeed the major gender difference in the underlying causes of violence was in the political sphere. Only few women fell victim to political violence. Meanwhile politics represented the single most important reason for which men, particularly black men, were murdered.

Although several blacks were killed because they protested while whites were taking their wives away, there are as many cases where black men saw their lives saved by their wives who did not hesitate to intervene as white men attacked their husbands. The most notable case was that of James Sparkes, who was pursued by white men be-

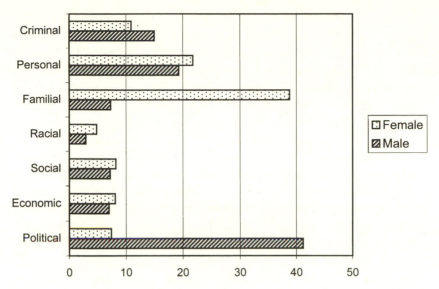

Figure 5.1 Motives Underlying Homicide by the Victims' Gender (percentages)

cause he decided to leave his former master and search for work elsewhere. Sparkes's life was saved by his wife and mother who decided to accompany the group of whites who had kidnapped him. In many more instances black women were killed for refusing to say where their husbands were hiding. A black woman named Judy Asher was killed in Caddo parish in October 1868 because she tried to protect her husband from a band of masked men. Nancy Goss, Maria Vance, Rose Boone, and the wife of Spencer White met the same fate for refusing to say where their husbands were hiding.[15] Black women were also killed unintentionally as whites attempted to kill their husbands. Such was the fate that awaited the wife of Raymond Ricard, the newly elected sheriff of West Baton Rouge, as whites fired in 1873 into her house in an attempt to kill her husband.[16]

The whipping, beating, and killing of numerous blacks was related to breaches of social etiquette and to incidents of disorderly conduct. Offenses were considered particularly grave when white women were involved. Not only black men, but several black women were killed when they did not obey a white order quickly enough, talked back, failed to call a white woman mistress, refused to yield the road or sidewalk to a white, were "impolite" to a white woman, or simply had a quarrel with a white woman. For example, Miss Lucy Sames had all her bedclothes taken and was whipped nearly to death by John Vance in 1873 in Bossier parish because she had disputed the word of Mrs. Vance. Miss Williams was killed in 1867 by Miss Hempley, a white woman, because she did not call her mistress. Miss Tennessee Edward was whipped by James Foster, a white planter, for allegedly quarrelling with a white woman.[17] There were, for example, eight cases of blacks being killed for having laughed about a white woman.[18]

Black men and women working as field hands were regularly mistreated as they protested about the settlement of their crop or the refusal of the planters to pay for it. There were even a few cases of black women killed by white planters over crop settlement. The most notable case was the one of Miss Joe Anna, a black woman, who worked on the plantation of Dr. Johnson of Caddo parish. When she asked the doctor in 1875 to pay for her last year's cotton crop, the doctor told her he would settle his account with her right away. He then got his gun and killed her.[19]

The public role of women was limited to congregating in church on weekends to hear the pastor and to sing hymns. While these values were in line with Victorian morality and the maintenance of womanly virtue, their imposition may have a pernicious effect even on black families. A black woman who had divorced and remarried was killed in 1871 by her first husband who did not accept that his wife had left him for another man. In February 1884, Berry Johnson, a black from Caddo parish, became so angry when his wife refused to go to church that he choked her to death.[20]

The presence of a double standard around the social roles of men and women had an obvious impact on the number of homicidal incidents. While their wives and children went to church, men congregated in public places, courthouses, auction sales, racetracks, and brothels where they played games and drank alcohol. As a consequence, a substantial number of men, as the data show, were killed during drunken brawls.[21]

The relative scarcity of intrafamilial homicides in general, compared to modern industrial societies, raises another point of interest.[22] Evidence shows that, unlike contemporary America, mothers and fathers, brothers and sisters, or husbands and wives only rarely resorted to deadly weapons to settle their differences. People had a greater tendency to kill a stranger than a person to whom they were related by blood or matrimony. Even if a substantial number of the women killed were victims of domestic conflicts, the total number of victims of intrafamilial violence was rather small. Community values and family ties represented a powerful deterrent to family violence.[23]

Although intrafamilial homicides were infrequent, marriage for women was too often marked by disappointment, loneliness, personal frustration, and unhappiness. As men and women lived in two different worlds where intimacy and sharing were often absent, women did not find the romantic love that they had dreamed of during their youth. Marital squabbles were frequent and often degenerated into violence. The right of a husband to beat his wife and children "for their own good" or as a "means to regulate their behavior" was well-established in the Southern culture. When Maryland criminalized wife beating in 1882, it was the first state to do so.[24] Indeed women's lives were defined by both the Southern culture of honor and the Victorian moral code that justified their inferior status and encouraged them to be submissive to their husband. As a result, they were extremely vulnerable to the spousal abuses that made wife beating a common phenomenon.[25]

But although wife beating was frequent, it only rarely ended in death. Wife killing was considered one of the most atrocious and cowardly crimes, and when it occurred it was severely punished. Only a few cases of wife killing were reported, most of them in New Orleans. Several of these women died at the hands of their husbands, whether from gunshots or poison, or from having been choked to death. The reasons varied from refusing to go to church, to leaving their husband, to a simple marital dispute. Although in New Orleans most cases involved whites, blacks formed the majority of the reported cases in rural areas.[26] Even so, domestic and marital quarrels among blacks were far from being as bloody as was asserted in the white press. Still, many black women did fall victim to a jealous husband who could not accept his wife's seeing another man or choosing to leave him. The police were regularly called to put an end to ceaseless quarrels between black men and women that often ended by resorting to knives and pistols. Crimes of passion were not rare among blacks. On April 21, 1868, Paul Chevare, a free man of color, killed Mary Samally and afterward committed suicide because she wanted to leave him. Similar homicides occurred in Jefferson parish in 1871 and in St. Bernard parish in 1873.[27]

Both the Southern culture of honor and the Victorian moral code were based on a sexual double standard in which women, but not men, were required to remain chaste and pure.[28] This moral standard was particularly pernicious for the women's condition. Newspapers reported countless cases of young, attractive ladies from respectable families who fled their rural homes and took refuge in New Orleans after having been seduced. With their chastity they had lost their reputations, and were consequently reduced to a "life of sins in the splendors of the evil calling in New Orleans." A fifteen-year-old girl named Josephine Ray who came from a very wealthy antebellum family was charged in July 1868 by her sister with leading an abandoned life as she lived in a brothel. In June 1868 a young sixteen-year-old girl attempted to commit suicide in New Orleans after being seduced and deserted.[29] These stories always created much excitement in the city.

The need to preserve the reputations of wives and daughters meant that the male code of honor had to be strictly enforced. Occasionally the enforcement of the Southern honor values had tragic consequences. For example, in January 1873, a stranger who had just landed at Port Hudson, East Feliciana parish, offered $50 to a local woman. When the offended husband learned of the improper proposition, he hunted the stranger down. The latter was instantly killed after a volley of gunfire.[30]

Rape has always been considered the worst crime of male domination and violence against women. This major crime in nineteenth-century Southern society was considered even worse than today as the Victorian moral code put women on a pedestal of virtue, a synonym of chastity and purity. Of course this status was reserved only for white women. Still a close scrutiny of the period reveals only 180 rapes for the years 1866 to 1884. This number of rapes is rather low, if one considers the general atmosphere of violence that prevailed after the Civil War (table 5.2).

The general distribution of rapes along regional and racial lines is quite revealing. According to the data only 19 percent of the rapes occurred in New Orleans. Does this mean that the incidence of rapes in the metropolitan area was lower because New Orleans was better policed? Or was it because rapes were also distributed unevenly along racial lines? The fact that black women represented three-fifths (59%) of the victims of rape in Louisiana suggests that the answer rests in the second explanation. Not only were incidents of rape divided equally between white and black men, but 49 percent of white women raped were by black men, while 50 percent of black women were raped by white men.

Table 5.2
Number of Reported Rapes Committed in
Louisiana, 1866–1884

Race of Victims by Race of Offenders	N	%
Unknown by unknown	41	22.7
Unknown by whites	11	6.1
Unknown by blacks	18	10.0
Whites by unknown	1	0.5
Blacks by unknown	4	2.2
Whites by whites	23	12.7
Whites by blacks	22	12.2
Blacks by whites	30	16.6
Blacks by blacks	30	16.6
Total	180	99.6

Rape of black women by whites was more widespread than suggested by these numbers, because sexual assaults and rapes of black women by whites were clearly underreported. Sexual assaults on black women had been endemic under slavery as a way to humiliate black men, to show them their inability to protect their wives, and consequently to diminish their own sense of personal dignity. Though many rapes were committed by white men acting alone—victims in these cases were generally servants—black women were also victims of collective rapes, committed by small bands of whites as a way to show blacks that whites were still their masters. Blacks, and more particularly black women, found it difficult to obtain justice from the courts when the offenders were whites, since any complaint could bring further violence. It was almost impossible for blacks to bring whites to court under rape charges. Two white men charged with attempting to rape a young black girl were finally discharged in St. Mary parish in 1868.[31]

The rape of a black woman by another black was usually tolerated by the white community. Only a few cases in which black men accused of rape by black women were brought to court. Oscar Hughes, a black, was sentenced to death by a black jury for having raped a black girl of four years old in 1871. Another black man was killed in St. Landry parish in September 1868 while resisting arrest after having been charged with assaulting Charity Jackson, a freed black woman.[32]

Many whites tended to continue the sexual practices they had developed with their slaves. As black women were considered to have more sexual experience and a greater libido than white women, white men felt justified in continuing to seek out company, blaming in the process the victim for what was their own fault. Consequently black women were regularly subjected to violence if they refused to sleep with white men.[33] For example, in September 1871, John Fazende, the son of a wealthy Creole family of Jefferson parish, beat to death Marie Estelle, a young mulatto of fifteen years old, for refusing his sexual advances.[34]

If the white community tolerated the sexual abuse of black women, it strongly opposed regular sexual intercourse between blacks and whites. The idea that blacks and whites could form a family was completely rejected. Nine blacks were killed during Reconstruction for having been too intimate with a white woman or for living with her. A white woman and a black man who lived together were burned to death in their cabin in April 1868 in Ouachita parish by a band of disguised men. In Calcasieu parish a white woman and a black man who were living together met the same fate in July 1868. A Mexican named Brown was murdered in May 1874 in St. Mary parish for having a love affair with a black woman. Florin Johnson, a black man, was burned to death for being too intimate with a white woman. A black was murdered in Richland parish in 1881 because he was living with a white woman.[35]

Even so murders originating from rape, sexual assault, or sexual abuse were rather rare. Overall, only 56 people were killed for such alleged charges. Alleged sexual assaults by blacks on white women were not only rare during Reconstruction, but they did not excite public opinion. Only eight blacks were lynched during Reconstruction for having allegedly raped a white woman or a white girl. The lynching of a black man in April 1875 in St. Landry parish for the rape and murder of the wife of George Lanthier, and that of six blacks in Grant parish in November 1873 for the alleged rape and murder of Mrs. Lacour, proved to be the exceptions. March Mark, a black, was also lynched in De Soto parish in 1874 for having allegedly done wrong to a white girl, an euphemism for describing an alleged sexual assault.[36]

There were also few cases of women who were killed in the process of committing a crime or because they were accessories to a crime or members of a criminal gang. The most notable case was the killing of Mrs. Cyriaque Guillory in September 1873 in Catahoula parish. The Guillory gang had terrorized St. Landry and other surrounding parishes since 1867 and was responsible for no less than a dozen murders.

As a posse attempted to arrest Cyriaque Guillory and other members of his gang, a violent gunfight followed. In the process, all the members of the gang were killed, including Mrs. Guillory who had been shot in the abdomen. Although she was seven months pregnant, Mrs. Guillory was very active during the fight in distributing ammunition and charging guns for her husband and other members of the gang.[37]

Females as Offenders

Female felons are usually subjected to judicial codes and policies that reflect what the political authorities find either desirable or excusable. These codes and policies, based on accepted social values, define the roles and attitudes of law enforcement officers and explain why criminals are dealt with differently depending on their gender. As a consequence many illegal actions remain hidden or are dissimulated, particularly when they involve women. Moreover, as we saw in chapter 4, the repression of many crimes can become almost impossible during unstable periods such as Reconstruction Louisiana. This is particularly true of crimes committed by a group or a class that does not represent or is not seen as a threat to society.[38]

The records of the city workhouse, parish jails, and state penitentiary are most revealing about the attitude of the judicial authorities toward female felons. The courts did not hesitate to send women to the workhouse, but they were much more reluctant to send them to parish jails as well as to the state penitentiary. Women represented about 50 percent of prisoners in the city workhouse, but while they represented 48 percent of the prisoners sentenced to the New Orleans parish prison in 1869, their number tended to decrease over the years to about 15 percent by the mid 1870s. During early Reconstruction a majority of the female prisoners in the parish prison were whites, but by 1874 they were almost exclusively blacks. Data on 2,283 people sentenced to the penitentiary in Louisiana during Reconstruction show that only 101 (or 4.4%) were women, and almost all women sent to the penitentiary were black.[39]

When one looks at the main characteristics of offenders, gender differences emerge even more clearly. The high number of homicides committed by men show that this was essentially a male crime, a male phenomenon. With only 112 homicides, women were responsible for only 2 percent of all murders committed in rural parishes between

1866 and 1884 and 4 percent of those committed in New Orleans. Although the ratio of homicides committed by women seems extremely low, these numbers are comparable to those revealed in other studies.[40] Women represented only 1.4 percent of the murderers in Louisiana during Reconstruction and 3.7 percent of the offenders during the early Redemption era. As the male number dropped, the female share consequently increased. But homicide in both urban and rural Louisiana was clearly a man's affair,[41] and black and white women were overwhelmingly victims rather than killers.

The analysis of the collective nature of male and female homicides generates further interesting results. Three-quarters (76%) of women who committed a homicide acted alone compared to under half (49%) of men. Moreover, the difference in homicidal behavior between men and women yields further noteworthy information when analyzed from a racial perspective. While black men acted alone in 69 percent of the homicides in which they were involved, white men committed collectively 64 percent of their homicides. Similarly black females acted alone 80 percent of the time, compared to 66 percent for white women.

This analysis highlights how women's violence usually originated from family or neighborhood disputes. The evidence suggests that the victims of women's wrath were often children or other women, while male violence tended to be a tool of social and political control. Female aggression manifested itself domestically inside the house where women played a role.

Infanticide,[42] the murder of a newborn or infant, is one type of crime that is generally committed by women. But it is virtually impossible to estimate the extent of that crime, as it would have required that every mother declare her pregnancy. As unwanted pregnancy represented a very acute problem in nineteenth-century America, abortion became, particularly among middle-class urban woman, a general phenomenon. According to recent studies, between 20 to 25 percent of pregnancies among women of these classes were ended artificially by abortion. As women of the laboring classes had barely the necessities for surviving and were too often abandoned, they had not the luxury to resort to abortion. Consequently infanticide and child abandonment were types of crimes that were generally committed by women of the laboring class.[43]

New Orleans newspapers were reporting almost every two or three days that the body of a newborn child had been found. These reports reflect a tragic daily reality. Out of 44 deaths that occurred in New Orleans in December 1870, the city coroners reported that 11 were stillborn. Many newborn children died under either criminal suspicion or negligence. And yet the number of mothers arrested for infanticide was rather small.[44] Although cases of infanticide were almost exclusively reported from New Orleans, this does not mean, however, that rural areas were free from such crime. One of the most atrocious infanticides ever committed in Louisiana occurred in June 1871 in the parish of East Baton Rouge. Henrietta Johnson, a black woman working on James McHatton's plantation was arrested after she had shown complete indifference to the disappearance of her newborn child. It was found afterward that she had given her new baby to the hogs to be eaten.[45]

Crime against children was not limited to newborns. There were many reports about the abuse, beating, mistreatment, and murder of young children. In August 1875, Mary Bray was arrested after beating her son so badly that he fell down twelve feet from the gallery of her house. He had previously taken refuge in a neighboring house complaining about his mother's mistreatment.[46]

Although women committed fewer homicides than men, a larger number were arrested as accessories to murder. Official police statistics for New Orleans are particularly revealing about women's complicity in homicide. Year after year, several women were charged with such crimes. In 1868 the number of women arrested as accessories to murder reached a peak with seventeen.[47] One could argue that the importance of the number of women arrested for being accessories to murder, compared to the low number arrested for committing murder, is most revealing about the particular condition of Louisiana women and shows how they had accepted subordination to men even in committing a crime. Often women who committed crimes did so as members of criminal bands. The most notable such case occurred in Red River parish in early August 1875. Three men, a boy, and two women were implicated in the very vicious murder of a peddler named Marcus Young. Two of them were former members of the notorious West-Kimball gang.[48]

This finding confirms one modern sociological theory that the percentage of homicides attributed to women is generally higher when the general criminal homicide rates are low. The data indeed show that the higher the incidence of violence, the smaller the female share.[49] Furthermore, this low level rate of homicide and crime in general is

Table 5.3
Racial Distribution of Homicides by Gender

Race of Victims and Offenders	Male Offenders	%	Female Offenders	%	Total	%
Unknown by unknown	497	9.2	33	29.5	530	9.6
Whites by unknown	86	1.6	2	1.8	88	1.6
Blacks by unknown	83	1.5	0		83	1.5
Unknown by whites	346	6.4	7	6.3	353	6.4
Whites by whites	1,073	20.0	18	20.0	1,091	19.8
Blacks by whites	2,162	40.2	8	7.1	2,170	39.5
Unknown by blacks	139	2.6	9	8.0	148	2.6
Whites by blacks	265	4.9	1	0.9	266	4.8
Blacks by blacks	724	13.5	34	30.4	758	13.8
Total	5,375	100.0	112	99.8	5,487	99.6

probably one reason why female homicidal behavior has not usually attracted much scholarly attention.

In spite of the small number of female offenders, an analysis along racial lines is revealing (table 5.3). In 94 percent of the cases when a white woman committed a murder, the victim was male; this compares to 87 percent when a white man committed a murder. Only very rarely did a white woman kill another white woman. In 75 percent of the cases when white women killed blacks, the victims were black men; this also compares to 94 percent for white men. Meanwhile, in 97 percent of the cases when black men killed whites, the victims were men. However, we find no case of a black woman killing a white woman, and only one case of a black woman killing a white man.

Finally we can turn our attention to the specific circumstances surrounding homicide. Although the information concerning what motivated women to turn to acts of violence and murders against other people are sketchy, their motives seem similar to those of men: personal grudges, material gain, sadism, self defense, angers, and familial arguments. What stands out, however, is that there is no evidence of political violence among Louisiana women (fig. 5.2). The range of motives underlying female homicides reflected the very restricted role of women in Louisiana society after the Civil War. For example, only two women were charged with committing homicides in the process of a robbery compared to 227 for men.

Marital disputes represented the single most important reason compelling women to commit homicide. Although it was more usual for a man to murder his wife, the killing of husbands by their wives

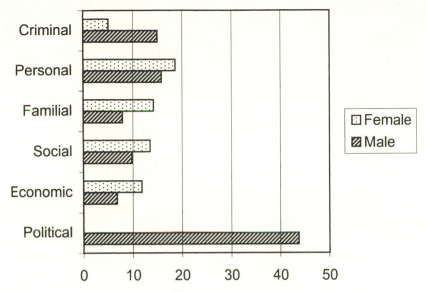

Figure 5.2 Motives Underlying Homicide by the Offenders' Gender (percentages)

did occur. For example, in October 1872, a black man named Johnson was killed by his wife, apparently because he had been drunk for the previous three days. In March 1884, William Demon, a black man from Assumption parish, was killed in the most brutal manner by his wife. They had been quarrelling at a social gathering, and upon their return home the quarrel was resumed. While Demon was seated at the table eating, his wife approached him from behind and struck him on the head with an ax. She followed up the initial blow repeatedly until the victim's head was completely severed from his body.[50]

Conclusion

The present analysis confirms what other studies of criminality have already shown: each gender has its own pattern of criminal behavior. Women play a substantially different role in crime than men, whether in terms of the method, the motivation, or the type of crimes committed. These differences point to distinct processes of socialization for men and women. Already largely determined by their biological conditions, women were further taught under the Southern culture of honor and by the Victorian code to be wives and mothers. As a result they tended to adopt a less aggressive and more submissive role in society. Women therefore committed fewer crimes than men not only because they were biologically less competitive than males, but also because it was less culturally acceptable for them to do so. The near absence of women either as victims or offenders in violent death is one of the major characteristics of the analysis of this study.

But while the criminality of women is certainly linked to the definition of gender roles in society, the low rate of female delinquency was also related to the particular political situation of Louisiana after the Civil War. Politics largely dominated the conflicts of that troubled period and women were for all intents and purposes, left out of the political arena.

Post–Civil War Louisiana was not in any way distinct from other societies with regard to the percentage of women involved in homicidal behavior. Homicide in Louisiana was clearly a man's affair. Furthermore, women's homicidal behavior reflects their very restricted role and, as such, it did not obey the same rules that applied to men. These data suggest that the victims of women's wrath were often children or other women, while male violence tended to be a means to attain social and political control. While Southern culture encouraged women to be submissive and granted them an idealized role as the symbol of purity, this status was clearly reserved for white women only. Not surprisingly the data contain numerous cases in which black women were brutally murdered by whites. Therefore, black women had the unenviable condition of representing a special target for violence because of both their gender and their race.

Gathering the dead and wounded after the Colfax riot of 1873. Originally published in *Harper's Weekly*. (New Orleans Historical Collection, 1974.25.9.196)

African Americans hiding in the swamps after the Colfax riot. Originally published in *Harper's Weekly*. (New Orleans Historical Collection, 1982.54.1)

The killing of African Americans during the New Orleans riot of 1866. Originally published in *Harper's Weekly*. (New Orleans Historical Collection, 1979.200)

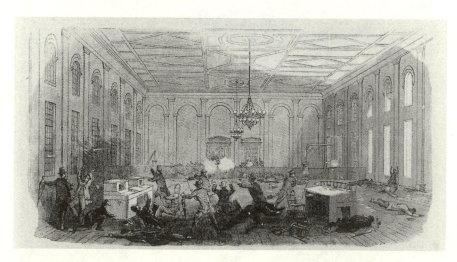

Interior of the Mechanics' Institute during the New Orleans riot of 1866. Originally published in *Harper's Weekly*. (New Orleans Historical Collection, 1979.200)

Scene of destruction in the Mechanics' Institute following the New Orleans riot of 1866. Originally published in *Harper's Weekly*. (New Orleans Historical Collection, 1979.200)

Carrying away the dead and wounded after the New Orleans riot of 1866. Originally published in *Harper's Weekly*. (New Orleans Historical Collection, 1979.200)

Julia Hayden, a schoolteacher murdered in 1874. Originally published in *Harper's Weekly*. (New Orleans Historical Collection, 1979.300i,ii)

A scene from the battle of Liberty Place, New Orleans, September 1874. Originally published in *Harper's Weekly*. (New Orleans Historical Collection, 1979.300i,ii)

6

Economic Conflict and Homicide

A major labor disturbance broke out in February 1875 on the plantation of William H. Arma in St. James parish. The trouble began as a local merchant attempted to seize the mortgaged crops of blacks who worked on shares. The blacks not only refused to give up the crop, but six of them opposed Adam Travis, the black deputy sheriff who attempted to arrest them. The workers were quickly backed up by other black hands. Then, Travis left and proceeded quickly to reassemble a posse of ten men, four white and six black. When Travis came back with his posse, a fight broke out during which a black member of the posse was killed and four other black members of the posse were wounded. As the news spread that the posse had been captured and was detained, Judge Félix P. Poche raised a force of several hundred men and proceeded quickly to arrest the workers and to release the posse.[1] This kind of labor violence was more frequent in northern than in southern Louisiana. As was noted in chapter 2, the study of homicidal behavior in southern Louisiana is particularly interesting, since the region was different from the rest of Louisiana due to its particular history, culture, language, religion, and economy.

Already settled before the Louisiana Purchase, the southern part of the state was largely inhabited by a population of French ancestry.[2] Although they shared a common history with the other areas of the South, the French population of southern Louisiana developed a set of values and a regional culture keenly different from those of most Southern people. The French population of southern Louisiana, and more particularly those who had Acadian roots, appeared to many foreign observers as an ignorant and monolithic group who remained aloof in order to keep their cultural identity alive. In the process this population had developed a particular way of doing things and a reputation for insouciance, sociability, a love of parties and horses and an indifference to state and national politics.[3]

These particular cultural characteristics make southern Louisiana one of the most interesting regions for the study of homicidal behavior in post–Civil War Southern society. Such a study raises several issues concerning the impact of cultural difference on the level and patterns of violence. Did this region follow the same patterns of violence as those settled by Anglo Saxon populations? Did blacks in southern Louisiana suffer the same level of violence as those in other parts of the state? What influence did the numerous bands of robbers and outlaws that plundered southern Louisiana have on regional homicide rates? What was the impact of the particular economic conditions within the southern Louisiana sugar industry on the violence in that region? These are some of the questions that need to be addressed.

Patterns of Violence

For the purpose of the present chapter, rural Louisiana is divided into two large regions, the first of which comprises the nineteen parishes of southern Louisiana, where the majority of the white population was of French descent. The southern region covers the Southwestern area, the South Central prairies, and the Sugar Bowl area. The second region is composed of the remaining thirty-eight parishes that were largely settled by old stock Americans. The southern parishes and the northern parishes each had a distinct pattern of violence that is revealed by the annual rate of homicides per 100,000 inhabitants (fig. 6.1). The difference was particularly obvious during Reconstruction, when the northern parishes had an annual homicide rate almost double that of the southern French parishes.

Differences in the racial patterns of homicide between the southern and northern parishes partly explain this discrepancy in the annual rates (table 6.1). Homicide in southern Louisiana was not only less frequent but it was also a more intraracial phenomenon for both whites and blacks. Meanwhile, interracial homicides, particularly whites killing blacks, were the main characteristic of homicidal behavior in the North. This was even more obvious during Reconstruction

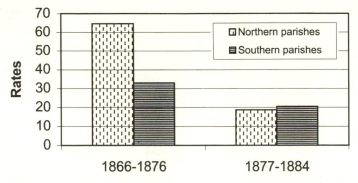

Figure 6.1 Annual Rates of Homicide per 100,000 Inhabitants

Table 6.1
Racial Distribution of Homicides in Rural Louisiana

	Southern Parishes		Northern Parishes	
	N	%	N	%
Unknown by unknown	138	14.4	340	10.7
Unknown by whites	65	6.8	151	4.7
Unknown by blacks	24	2.5	81	2.5
Whites by unknown	47	4.9	122	3.8
Blacks by unknown	52	5.4	264	8.2
Whites by whites	191	20.0	419	13.1
Whites by blacks	53	5.5	101	3.1
Blacks by whites	213	22.3	1,325	41.5
Blacks by blacks	172	18.0	383	12.0
Total	955	100.0	3,186	100.0

when blacks represented 78 percent of the people killed in northern Louisiana compared to only 61 percent in southern Louisiana.

Moreover, blacks committed only 18 percent of homicides in northern parishes compared to 28 percent in the southern counterpart. While 84 percent of black victims were killed by whites in the northern parishes, the percentage was lower in southern Louisiana at only 68 percent. Therefore, whites had relatively little to fear from blacks in both southern and northern Louisiana. The probability that a white would fall victim to a black murderer was rather small: less than 20 percent of whites killed in both regions were murdered by blacks.

This situation changed dramatically with the end of Reconstruction, however. Violence throughout the state became more intraracial

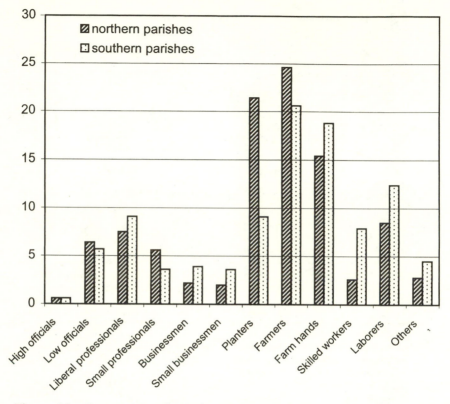

Figure 6.2 Occupations of People Committing Homicide in Northern and Southern Louisiana, 1866–1884 (percentages)

in character. Blacks still represented 60 percent of those killed in both regions, but the percentage of blacks killed by whites dropped substantially to 43 percent in northern parishes and to 35 percent in southern Louisiana. Outbreaks of racial violence became less frequent, despite the withdrawal of Federal troops from the state. And yet, from the smallest incident arose the danger of racial violence in the region. For example, white people of St. Landry parish were greatly agitated in 1882 by an apprehended black outbreak. In 1883 a drunken white narrowly missed involving the town of Thibodeaux in a riot when he assaulted several black people.[4]

The disparity in the number of farmers and planters is one of the most interesting aspects about the occupational distribution of the people charged with homicide in rural Louisiana (fig. 6.2). Farmers and planters represented 46 percent of the people who committed

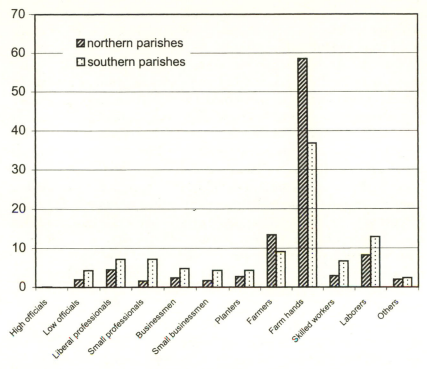

Figure 6.3 Occupations of the Victims of Homicide in Northern and Southern Louisiana, 1866–1884 (percentages)

homicide in northern parishes, compared to only 30 percent in southern Louisiana. Meanwhile, farmhands represented 59 percent of the homicide victims in northern parishes, compared to 37 percent for southern Louisiana (fig 6.3). As we will see later, confrontation between planters and black field hands was indeed more prevalent in the cotton fields than in the sugar land.[5]

The Motives Underlying Homicides

An analysis of the motives for homicides in both regions should unveil that robberies and crimes against property were at the root of most homicidal behavior in the southern parishes. Long before the Civil War, the region had already gained a reputation as a smuggling center and a paradise for cattle thieves. Southern Louisiana was, with its numerous lakes, bayous, and swamps, almost impenetrable and offered an ideal refuge where criminal bands could flourish. Not surprisingly, the region emerged during the Civil War as a major center of guerrilla and jayhawker activities.[6]

After the war thousands of rural people, particularly blacks, moved to the towns and villages of southern Louisiana, which were also invaded by tramps and beggars who could only survive through stealing. Not surprisingly rural newspapers hysterically claimed that barely a night passed without some evidence of the thieves' daring escapades. They asserted that nearly every store and residence in these towns was struck and the thieves often succeeded in escaping with considerable bounty.[7] Bands of thieves and outlaws rode through the surrounding countryside and developed large networks for disposing of the stolen property. During the early 1870s one gang of black thieves extended its operations throughout the region from New Iberia to Brashear City.[8]

As robbers appeared in a parish or moved to a new area and began to operate their illicit trade, the most improbable stories about them arose and became exaggerated. Rumors could inflate the size of a five-member band to fifty, describing the thieves as armed to the teeth and eager to perpetrate any act of violence. The entire region would then became worked up to a pitch of excitement. Many papers advised the rural people of southern Louisiana to keep their guns well loaded and to resort to summary punishments whenever a thief was caught stealing.[9]

Cattle stealing and killing became so common in the late 1860s that it was considered the most serious obstacle to raising stock in the region. In some parishes the number of animals killed would have been sufficient to supply local towns with milk, butter, and meat. In the prairies of southwestern Louisiana, three-quarters of the livestock roaming at large had been illegally slaughtered by 1868. A planter in East Baton Rouge parish lost 27 of his 33 hogs at the hands of thieves in early December 1867. His cows, goats, and sheep disappeared in the same manner. Another planter saved 60 of his 110 hogs from theft by killing them himself. Cattle and even horses were often shot and killed during the night. There seemed to be no safety for stock of any kind.[10]

But criminal activities in southern Louisiana were not limited to robbery and cattle thefts. Bands of disguised men, prowling the roads and committing all kind of outrages, did often "blood" their hands at the slightest provocation. In August 1868 a gang of black thieves regularly lay in ambush and fired on the passing trains in Terrebonne

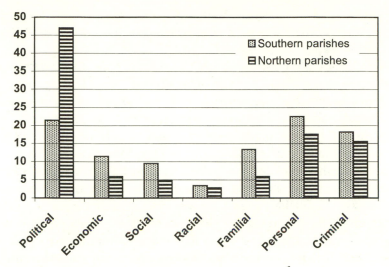

Figure 6.4 Motives Underlying Homicide in Northern and Southern Louisiana (percentages)

parish. In the process the community became much excited, especially because three whites had been killed.[11] But these activities were not limited to black bands alone. On the contrary, white gangs were just as common and just as brutal. A group of masked white men broke into the house of a respectable black family one night in August 1868 in St. Mary parish. They dragged the whole family into the woods where they killed the father and mother in the most vicious manner, cutting their throats from ear to ear. A similar band was terrorizing blacks in Lafayette parish in 1867.[12]

And yet despite the notorious reputation of the region, criminal activities, and more particularly robbery, were at the root of only 18 percent of the homicides that occurred in southern Louisiana, compared to 16 percent in the northern parishes (fig. 6.4). After the Civil War, politics represented the main cause of violence in southern Louisiana, as in other regions.

Southern Louisiana represented a particular fertile region for the proliferation of paramilitary organizations dedicated to maintaining white supremacy in the state. The presence of various Ku Klux Klan organizations in Lafayette, St. Martin, St. Mary, St. Landry, and Terrebonne parishes created much apprehension among the black population during the summer of 1868. As masked white bands roamed in the still hours of the night, prowling through the woods behind certain

plantations, blacks became frightened and terrorized, strongly believing that whites intended to assassinate or drive away every Yankee
and black leader.[13]

The black community of southern Louisiana saw their worst fears
confirmed in the Opelousas riot of September 1868. During that riot,
only blacks who were accompanied by a white, or who had joined a
Democratic club, or who were carrying protection papers had their
lives saved.[14] Further, the assassination of Sheriff Henry Pope and Parish Judge Valentine Chase of St. Mary, the sacking of the parish courthouse, and the destruction of Emerson Bently's press, demonstrated
to the local black community that even their white allies were not safe.
Local White Camelia Council leaders in fact selected targets all over
southern Louisiana, as they did in other regions, among prominent or
politically active black and white Republicans.[15] In the maelstrom of
1868, political intimidation and violence was not directed only at
black and white Republicans. Many poor Cajuns and white Creoles,
reputed to be favorable to the Republican ticket, were prevented
from voting.[16]

Political violence erupted again in November 1870 when the cities
of Baton Rouge and Donaldsonville were each struck by a riot on
election day. Mayor Schonberg and Parish Judge Laws, two whites,
were the only people killed during the Donaldsonville riot. Meanwhile, only two blacks were killed during the Baton Rouge riot,
including Joseph Lofficial, an elected representative.[17] But this was
nothing compared to the major wave of violence that shook southern
Louisiana during the spring of 1873. At this time, former Confederate
Colonel Alcibiade Deblanc led an insurrection in the three Cajun parishes of Lafayette, St. Martin, and Vermilion against the new Republican government of Governor William P. Kellogg. Colonel Deblanc,
reinforced by citizens from Lafayette and St. Landry, gathered his
small force in St. Martinville. Using two small guns, he offered open
resistance to a detachment of the New Orleans Metropolitan Police
who had been dispatched to the region as a militia unit to restore
order.[18]

Southern Louisiana witnessed a new wave of political violence in
1874. The White League movement, first launched in St. Landry parish in April 1874, was particularly active all over the Teche area. Some
850 people joined the White League in Lafayette parish and 875
in Iberia parish. Alcibiade Deblanc assumed leadership of the White
League in the region and transformed the area into a White League

stronghold. In the course of his campaign of political intimidation, several black churches were burned and numerous black religious services were disrupted, particularly in Iberia and St. Martin parishes. Moreover, several blacks were either "found dead," "lynched," or "foully dealt with." [19] Many conservative planters, following instructions issued by the White League, discharged blacks who had voted for the Republican ticket. Meanwhile, 160 and 15 black families were discharged in November 1974 in Iberia and Lafayette parishes respectively. The policy of discharging black workers for participating in politics and for voting Republican was not new. It had already been used in 1868, but in southern Louisiana, this policy never reached the level it did in northern Louisiana. [20]

The only notable incident of political violence in southern Louisiana after 1874 occurred in November 1884. The Loreauville riot had its origins in the determination of the Bourbon Democrats to overthrow Republican rule in southern Louisiana, the last stronghold of republicanism. During the state election of April 1884 white Democrats refused all compromise and carried the election by fraud, intimidation, and ballot stuffing. But because Republicans in Iberia parish refused to yield power, the parish was in trouble during the whole summer. A black posse under the leadership of ex-sheriff Theogène Viator proceeded to occupy the courthouse in July. On two occasions, detachments of the state militia were sent to New Iberia to quiet down the situation. [21] As the presidential election of 1884 approached, Democrats were more determined than ever to carry the day. On November 1, 1884, a group of whites disrupted a black political meeting held in the small village of Loreauville. The skirmish quickly turned into a bloodbath in which two whites and some twenty blacks were killed. [22]

Still, the number of white Republicans killed in southern Louisiana during Reconstruction was rather small. The murder of black political leaders was even more exceptional. Indeed, political violence in the southern parishes never reached the level of northern Louisiana. The beating to death in May 1869 of Alexander François, a black senator from St. Martin, by Colonel Fournet was the most notable political murder in southern Louisiana. [23] This explains why the region had a lower rate of homicide than the northern parishes.

Politics, then, certainly explain why homicides were less prevalent in southern Louisiana than in the northern part of the state, but we still need to know why political violence was less common in southern Louisiana. The answer lies in the particular economic situation of the region. The adjustment to emancipation and to the post–Civil War economy was much different in southern Louisiana than in the northern parishes. Because sugar planters were more dependent on their field hands than were cotton planters, they were more reluctant to resort to violence and intimidation against blacks.

A Plantation Economy In Crisis

The plantation economy underwent a period of deep depression and transformation after the Civil War. Ruined by the war, many planters and farmers could no longer afford to grow cotton and to buy all of their supplies of meat and corn, of working stock and other things necessary for farming. The economic depression of the mid-1870s, combined with the poor crop of 1873 and the flood of 1874, had disastrous effects on the ability of the planters to keep their land. The 1880 federal census reveals the extent of the disintegration of the old plantation system in this period. In Rapides parish alone, the number of units with less than 50 acres climbed from 516 in 1860 to 1,349 in 1880. In many parishes small subsistence farms replaced large cotton plantations.[24] The sugar planters were confronted with many of the same problems: the low price of sugar, poor crops, bad weather, lack of capital, seed rot, freezing, and high credit charges.[25]

Unlike cotton plantations, though, sugar estates in southern Louisiana remained largely intact, although ownership shifted greatly. The main reason for this difference lay in the large amounts of capital needed to keep sugar plantations in operation. Indeed, sugar culture required far more equipment and training of the labor force than did cotton plantations. Sugar production required not only implements for cutting the cane, but also vaults to guide the cane, kettles to boil the cane juice, and draft animals to bring the cane from the field.[26]

The sugar planters were faced with an even worse problem: the falling price of sugar on the American market. For example, a hogshead of sugar that sold for more than $200 at the end of the war, yielded $100 by 1876, and only $60 by 1878. The low price of sugar discouraged many planters and forced radical changes in the production system.[27] Many planters barely survived only because the American tariff on sugar insured them a minimal protection against foreign competition.

But at this same time the fluctuation in the sugar tariff after the war added to the difficulties many planters had in adjusting to the new situation. The tariff on sugar, which had been fixed at 3¢ per pound after the war, was reduced to 1.5¢ during the early 1870s. Increased to 2.8¢ in 1875, the tariff was again reduced to 2¢ in 1884. This fluctuation of the tariff did much to upset the internal sugar trade and to increase the financial vulnerability of the sugar planters. Consequently, in the late 1870s and early 1880s, the planters formed an association to protect their industry. While the new association represented a powerful lobby aimed at maintaining the sugar tariff, it also became a dynamic force in improving methods of cultivation and in modernizing the sugar industry in general.[28]

By the early 1880s most Democratic leaders in the Northern states saw the sugar tariff as a special privilege granted to a particular region. The opposition to it was particularly strong among sugar refiners who had a preference for cheap imported sugar. But opposition to the tariff was not limited to northern Democrats.

Most Southern Democrats were consistently in favor of reducing the tariff on Louisiana sugar. Even newspapers in northern Louisiana and other cotton areas seemed insensitive to the crushing blow a reduction or an abolition of the tariff would mean for southern Louisiana. Reductions in the sugar tariff could cause planters either to reduce wages or to cut the number of acres cultivated in order to avoid bankruptcy. The Sugar Planters' Association maintained that the complete abolition of the tariff would have compelled 50 percent of the sugar plantations to convert to cotton or rice production. The loss would have been substantial, considering that some 260,000 people were dependent on the sugar industry.[29]

The Congress elected in 1882 was clearly free-trade in its commercial orientation as far as the sugar tariff was concerned. As the reduction of the sugar tariff had become a partisan issue, it was put on the agenda of the new Congress. In December 1882 a bill was introduced that aimed at reducing the tariff on sugar by 20 percent. The measure generated bitter opposition in southern Louisiana. A convention was held in New Orleans in January 1884 to devise means to preserve the tariff. Many planters threatened to leave the Democratic party. The tariff became an important issue during the gubernatorial election of April 1884, which saw the Republicans attempt to profit from the dissension it had created among Democrats.[30]

Southern Louisiana planters did not stand alone in their appeals to the Congress for the maintenance of the sugar tariff. Following a meeting held in New Orleans, black workers in Louisiana's sugar industry addressed a circular to their fellow citizens in January 1884. The circular called upon them to appeal to Congress to resist the attempted effort to reduce the tariff upon sugar. The disappearance of the tariff, they argued, would mean a reduction of 50 percent in the workers' wages.[31]

Economic differences between southern and northern Louisiana had political ramifications that had divided the two regions since the antebellum period. Although they shared with the planters of northern Louisiana the same racial prejudices, white planters in southern Louisiana were compelled by economic necessity, given the support of the National Republican Party for a sugar tariff, to take a different stand as far as national politics was concerned. The tariff issue and the need of black labor largely explain why southern Louisiana remained a Republican stronghold long after the end of Reconstruction.[32]

A Region Plagued with Labor Shortages

The abolition of slavery brought not only the development of new business methods, but also radical changes in the labor relationship between planters and their hands. Indeed, with emancipation, control over labor became the greatest question that Southern planters had to face. It was vital for planters to adjust quickly to the new economic realities if they wanted to keep their field hands and to remain in operation. At first they resorted to the payment of fixed wages, but this system was quickly abandoned as planters lacked the capital needed to pay regular wages.[33]

Meanwhile sharecropping, which replaced the wage system, presented many advantages for blacks. It allowed black laborers to escape the gang system and it made it possible for them to work on their own and to participate in the commercial economy. Still, indebtedness was an inescapable ingredient of sharecropping. Under the sharecropping system blacks became dependent on the local store owners who advanced them the necessary goods for the coming year. Although sharecropping had its shortcomings, it became the favorite system in the cotton belt, where emancipation had compelled planters to devise new business methods and new means of dealing with laborers.[34]

Several attempts were made to introduce sharecropping in southern Louisiana, but except for a few successful experiments, the system proved to be more or less a failure. The payment of fixed wages seemed more appropriate to the sugar economy and represented a better way for planters to secure reliable hands. This system was also preferred by many black hands, afraid to be reduced to a condition of semislavery by debt. Finally, the wage system was less ruinous for the planters who could hire the supplementary hands they needed in harvesttimes.[35]

Still, sugarcane culture was constantly plagued with labor shortage after the war. Sugar production was the most labor intensive of the crops grown in the state. And the difficulty of obtaining good and reliable hands at the beginning of the year caused many problems in the region. In 1871 the situation became so serious in the parish of West Baton Rouge that planting had to be postponed. The coming crop was endangered and was only saved because the new hired hands agreed to work extra hours to make up for lost time.[36]

The planters could not count on the state government for a close control of the black population. The Republican authorities were reluctant to coerce blacks to work on plantations. But from the planters' point of view, the need to control black labor remained paramount. The desire of blacks to improve their condition by moving to other plantations was a real problem, even in southern Louisiana. Many blacks deserted plantations after the war and moved to neighboring towns or to New Orleans. As late as the early 1880s, blacks were still moving to towns or even changing regions. Laborers were reported leaving Terrebonne and going to the Attakapas region, where better wages were paid.[37]

In several instances planters who had difficulty adjusting to labor competition resorted to violence to prevent blacks from leaving their plantations. In October 1881, Israel Dotson, the new owner of the Excelsor plantation, attempted to prevent George Ashley, a black field hand, from leaving the plantation with his wife and son. Ashley resisting along with his son, shot Dotson dead. A force of one hundred men was sent to capture the two blacks.[38] Not surprisingly, sugar planters hoped that the end of Reconstruction would bring tighter controls over labor contracts. This is shown clearly by a petition they submitted to the Louisiana State Assembly in January 1878.[39]

Meanwhile, the scarcity of labor brought stiff competition among planters for the hiring of good hands. Regularly, planters attempted to entice laborers away from neighboring plantations by making better offers. The competition once in a while degenerated into open conflict and bloody fighting. In 1881, for example, the planters of West Feliciana resorted to a campaign of terror to prevent several wealthy merchants from establishing new plantations. The planters were afraid of losing their best laborers, because the new planters were offering blacks better terms than the usual ones in the parish.[40]

Therefore, white planters were compelled to offer inducements to keep blacks on their plantations. In 1869, P. Harnan was offering $40 a hand plus board. Yet he was unable to find the number of workers he needed. Confronted with this great scarcity of labor, many planters began to offer blacks better quarters and the privilege of raising poultry and some stock. In spite of these improvements, many blacks searched for work on levees and railroads, jobs which were more remunerative than field labor. For many blacks, leaving the plantations became a way to improve their working conditions. This situation only amplified the shortage of labor on the plantations.[41]

As the scarcity of labor remained chronic, sugar planters were compelled to devise new means to attract white laborers. Immigration societies were launched in an attempt to attract immigrants, mainly from France and Canada. As late as 1880, planters attempted to lure European immigrants and white Creoles to work on their plantations by offering them not only good wages but the privilege of raising all the poultry they desired, of keeping some hogs, cows, and horses, and of cultivating potatoes and vegetables.[42] Although many planters looked at white immigration as a solution, experience showed that both white Creoles and white immigrants found field work too monotonous.[43]

Labor Strikes on Sugar Plantations

As black laborers on sugar plantations discovered the inherent power they had because of the shortage of trained hands, they did not hesitate to exercise their newly won power to improve their working and living conditions. Even so, the *Donaldsonville Chief,* a Republican newspaper, asserted that black hands had not enough leadership, sense of organization, and material means to launch and to support a systematic strike for a sustained period of time.[44]

The years 1867–68 were underlined by many spontaneous small-scale strikes on the sugar plantations of southern Louisiana. But these labor skirmishes were easily dealt with by the local agent of the Freedmen's Bureau. The first real strike on sugar plantations occurred in November 1870, when black hands asked for a new contract, even though they had not completed their existing one. Conceived by blacks as a way of bargaining for better terms, it was perceived by whites as a sign of dishonesty and bad faith. Above all, it demonstrated the extent to which white planters depended on blacks for their crop, particularly in harvesttimes.[45] Several unsuccessful strikes were staged in southern Louisiana in October and November 1872.[46] Although blacks on sugar plantations demanded better wages, their current wages, at $20 a month plus rations, were higher than in the cotton fields. Furthermore, sugar hands had better living conditions than those working on cotton plantations.[47]

The situation changed dramatically, however, with the depression of 1873. Sugar planters were no longer willing to continue paying the prevalent wages. The movement to reduce wages began in Terrebonne parish in November 1873 and quickly spread to all of southern Louisiana. By 1874, wages on sugar plantations were generally reduced to $13 a month with rations, or $17 a month without rations.[48] As planters lowered the wages, blacks protested and attempted to resist, forming the first trade-union among sugar workers. A posse of blacks and whites led by the black sheriff of Terrebonne parish confronted the strikers before the militia even arrived in the parish. Meanwhile, such black leaders as Senator Cage and Representative Keys tried to quiet down black excitement. In the process the black sugar workers felt betrayed by their political leaders who joined with the planters to break down the strike.[49]

Although the cost of living increased with the return of prosperity, wages did not. In 1878, workers' wages still remained low as they varied between 13 and 18 dollars per month, two-thirds to be paid at the end of the month, the balance after the rolling season. Three prices were usually paid: from $1 to $1.50 per day for planting the cane, $0.75 for the regular season, and $1.50 for rolling the crop.[50] Consequently, a movement to strike for better wages was launched in Assumption parish in late February 1880 and quickly spread to St. Charles and St. John the Baptist parishes in March. By April the strike affected the parishes of Ascension, Jefferson, and St. James. In May the movement had spread to Iberville, St. Bernard, and Plaquemines parishes.[51]

These strikes started the same way in each parish. Some black field hands left work, demanded a wage increase, and were met with a prompt refusal. Some hands then decided to leave the plantations and to convince workers on other plantations to do the same. As they moved from plantation to plantation with their wives and children, they gradually gathered several hundred workers who joined them to support their demand for higher wages. Although described as an insurrection, the strikes did not represent a deliberate movement. Most of the time, the strikes lasted only one or two days and, in spite of vague rumors of a general strike, blacks agreed to return to work under the conditions imposed by the planters. Moreover, the demonstrations only rarely became violent. Once in a while violence erupted when hands refused to leave work; strikers threatened to burn their cabins if they refused to join the movement. Three black workers were even killed in St. Charles when proponents and opponents of the strike confronted each other.[52]

And yet, as local authorities felt they could not handle the situation, they called on Governor Wiltz for help. The reaction of the state authorities was swift and based on the not unjustified fear of the contagious effect of the strike movement. Four companies of the state militia and a detachment of artillery were sent to St. Charles parish in late March. Another detachment was sent to St. John the Baptist parish with orders to arrest the strike leaders on charges of trespassing, inciting a work stoppage, and intimidating nonstrikers. As the labor strike spread to other parishes, the governor was required to send militia to these new trouble spots. In April 1880 the secretary of state met 300 blacks in St. John the Baptist parish in an attempt to reach a compromise. When it became obvious that no agreement could be reached, a company of artillery and another of riflemen were sent to the parish. Arresting the leaders not only caused much anger among black laborers but incited them to resist the militia in St. Bernard and Plaquemines parishes in April and May 1880. Blacks were compelled by military force to go back to work at the same wages as before the strike. When talks failed, judicial proceedings were taken against the leaders. In the end, Governor Wiltz used his pardoning power to quiet down the situation on the sugar plantations.[53]

The strike movement did not stop in 1880. One year later, some 300 to 400 blacks led by a Spaniard, went from plantation to plantation to compel laborers to stop work until planters consented to pay the wages they demanded. In 1884 great excitement prevailed in Iberville parish when a proposition for a wage reduction was submitted. In August a similar decision by planters in Iberia parish reduced the wages from 85 to 65 cents a day. The change sparked a strike by the

Table 6.2
Labor Strikes in Rural Louisiana, 1866–1884

Regions	1866–1876		1877–1884		Total	
	N	%	N	%	N	%
Northern Louisiana	10	33.3	9	45.0	19	38.0
Southern Louisiana	20	66.7	11	55.0	31	62.0
Total	30	100.0	20	100.0	50	100.0

sugar laborers, but after a few days the resistance trailed off.[54]

The strikes of the spring of 1880 took on greater significance because they affected several parishes. Although the main demand was for wage increases, the strikers also adopted a political program in which they asserted they formed a nation and which called for working-class solidarity.[55] In that sense, black sugar laborers showed a growing sense of class consciousness and an ability to organize that planters did not foresee. And yet, while the strikes did reflect the current political situation, they did not represent an uprising against the local or state authorities. State and local newspapers did try to blame Republicans for allegedly organizing a labor union among the black hands, but the charge did not fly far.[56] All the various parties involved—the black laborers, the planters, and the state authorities—worked diligently to limit the strike movement to what it was, a labor conflict. As a consequence labor conflicts in southern Louisiana took relatively few lives compared to labor disturbances in northern Louisiana.

One of the most interesting aspects of violence in post–Civil War Louisiana was that strikes in cotton fields seemed simply not to exist. Not only did northern Louisiana have a smaller share of strikes than southern Louisiana in proportion to its population (table 6.2), but none of these northern strikes took place in the cotton fields, while most strikes in southern Louisiana were fought by sugar hands.[57] This difference with the sugar region appears to have been closely linked to differences in crop systems. The sharecrop system that prevailed on cotton plantations limited the possibility of worker organization. Each field hand worked his piece of land on which he lived with his family. As a consequence he had no reason to strike except to protest about the crop settlement at the end of the year.[58]

This did not mean, however, that the cotton fields of northern Louisiana were free from labor trouble. In October 1868 six blacks, armed with shotguns, muskets, and pistols, went to the house of a planter for whom they worked in West Feliciana parish and demanded an immediate settlement of their crop. In February 1878 some three hundred blacks in Grant parish, who were protesting against their working conditions, seized and threatened to kill a white overseer. The incident stirred up the surrounding region. Blacks finally chose to release the overseer and to return to work as whites threatened to unleash a massacre similar to the one at Colfax in 1873. These two examples are a good illustration of white reaction to labor conflict in northern Louisiana. Any labor disturbance in that region was quickly described as a black uprising, riot, or insurrection, and as such it raised among whites their worst pre-antebellum fears.[59]

Conclusion

After the war, southern Louisiana was incontestably a paradise for robbers and outlaws and had its share of political riots and disturbances. And yet the regional distribution of homicide shows that southern Louisiana did not experience the same intensity of violence as the English-speaking parishes. With the exception of the Opelousas riot of 1868 and the Loreauville riot of 1884, violence there never degenerated into mass murder as it did in other regions of Louisiana.

By 1884 the only Republican stronghold in Louisiana was to be found in the southern parishes. This particular regional situation can be explained by the fact that even if the planters and freedmen disagreed about wages and working conditions, they generally agreed about politics. Not only were many plantations owned by white Republicans and Northern businessmen, but many Democratic planters opposed their party's platform on the tariff question and lobbied the Federal Administration to protect them against foreign sugar imports.[60] As a consequence white Conservatives in southern Louisiana did not resort to political violence and did not coerce as many blacks to vote Democratic as in the northern parts of the state.

This view was shared by a congressional committee that investigated violence in Louisiana in 1879. The members of the committee found it a "significant fact that the illegal, brutal methods of electioneering that are now known as bull-dozing have been confined for the most part since 1868 to the cotton-growing regions of the South." The fact that "the larger proportion of French descendants, with whom difference of color and race has never been reckoned a disqualification for the equal enjoyment of human rights and political prerogatives" represented for the committee only part of the explanation for the lower degree of political violence in southern Louisiana. The committee asserted further that because of "the exigence of the cane crop, there have been no serious or systematic attempts made in the sugar-growing parishes to control by violence the negro vote." The committee concluded that the demoralization of agricultural labor that followed the attack on Fairfax House in Tensas parish, the hangings in Pointe Coupée, and the massacres of Bass's Lane and Caledonia in Caddo parish of the fall of 1878 would have brought ruin to hundreds of wealthy planters in the sugar-growing regions.[61]

PART IV

Racial Violence

Black Violence in Post–Civil War Rural Louisiana

The *Franklin Planter's Banner* called on the state authorities for the imposition of martial law in St. Mary parish in December 1871. The white conservative paper pointed out that fifty blacks had been killed in that parish since 1868, and it complained about the failure of the Republican press to notice such a horrible state of affairs because these blacks had been killed by other blacks. The paper went on to add that blacks in St. Mary rarely harmed white people and that white people rarely killed blacks. Finally, the *Planter's Banner* concluded that some of these murders were of the most horrible character and that most of them were committed for trivial reasons, often without any provocation.[1] By its statement, the *Planter's Banner* was showing that if whites had little to fear from black violence they were not completely indifferent to black homicides. In doing so, it also reflected the fact that after emancipation, blacks represented an important component in the picture of violence.

When the question of racial discrimination and civil rights surfaced as a national concern in North America during the 1950s and 1960s, historians could not avoid the debate. A new generation of historians began to reexamine the Civil War and Reconstruction period and to offer new interpretations of those turbulent days. These scholars provided new insights into the living conditions of blacks under slavery and their difficult adjustment to freedom. They also placed new emphasis on the active role played by blacks in their fight for freedom and their involvement in forging new institutions and redefining their social and economic status. As a consequence the nineteenth-century black experience has emerged as one of the most striking features of recent North American historiography and particularly the social history of the Civil War and Reconstruction period.[2]

Twentieth-century social scientists have consistently noted a propensity to murder among Southern blacks that was four to ten times greater than that of Southern whites. Further, they have found that most of the violence had been intra- and not inter-racial. Some social scientists have argued that the higher level of violence among blacks can only have resulted from structural factors caused by illiteracy and poverty. Others have attributed it to psychological factors resulting from black exclusion from society. Yet all have agreed that black assaults and intraracial killings represent the traditional response of the community to intolerable pressure and insoluble conflicts.[3]

Violence and criminality are important features of the post–Civil War period and shed considerable light on the nineteenth-century black experience, especially concerning the adjustment to freedom. Though white violence has received much attention, no historian has systematically studied black violence and criminality in the South during the post–Civil War years. Indeed fearing the charges of being racists, most social scientists and historians have been reluctant during the last forty years to study behavior that could seem offensive for a particular race.[4] The present chapter will take an empirical approach to this issue by analyzing salient trends of black homicidal behavior in rural Louisiana. Special attention will be paid to the rate of black homicides, the kind of blacks who became murderers, the social context in which murders were committed, and the circumstances surrounding these crimes. References to white homicides will regularly be made in order to place black violence in a broader perspective. Black homicidal behavior reveals much about the tensions within the black community. It also illustrates how blacks adjusted to freedom and responded to white violence in the period after the Civil War.

Black Violence as Seen by Contemporaries

How violent was Louisiana after the Civil War? This question has been the focal point of a major controversy involving both eyewitnesses and later historians. For post–Civil War white Louisianians, the whole question of violence was a sore point. Conservative Democrats and local conservative newspapers were reluctant to acknowledge that much violence existed in Louisiana and quick to deny any suggestion that it might be racially or politically motivated. Charges of violence presented by blacks and Republicans were dismissed as politically oriented "allegations" made to maintain their positions in power by bringing further federal intervention into the local affairs of Louisiana. To support their point of view, conservatives did not hesitate to bring before congressional committees their own witnesses who denied that there had been any racial or even political violence in Louisiana.[5]

The question raised here is whether or not local newspapers and conservative whites in Louisiana demonstrated the same reluctance to discuss black-on-black violence. Furthermore, can traces of black intraracial violence be found in nineteenth-century Louisiana society? Were white newspapers interested in black intraracial violence or did they simply ignore it? Did blacks succeed in dissimulating their internal conflicts, even those that led to a deadly conclusion?

One might argue that because of their overt racism whites and local newspapers would often have ignored black violence.[6] Such an assumption, however, would be incorrect. Rather, a thorough screening of all local newspapers in Louisiana supports the *Jefferson State Register's* assertion that "if one colored man kills another, it is once reported and doubled in every Democratic paper in the state, and probably some silly joke or state wit is repeated with the fact."[7] Indeed conservative newspapers all over Louisiana were quick to blame blacks for the alleged increase in postbellum violence. Not only were blacks and Republicans blamed for provoking whites, but they were also charged with committing most of the violence. Week after week, year after year, the charges continued. If one were to believe the conservative press, blacks were constantly quarrelling and resorting to murder and attempted murder, stabbing and shooting to resolve their childish and foolish quarrels.[8]

Because of their alleged "murderous proclivities," blacks were frequently charged with being the main perpetrators of violence in Louisiana. Repeatedly local newspapers printed descriptions of black murders, often concluding with such statements as "we regret to notice that among the colored people human life is held in but light estimation in this parish," or, "if negroes continue to slaughter each other, we will have to conclude that Providence has chosen to exterminate them in this way." Clearly the conservative press explained the high level of homicides occurring in Louisiana by the black propensity to kill each other, blaming them for the bad publicity that was then tainting the state's reputation.[9]

Moreover, the conservative press regularly complained about the numerous black disturbances and reported any row or trouble that may have occurred between blacks. These papers objected in particular to the behavior of black farm laborers who spent Saturday nights in town drinking and who, in the process, got involved in fights and made the "night hideous with yells, shouts and pistols fired." The conservative press also condemned what they described as the blacks' habit of entering stores in gangs, drinking too much, and getting into quarrels. These drunken disputes, they argued, too often ended with violent deaths. In many instances large numbers of blacks were reported to have been engaged in riots in which sticks, knives, and other weapons were used. As a consequence the local police forces were regularly asked to intervene in order to quell black disturbances.[10]

The conservative press not only argued zealously that local crime was almost entirely confined to blacks, it also sought to explain this situation. First, the newspapers argued, emancipation had led the formerly "good" slaves to become relentless criminals: "They kill those of their own color to an extent that shocks all who remember how few homicides or grave crimes were committed by this race when they were in a state of slavery. Freedom with them means license and indolence." Second, the prevailing political situation was held to have incited blacks to become criminals: "One year of radical rule in St. Mary has produced more lawlessness among the black population than ever existed among them before. They shoot and kill each other for the most trifling insults and provocation. And when one negro kills another . . . the radical authorities pay little attention or no attention to it." Finally, blacks committed more crime, it was argued, because, "as the courts are now organized, they are in very little danger of either arrest or conviction no matter what may be the nature of the crimes they commit."[11]

According to the conservative press, this deplorable situation persisted after the end of Reconstruction. In 1880 the *Shreveport Daily Standard* asserted that "there seems to be 'blood in the moon' for the negroes in this section lately, and they are engaged in a war to exterminate their own species."[12] Blacks were reported shooting each other every day in Assumption parish in the early 1880s. Five blacks were reported as having been killed by other blacks in that parish in July 1882 alone.[13] The *Iberville South* stated in 1883: "It appears that it is becoming fashionable among our colored population to cut, shoot, and kill one another."[14]

At the same time, blacks were charged with monopolizing the criminal calendar and overloading the judicial system. One journalist expressed the hope that at "some time in the future, say a hundred years, here, our colored citizens will lose their ambition to appear in the court." Conservative newspapers charged that blacks were responsible for 75 percent of all crimes committed in post–Civil War Louisiana and for two-thirds of the murders.[15] Any thorough investigation, they argued, would not only show that "three-fourths of the murders in Louisiana were committed by negroes," but "that two-thirds of the remainder grew out of causes entirely foreign to politics."[16] For example, in February 1875 the *Louisiana Democrat,* after examining the Rapides parish court records, fixed the number of people killed in Rapides between January 1868 and January 1875 at fifty-seven. The paper obtained this number the following way: three whites killed by blacks, ten blacks by whites, nine whites by whites, twenty-eight blacks by blacks, and three whites and two blacks killed by unknown parties. A total of fifty-seven was reached by adding two cases of suicide.[17]

Although not all historians have shared this view on post–Civil War violence,[18] these sensational accounts have nonetheless found their way into many historical studies. Distinguished historians such as Joe Gray Taylor and Joel Williamson have adopted and reinforced this impressionistic and often distorted image of post–Civil War black criminality. After scrutinizing conservative newspapers, Joe Gray Taylor arrived at the following conclusions: that "more black men were killed or wounded by black men than by whites during all the years from 1865 through 1878"; that "most violence inflicted upon black people in Louisiana, and elsewhere for that matter, was inflicted by black people"; and that "for every black man killed by a white for political or other reasons, two men were killed by other black men." Similarly, Joel Williamson asserted that "the great truth is that most blacks died by black hands" as "black life was cheapened in the elimination of black tensions."[19] As I will show, the statistical analysis of black homicidal behavior in post–Civil War rural Louisiana tells a different story.

Patterns of Black Homicidal Behavior

Information compiled on 557 black homicides committed against other blacks provides comprehensive evidence of the frequency of black intraracial homicides in rural Louisiana. This data becomes an even more significant record of real physical violence in rural Louisiana when black intraracial homicidal behavior is compared not only to black homicides committed against whites, but also with white homicidal behavior.

Against the scattered evidence of contemporary prejudices and perceptions, one must set the hard statistics concerning black homicide. The black community certainly had its criminal elements, but in spite of the economic, social, and political emancipation that they gained through enfranchisement, blacks, with some minor exception, were less prone than whites to violence. Indeed, whites had little need to fear from blacks. The cases were rare and were mostly related to either robbery or work relations. For example, Irwin Garrett, manager of the plantation owned by his uncle Captain Stephen Garrett in Assumption parish, was killed by a mulatto named Yankee on November 6, 1882, after the mulatto had a quarrel with the plantation manager over his wages.[20] The evidence provided by the quantitative analysis is overwhelming. Although they formed 60 percent of the population, blacks were responsible for only 25 percent of all murders committed in rural Louisiana between 1866 and 1884 (table 7.1). In the same period they were victims of 72 percent of all homicides. The situation was even more striking during Reconstruction, when blacks committed less than 20 percent of the homicides, but were the victims in 80 percent of all murders. Furthermore, only 20 percent of whites killed during the whole period died at the hands of blacks, while 75 percent of black victims were killed by whites.[21] Thus, though black homicides were a feature of the period, their importance was minimal compared to white homicides.

The figures in table 7.1 show important differences between black homicides and those involving both whites and the total population. Most black homicides were also intraracial in nature. Almost all black homicides were perpetrated against other blacks during Reconstruction (77%) and the early post-Reconstruction period (83%). In contrast white homicides were largely interracial during Reconstruction (77%). Only after 1876 were more than half of white homicides directed against other whites (56%). When a fatal dispute occurred be-

Table 7.1
Racial Distribution of Homicides in Rural Louisiana, 1866–1884

	1866–76	%	1877–84	%	Total Pop.	%
Unknown by unknown	250	8.1	281	25.2	531	12.5
Unknown by whites	148	4.8	80	7.2	228	5.4
Unknown by blacks	68	2.2	41	3.7	109	2.6
Blacks by unknown	265	8.5	51	4.6	316	7.5
Whites by unknown	125	4.0	44	3.9	169	4.0
Whites by blacks	101	3.3	55	4.9	156	3.7
Whites by whites	426	13.7	190	17.0	616	14.6
Blacks by whites	1,393	44.9	153	13.7	1,546	36.6
Blacks by blacks	326	10.5	231	20.7	557	13.1
Total	3,102	100.0	1,126	100.0	4,228	100.0

tween a white and a black, blacks were, as noted in previous chapters, most frequently the victims. Blacks only rarely killed whites, and when they did, it was usually a desperate act committed as a last resort.[22] As indicated above, homicide rates were markedly different between races. Even so the fundamental difference between Reconstruction and the early Redemption period was that for both races violence was becoming a more intraracial phenomenon.

Indeed the most striking conclusion that can be drawn from the data is that black homicides constituted a smaller proportion of all homicides in Louisiana after the Civil War. The black criminal, granting that his opportunities were not always equal, was less likely to be violent. It is abundantly clear that just as blacks were more likely to kill other blacks than whites, so too were they also more likely to fall victims of a white, rather than a black, killer.

Indeed the greatest difference in the distribution of homicide between whites and blacks rests precisely in the approach adopted by the criminal justice system toward each of them. Thus "the murder committed by a black is considered as a crime and severely punished, while the same act committed by a white is considered as a personal and private affair."[23]

Another characteristic that emerged from this analysis is the fact that blacks only rarely killed whites. The pattern of murders indeed followed the racial lines and become more intraracial in character after 1876 as the number of blacks killed by whites decreased substantially.[24] Significantly, as blacks lived in a world they could not change, they tended to express their anger and their endemic frustration not in encounters against whites but in violence within the black community.[25]

Whatever the conservative newspapers may have said about black homicidal behavior, the evidence clearly shows that black intraracial homicide rates were lower than white rates during both periods. The data show that there were fewer black murders per 100,000 persons than there were white. While black homicidal behavior decreased slightly, with rates of 8.9 per 100,000 during Reconstruction and 6.6 in the early Redemption period, white intraracial homicide rates dropped from 17 to 8.[26] The last noteworthy feature to emerge from these data is the apparent stability of black homicidal behavior as a proportion of all homicides in the twenty years with which we are concerned. But the question arises why black homicide rates remained more stable while those of whites strongly decreased.

Data in table 7.1 show that the overall homicide rates in Louisiana actually declined as Reconstruction ended. Though the evidence certainly shows that blacks were far less prone to homicides than whites, they were far from being upright and law-abiding as shown by their involvement in property crimes.[27] Still, the figures in table 7.1 show clearly that black patterns of homicidal behavior diminished only slightly through the years, while white rates went through a slow but constant decline.

Blacks, then, were less likely to resort to murder. Moreover, when they did, blacks acted alone. Indeed, 86 percent of black intraracial homicides involved only one assailant. This was also true for black interracial violence; in 66 percent of such cases, a lone black killed a white. In sharp contrast, white intraracial (33%) and interracial (70%) murders tended to involve two or more assailants (fig. 7.1). Clearly, homicide among blacks followed different patterns and thus had different consequences and meanings than among whites.

As we have seen in chapter 5, a striking feature of this analysis is the absence of women as either murderers or murder victims. Women represented only 4 percent of the 156 whites killed by blacks, they comprised 10 percent of the victims of black intraracial violence. Meanwhile, white and black women represented 3.4 percent and 3.5 percent respectively of the victims of white violence. The higher number of black women dying at the hands of other blacks may imply a greater tendency amongst blacks to turn their aggression against themselves rather than against whites. The absence of women as assailants is even more evident. Indeed, women, whether black or white, represented less than 1 percent of the people committing homicides.[28]

One must not forget that a large portion of the black population

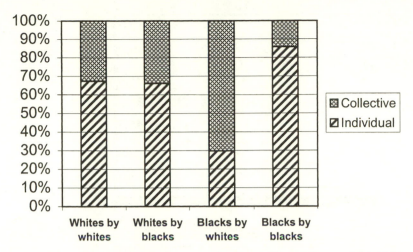

Figure 7.1   Racial Nature of Homicides in Rural Louisiana, 1866–1884

was young and consequently fell into the age group that tended to be more prone to violence. Not surprisingly these data indicate that younger members of the black population had a greater propensity to commit homicides than did their elders. This is even more obvious when compared to the rates for young whites. Thirty-four percent of blacks who killed other blacks were less than 24 years old, compared to only 23 percent of whites who killed other whites. Furthermore, only 15 percent of blacks involved in intraracial homicides were 45 years old or more, compared to 26 percent for whites. The analysis of interracial homicides gives similar numbers for each racial group. For blacks, being young and male were the conditions most consistently associated with the risk of becoming involved in a murder. This may suggest that younger blacks were more free from the restraint of slavery, less submissive to whites, and consequently less afraid to resort to violence to solve their disputes.

The data reveal few cases of homicide among the black elites. The killing of William Weeks, the assistant secretary of state, by George Paris, a former member of the state legislature and a member of the state board of assessors, represented the most notable case.[29] But such bloody incidents among the black elites were rather rare. Most black intraracial homicides involved people from the lower social strata of the black community in both the city and the rural areas.

Meanwhile white intraracial homicides were spread more evenly through the different levels of white society (fig. 7.2). This finding

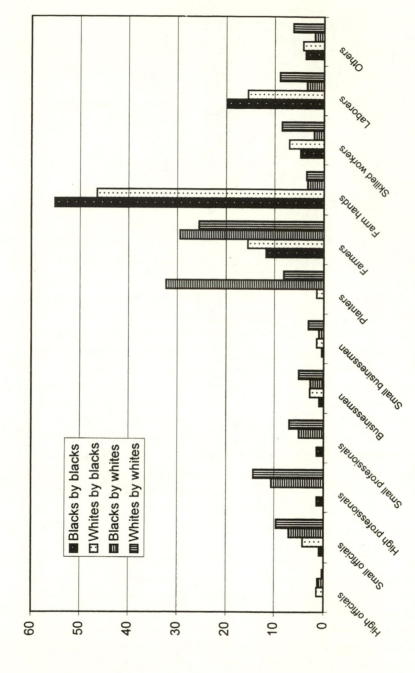

Figure 7.2 Occupation of Perpetrators of Homicides in Rural Louisiana (percentages)

contradicts studies of twentieth-century North America and sheds light on attitudes prevailing within white society after the Civil War. The involvement of a large number (33%) of members of the social and economic elites is an important characteristic of white intraracial homicide. Finally, the presence of large numbers of skilled workers, day laborers, businessmen, professionals, and public officials seems to support the hypothesis that a great number of homicides, for both races, took place in towns and villages.[30]

More than a century ago Horace Redfield demonstrated the existence of a great variety of patterns of violence among the Southern states. The statistical breakdown shows that black and white intraracial homicides in Louisiana varied greatly from one area to another. Indeed the geography of homicides shows that a disproportionate number of incidents occurred in the northwestern part of the state. Significantly, black intraracial homicide varied from a low rate of 2 per 100,000 inhabitants in the Central Hill area to 16 in the Red River Delta area (fig. 7.3). Meanwhile the white rate went from 5 in the Bayou area to 40 in the Red River Delta area (fig. 7.4). Moreover, a cross-sectional correlation between regional homicide rates and the proportion of blacks in the population yields conflicting results. Interestingly, levels of homicides between whites and blacks were not completely independent of one another, since the most violent area for both races was the Red River parishes. Although the region had only 13 percent of the rural population of Louisiana, 34 percent of homicides and 59 percent of white homicides against blacks occurred there. Indeed the black homicide rate tended to be higher in regions that had a higher rate of white violence. The physical environment of the blacks varied somewhat depending upon the region of Louisiana where they lived.

The Circumstances and Significance of Black Homicidal Behavior

What motivated blacks to resort to violence and to murder other blacks? It is not easy to identify the circumstances surrounding these incidents. Almost half of the disputes did not have any clearly specified cause, and the underlying causes of many trivial disputes are difficult to detect in newspapers and other primary sources. Finally, many homicides were reported as having mysterious causes.[31] Still,

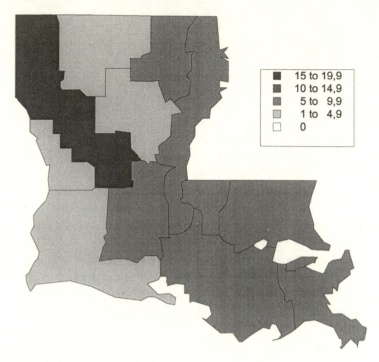

Figure 7.3 Annual Rate of Blacks Killed by Blacks per 100,000 Inhabitants, 1866–1884

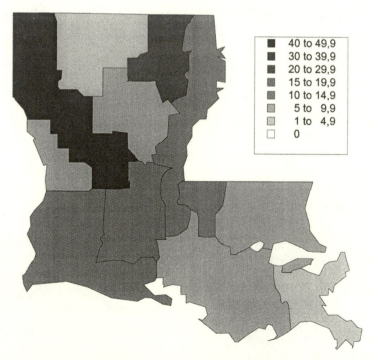

Figure 7.4 Annual Rate of Whites Killed by Whites per 100,000 Inhabitants, 1866–1884

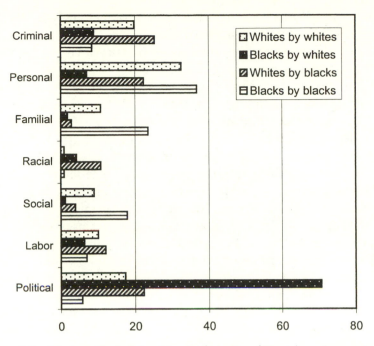

Figure 7.5   Motives Underlying Homicide in Rural Louisiana (percentages)

these data furnish enough details to get a fair idea of the origins and circumstances behind much of this violence (fig. 7.5).

Not surprisingly, politically or economically motivated homicides among blacks, compared to whites, were unusual. Blacks rarely resorted to murdering either whites or other blacks for political or economic reasons. Conservative whites tended to see such acts as threats to the whole social order and would often bring heavy retribution against their perpetrators. In contrast, 70 percent of white interracial homicides were political in origin. These murders were aimed at preserving the old social and economic order. Since black intraracial homicides did not represent a threat to white supremacy, they were tolerated by whites during and after Reconstruction. Rather than challenging white domination, then, most blacks found it easier to turn their frustration against their own kind.

Because black homicides have been especially common in the United States, the phenomenon has to be considered in terms of the black experience. The standard explanation for the high rates of murders among blacks is as follows: "Negroes murder and assault each other with such appalling frequency because of their daily frustrations in dealing with white men. Because aggression against white men would call forth extreme negative sanctions, frustrated negroes transfer their aggressive feeling to other negroes."[32]

Although the conservative press asserted that blacks regularly killed each other for trivial matters, my data show that the prime motives for black intraracial homicide were similar to those which moved whites to kill each other. Blacks (37%), as well as whites (32%), killed each other over personal grudges, in self-defense, and over trivial matters, as violence became an extralegal means of defending their honor and gaining respect within their own communities. Blacks lived in a world they could not change. The endemic frustration of black life and their particular code of honor were expressed not in encounters against whites but in violence within the black community.[33]

Blacks expressed this particular code of honor in several instances as they showed a great sensitivity to insult and fought to gain respect within their own community.[34] For example, a black was killed in Iberia parish in November 1870 in a dispute with another regarding which one was to act as fireman. Two blacks were killed in a quarrel over 30¢ in Natchitoches parish in August 1874. Ten cents was the center of a dispute between two blacks that ended with a death in Iberville parish in April 1883. In June 1881, Peter Phillips shot and killed Albert Delisle for a morsel of bread. Furthermore, the story of the brutal murder of Thomas Williams by Daniel Johnson, a black ex-convict, in February 1880 in Rapides Parish, provides a good example of the particular black code of honor. In his role as boss on the premises of his employers, Johnson ordered another black, Thomas Williams, to leave the place. Rather than comply with the order, Williams went to a black ball that was in progress on the property. Johnson, finding William at the ball, drew his pistol and deliberately shot the other man, walked to where the deceased lay, and fired more bullets into his body.[35]

Familial and marital quarrels were the second major category of criminality among blacks. Quarrels over women and disputes of passion were one of the main causes for which blacks killed each other. As shown in chapter 5, there were also a few instances of wife-killing. The killing of men by their wives did occur, but very infrequently.[36] Overall, the relative scarcity of black intrafamilial homicides is striking when compared to modern industrial societies.

A major complaint in the conservative press was that blacks consumed too much whiskey, particularly on Sundays. As a consequence, they were alleged to be constantly quarreling and disturbing the lives of peaceful town citizens. Indeed whisky consumption by blacks was perceived to be astonishingly high after the war. Blacks tended to congregate in towns on Sundays around billiard halls, barrooms, and groceries stores which, in late nineteenth-century rural Louisiana, were the only places of amusement. Conservative papers charged that because black laborers were drinking and idling on Sundays, they were involved in frequent quarrels. As we have seen before, newspapers regularly condemned the black gangs that entered stores to buy whisky and drink heavily; these manifestations inevitably ended in disputes, fights, and too often in violent deaths.[37] Whites regularly complained about and denounced the troubles caused by blacks. Saturday nights represented a special moment for blacks who left the plantations and went to villages and towns, often to provoke troubles.[38] Furthermore, local newspapers asserted that one half to two-thirds of all homicides in rural Louisiana were directly or indirectly linked to heavy drinking. Even so, the problem of heavy drinking was not limited to the black community. Evidence indicates that it also largely affected the white population and that all rural Louisiana suffered from widespread drinking.[39] However, the data do not support or confirm the press assertion that whisky consumption was the main cause of homicides in rural Louisiana.

Gaming also appears to have been a major cause of homicides among blacks. Many tried their luck at draw poker and other card games. Often the losing party disputed the outcome, sometimes violently enough to kill the winning player. The story of George Walker was not uncommon. Arrested in New Orleans on February 1, 1876, Walker was charged with having stabbed and killed John Mackley, another black, over a dispute about a card game three days earlier on the West Dover plantation in the parish of West Baton Rouge.[40] Rural areas experienced high levels of gaming and gambling, as every town and every street corner became sites for such activities.

But neither alcohol nor gaming alone caused the most violence. Whiskey and poker had to be combined with pistols to become lethal. These three elements were reported to be at the origins, mostly on Sundays, of three-quarters of all black intra-racial homicides in the countryside. Most observers linked the frequency of crime and the high rates of black and white homicides to the general custom of carrying concealed weapons and the practice of gambling in public places where intoxicating drinks were freely sold.[41]

Conservative newspapers in rural areas regularly complained about the blacks' practice of carrying concealed weapons, even when working in the fields. Although blacks did carry weapons as a means of self-defence and to enhance their self-esteem, the conservative press argued that frequent accidents and brutal murders were the result. However, this practice was not limited to blacks. Evidence for both races show that people act violently at the slightest provocation, or even with no provocation. The practice of carrying concealed weapons made quarrels among both races more numerous and more bloody. Pistols and other concealed weapons could turn trivial disputes into deadly encounters.[42]

In spite of the conservative presses' allegations that blacks had become inveterate criminals and that they monopolized the criminal calendar, the data presented here show that they were less prone to resort to homicide in the course of another crime. Only a few homicides could be linked to other forms of black criminal behavior. Although robberies were regularly committed by blacks in rural Louisiana, evidence shows that blacks rarely committed murder while perpetrating theft. Only 34 black homicides, of which 19 were against whites, were linked to robbery. Meanwhile, 61 white homicides originated with robberies, and 37 of these were intraracial in nature. The fact that so few homicides were related to robbery is in itself rather surprising.[43]

When all of the evidence is evaluated, one is left with the impression that most intraracial homicides, for both races, were not premeditated but rather spontaneous acts arising from disputes between individuals who knew each other. These data confirm the view that both blacks and whites in nineteenth-century Louisiana had quick tempers and an exaggerated sense of honor. When these two elements combined with whisky, gaming, and pistols, they became highly explosive. Indeed, these were the cultural characteristics that made intraracial homicides a daily occurrence for both races in rural Louisiana.

Conclusion

Twentieth-century social scientists have fully examined the various factors that underlie black and white violence. They have demonstrated by sophisticated analysis how violence was deeply rooted in poverty, lack of education, poor housing, and disrupted family. Nevertheless few historians have examined nineteenth-century black violence, except in very general terms. Since intraracial homicide rates have been especially high among African Americans in the United States during the last century, these historians have concluded, without detailed study, that the same was true for the nineteenth-century rural South. They were therefore rather quick to draw sweeping conclusions and to adopt the impressionistic portrayals of black violence that they found in the local conservative press.

The foregoing analysis of the general patterns of homicide and the statistical breakdown between races show that these historians have been too hasty in blaming blacks for the high level of violence that marked the period. In fact, whites were largely responsible for the general atmosphere of violence that prevailed. Proportionately they killed each other in greater numbers than did blacks. Evidence presented here clearly shows that there were fewer black intraracial homicides per 100,000 persons than there were among whites.

This data set also reveals several important characteristics of post–Civil War homicidal behavior in Louisiana. First, violence became more intraracially oriented with the end of Reconstruction. Second, white intraracial homicide rates declined significantly with the end of Reconstruction, while black homicide rates also fell, but much less sharply. Third, white and black intraracial rates varied within the various areas of the state and were closely linked to the general rates of violence that prevailed in those regions.

The sharp decline of white interracial violence was due to a greater consensus among whites about the black issue, the fall from power of the Republicans, and the appeasement of the social and political disruption generated by the Civil War. Paradoxically, the same factors that eased the tension within the white community were responsible for the relative stagnation of black homicidal behavior. As blacks became more socially and politically alienated, violence remained a dominant feature of their community.

The Black Response to White Violence

On a Sunday afternoon in July 1874, the black population of Homer, Claiborne parish, went to town as they usually did on Sundays for trading, this being the time they were relieved by contract from work. But this Sunday took a violent turn when a black was killed after having a personal dispute with the town's white barber. The almost two hundred blacks who were in the town quickly assembled in the vicinity where the shooting had occurred and demanded that the white man be delivered to them. The local white population not only rejected their demand; they also gave the black crowd fifteen minutes to leave town, which the blacks did after some hesitation.[1] This case could be seen as an isolated incident, but it takes on greater significance in light of blacks' new assertiveness and the difficulty experienced by whites in adjusting to the new economic and political conditions generated by emancipation.

As we have seen in previous chapters, revisionist historians have produced, in their search to explain the tensions and conflicts that characterized this period, new, comprehensive studies that show how both races struggled to adjust to the changes in economic, social, and political conditions of the postwar years. In the process, blacks emerged as an independent force in a post–Civil War period distinguished by complex interpenetration of racial, class, and social conflict. However, few historians have shown much interest in the way blacks reacted to white encroachment and white violence after the war.[2] As we will see, blacks did not remain passive but were active participants in the drama that shaped their destiny. The black reaction combined self-defense, militancy, and restraint. Confronted by strong adversity, blacks proved very imaginative in devising various means to resist white violence and to counter the white effort to bring them back under subjugation.

Blacks Assert Their Rights

From today's perspective it is easy to minimize the importance of the upheaval caused by Reconstruction policies in Louisiana, as elsewhere in the South. However, P. B. S. Pinchback, a black politician and former lieutenant-governor of Louisiana, told a Cincinnati audience in September 1874: "The introduction of the colored element into the political body had brought extraordinary changes" and "had also resulted in creating a bitter antagonism of race." Echoing the comment made almost a century earlier by Pinchback, John Hope Franklin wrote in 1961: "The entrance of negroes into the political arena was the most revolutionary aspect of the Reconstruction program."[3]

During the years immediately after the Civil War, blacks attempted to unravel the complex racial and cultural changes that occurred as a result of emancipation. Of perhaps greater significance, however, was the determination of blacks to ensure their survival, their welfare, and the fulfillment of their personal and group aspirations by assuming as much responsibility as the circumstances would allow. This is especially true for free blacks in New Orleans who were at this time "moved by truly revolutionary concepts in redefining social relations." These men shared a genuine liberal concern for social, political, and economic equality. While the Reconstruction policy was being defined, they felt that emancipation and the right to vote were not enough and that blacks should also have the right to hold office, to operate their own school system, and to define their economic future.[4] The demand of the Louisiana black community for universal suffrage and civil rights was first voiced during the Civil War and more particularly at the National Equal Rights League convention that met in New Orleans in January 1865.[5]

Nothing reflected more clearly the social and political revolution that swept Louisiana after the Civil War than the 1868 state constitution's introduction of universal manhood suffrage, the right of any citizen to hold office, and a formal bill of rights. The new constitution provided such fundamental rights as freedom of the press, freedom to assemble and to petition, and protection from the state against oppressive fines, cruel punishments, and unreasonable searches. It also guaranteed the right to a speedy trial before an impartial jury for any person charged with a criminal offense. Finally, the new constitution prohibited the legislature from enacting a retroactive law on any law that would fix the price of manual labor or that would establish a religious test. Black delegates played a major role in the constitutional convention for the adoption of this civil rights program.[6]

The articles that prohibited public discrimination based on race or previous status became the most controversial provisions of the new constitution. Articles 13 and 135 granted the former slaves the same rights as their former masters. They were afterward seen by the conservative press as a monstrous and unnatural interference into the personal liberty and privacy rights of individuals.[7] Even Republican Governor Henry C. Warmoth was quick to show, by his veto of a civil rights bill in 1868, that his administration did not intend to yield power to help the black cause or to alleviate the black masses.[8]

Still, in spite of the strong opposition of white conservatives and Governor Warmoth, a civil rights law was finally enacted in 1869. The new law prohibited discrimination on the basis of race or color in public places, hotels, and common carriers in the state. The legislature reinforced the new law in 1873 by making guilty parties liable to be sued and to pay such damages as a court might award.[9] Not surprisingly the new laws created a great divide between the black and white communities. White resistance to racial equality persisted throughout the entire period. For example, in 1869, Lieutenant-Governor James O. Dunn was refused a first-class place on the New Orleans and Jackson Railroad and compelled to make his journey to Washington on a "nigger car"; in Northern cities he could stay in first-class hotels. In 1873, two black men, Cain Sartain, a member of the legislature, and Davis Jackson, a clerk of the court, attempted to be served in the first-class section on a steamer. Their request provoked open resistance by the white passengers. The ensuing brawl ended with the arrest of the two black protagonists.[10]

At a black convention in February 1872, black leaders showed their determination to ensure the election of a greater number of black officeholders by consolidating the black vote. Still, black ministers opposed the formation of a black political coalition and instead pressed their political leaders to push for the reform of abuses in the Republican party. Even so, the 1873 black convention articulated the complaints of the black community around the fair distribution of local and state offices. In July 1873, Henri Burch, a prominent black politician, asserted the willingness of black leaders to join whites for better government, but only after whites accepted the right of blacks to be admitted on equal footing.[11]

Blacks also voiced their political grievances in their community associations and organizations. One of those associations was "L'association des hommes couleurs de la Nouvelle-Orléans," which in 1878 expressed the black community's sense of betrayal and abandonment by the Federal administration. Moreover, the association proposed that black votes be used solely for electing black officials.[12] A similar stand was adopted by the Grand Council of the Colored Men's Protective Union of the State of Louisiana. In February 1884 the council issued a call to black voters to register and to vote only for black Republican candidates at the election to be held the following April.[13]

The recurrent demands of black people for the recognition of their civil and political rights antagonized whites, particularly in the rural parishes. In the countryside the fear of being overwhelmed by the black masses added to the recurrent fear of a black insurrection. Violence, therefore, became the ultimate instrument in forcing blacks into submissiveness, in preserving as much as possible of the old plantation order, and in maintaining Louisiana as a "white man's country." Consequently, as we have noted in previous chapters, politics were not only at the root of most of the violence in Reconstructed Louisiana, but much of the white anger was directed against blacks who had begun to engage in political activities, join Republican clubs, and assert their right to vote. To be a member of the constitutional convention or the legislature or a candidate for the legislature did not protect blacks from murder. Indeed three black members of the state house, one black member of the state senate, and two black elected house members were killed during Reconstruction in Louisiana.[14] As we have seen previously, countless blacks who held other public offices were killed because of their political commitment.[15]

Black Armed Resistance to White Violence

Although the black population in various parishes was subjected to a reign of terror, many black leaders refused to be cowed. Under slavery, blacks had learned the consequence of open rebellion, and therefore they did not usually seek out open confrontation with their former masters or other whites. Passive resistance was the preferred strategy. Yet, confronted with post–Civil War white violence, blacks regularly organized and increasingly met their aggressors with open resistance.

Black resistance usually took the form of spontaneous responses to emergency situations rather than the result of planned interventions. Still, when blacks felt threatened, they did not hesitate to form bands ranging in size from ten or fifteen to more than one hundred armed people. When rumor spread in the Atchafalaya regions in 1876 that white people were getting ready to attack them, blacks left their fields, procured arms, and organized themselves as well as possible, throwing out pickets to give the alarm and deserting their homes. Although they suffered no attack, blacks remained apprehensive and returned to their homes only several days later. Meanwhile, leaders of the two communities met to find ways to identify the source of the rumor and to attempt to quell the tension.[16]

On numerous occasions bands of blacks moved into towns to assert their rights or to demand retribution for some great injustices or wrongs that had been committed against them.[17] Blacks were particularly sensitive to what they considered arbitrary arrests. In several instances gangs of blacks attempted to rescue others who had been arrested by whites and charged with stealing, murder, or other crimes.[18] Conservative whites would often bring heavy retribution against such perpetrators.[19]

Faced with white violence, blacks also responded by carrying weapons not only to their public and political meetings,[20] but also when at work in the fields.[21] Although black leaders asserted that this was done as a means of self-protection,[22] whites became particularly inflamed when they saw blacks bearing arms, walking to the polls in military formation, or practicing drills during the night.[23] But the claims that black men attended political meetings heavily armed were not always founded, as Lieutenant L. M. Keller discovered in St. Mary parish after canvassing whites who had been present at the alleged meeting.[24]

The idea that blacks could bear arms gave life to the greatest white fears and confirmed the worst antebellum prophecies. Since these blacks did not conform to the traditional white racist conceptions, the white community feared revolt and insurrection. Even the most trivial incidents could provoke wild rumors in a society such as this, where oral communication predominated. Indeed each time that they attempted to overturn the Republican domination of the state and parish political apparatus, or to limit the political rights of the blacks, whites became afraid of a black reaction. This profound fear that blacks would one day strike back against the whites was at the root of many rumors of black uprisings.[25]

This was especially true during periods of political tension or when blacks showed a strong determination to resist white encroachment. Blacks regularly assembled under arms and offered open resistance when whites attempted to intimidate or to compel them to vote Democratic. But too often, black resistance ended in massacres, as during the riots in New Orleans in 1866 and 1868, in St. Landry, St. Bernard, and Bossier in 1868, in Colfax and Coushatta in 1873 and 1874, in Caledonia, Natchitoches, and Tensas in 1878, and in Loreauville in 1884. During these racial clashes the lives of hundreds of blacks were sacrificed to white fury.[26]

Arson and the destruction of property more generally became the preferred retaliation of blacks, being that they were less likely to be caught while committing these crimes. For example, Joe Griss, a black who worked on the L'Argent plantation in Tensas parish threatened to burn the plantation for being discharged. On the same night, Griss began to execute his threats by burning his former cabins and the plantation's stable, which contained corn, hay, and farming implements. Finally, he shot and killed four mules before escaping.[27] Not only did arson provide a thorough revenge, but blacks felt less fear since arsonists were rarely caught.[28] Still, arson represented a double-edged sword as white conservatives often used this same tactic as a means to intimidate blacks and white Republicans.[29]

Black leaders quickly discovered the futility of armed resistance, which only brought heavy reprisals against their community. Therefore, they not only denied that blacks had any will to be hostile toward white people, but they cautiously advised black people not to make any violent demonstrations. Black leaders also held meetings to condemn lawlessness, arguing that black people were peaceful and law-abiding and were only asking for justice before the law and for political equality.[30]

Blacks Plead for State Protection

During the peak of the racial violence in 1868, Governor Warmoth remained almost helpless. Acknowledging the bad conditions that prevailed in many parishes, Warmoth asserted that "there exists no protection for the citizens in the courts," and that "men are shot down in the streets, in their homes and elsewhere without a question being asked, or any step taken to bring the offenders to justice."[31] As the presidential election approached the situation worsened. Violence swept the rural parishes and hundreds of blacks were killed during the riots of September and October 1868. The survival of both black rights and Republican government became paramount.

In the wake of the violence, blacks and their white allies pressed the state legislature to launch an unprecedented investigation into the particular conditions that had prevailed in New Orleans and rural areas during the previous presidential election. Hundreds of blacks came forward to testify before a joint committee of the state legislature. In response to that investigation, and in order to prevent a repetition of the events of 1868, the state legislature enacted an election law that created a Returning Board,[32] along with a new riot law. The latter measure empowered the governor to issue warrants for the arrest of people suspected of committing crimes punishable by death or imprisonment in cases where local officials had failed to make the arrest.[33]

In this heated context blacks showed a willingness to collaborate with the justice authorities.[34] But these authorities proved reluctant to accept their affidavits against whites. When a black man was killed, civil authorities too often made no special record of it and made no effort to solve the crime.[35] The arrest of a white for killing a black was a rare occurrence. When it happened, it created great excitement within the community and the person charged was usually acquitted, often without even being indicted. District Judge A. B. Levisse testified before a congressional committee in 1875 that when a black was found dead "a simple mention is made of it, perhaps orally or in print, and nothing is done. There is no investigation made. The coroner is sent, perhaps to hold an inquest and we have him buried."[36] Decidedly there was no justice for blacks in post–Civil War Louisiana.

The state legislature authorized Governor Warmoth to use the New Orleans Metropolitan Police as a militia unit until the establishment in June 1870 of a state militia under the command of former Confederate General James Longstreet. The new militia represented a mixture of white and black troops, the latter forming the larger part with 2,500 members in 1872. The support of the Republican program, the defense of personal freedom, the steady wages, and the desire to break away from the plantation routine were the main motives behind black enlistment in the militia.[37]

The maintenance of a black militia was essential to the survival of blacks' right to vote and to hold office. But nothing incited whites to violence more than the sight of black soldiers and civilians openly carrying weapons.[38] Consequently, in spite of its substantial numbers, the new militia proved to be no match for the white paramilitary organizations of 1873 and the White League of 1874. Blacks therefore continued to depend largely on the presence of the Federal troops for protection.[39]

Blacks Call on the Federal Government for Support

During the years immediately after the war, the major problems confronting Federal and military officials included the excesses of planters and their confederates attempting to impose pre–Civil War behavior on blacks. Confronted with repeated reports of atrocities and other acts of violence coming from the South, the Federal authorities devised new methods of ensuring better protection of the blacks' political and civil rights.

Created by Congress in February 1865, the Bureau of Freedmen, Refugees and Abandoned Lands—better known as the Freedmen's Bureau—became the first and the main tool devised by the Federal government to transform former slaves into American citizens. The bureau played an essential role in that transitional period by furnishing freedmen with basic medical care, education, and other primary services. Above all, the bureau's influence was most visible in protecting blacks' rights. The bureau appointed an agent in each parish of the state whose main duty was to receive the complaints of freedmen and to report on the state of race relations in the district. In their monthly reports and their general correspondence, these agents noted countless cases of abuses and acts of violence perpetrated by whites against blacks. The agents also played a major role as brokers between planters and freedmen. Their swift intervention prevented riots from breaking out in many instances.[40]

However, the ability of the Freedmen's Bureau to protect blacks was limited. If an agent was too radical or too sympathetic to blacks, he was often removed as a result of white political pressure. Thomas M.

Conway, the state superintendent, was removed in October 1865 because of his radical views; he was replaced by the more conservative General James S. Fullerton.[41] Furthermore, the Freedmen's Bureau agents had no restraining power. They could only register freedmen's complaints, once they had investigated them. Moreover, the agents' power did not extend to the field of politics. They were usually only called on to settle employee-employer disputes. Finally, most agents were former Union army officers who shared many of the racial prejudices of Southern whites and who, consequently, often sided with whites in labor or other disputes.[42]

During and immediately after the war, the Union army offered the second best protection to blacks. Slaves fled plantations and took refuge in army camps, while large numbers of blacks enlisted in the Federal army. In times of trouble, blacks petitioned for troops, and the mere presence of an army officer created great joy in local black communities. Further, blacks did not hesitate to go to the nearest military post and register their complaints with the military officer in charge. As a consequence army officers were often called on to investigate allegations of violence against blacks. Towns and parishes where troops were stationed usually suffered the least from violence.[43]

During the early days of Reconstruction, military authorities overshadowed civil authorities, interfering regularly in civil affairs. The role of the military authorities was enhanced when Congress adopted, over President Andrew Johnson's opposition, several radical measures that climaxed with the Military Reconstruction Acts of 1867. Acting in accordance with this new Reconstruction policy, Generals Philip H. Sheridan and Joseph A. Mower proceeded with the registration of freedmen and the disfranchisement of former Confederate officers and officials. The military authorities not only supervised elections, they also overruled civil officials and dictated policy on matters as diverse as schools and education, labor and civil rights, and the operations of railroads and banks. They also required that freedmen serve on juries and forced the desegregation of the New Orleans streetcars and New Orleans public school system. Finally, they did not hesitate to remove uncooperative Democratic officials.[44]

The role of the military changed with the political readmission of Louisiana by Congress in the summer of 1868. The military authorities saw their role reduced to that of a policing force that could periodically be called upon to support civil authorities. Federal troops still served as guards at the polls, but they were mainly used to protect

Republican officials from attacks by Democrats, to insure freedmen's safety, and to assist provost marshals in bringing criminals to court.[45]

Despite the enactment by Congress of the Military Reconstruction Acts, the army proved unable to ensure even minimal protection for freedmen in rural areas. First, Congress proceeded quickly with a large demobilization program that left army commanders with almost no troops. By 1867 only 716 men and officers were stationed in Louisiana. Although the number of troops rose to 2,000 in 1873, the state was left with less than 150 troops in the summer of 1874, on the eve of the White League uprising. With so few soldiers it became nearly impossible for military officials to intervene swiftly when a crisis emerged, let alone to maintain order.[46] For many district commanders the protection of blacks was not paramount. Such commanders preferred to remain inert, as General Lowell Rousseau did during the fall of 1868 when he was afraid to use troops. After 1868 officials in Washington were even more reluctant to authorize the use of soldiers as policemen.[47] Therefore, blacks were compelled after 1867 to look out for themselves and were left with no military protection in the rural parishes.

Still, blacks petitioned Congress and attempted to confront the Federal government and Northern public opinion with the brutality of the Southern violence committed against them. Indeed, blacks played a major role in collecting evidence for congressional committees. From field hands to members of the state legislature, blacks came by the hundreds to testify before congressional committees about the perils of their lives.[48]

Despite the personal commitment of President Grant, the support of the Federal administration to civil rights experienced a slow but steady decline in the early 1870s. The ability of the Federal troops to perform their duty in preserving peace was greatly diminished by the conservative attitudes of both Congress and Northern public opinion. The number of troops was greatly reduced and military spending was drastically cut, as Congress attentively scrutinized the use of Federal soldiers in Louisiana. President Grant was asked more and more often to justify his policy in the South and more particularly in Louisiana.[49]

Louisiana's laws required that homicides and other violent crimes be dealt with in the district and parish courts where the crimes were committed. But these laws were superseded by the civil rights bill and the enforcement act adopted by the Federal government in cases involving freedmen. By making violent crimes against freedmen a federal offense, justice could not be obtained in the local state courts. Consequently the United States commissioner was authorized to intervene in most criminal cases and to order the arrest of those who committed such crimes. Periodically, whites were arrested after a riot and brought before a Federal court, but Federal authorities proved reluctant to prosecute whites for aggression against blacks. Only a few whites were charged by U.S. grand juries with federal offenses for violating blacks civil rights and tried before Federal courts. Almost none of them were ever convicted. Trials languished, ending either in mistrial or in *nolle prosequi*.[50] Moreover, in 1874 Congress limited the rights of blacks to serve on juries by requiring proof that the candidates were able to read and write. Finally, in 1875 the United States Supreme Court declared part of the enforcement acts unconstitutional, further reducing the ability of the Federal government to intervene.[51]

In response, Louisiana freedmen submitted a petition to President Grant in May 1875 in which they expressed their dissatisfaction with the National Republican Party's empty promises. They particularly complained about the fact that whites voted for laws that they disobeyed, while blacks "have tried to obey and be governed by the laws that have been made, and we see very little credit for it." The petitioners further argued that blacks voted for the Republican ticket only to be left without protection and subjected to a reign of terror with much the "same old whipping and murders" as before the war.[52] A "colored association" published in 1878 a manifesto in which they complained about the ingratitude of the Federal administration that they charged with having abandoned and betrayed black people in a cowardly way.[53]

Blacks Look for Compromise

As state and federal protection offered only limited safeguards, particularly in rural areas, many black leaders searched for political solutions. Prominent blacks in both New Orleans and the countryside became increasingly convinced of the need to compromise with white conservatives. By adopting a more moderate stance in their demands for reform, blacks hoped to maintain part of their political influence without unduly antagonizing large segments of white society. Yet they were not willing to compromise at any price. R. I. Cromwell, a black carpetbagger born in Virginia but who had lived most of his life in the North, attempted in his public eulogy of former Lieutenant-Governor Oscar J. Dunn, to summarize the moderate view shared by most black leaders. "Black Republicans," he asserted, "were in favor of peace with white people, harmony among the colored people, full and free enjoyment of all rights under the Federal Constitution, and finally no discrimination based on colour."[54]

Once these requirements were accepted, many black leaders were anxious to make a political alliance with whites, even white conservatives. Already in September 1868, P. B. S. Pinchback expressed this objective when he asserted before the state senate that blacks asked only for justice before the law and political equality. He added that if another party promised his race more than the Republican party had done and kept its promise, he would join that party, no matter its name. Finally, he called for reenfranchising whites who had been disenfranchised by Congress as a measure of good will.[55]

The Unification Movement, launched by former Confederate General P. G. T. Beauregard in 1873 and several New Orleans black leaders, illustrates the distance travelled by many white conservatives in appeasing black people. The movement attempted to break up black support for radical policies by offering them "the privilege of cooperating with their white superiors." The offer to end all forms of discrimination did not generate enthusiasm among the white population and appeared rather remote to most blacks. Consequently the movement quickly faded away as it did not offer blacks any tangible gain.[56]

A year later, however, black leaders and white conservatives in the rural areas found new motives for compromise. As white conservatives launched a bitter campaign for white rule that culminated in the White League uprising of September 1874 and the reinstallment of Republican officials by the Federal army, a political solution was needed more urgently than ever. By then white conservatives in parishes where blacks held an overwhelming majority of the population were ready to compromise by proposing the formation of common tickets. The first such compromise occurred in October 1874 in the district covered by the parishes of Assumption, Lafourche, and Terrebonne and became known as the Terrebonne plan. Under the compromise conservatives nominated one candidate for the state house, one for the senate, and three for the police jury, while Republicans nominated one candidate for the state house, one for parish judge, one for sheriff, one for coroner, and two for the police jury. Furthermore, Republicans divided the offices assigned to them between black and white candidates.[57] Similar agreements were reached between black leaders and white conservatives in other French parishes of southern Louisiana such as Ascension, St. Charles, St. James, and St. Mary. The movement finally spread to some other parishes such as East Baton Rouge, East Feliciana, Jefferson, Rapides, and West Feliciana.[58]

By compromising with white conservatives, blacks saw an opportunity to curb white violence while ensuring the survival of their right to vote and to hold office. White Republicans who wanted to maintain their hegemony over the black masses strongly opposed the formation of a common ticket with white conservatives, while many black leaders were ready to support it. Such was the case in St. Mary parish where black Republicans led by Andrew J. Gordon, a former member of the antislavery movement from Philadelphia, agreed in October 1874 to form a common ticket with white Conservatives in spite of the opposition of white Republicans who chose to present a regular ticket.[59] Consequently the compromise plan partly unravelled because the Returning Board threw away election results in those parishes, thus giving the victory to the regular Republican ticket.[60]

But the search for a political solution remained the order of the day. A congressional committee imposed a statewide compromise, known as the Wheeler Compromise or Wheeler Adjustment Plan, during the spring of 1875, in an attempt to put an end to the Louisiana imbroglio.[61] As blacks felt increasingly abandoned and betrayed by white Republicans at the state and national levels, they became ready to reach a compromise with white conservatives. In 1876, Pinchback had already suggested the idea of splitting the black vote between the Republican and Democratic parties as a means of maintaining the fundamental political rights of blacks.[62] With the end of Reconstruction, black leaders were even more ready to compromise in order to preserve their minimal political influence,[63] but it was the white conservatives that often were no longer willing to do so. For example, Alfred Fairfax, a black candidate for Congress in 1878, proposed the formation of a compromise ticket with Democrats, but the proposition was rejected by the Democrats who resorted to violence to intimidate the large black majority in Tensas parish and other surrounding parishes. Thirty blacks were killed in the aftermath of the "negro hunt" that followed.[64]

Blacks Abstain from Voting or Vote for Democrats

When white violence reached its paroxysm of rage during the terror campaign of the Knights of the White Camelia in 1868 and the White League uprising of 1874, large numbers of blacks chose to remain passive and to abstain from voting. The election results of November 1868 showed a dramatic change in the black vote from the previous election. Seven parishes that in April had given 4,707 votes to Warmoth gave no votes to Grant. Eight parishes saw their Republican vote drop from 5,520 to only 10. And in another 21 parishes, Grant received only 501 of the 26,814 Republican votes cast in April.[65] If the White League campaign of 1874 was less bloody than that of the White Camelia in 1868, the intimidation of black voters was nonetheless the cornerstone of its policy. All over the state, merchants and planters signed pledges not to hire blacks and to discharge those who voted Republican in 1874. Lists of blacks who voted Republican were drawn up in several parishes. In many parishes hundreds of blacks were run off the plantations after the election. Not surprisingly, blacks in their hundreds did not even bother to register in many parishes. As a result of the White League violence, 1,200 blacks did not register in Iberia parish alone. Some 150 of those who registered were compelled to vote for the Democratic ticket for fear of losing their employment.[66] The terror and intimidation had long-lasting effects. Following the 1868 riot in St. Landry, blacks always put leading whites on the Republican ticket. John Simmes was the only black elected to hold an office of any consequence in that parish between 1868 and 1874.[67]

By 1876 Republican rule had become a great disappointment for many blacks. Several prominent blacks were reported to have crossed party lines and joined the Democrats. In many parishes Democratic clubs registered hundreds of blacks in their "colored clubs," and Republicans had trouble finding suitable black candidates to put on their tickets. Although many blacks attended Democratic meetings, it is almost impossible to determine, as Marguerite Leach has argued, whether or not black voters were sincere in rallying behind the Democratic party. "From long experience the negroes had learned that when the whites entered upon a campaign of intimidation it was better to yield gracefully. They became the best of Democrats."[68]

Beyond the limited possibility of holding an office under the Democratic banner, many other factors help explain this shift in party allegiance. William Scott, for example, had been a leading black

Republican in Ouachita until 1876. He became a Democrat during the summer of 1876 because he felt he had not received the reward he deserved for supporting the Republican cause. Richard Barrington, a rich black farmer from Ouachita parish who was disappointed by white Republicans, joined the Democratic party in 1876. He did so in spite of the fact that his own son was running for a legislative seat under the Republican ticket. Richard Everett, a well-educated freedman and skilled worker, became a Democrat by following his former master who had always treated him fairly. But it was former state senator and house member Robert Poindexter who became the most well-reported case of crossover to the Democratic party.[69]

Attempts to lure blacks to vote Democrat became an important part of the white conservative strategy in 1876, but intimidation remained the main tool of white policy by which black votes were turned into Democratic votes. Consequently the main issue surrounding the 1876 election, as far as Louisiana is concerned, is not so much why so many blacks voted for the Democrats, but why so many stayed home on the election day. Blacks had learned hard lessons from previous elections; thousands of registered blacks preferred to stay home than to be coerced to vote Democratic.[70] In an attempt to win black votes, Democrats stopped talking of "negro rule" in 1876 and put more emphasis on the need to reform the abuses generated by a corrupt government.[71]

After the end of Reconstruction, Democrats continued to resort to various tricks in their attempts to deceive black voters. In 1879, for example, prominent Democrats of St. Landry parish produced a fake Republican ticket in an attempt to divide the black vote.[72] But coercion remained, even after the end of Reconstruction, the principal means of diverting black votes to the Democratic party and of ending Republican rule at the local level. Such was the case in Tensas parish in 1882 where blacks participated with considerable zeal in the election, casting their votes for the Democratic nominees.[73] By the spring of 1884 the state Democratic leaders were determined to transfer the large Republican majority of southern Louisiana to the Democratic ticket. To achieve this goal they resorted to the same old means of violence, intimidation, and ballot stuffing that had been so successful in northern Louisiana.[74]

The conservative strategy did not really work since only a few black leaders joined the Democratic party. Indeed, the data reveal the presence of only 30 Democratic black leaders during Reconstruction and

105 for the years 1877 to 1884. Of those black Democrats only 7 held an office during Reconstruction, although 35 did so in the latter period.[75] Yet, on the whole, what is even more amazing is the courage and determination shown by the tens of thousands of blacks who appeared at the polls and voted Republican throughout the Reconstruction and early Bourbon periods.

Blacks Move to Other Lands

By the end of Reconstruction, blacks had encountered all the difficulties of being free men in post–Civil War Louisiana. They were threatened, assaulted, brutalized, and often murdered for trying to exercise their political rights. Cowed by white conservatives, abandoned by the Federal government, and betrayed by their white allies, by 1876 blacks no longer knew who their friends were. To move away from such an inhospitable state became for many the only reasonable survival strategy.

Blacks learned that in times of political turmoil they were better off to lay low. Each time that violence broke out hundreds of blacks ran to the woods and fields or took refuge in swamps and other hiding places.[76] When white terror became too great, frightened blacks left their parishes for others; they left St. Martin for Iberia in 1868, for example, and moved from the two Felicianas to Pointe Coupée in 1874 and 1875.[77]

A limited number of blacks had previously attempted to improve their condition by moving to the North, to Canada, or to Africa. Some 3,000 black families managed to leave Louisiana for Texas during the mid-1870s, but this emigration was small when compared to the 1879 exodus.[78] Although the 1879 emigration, better known as the "Kansas exodus," was not limited to Louisiana, it nevertheless represented the final response of blacks in that state to white violence. Indeed, the exodus was the strongest in the parishes of Caddo, Concordia, Madison, Natchitoches, and Tensas where blacks had been particularly bulldozed during the election campaign of 1878. The exodus received a great impetus in February 1879 in the northern portion of the state, when whites who had been charged for their involvement in the Natchitoches riot of 1878 returned home with two small cannons after being acquitted. These cannons were fired at each landing along the river, spreading terror among blacks along their path. In each of these parishes hundreds and even thousands of blacks left for Kansas. In all, Louisiana lost tens of thousands of its black population during the exodus.[79]

The second most important cause of the exodus was the rumors spread concerning the forthcoming constitutional convention. Many blacks strongly believed that the new constitution would relegate them to slavery, abolish the public school system, or disenfranchise blacks by a heavy poll tax. A meeting of blacks and whites was held in Vidalia, Concordia parish, in April 1879 to investigate the causes of the exodus. The organizers of the meeting could find no other cause than the current political situation and the fears raised by the coming constitutional convention.[80]

But the exodus was not caused by politics and violence alone. It also had its roots in the prevalent economic situation in northern Louisiana. Many blacks were dissatisfied with the sharecropping system. They felt that they paid too much rent for the use of lands and that they were cheated by country merchants and traders. Often they were reduced to abject poverty by heavy debt loads. As such, the Kansas exodus furnished an ideal opportunity to improve their economic condition.[81]

The absence of emigration from the sugar parishes further confirms the economic nature of the migration as labor there was better treated and better paid. Blacks in the parishes of West Baton Rouge, Avoyelles, and St. Landry proved to be more cautious than the ones of northern Louisiana. Not only did they hold meetings during the spring of 1879 to discuss the opportunity to move to Kansas, but they also chose before acting on such a decision to send delegates to Kansas. Once they received the reports of their delegation, they decided that Louisiana offered better prospects than Kansas.[82]

The 1879 exodus, anything but spontaneous, had been well planned in secret. Such prominent black leaders as Ranford Blunt and William Murrell were directly involved in the organization of the emigration. Henry Adams, who fought for civil rights throughout Reconstruction and regularly came forward to testify before congressional committees, also played a major role. Under his leadership the Colonization Council grew from 500 to 98,000 members.[83] Louisiana black leaders convened in New Orleans in May 1879 and confirmed their support for the Kansas exodus while they also examined the expediency of organizing a general exodus to Africa.[84] However, the Kansas migration had by then attracted such national attention that Congress was compelled to investigate the causes of the phenomenon.[85]

White planters drew hard lessons from the exodus. It proved that mistreated blacks would move not only from the plantation or the parish, but even from the state. The 1879 exodus reached such a level as to create a shortage of workers in northern Louisiana. All over the state calls were issued to protect blacks and to convince them that their political rights were not endangered. Planters in Tensas, a parish where blacks had been widely terrorized in 1878 and where the exodus had been particularly intense, signed a pledge in May 1879 to protect blacks against further intimidation and violence. A month later the planters petitioned district judicial authorities not to hold the coming court term in order to not further excite blacks. In other parishes leading white Democrats decided to take steps to prevent bulldozing. Not only did they strongly criticize the bulldozing of blacks but they organized vigilance groups to arrest and punish bull-dozers.[86] Meanwhile, in many parishes, planters either reduced rents, lightened the obligations of sharecroppers, or raised wages in order to convince blacks to stay.[87]

Despite these measures, political violence was not completely absent from many parishes when Louisiana held an election for a new administration and to ratify a new constitution in December 1879. As a result blacks once again resorted to the migration strategy, but on a smaller scale than in 1879. This time the trend affected all of the Florida parishes in southern Louisiana, a region particularly unsettled by the lynching of four blacks on December 31, 1879 in Amite City.[88]

Conclusion

In this chapter the main issue has been not so much how violent Louisiana was, but how blacks responded to the white reign of terror. The analysis shows that the black reaction combined self-defense, militancy, and restraint; blacks devised various strategies to resist white violence. Black leaders attempted to curb armed resistance, cautiously advising blacks to restrain themselves. Conscious of the impact that white violence was having on Northern public opinion, blacks regularly came before congressional committees to testify; they also petitioned both the state and Federal governments for better protection. Black leaders showed their readiness to compromise and to share offices with white conservatives in order to preserve their fundamental rights and to curb the level of violence. With the end of Reconstruction and the resumption of white violence during the 1878 election, however, many blacks felt abandoned and betrayed and saw no other alternative than to leave the state.

Faced with severe adversity, Louisiana's blacks in this period proved very imaginative in devising means to resist white violence and to counter white efforts to bring them back under subjugation. Although they were ultimately unable to curb white violence, blacks at least left a legacy of a daily and heroic resistance to white encroachment. In the process they had some limited success in preserving their fundamental rights and in forcing whites to change their strategy. Above all blacks showed that they shared, in spite of the dark days of Reconstruction, the basic democratic values of North American society. Yet, in the end, blacks emerged as the tragic figures of the period. Their failure to preserve their political rights was the failure of the entire nation, as their tragedy was the tragedy of the whole nation.

Aftermath

Between July 23 and 27, 1900, New Orleans witnessed the five most violent days in its history. Over these five days the Crescent City was struck by a major race riot. The disturbance began on the night of July 23 when two black men, Robert Charles and Lenard Pierce, who had been waiting for a black woman, resisted two white policemen who attempted to arrest them on the charge of being suspicious characters. After enduring a severe beating, Charles drew a pistol and fired at one of the policemen, who fired back. Both Charles and the policeman were wounded. As calls for police reinforcement were issued, Charles managed to escape.

The police, supported by a crowd of whites, launched a vast search for the rebellious black. The incident quickly aroused the entire white community and became an excuse for whites to riot. Bands of hundreds of whites, virtually unchecked by the police, roamed the streets of New Orleans for three days shooting, looting, and burning properties and assaulting blacks, killing several blacks in the process. By the third day more than 1,500 whites had joined a voluntary police force. Meanwhile the governor had ordered a detachment of the state militia to New Orleans to support the local authorities. Finally, on the fifth day, a black informed the police that Charles was hiding at 1208 Saratoga Street. As the news of Charles's hideout spread, a crowd of some 10,000 people gathered around the place, including 1,000 fully armed men. Despite the odds Charles remained defiant. During the fight that followed some 5,000 shots were fired toward the hideout. Charles was finally shot and killed, but only after he had shot nearly thirty white people, including four policemen.[1]

Following the riot, the white press unleashed its racist invectives, describing Charles not only as a "monster," a "bad nigger," and a

193

"brute," but also as a "bloodthirsty champion of African supremacy."
To a contemporary historian, Charles appears "as one of the proudest
black martyrs in American history." In William Ivy Hair's view, "Robert Charles was neither hero nor fiend incarnate, but a human being
of rather more than ordinary courage."[2]

This terrible tragedy, however, goes beyond the courageous resistance of one black individual to white oppression; its significance goes
much further. It clearly demonstrates, for example, the particular
climate of lawlessness that prevailed in late nineteenth-century Louisiana and in the South in general. And above all, this riot, which
occurred only four years after the United States Supreme Court had
upheld segregation and two years after Louisiana had disenfranchised
blacks, tells the story of the general degradation in race relations
that had occurred in Louisiana and in other Southern states since
emancipation.[3]

The present study has attempted to establish the most salient patterns in homicidal behavior in post–Civil War Louisiana. In the process I have examined homicide from various perspectives and studied
its underlying causes. The study reveals that Reconstruction saw the
emergence of several new patterns of homicide and violence. In this
period the white community, broadly speaking, regularly resorted to
campaigns of terror—and even to mass murder—in order to regain
political hegemony over the state and to maintain economic control
over the black labor force. These new patterns of violence had long-lasting effects on race relations and the general evolution of Louisiana
society. In the process the Southern culture of violence not only came
out reinforced, but it had also two unexpected consequences as it permeated the black community both in the South and in the Northern
cities as we will see in the following pages.

Toward the Disenfranchisement of Blacks

Considered in a long-term perspective, the late 1870s and the early
1880s clearly emerges as a period of transition. The patterns of violence between 1865 and 1884 gradually changed, as did the implication of the state government. During Reconstruction, despite the
weakness and the inability of the state government to maintain order
completely, it nonetheless attempted to ensure a minimal protection
for the black population. The Republican authorities regularly sent

detachments of the metropolitan police or of the state militia to rural areas. They adopted riot laws to curtail violence. They repeatedly launched investigations of violence. And they called upon Federal troops for assistance in the most severely affected districts. But the attitude of the state government had dramatically changed by the early 1880s.

One might suggest that once the Republican regime had been overthrown, political violence was no longer necessary. Indeed, while Reconstruction had been marked by numerous major political riots, many of which degenerated into mass murder, it went otherwise during the two last decades of the nineteenth century. In this period Louisiana had only one major political riot: the Loreauville riot of 1884. Yet this did not mean that political violence and intimidation had completely disappeared. Indeed, white conservatives still needed to coerce blacks into voting for the Democratic party, and violence remained an important tool for white conservatives who were at first rather reluctant to adopt a too radical stand on racial issues.[4]

So in spite of their countless speeches about white supremacy, their reactionary attitude, and their negrophobia, the Bourbons were not yet willing to go as far as disenfranchising the black population. The decision of the Bourbons to vote down a proposal to limit suffrage during the 1879 constitutional convention was motivated by several factors. By the spring of 1879 planters in northern Louisiana had already lost tens of thousands of field hands to the Kansas exodus. They were afraid that such a proposal would accentuate the emigration movement. Meanwhile many white conservatives were afraid of the reaction that disenfranchisement of blacks would provoke in Northern public opinion. Finally, the Democratic leaders believed that the black vote, if it was well controlled and manipulated, could become an important tool to overcome white dissidents in many parishes.[5] During Reconstruction, Louisiana Republicans had already shown how control of the state government could allow a party to determine the official results of an election. The Bourbons had not forgotten the lesson, and control of the electoral process quickly became a crucial element of their maintenance in power.

During Reconstruction the Louisiana legislature entrusted a state board with the power to compile election returns and empowered the governor to appoint a supervisor of elections. Returning electoral matters to local authorities became one of the main demands of the white conservatives. This was accomplished in April 1877 when the state legislature enacted a new law returning control of elections to the police juries. Under the new law the police jury was to appoint three commissioners of elections for each polling place fifteen days prior to an election.[6]

But in order to ensure for the state administration complete control over the electoral process, the Democratic legislature adopted a new elections law in 1882. Act 101 removed the exclusive power of choosing polling places and commissioners of elections from the police juries, giving it to a parish supervisor appointed directly by the governor. The new law, which had been personally sponsored by Governor Samuel D. McEnery, allowed the state authorities to subvert the democratic character of all local and state elections and to reverse the public choice. White conservatives could therefore hope to control all local and state elections and even to carry any parish by resorting, if necessary, to widespread fraud, bribery, and ballot stuffing. As a consequence the new law installed a system of political fraud that made a mockery of elections in late nineteenth-century Louisiana.[7]

Furthermore, vote fraud, which had represented a powerful tool to overthrow the radical government and to limit the political influence of both blacks and the Republican party even at the local level, became a means of controlling the Democratic state and local conventions. Under a new set of rules the number of delegates attributed to each parish was based on the vote received by the Democratic party in the last election. As a result stuffing ballot boxes and intimidating blacks to vote Democratic was a means not only of ensuring a Democratic hegemony over the state government, but of guaranteeing Bourbon control over the Democratic party.[8]

Reconstruction had consolidated behind the Bourbons and their white supremacy policy not only planters, merchants, and other entrepreneurs, but also poor whites and small farmers. The fear of black competition had brought poor whites and small farmers into the white supremacist coalition.[9] Meanwhile, after 1876 the Bourbons succeeded through physical coercion and economic intimidation in transforming the large Republican majority in black parishes into support for their policies.[10] However, the myth of white solidarity was deeply challenged during the early 1890s by the People's party, most commonly known as the Populist movement.

The development of the Populist movement presented a major threat to the policy of white supremacy. The ideology of white supremacy attempted to establish a society that separated blacks and whites with a clear caste line. However, the agrarian movement, which blamed the Bourbons for their ties with the Northern capital, split from the Democratic party during the early 1890s. As the agrarian movement showed a certain readiness to forge an alliance with blacks, the Populism movement and its black allies were seen as a political threat that could challenge the Southern caste system.[11]

Populism arose in Louisiana while both the Republican and Democratic parties were deeply divided by internal factionalism. The Populists proved able to catalyze the various forces of reform in both New Orleans and the rural parishes. The growing influence of the Populists became obvious during the state election of 1892, when the Populists and their antilottery allies in the Democratic party won a majority of the seats in the legislative assembly. The Populists then proceeded to enlarge their coalition by launching a campaign aimed at overcoming racism among poor whites, appealing to blacks, and collaborating with the Republican party. Consequently the Populist party quickly emerged as a strong contender in Louisiana politics, threatening the hegemony of the Bourbons over both the state government and the legislative assembly.[12] During the congressional election of 1894 and the state election of 1896, only widespread fraud and violence enabled the Bourbons to prevent a victory of the Fusion ticket—an alliance of Republicans, Populists, and the antilottery wing of the Democratic party—in order to defeat the Bourbon Democrats.

While the election of 1894 had been the most violent since 1878, the election of 1896 was even worse. During the campaign of 1896 armed bands of Democratic regulators terrorized many parishes in both northern and southern Louisiana. Political violence broke out in East Baton Rouge where several black people were killed, while one Populist candidate was shot and another had his barn burned. St. Landry was the Southern parish that suffered the most from political trouble. As a result of the Fusionists having registered large numbers of blacks, white conservatives launched a general campaign of racial terror. In the meantime several political disturbances occurred in northern Louisiana, particularly in parishes with large black majorities. Consequently the year 1896 saw the state establish the unenviable record of twenty-one lynchings, the highest number in the South for any year during the 1890s. The Bourbons did not hesitate to use the full powers of the state government, including the use of militia units, to implant their policy of white supremacy.[13]

The gubernatorial election of 1896 was a reminder of the heyday of Reconstruction, with its bitter passions and its several outbreaks of political violence. Still, political violence was not sufficient to ensure the victory of the Bourbons. Only massive fraud in several black parishes allowed them to carry the day.[14] The Populists in several parishes, both white and black, were infuriated by the rigging of the election. The governor was compelled to send the militia to six different parishes to suppress riots or to restore order.[15] Meanwhile, white conservatives drew a lesson from the Populist uproar. Faced with the danger of an alliance between poor whites and blacks, the Bourbons saw in disenfranchisement an easy way to ensure their perennial domination over the state government.[16] The Populists, disappointed by the lukewarm support they had received from blacks, were prepared to back the measure. The process was made more acceptable because it was described as a reform measure, a way to put an end to ballot stuffing, electoral fraud, and political violence. Still, disenfranchisement was made possible only after white conservatives had stirred up the negrophobia of the white community.[17]

Disenfranchisement became a reality in Louisiana in 1898. With the exception of the modification of the franchise articles, the constitutional convention of 1898 merely reprinted the 1879 constitution. With the introduction of a literacy test and a grandfather clause, "blacks were simply removed as a direct political factor" in Louisiana: the number of black votes was reduced by 96 percent between 1896 and 1900 (from 130,344 to 5,320). But disenfranchisement in Louisiana was not limited to blacks as 24 percent of whites also lost their franchise rights.[18]

With disenfranchisement the Southern white community not only reduced the threat of a possible alliance between blacks and poor whites, but it also took a strong commitment to the ideology of the white supremacist Democrats and to the enforcement of racism.[19] With segregation upheld in 1896 by the United States Supreme Court and the disenfranchisement of blacks in 1898, Louisiana had become part of the new solid South.[20] The political failure of Populism had a long-lasting effect as blacks had to wait until the 1960s to see their political rights fully restored in Louisiana and in other Southern states.

The Rationale for Black Economic Subordination

The determination of white conservatives to maintain tight control over blacks was not limited to the political arena. The labor conditions that prevailed in New Orleans were much different than those in the rural parishes. The racial harmony that prevailed among New Orleans workers during the 1880s and early 1890s contrasted singularly with the general climate of racial tension of the period. By the early 1880s organized labor among both black and white workers had become a central part of the social and economic life of the city. White workers were quite conscious that they could not obtain wage increases and better working conditions if black workers were ready to work for less. As a consequence both races found working closely together advantageous.[21] This spirit of racial collaboration reached its pinnacle during the general strike of 1892, when black and white laborers cooperated across racial lines.

As demonstrated in chapter 3, city workers became increasingly militant during the 1880s and regularly resorted to strikes to obtain better wages and shorter working hours. Already established in New Orleans since 1886, the American Federation of Labor (AFL) launched a vast campaign to charter new affiliates in 1892. Some thirty new unions were created, giving the city a total of ninety-five unions, of which forty-five had joined the AFL together under the Workingmen's Amalgamated Council. The November 1892 labor conflict turned the new labor council against the Board of Trade that represented the business community.[22]

A conflict became unavoidable as the Board of Trade refused to recognize the representatives of the new labor council and were even less ready to acquiesce to their demands for "a ten-hour day, overtime pay and the preferential closed shop." As a consequence forty-two unions affiliated with the AFL and encompassing about 20,000 workers launched a general strike on November 8, 1892. Economic activities in the city were virtually paralyzed. Yet the Board of Trade remained adamant in its refusal to make any concessions, threatening to import outside workers.[23]

Paradoxically trade unions in New Orleans had experienced substantial growth during the 1880s under the umbrella of the Democratic party, as the city machine courted the working class. Moreover, Mayor John Fitzpatrick, the son of an Irish immigrant, who had been elected in early 1892 with the support of the city workers, was openly sympathetic to the demands of the strikers.[24] But for political and personal reasons Governor Murphy J. Foster chose to side with the Board of Trade rather than the strikers. He therefore issued a proclamation calling for an immediate return to work and threatened to use the state militia to break the strike, even though there had been no act of violence. The governor's proclamation broke the labor resistance as trade unions were not ready to face the militia. The strike ended with a compromise in which labor made some gains in terms of wages and work hours, but failed to obtain concessions from the Board of Trade concerning the principles of collective bargaining and the closed shop.[25]

City merchants and shippers, however, would use the 1893 economic depression to break up the racial harmony that had prevailed during the 1892 strike. In October 1894, when English shippers attempted to hire black workers to load cotton bales on oceangoing ships, replacing white crewmen, the New Orleans harbor became the scene of major labor disturbances. The racial warfare on the levees was renewed in March 1895 with greater violence: property worth more than $750,000 was destroyed, 25,000 cotton bales were burned, the levees were severely damaged, and several men were killed, most of them blacks. The violence ended only after Governor Foster ordered the state militia to the city to restore order. The racial harmony among New Orleans labor had been irreparably broken.[26]

The reaction of the state authorities to the numerous strikes that troubled southern Louisiana during the 1880s showed how the control of black agricultural labor was paramount. The sugar planters, despite their support for the National Republican Party, were not ready to relinquish control over black labor. Here again the pattern of using violence to break the sugar workers' strikes was established during the late 1870s and early 1880s. As shown in chapter 6, the sugar hands were compelled during those strikes to return to work under the conditions fixed by the planters, having made no gains whatsoever. The breaking of the strikes of the early 1880s in southern Louisiana had revealed how desperately black sugar hands needed organized support in order to resist the deterioration of their working conditions. With the arrival of the Knights of Labor in Louisiana in the early 1880s, the black sugar hands found the organized support they needed.[27]

By 1886 the Knights of Labor were well implanted in southern Louisiana, having organized nearly 10,000 sugar workers, most of them blacks. In October 1887 the sugarcane workers of Iberia, Lafourche, St. Martin, St. Mary, and Terrebonne parishes held a district meeting in Morgan City. The local branch of the Knights of Labor then agreed on a wage scale of $1.25 per day without board or $1.00 per day plus board, and of $0.60 for six hours of night work. Furthermore, they demanded that wages be paid every two weeks and agreed to refuse wages paid in script.[28]

The planters refused even to discuss these demands, which were delivered to them at a meeting in Thibodeaux on October 24, 1887. Furthermore the planters adopted an intransigent position: they would not hire any worker who had been discharged for refusing to work, and they would require that such workers leave their plantations within twenty-four hours. In protest the Knights of Labor launched a general strike in southern Louisiana that mobilized between 6,000 and 10,000 of its members.[29]

Although the strikers had not resorted to violence and no trouble had yet erupted, Governor McEnery quickly responded to the demands of the Sugar Planters Association by sending detachments of the state militia to the region. In early November several disturbances broke out. The most significant one occurred at Pattersonville on the November 5, when four Knights of Labor leaders were killed and several others were wounded by a white posse.[30] Following a freeze that damaged the uncut cane, Judge Taylor Beattie, a planter and a former Republican candidate for governor in 1879, supported the planters' demands by declaring martial law in the district on November 22. This opened the door to an outburst of violence in the region. Soon after Beattie's declaration, a group of some three hundred armed whites attacked the black quarters in Thibodeaux, firing at every black they saw. The assault lasted all night and degenerated into a "negro hunt." During the attack, two black Knights of Labor leaders who had been previously arrested were taken from the jail and lynched.[31] The strike was broken by a wave of violence that had tacit official support; the state authorities refused to even investigate the riot.[32] No official count was made of the number of blacks killed, but, as shown by a recent study, the Thibodeaux massacre left at least fifty people dead.[33]

The Thibodeaux massacre was the most serious labor disturbance, in terms of the number of victims, that occurred in Louisiana in the second half of the nineteenth century. However the massacre was in continuity with the strike-breaking policy of the sugar plantations that had been implanted during the early 1880s. The sugar planters had not resorted to political violence on a large scale during Reconstruction for economic reasons, as was shown in chapter 6, but they were not ready to recognize the rights of field hands to negotiate their working conditions, and were even less inclined to accept the formation of a trade union among the sugar workers of the region. The Thibodeaux massacre, then, reveals the determination of the planters to maintain tight control over their workers. The 1887 labor disturbance had long-lasting effects: not only did it break up the labor union in southern Louisiana, but it also ensured the white planters complete control over the labor force. There would be no further attempt to organize sugar workers for the next sixty-five years. Furthermore with black workers now abandoned even by their white Republican allies, the massacre brought a renewal of the black exodus. Finally, the massacre showed that if not all whites living in rural parishes had rallied behind white solidarity for political reasons, many more were ready to do so on economic grounds.[34]

Labor conflict in rural Louisiana was not limited to sugar plantations, though. In Louisiana, as in other Southern states, the competition of poor whites with blacks for labor generated deep conflict that often erupted in open violence. As shown by the split labor market theory, planters had no interest in seeing the development of a free labor market, as they urgently needed a large pool of cheap agricultural workers to maximize their profit. The freedmen could furnish the basis of the plantation labor, as long as they remained under strict control. But planters could also turn to white labor. During the late 1880s and early 1890s, as a consequence of the Lafourche strike of 1887, planters in southern Louisiana hired 60,000 Sicilians to lessen their dependency on black labor. If this was true during Reconstruction and the early Redemption period, it became even more apparent by the turn of the century as large number of small white farmers lost their farms and became tenant farmers. Fighting to survive under difficult economic condition, poor whites saw blacks not as allies, but as competitors. As a consequence both planters and poor whites had interests, albeit for opposite reasons, in restricting the economic opportunities for blacks and keeping them in subordination.[35]

Violence had been repeatedly used, as we have seen, during Reconstruction to prevent blacks from owning lands. During the late nineteenth and early twentieth centuries, both planters and poor white farmers regularly resorted to violence against more enterprising blacks. In 1890, for example, white landowners who were strongly opposed to the idea of seeing black ownership of lands, conducted a campaign of terror against blacks who had been able to accumulate property in the vicinity of Baton Rouge.[36]

The whitecapping movement that struck several Southern states during the 1890s and the early twentieth century was a terrorist organization that resorted to intimidation, psychological terror, and murder as it functioned "as a direct outgrowth of the Ku Klux Klan."[37] As a consequence the whitecapping movement represented a serious threat. Not only did it terrorize local communities in the Florida parishes, but it also paralyzed local economic activity. Although it was also directed against Jewish merchants, blacks still remained the main target of the violence. Whitecap brutality struck particularly at blacks who owned lands or those who competed with whites for jobs. As poor whites strongly competed against blacks for work in Avoyelles during the early 1890s, the whitecapping movement particularly disturbed that parish in 1892.[38]

As the rivalry between black and white workers largely intensified by the early twentieth century, antiblack violence played a paradoxical role. As antiblack violence generated an unprecedented emigration movement within the black community, it created a labor shortage, and as a consequence it reduced the competition between blacks and poor whites. If planters suffered from the black emigration, poor whites largely benefitted from it. Therefore, poor whites had little desire to diminish their antiblack hostilities.[39] Violence remained during the early twentieth century as an essential means to perpetuate the economic oppression of blacks.[40]

A General Atmosphere of Lawlessness

Various observers of the period noted that if the 1880s in Louisiana and in other Southern states had been relatively calm, it went otherwise for the 1890s, which were underlined by an upsurge in personal assaults and homicides. The number of people charged with homicide in Louisiana increased from 178 in 1880 to 328 in 1890, or from a ratio of 18.5 per 100,000 persons to 29.3. The general atmosphere of crime and violence did affect New Orleans, which maintained its reputation as a paradise for criminals, but the most salient features of Louisiana homicidal behavior during the post–Civil War period were that it was mainly rural and that it was defined along racial lines. Official statistics and general studies suggest that this pattern of homicides continued during the 1890s, when 90 percent of homicides occurred in rural areas. However, according to these studies, the

Louisiana black population suffered more from violence than was the case for any other Southern state during the 1880s and 1890s.[41]

The murder of white men by members of their own race still remained an important feature that was not limited to the lower classes. W. J. Ramage reported during the 1890s, "that in the Southern States men of a certain amount of education, and often enjoying the highest social standing, are not infrequently guilty of the most shocking homicides that ever stained the calendar of a court."[42] Samuel C. Hyde shows in his recent study how powerful families in the Florida parishes perpetuated the local tradition of violence by entering into bloody feuds during the 1880s and 1890s. Professor Hyde relates no less than thirty-five murders that occurred in that region between 1883 and 1899 due to family feuds.[43] Indeed most of the time, a white murderer, either acting alone or within a family feud, could generate enough sympathy from the community in order to obtain an acquittal verdict by pleading self-defense. This situation lasted so long only because of the Southern apathy toward its homicide record and because Southern people, no matter their social classes, thought it was degrading to appeal to the court when their honor was involved.[44]

Meanwhile, black intraracial homicides had become an important component of the general atmosphere of lawlessness in the South as the degradation of social, legal, and political conditions that characterized the Redemption period increasingly alienated blacks.[45] The late nineteenth century saw the emergence of the image of the "bad nigger" who was no longer docile, who was not afraid to stand on his own, and who did not hesitate to resort to violence to defend his honor. This emergence of more assertive blacks reflected a profound change that affected many segments of the black community in Louisiana and in other Southern states.[46] W. E. B. Du Bois, a world reputed black historian and a keen observer of the black community during the early twentieth century, noticed the increase of violence and criminality within the black community. But Du Bois directly linked the emergence of crime and professional criminals within his community to racism and racial oppression.[47] Indeed as the black community was confronted by large-scale discrimination and racism by the late nineteenth century, it suffered from the lack of institutional support and police protection. The fact that black violence against blacks was much tolerated by whites had a tremendous psychological impact on blacks. As a consequence even law-abiding blacks were compelled to resort to violence to settle problems within their own community.[48]

The general atmosphere of lawlessness was particularly palpable in rural parishes where the inability of formal mechanisms of law enforcement to deal with criminal offenders was most tangible. And yet Bourbons could no longer put the blame on Republican officials as they did during Reconstruction when they asserted that Republican rule was responsible for the high level of violence and crime. Newspapers all over the state continued to complain about the inefficiency of the court, the incompetency of district attorney in prosecuting criminals, and the inability of sheriffs to arrest law offenders.[49] But law enforcement officers were almost powerless, despite the fact that in 1882 the state legislature had adopted a law by which a person resisting an officer carrying out his duty could be arrested and charged without a court warrant.[50] But if lawlessness had been a main justification for lynching during Reconstruction, it was less so during the early Redemption period.

Reconstruction had indeed established the pattern for lynching in Louisiana. The percentage of blacks lynched during the 1880s and 1890s did not vary substantially from that found in the data on Reconstruction and the early Redemption era.[51] The storming of the New Orleans parish prison in March 1891 and the killing of eleven Italians found not guilty of the murder of the city police chief was the most notable lynching of whites during that period.[52] And yet what made lynching particular to the Redemption period was that it was almost completely directed against blacks. Moreover, lynching was more than simply an hysterical manifestation of a white community outraged by alleged black criminal behavior. Not surprisingly, as lynching expressed the deep racial prejudices of many whites living in rural areas, it degenerated more and more frequently into a ritual that included sadism, slow torture, and other acts of racial barbarism.[53] Lynching gradually emerged during the Redemption period as "the most dramatic and brutal method of racial control" and represented with other forms of antiblack violence a way to repress blacks as they represented a political or economic threat.[54] As Robert Zangrando asserts, "Lynching was a means to intimidate, degrade, and control black people throughout the southern and boarder states, from Reconstruction to the mid-twentieth century."[55]

The regional distribution of lynchings corroborated this study's analysis of the regional variations in homicidal behavior. Indeed lynchings tended to recur in areas where a previous lynching had happened.[56] Furthermore, the frequency of lynchings in each region was directly linked to the proportion of blacks in its population. These variations reveal how mob violence was inherently used by local white communities as a means to control the black population. The perceived need for such violent measures was greater or lesser depending on the size of the local black community.[57]

During the Redemption period, lynching emerged as an important tool in the hands of white conservatives preoccupied with making sure that blacks knew their status within Southern society. Lynching became part of a widely accepted, or at least tolerated, policy within the white community. As a consequence state and local authorities gave their tacit approval to lynching, showing a great unwillingness to intervene to prevent a lynching or to send troops to maintain order and to protect the intended victims. Furthermore, local and state authorities rarely indicted or prosecuted a person for having organized a lynching and were even less willing to find a person guilty of such a crime.[58] Therefore, one must not minimize the importance of such antiblack violence, as lynching, in maintaining white supremacy.[59]

This study also points to a clear dichotomy between the general lawlessness of whites and the relatively nonviolent attitude of blacks during Reconstruction. This racial discrepancy might be explained by several factors. It could be argued that the effect of the war was greater on whites, that blacks were less likely to possess guns and other weapons as they were too poor to buy them, or that whites were ready to resort to violence as a means to make Louisiana a "white-man's country." However, data show that while blacks were less violent than whites, the latter were also becoming less violent after the end of Reconstruction. One plausible interpretation is that race relations had been channelled into other forms and was now under better control. By 1877, when whites had achieved their ultimate goal of redeeming the state, the use of violence for political motives became less necessary as blacks represented less of a political threat.[60]

As a result, violence had become more intraracial in character by the end of Reconstruction. The data show an important decline in white intraracial homicide rates at the end of Reconstruction, while black homicide rates decreased much less sharply. The social and political disruption generated by the war quieted down, as blacks became subdued and their white allies lost their political influence. In this context the white community was able to achieve a wider consensus about the future of the Louisiana society than during Reconstruction.

Still antiblack violence remained an important feature of the late nineteenth and early twentieth centuries in Louisiana and in the South. Whites resorted periodically not only to lynching but also to other forms of mob violence as shown by the repeated riots that struck the South by the turn of the century: in Wilmington and Phoenix in 1898, in New Orleans in 1900, in Atlanta and Brownsville in 1906, and in Waco in 1910.[61] The number of riots, when compared to the Reconstruction period, was on the decline. And yet white violence and racial discrimination showed that, by the turn of the century, the future of blacks in the South was rather grim.

By the turn of the twentieth century, blacks who formed less than 50 percent of the population in the South, represented 90 percent of the people who suffered lethal violence in the form of lynchings or in the hands of the white criminal justice system.[62] Faced with continuous white violence and racial oppression, blacks could only offer a courageous but futile resistance or remain docile. Confronted by such a dilemma, hundreds of thousands of blacks in Louisiana, as in other Southern states, chose between 1900 and 1960 to leave the rural areas for the cities and, afterward, the South for the North. Contemporary observers noticed a close link between black emigration and lynching, showing that year after year the heaviest emigration came from towns and counties where an upsurge of lynching occurred. As the emigration strategy struck at the core of white oppression—the need for black labor—it brought, as in 1879 and in 1887, a substantial decline in the number of lynching incidents as local white planters issued calls for a reduction of antiblack violence. Still the great migration movement largely transformed the life of the black communities in both the South and the North.[63]

Conclusion

In order to explain the persistence of a high rate of homicide in the South, twentieth-century social scientists have consistently resorted to the existence of a regional subculture of violence based on honor. Under the subculture of violence theory, the South shares a set of values that requires a response to an affront, an insult, or a lack of respect.[64] However, social scientists have been more puzzled by the increase of homicide rates in the large metropolitan areas of the United States during the twentieth century. Although they were rather quick to link that phenomenon to the emergence of black ghettos in the Northern and Western cities,[65] they strongly disagree on the roots of black homicidal behavior in large metropolitan areas.

Some social scientists find in the subculture of violence theory a comprehensive understanding for the development of patterns of violence among the black communities outside of the South. As rural blacks migrated to the North in increasing numbers during the first half of the twentieth century, these social scientists argued that blacks brought with them a set of cultural values that accepted violence, which flourished in the environment of the black ghettos.[66] But for many this interpretation is too controversial.

Not surprisingly some other social scientists have acknowledged that the massive arrival of black emigrants in Northern cities created an antiblack feeling during the early twentieth century. They have linked the emergence of large black ghettos in Northern cities to white hostility and, more particularly, to the discriminatory practices, the lack of institutional support, and the racial prejudice to which blacks were confronted in the North.[67] As a consequence the Northern urban life, with its large population size, its anonymous, transitory, and superficial relations, its weakening social control, its family disintegration, and its endemic poverty in some of its districts, represented a ground favorable for the development of delinquency.[68] Therefore, these social scientists argued that high black homicide rates in the large American city are not the product of a subculture of violence imported from the South, but could be directly linked to poverty and the particular demographic characteristics of the ghettos.[69]

Sociologists and criminologists have clearly demonstrated how twentieth-century African American violence in the inner city was linked to economic pressures and cultural forces. And yet their explanation of violence among African Americans falls short. Without denying the influence that modern urban conditions have on high homicide rates, the present study shows that violence in the city has deeper historical roots. The race-based gap in homicide rates that have captured the attention of modern scholars emerged well before the deterioration of North America's inner cities. In fact, the first signs of this gap even predated the great migration of blacks to Northern cities. Rather it was in the political and economic conditions of the Reconstruction era that the roots of modern African American violence can be traced.

Notes

Introduction

1. Guy H. Cardwell, "The Duel in the Old South: Crux of a Concept," *South Atlantic Quarterly*, 66, Winter 1967, 50–69; John L. Harr, "Law and Lawlessness in the Lower Mississippi Valley, 1815–1860," *Northeast Missouri State College Studies*, 19, June 1955, 51–70; W. Stuart Harris, "Rowdyism, Public Drunkenness, and Bloody Encounters in Early Perry County," *Alabama Review*, 33, no. 1, January 1980, 15–24; Michael S. Hindus, *Prison and Plantation: Crime, Justice, and Authority in Massachusetts and South Carolina, 1767–1878*, Chapel Hill, 1980; John Hope Franklin, *The Militant South, 1800–1861*, New York, 1964; Richard Slotkin, *Regeneration Through Violence, The Mythology of the American Frontier, 1600–1860*, Middleton, 1973; Jack Kinney Williams, *Vogues in Villainy, Crime and Retribution in Antebellum South Carolina*, Charleston, 1959.

2. Richard Maxwell Brown, "Southern Violence—Regional Problem or National Nemesis?: Legal Attitudes Toward Southern Homicide in Historical Perspective," *Vanderbilt Law Review*, 32, 1979, 219–33; Henry C. Brearly, *Homicide in the United States*, Chapel Hill, 1932; Charles A. Ellwood, "Has Crime Increased in the United States Since 1880," *Journal of Criminal Law and Criminology and Police Science*, l, 1910–1911, 382–83; Frederic Hoffman, *The Homicide Problem*, Newark, 1925; J. J. Kilpatrick, "Murder in the Deep South," *Survey Graphic*, 32, October 1943, 395–97; Stuart Lottier, "Distribution of Criminal Offences in Sectional Regions," *Journal of Criminal Law*, 29, May-June 1938, 329–44; B. J. Ramage, "Homicide in the Southern States," *Sewanee Review*, 4, 1895–1896, 211–25; Lyle Shannon, "The Spatial Distribution of Criminal Offences by States," *Journal of Criminal Law*, 45, September-October 1954, 264–73.

3. Horace V. Redfield, *Homicide, North and South*, Philadelphia, 1880; see also Brown, "Southern Violence," 229–31.

4. Wilbur Cash put particular emphasis on the legacy of the frontier with its lack of social restrictions, its individualistic culture, its particular

code of honor, its adulation of the self-made man, its emphasis on the ability of any man to confront adversity and solve his own problem. Wilbur Cash, *The Mind of the South*, New York, 1941, 32–34, 44–52, 115–23.

5. Cash, *The Mind of the South*, 424–26; see also Joel Williamson, *The Crucible of Race: Black-White Relations in the American South Since Emancipation*, New York, 1984, 1–3. Such historians as W. E. B. DuBois, David Brion Davis, and John Hope Franklin endorsed this view, but since they believed that the long tradition of violence in the South was deeply rooted in slavery, they tended to blame the plantation economy. W. E. B. DuBois, *Black Reconstruction*, New York, 1975; David Brion Davis, *From Homicide to Slavery, Studies in American Culture*, Oxford, 1986; John Hope Franklin, *Reconstruction After the Civil War*, Chicago, 1961.

6. Larry Baron and Murray A. Straus, "Cultural and Economic Sources of Homicide in the United States," *Sociological Quarterly*, 29, no. 3, 1988, 371–90; Judith R. Blau and Peter M. Blau, "The Cost of Inequality: Metropolitan Structure and Violent Crimes," *American Sociological Review*, 47, 1982, 114–29; Andrew F. Henry and James F. Short Jr., *Suicide and Homicide: Some Economic, Sociological and Psychological Aspects of Aggression*, New York, 1964, 13–19; Robert Nash Parker, "Poverty, Subculture of Violence, and Type of Homicide," *Social Forces*, 67, June 1989, 983–1007.

7. Baron and Straus, "Cultural and Economic Sources of Homicide," 372; Lin Huff-Corzine, Jay Corzine, and David C. Moore, "Southern Exposure: Deciphering the South's Influence on Homicide Rates," *Social Forces*, 64, June 1986, 1906–24; Martin Daly and Margo Wilson, *Homicide*, New York, 1988, 286–88; Austin L. Porterfield, "Indices of Suicides and Homicides by States and Cities: Some Southern–Non-Southern Constitutions with Implications for Research," *American Sociological Review*, 14, 1949, 488; John S. Reed, "To Live—And Die—In Dixie: A Contribution to the Study of Southern Violence," *Political Science Quarterly*, 86, September 1971, 429–43; Leroy C. Schultz, "Why Negroes Carry Weapons," *Journal of Criminal Law: Criminology and Police Science*, 53, December 1962, 476–83; Kirk R. Williams, "Economic Sources of Homicide: Reestimating the Effects of Poverty and Inequality," *American Sociological Review*, 49, April 1984, 283–89; Marvin Wolfgang and Franco Ferracuti, *The Subculture of Violence, Toward an Integrating Theory of Criminality*, 1967, 263–64.

8. Raymond P. Gastill, "Homicides and a Regional Culture of Violence," *American Sociological Review*, 36, 1971, 412–27; Sheldon Hackney, "Southern Violence," *American Historical Review*, 74, February 1969, 906–25; Steven F. Messner, "Regional and Racial Effects on the Urban Homicide Rates: The Subculture of Violence Revisited," *American*

Journal of Sociology, 88, 1983, 997–99; Fox Butterfield, *All God's Children: The Bosket Family and the American Tradition,* New York 1995, 7–14; see also Brown, "Southern Violence," 226; Franklin, *The Militant South,* 12–13; Richard E. Nisbett and Dov Cohen, *Culture of Honor: The Psychology of Violence in the South,* Boulder, Colo., 1996.

9. Gastill creates an "index of Southernness" that includes a number of socioeconomic and demographical variables by which he associates culture and homicide rates. By various correlations, he examines the influence of the index of Southernness on homicide rates and concludes the existence of a Southern culture of violence. Although no one will deny the existence of a cultural difference that is particular to the South, the methodological approach used in verifying such an ambiguous concept as culture by means of a quantitative approach raises many questions. Brown, "Southern Violence," 225–27; Colin Loftin and Robert H. Hill, "Regional Subculture and Homicides: An Examination of the Gastill-Hackney Thesis," *American Sociological Review,* 39, October 1974, 714, 722–23; Daly and Wilson, *Homicide,* 286–91; Kenneth C. Land, Patricia L. McCall, and Laurence E. Cohen, "Structural Covariates of Homicide Rates: Are There any Invariances across Time and Social Space?" *American Journal of Sociology,* 95, January 1990, 922–63; Messner, "Regional and Racial Effects on the Urban Homicide Rates," 999.

10. Edward L. Ayers, *Vengeance and Justice: Crime and Punishment in the 19th-Century American South,* New York, 1984; Dickson D. Bruce Jr., *Violence and Culture in the Antebellum South,* Austin, 1979; David Grimsted, *American Mobbing, 1828–1861, Toward Civil War,* New York, 1998; Samuel C. Hyde, Jr., *Pistols and Politics, The Dilemma of Democracy in Louisiana's Florida Parishes, 1810–1899,* Baton Rouge, 1996; Grady McWhiney, *Cracker Culture, Celtic Ways in the Old South,* Tuscaloosa, 1988, 146–70; Bertram Wyatt-Brown, *Southern Honor, Ethics & Behavior in the Old South,* New York, 1982.

11. John B. Boles and Evelyn T. Nolen eds., *Interpreting Southern History, Historiographical Essays in Honor of Sanford W. Higgenbotham,* Baton Rouge, 1987, 162–307; Eric Foner, *Reconstruction: America's Unfinished Revolution, 1863–1877,* New York, 1988; William Gillette, *Retreat From Reconstruction, 1869–1879,* Baton Rouge, 1979; Stetson Kennedy, *After Appomattox: How the South Won the War,* Gainesville, 1995; Leon F. Litwack, *Been in the Storm So Long: The Aftermath of Slavery,* New York, 1979; Michael Perman, *The Road to Redemption: Southern Politics, 1869–1879,* Chapel Hill, 1984; Howard N. Rabinowitz, *Race Relations in the Urban South, 1865–1890,* Urbana, 1980; Howard N. Rabinowitz, *Race, Ethnicity and Urbanization, Selected Essays,* Columbia, 1994; Armstead L. Robinson, "Beyond the Realm of Social Consensus: New Meanings of Reconstruction for

American History," *Journal of American History*, 78, September 1981, 276–97; Mark W. Summers, *The Era of Good Stealings*, Oxford, 1993; Michael Wayne, *The Reshaping of Plantation Society, The Natchez District, 1860–1880*, Baton Rouge, 1983; Jonathan Wiener, *Social Origins of the New South, Alabama, 1860–1865*, Baton Rouge, 1978; Joel Williamson, *Crucible of Race*; Forrest G. Wood, *Black Scare: The Racist Response to Emancipation and Reconstruction*, Berkeley, 1968.

12. William Dunning, John Burgess, and their students were the first historians to elaborate an interpretation of Reconstruction. Under their pen, Reconstruction was described as a sordid period of corruption and "the darkest page in the saga of American history" as "unscrupulous" Northern whites and "unprincipled scalawags" dominated the South by manipulating ignorant freedmen. Therefore violence became the ultimate tool used by the Southern white community to overthrow the Republican regime and restore "home rule." Eric Foner, *Reconstruction*, xix–xxvi, 609.

13. Carolyn E. Delatte, "The St. Landry Riot: A Forgotten Incident of Reconstruction Violence," *Louisiana History*, 17, Winter 1976, 41–49; Melinda M. Hennessey, "Race and Violence in Reconstruction New Orleans: The 1868 Riot," *Louisiana History*, 20, Winter 1979, 77–92; Melinda M. Hennessey, "Political Terrorism in the Black Belt: The Eutaw Riot," *Alabama Review*, 33, January 1980, 112–25; George C. Rable, *But There Was No Peace: The Role of Violence in the Politics of Reconstruction*, Athens, Ga., 1984; Herbert Shapiro, *White Violence and Black Response, From Reconstruction to Montgomery*, Amherst, 1988; Albert C. Smith, "'Southern Violence' Reconsidered: Arson as Protest in Black Belt Georgia, 1865–1910," *Journal of Southern History*, 51, November 1985, 526–64.

14. Charles L. Flynn, "The Ancient Pedigree of Violent Repression: Georgia's Klan as a Folk Movement," in *The Southern Enigma: Essays on Race, Class, and Folk Culture*, edited by Walter J. Fraser and Winfred B. Moore Jr., Westport, Conn., 1983; Ray Granada, "Violence: An Instrument of Policy in Reconstruction Alabama," *Alabama Historical Quarterly*, 30, Fall-Winter 1968, 191–202; Ralph L. Peek, "Lawlessness in Florida, 1868–1871," *Florida Historical Quarterly*, 40, October 1961, 164–85; Herbert Shapiro, "The Ku Klux Klan During Reconstruction: The South Carolina Episode," *Journal of Negro History*, 49, January 1964, 34–55; John Z. Sloan, "The Ku Klux Klan and the Alabama Election of 1872," *Alabama Review*, 18, April 1965, 113–24; Allen W. Trelease, *White Terror: The Ku Klux Klan Conspiracy and Southern Reconstruction*, New York, 1971; Wynn Craig Wade, *The Fiery Cross: The Ku Klux Klan in America*, New York, 1987.

15. John A. Carpenter, "Atrocities in the Reconstruction Period,"

Journal of Negro History, 47, October 1962, 234–47; Barry A. Crouch, "A Spirit of Lawlessness: White Violence; Texas Blacks, 1865–1868," *Journal of Social History,* 18, Winter 1984, 217–32; Gregg Cantrell, "Racial Violence and Reconstruction Policy in Texas, 1867–1868," *Southwestern Historical Quarterly,* January 1990, 333–55.

16. Joe Gray Taylor, *Louisiana Reconstructed, 1863–1877,* Baton Rouge, 1974; Ted Tunnell, *Crucible Reconstruction, War, Radicalism and Race in Louisiana, 1862–1877,* Baton Rouge, 1984.

17. Ann Patton Baenziger, "The Texas State Police During Reconstruction: A Reexamination," *Southwestern Historical Quarterly,* 72, April 1969, 471; Crouch, "A Spirit of Lawlessness," 217–32; Cantrell, "Racial Violence," 333–55; Redfield, *Homicide, North and South,* 11; Taylor, *Louisiana Reconstructed,* 418–23; Trelease, *White Terror,* 127–36; Frank J. Wetta, "'Bulldozing the Scalawags': Some Examples of the Persecution of Southern White Republicans in Louisiana During Reconstruction," *Louisiana History,* 21, Winter, 1980, 43–58.

18. 43rd Congress, 2nd sess., House Report no. 261, 333; Henry C. Dethloff and Robert R. Jones, "Race Relations in Louisiana, 1877–1898," *Louisiana History,* 9, Fall 1968, 307; Charles Vincent, "Black Louisianians During the Civil War and Reconstruction: Aspects of Their Struggles and Achievements," in *Louisiana's Black Heritage,* edited by Robert R. Macdonald, John R. Kemp, and Edward F. Haas, New Orleans, 1979, 85; Taylor, *Louisiana Reconstructed,* 91.

19. V. A. Gatrell and T. B. Hadden, "Criminal Statistics and Their Interpretation," in *Nineteenth Century Society: Essays in the Use of Quantitative Methods For the Study of Social Data,* edited by E. A. Wrigley, Cambridge, 1972, 336–96; Michel Perrot, "Délinquences et systèmes pénitentiaires en France au XIXe siècle," *Annales, Économie, Société, Civilisations,* Janvier-Février 1975, 67–91; Howard Zehr, "The Modernization of Crimes in Germany and France, 1830–1919," *Journal of Social History,* 8, 1975, 117–41.

20. Theodore W. Ferdinand, "The Criminal Patterns of Boston Since 1849," *American Journal of Sociology,* 73, July 1967, 86; Roger Lane, *Violent Death in the City: Suicide, Accident & Murders in Nineteenth-Century Philadelphia,* Cambridge, Mass., 1979, 64; Eric H. Monkkonen, "The Organized Response to Crime in Nineteenth and Twentieth Century America," *Journal of Interdisciplinary History,* 14, Summer 1983, 113–28.

21. Donald J. Black, "Production of Crime Rates," *American Sociological Review,* 35, August 1970, 733–47; Gatrell and Hadden, "Criminal Statistics and Their Interpretation," 336–96; Roger Lane, "Crime and Criminal Statistics in Nineteenth-Century Massachusetts," *Journal of Social History,* Winter 1968, 156–63; Michael D. Maltz, "Crime Statistics:

A Historical Perspective," *Crime and Delinquency,* January 1977, 32–40; Eric H. Monkkonen, "Systematic Criminal Justice History: Some Suggestions," *Journal of Interdisciplinary History,* 9, Winter 1979, 451–64; Robert A. Nye, "Crime in Modern Societies: Some Research Strategies For Historians," *Journal of Social History,* 11, Summer 1978, 491–507; Samuel Walker, "Counting Cops and Crime," *Review of American History,* 10, June 1982, 212–17.

22. Black, "Production of Crime Rates," 733–47; Gatrell and Hadden, "Criminal Statistics and Their Interpretation," 336–96; Lane, "Crime and Criminal Statistics," 156–63; Lane, *Violent Death in the City,* 56; Maltz, "Crime Statistics," 32–40; Monkkonen, "Systematic Criminal Justice History," 451–64; Nye, "Crime in Modern Societies," 491–507; Walker, "Counting Cops and Crime," 212–17; Howard Zehr, *Crime and the Development of Modern Society: Patterns of Criminality in Nineteenth-Century Germany and France,* London, 1976, 86.

23. J. S. Cockburn, "Patterns of Violence in English Society: Homicide in Kent 1560–1985, *Past & Present,* 130, February 1991, 70–106; Daly and Wilson, *Homicide,* 12; Lane, *Violent Death in the City,* 56; Monkkonen, "Systematic Criminal Justice History," 451–64; Nye, "Crime in Modern Societies," 491–507; Pieter Spierenburg, "Faces of Violence: Homicide Trends and Cultural Meanings: Amsterdam, 1431–1816," *Journal of Social History,* 27, Summer 1994, 701–16.

24. Lane, *Violent Death in the City,* 56; Monkkonen, "Systematic Criminal Justice History," 451–64; Nye, "Crime in Modern Societies," 491–507.

25. Lane, *Violent Death in the City,* 53, 55; Zehr, *Crime and Modern Society,* 85.

26. Williams, *Vogues in Villainy,* 34. See also Cockburn, "Patterns of Violence," 73; Spierenburg, "Faces of Violence," 706.

27. Redfield, *Homicide, North and South,* 172; see also Lane, *Violent Death in the City,* 58.

28. *Shreveport Times,* January 25, 1875; Gilles Vandal, "'Bloody Caddo': White Violence Against Blacks in a Louisiana Parish, 1865–1876," *Journal of Social History,* 25, December 1991, 374.

29. Cockburn, "Patterns of Violence," 73; Lane, *Violent Death in the City,* 55–56; Michael L. Radelet and Glenn L. Pierce, "Race and Prosecutorial Discretion in Homicide Cases," *Law & Society Review,* 19, 1985, 587–621; Spierenburg, "Faces of Violence," 706; Zehr, *Crime and Modern Society,* 85.

30. Cockburn, "Patterns of Violence," 72–73; Spierenburg, "Faces of Violence," 706; Zehr, *Crime and Modern Society,* 85.

31. Harvey J. Graff, "A Reply," *Journal of Interdisciplinary History,* 9, Winter 1979, 468; Eric H. Monkkonen, "New York City Homicides: A Research Note," *Social Science History,* 19, Summer 1995, 203–5.

32. Brown, "Southern Violence," 226; Zehr, *Crime and Modern Society,* 157–58.

33. Lane, *Violent Death in the City,* 55; Monkkonen, "Systematic Criminal Justice History," 452; Spierenburg, "Faces of Violence," 702.

34. Lane, *Violent Death in the City,* 56.

35. Lane, *Violent Death in the City,* 55; Spierenburg, "Faces of Violence," 702–5; Monkkonen, "Systematic Criminal Justice History," 452.

36. Monkkonen, "New York City Homicides," 203; Spierenburg, "Faces of Violence," 706; Zehr, *Crime and Modern Society,* 85.

37. Gastill, "Homicides and a Regional Culture," 412; Monkkonen, "New York City Homicides," 205.

38. The law of 1855, which remained in force during the whole period under study, defined three kinds of homicide: First, there was the deliberate and intentional homicide, the particularly brutal, or the one that occurred when the offender was in the process of committing a crime. Such homicides were usually defined as murder, and the offender was subject to capital punishment. Second, the law defined the unintentional homicide that occurred during a brawl, a private quarrel, or a domestic dispute, which was often defined by the courts as manslaughter. In such cases the offender was subject, if found guilty, to a sentence of hard labor in the state penitentiary ranging from a few years to life. Third, the statutes recognized cases of justified homicide. The defendant was found not guilty if it could be determined that he had perpetrated the deed in self-defense. This latter category also included homicide committed by officers of the law while performing their duty. Furthermore, since the 1855 law was vague about what should be the punishment for manslaughter and failed to define different degrees of punishment, there were numerous acquittals of people who had committed the offense to a less aggravated degree. Annual Report of the Attorney General to the General Assembly of the State of Louisiana, 1867, 3, 1878, 8; John Ray, *Revised Laws and Statutes of the State of Louisiana,* vol. 1, New Orleans 1870, 385. Cockburn in his study of homicide in England uses a similar definition of homicide. Cockburn, "Patterns of Violence," 76.

39. Daly and Wilson, *Homicide,* 14.

40. Miscellaneous Reports, no. 1318, and Register of Murders and Outrages, no. 1322, Bureau of Freedmen, Refugees and Abandoned Lands (hereafter cited as BFRAL), Reg. 105, War Department, National Archives, Washington, D.C.

41. The following documents are all found in the archives of the Louisiana State University in Baton Rouge: Report of the Joint Committee of the General Assembly of Louisiana on the Conduct of the Late Election and on the Condition of Peace and Order in the State, New Orleans, 1868; Supplemental Report of the Joint Committee of the General Assembly of Louisiana on the Conduct of the Late Election and the

Condition of Peace and Order in the State (hereafter cited as Supplemental Report), New Orleans, 1869; Report of the General Assembly of Louisiana on the Conduct of the Election of April 17, and 18, 1868, and the Condition of Peace and Order in the State, New Orleans, 1868.

42. Annual Report of the Louisiana State Attorney General to the General Assembly for the years 1867 to 1877, 1881, 1883.

43. Annual Report of the Board of the Louisiana State Penitentiary to the General Assembly for the years 1865 to 1877, 1879.

44. House Executive Documents, 39th Congress, 2nd sess., no. 68; 40th Congress, 2nd sess., no. 209; 41st Congress, 2nd sess., nos. 142, 209, 268; 42nd Congress, 3rd sess. no. 91; House Miscellaneous Documents, 41st Congress, 1st sess., nos. 12, 13, 16; 41st Congress, 2nd sess., nos. 152, 154; 42nd Congress, 2nd sess., nos. 104, 211; 44th Congress, 2nd sess., no. 34 (three parts); 45th Congress, 2nd sess., no. 52; 45th Congress, 3rd sess., no. 31 (three parts); House Reports, 39th Congress, 1st sess., no. 30; 39th Congress, 2nd sess., no. 16; 41st Congress, 1st sess., no. 27; 42nd Congress, 2nd sess., no. 92; 43rd Congress, 1st sess., nos. 597, 732; 43rd Congress, 2nd sess., nos. 101, 261; 44th Congress, 1st sess., nos. 442, 816; 44th Congress, 2nd sess., nos. 30, 44, 100, 156; 45th Congress, 3rd sess., no. 140; Senate Executive Documents, 39th Congress, 1st sess., no. 2; 39th Congress, 2nd sess., no. 6; 40th Congress, 1st sess., no. 14; 40th Congress, 2nd sess., no. 53; 40th Congress, 3rd sess., no. 15; 42nd Congress, 3rd sess., no. 47; 43rd Congress, 2nd sess., nos. 13, 17; 44th Congress, 2nd sess., no. 2; Senate Reports, 42nd Congress, 2nd sess., no. 41; 42nd Congress, 3rd sess., nos. 417, 457; 43rd Congress, 2nd sess., no. 626; 44th Congress, 2nd sess., no. 701 (4 parts); 45th Congress, 3rd sess., no. 855 (3 parts); 46th Congress, 2nd sess., no. 693; Senate Miscellaneous Documents, 43rd Congress, 2nd sess., nos. 45, 46.

45. More than fifty state and local newspapers have been consulted. Alexandria, *Alexandria Caucasian*, 1874–1875; Alexandria, *Louisiana Democrat*, 1865–1884; Alexandria, *Rapides Gazette*, 1871–1873, 1876–1878; *Amite Independent*, 1874–1876; *Assumption Pioneer*, 1865–1884; *Baton Rouge Capitolian Advocate*, 1884; *Baton Rouge Louisiana Capitolian*, 1879–1882; *Baton Rouge Tri-Weekly Advocate*, 1865–1871; *Baton Rouge Tri-Weekly Capitolian*, 1881–1883; *Baton Rouge Tri-Weekly Gazette & Comet*, 1865–1868; *Baton Rouge Weekly Advocate*, 1869–1872, 1878–1884; *Baton Rouge Weekly Truth*, 1882–1884; Bossier, *Bellevue Banner*, 1866–1884; *Carroll Conservative*, 1879; *Carroll Record*, 1868–1869; *Carroll Republican*, 1873–1876; *Carroll Watchman*, 1875; *Claiborne Guardian*, 1879–1881; *Colfax Chronicle*, 1876–1884; *Franklin Planter's Banner*, 1867–1872; *Iberville South*, 1865–1869, 1871, 1876–1884; *Jefferson State Register*, 1872–1874; *Lafayette Adver-*

tiser, 1869–1870, 1873–1874, 1877–1878, 1882; Lafayette, *Louisiana Cotton Boll,* 1873–1877; *Madison Times,* 1884; *Marksville Weekly Register,* 1868–1869; *Monroe Bulletin,* 1880, 1882–1884; *Morehouse Clarion,* 1879–1881; Morgan City, *Attakapas Register,* 1876–1878; *Natchitoches People's Vindicator,* 1874–1881; *Natchitoches Semi-Weekly Times,* 1866–1867; *Louisiana Sugar Bowl,* 1870–1881; *New Orleans Bee,* 1852–1884; *New Orleans Black Republican,* 1865; *New Orleans Bulletin,* 1874–1876; *New Orleans Commercial Bulletin,* 1865–1871; *New Orleans Crescent,* 1852–1868; *New Orleans Daily Picayune,* 1852–1884; *New Orleans Democrat,* 1876–1881; *New Orleans Republican,* 1867–1876; *New Orleans Semi-Weekly Louisianian,* 1871–1882; *New Orleans Southern Star,* 1865–1866; *New Orleans Times,* 1865–1881; *New Orleans Times-Democrat,* 1881–1884; *New Orleans Tribune,* 1864–1867, 1869; *Ouachita Telegraph,* 1871–1883; *Pointe Coupée Democrat,* 1884; *Rapides Democrat,* 1877–1883; *Richland Beacon News,* 1872–1882; St. Charles, *L'Avant-Coureur,* 1866–1869, 1871–1872; St. James, *Le Louisianais,* 1871–1876; *St. James Sentinel,* 1873–1875; St. John the Baptist, *Le Foyer Créole,*1865–1884; St. John the Baptist, *Le Meschaceebe,* 1865–1881; *St. Landry Democrat,* 1877–1884; St. Landry, *Le courier des Opelousas;* St. Landry, *Le journal des Opelousas,* 1868–1878; St. Mary, *Brashear News,* 1875; *St. Tammany Farmer,* 1878–1884; *Shreveport Daily Standard,* 1878–1881; *Shreveport Southwestern,* 1865–1871; *Shreveport Times,* 1871–1877, 1879–1884; *Tangipahoa Democrat,* 1874; *Tensas Gazette,* 1872–1874, 1879–1884; *Thibodeaux Sentinel,* 1865–1884; Vermilion, *Abbeville Meridional,* 1877–1881; *West Baton Rouge Sugar Planter,* 1866–1870; Winn, *The Southern Sentinel,* 1884.

46. Although there is no way of knowing if his investigation method was accurate, Redfield estimated that 90 percent of all homicides committed in the South found their way into news columns of local and state newspapers. Redfield, *Homicide, North and South,* 13, 171–75.

47. Redfield, *Homicide, North and South,* 176.

48. Nye, "Crime in Modern Societies," 495.

49. Brown Mexial, a black man, was found dead in the woods of the parish of Iberia in August 1874 and his death has remained shrouded in mystery. The head of the deceased was riddled with buckshot. The *Richland Beacon News* reported a similar murder that had occurred in Bossier: "On Friday morning, June 11th in this parish, John Bratton (a colored man) was found in his field shot through the head by some unknown person." The number of cases continue. 39th Congress, 1st sess., House Report no. 30, 153; 41st Congress, 2nd sess., House Misc. Doc. no. 154, part 1, 33, 36, 39, 55, 78, part 2, 117; 43rd Congress, 2nd sess., House Report no. 261, 175, 366–67, 783; 44th Congress, 2nd sess., House Re-

port no. 30, 77, 408; *Richland Beacon News*, June 26, 1875; Bellevue, *Bossier Banner*, June 17, 1875; *New Orleans Times*, January 22, 1875.

50. Several historians have excluded infanticides from homicide data because of the peculiar nature of this crime. Cockburn, "Patterns of Violence," 71, 96–97; Spierenburg, "Faces of Violence," 707.

51. The way that I identified each homicide included in the data set was simple. I proceeded first with a thorough reading of all congressional reports and documents and noted all the information that was reported on any particular homicide. Second, I proceeded in the same manner, reading the correspondence and other documents of the War Department and the Freedmen's Bureau. Third, I read the legislative reports of two state committees that investigated the violence that underlined the 1868 election. Finally, I went through all the local and state newspapers between 1865 and 1885. Each time a homicide was reported I entered all the information pertaining to it on an individual sheet of paper. The sheets were then arranged in alphabetic order by the victim's name to see if a case was reported more than once. I then compared the details on the sheets that bore the same name to see if they were related to the same case. In this way the repetition of cases was avoided. In the few cases where these accounts contradicted each other—usually on minor points—a reasoned judgment had to be made as to the quality and coherence of the information. It occasionally occurred that a homicide was reported by a newspaper and subsequently disavowed. In these cases I concluded that the murder had never taken place and no entry was made in the data set.

52. Redfield, *Homicide, North and South*, 150.

53. Philip H. Sheridan to William W. Belknap, Telegram of January 10, 1875, Sheridan Papers, Library of Congress; see also 43rd Congress, 2nd sess., Senate Exec. Doc. no. 13, 29–31.

54. Ramage, "Homicide in the Southern States," 223.

55. In August 1871 the Census Office published the statistics of homicides by states for the preceding year. Louisiana ranked second after Texas with 128 official homicides. Meanwhile, Redfield compared Maine and Louisiana over a ten-year period, two states with approximately the same population. He showed that Maine had a homicide rate ten times lower than the rate in Louisiana. The Federal Census Report of 1880 gave Louisiana an official homicide rate of 19 per 100,000 compared to 4.4 for Maine. Ramage, "Homicide in the Southern States," 222–23; Redfield, *Homicide, North and South*, 147–50.

56. The term "Bourbon" had been largely used by Louisiana historians to define the period of 1877 to 1900. The white conservatives are compared, for their refusal to accept the changes brought by the Civil War and Reconstruction, to the French Bourbons who came back to

power after 1815 and seemed to have learned nothing and forgot nothing. Although periodically this study refers to the white conservatives as Bourbons, the term "Redemption" is retained for the present study, which is more commonly used by historians, to characterize the post-Reconstruction period.

Chapter 1: Rural versus Urban Patterns of Homicide

1. *New Orleans Bee,* April 14, 1874.

2. J. M. Beattie, "The Patterns of Crime in England, 1660–1800," *Past and Present,* 62, February 1974, 47–95; Cockburn, "Patterns of Violence," 70–106; David Cohen and Eric A. Johnson, "French Criminality: Urban-Rural Differences in the Nineteenth Century," *Journal of Interdisciplinary History,* 13, no. 3, Winter 1982, 477–501; Harvey J. Graff, "Crime and Punishment in the Nineteenth Century: A New Look at the Criminal," *Journal of Interdisciplinary History,* 7, Winter 1977, 477–91; Eric A. Johnson, "Cities Don't Cause Crime: Urban-Rural Differences in Late Nineteenth and Early Twentieth-Century German Criminality," *Social Science History,* 16, Spring 1992, 129–76; David J. V. Jones, *Crime in Nineteenth-Century Wales,* Cardiff, 1992; Eric Van Young, "Islands in the Storm: Quiet Cities and Violent Countryside in the Mexican Independence Era," *Past And Present,* 118, 1988, 130–155; Zehr, *Crime and Modern Society,* 9–30.

3. Henry Allen Bullock, "Urban Homicides in Theory and Fact," *Journal of Criminal Law, Criminology and Police Science,* 45, 1955, 565–75; R. C. Benning and O. J. Schroeder, *Homicides in an Urban Community,* Springfield, Ill., 1960.

4. The city was markedly heterogeneous as 38 percent of its population was foreign-born with 24,400 Irish, 19,500 Germans, and 10,500 French. Allan Conway, "New Orleans as a Port of Immigration, 1820–1860," *Louisiana Studies,* 1, Fall 1962, 1–17; Joseph G. Tregle, "Early New Orleans Society: A Reappraisal," *Journal of Southern Society,* 18, February 1952, 21–36; William W. Chenault and Robert C. Reinders, "The Northern-born Community of New Orleans," *Journal of American History,* 51, September 1964, 232–47.

5. *New Orleans Bee,* July 4, 7, 1865; *New Orleans Crescent,* November 14, 17, 1865; *New Orleans Daily Picayune,* June 22, 1865, October 24, 1866, February 10, 1867, April 15, 26, 1868; John W. Blassingame, *Black New Orleans, 1860–1880,* Chicago, 1973, 51, 221; Roger W. Shugg, *Origins of Class Struggle in Louisiana, A Social History of White Farmers and Laborers During Slavery and After, 1840–1875,* Baton Rouge, 1969, 251; Taylor, *Louisiana Reconstructed,* 326, 384.

6. New Orleans ranked fourth in the world for the magnitude and value of her commerce being exceeded only by London, Liverpool, and New York. On the eve of the Civil War, New Orleans business reached $324 million, practically all of it connected with the harbor. James P. Baugham, "Gateway to the Americas" in *The Past as Prelude, New Orleans, 1718–1968*, edited by Hodding Carter, New Orleans, 1969, 268–83; Harold Sinclair, *The Port of New Orleans*, New York, 1942, 175, 293.

7. *New Orleans Bee*, April 24, 1851, January 4, 1861, January 4, 1872; *New Orleans Daily Picayune*, January 4, April 3, August 5, 20, 1869, May 14, July 13, 31, December 10, 1870, and August 31, 1871.

8. *New Orleans Daily Picayune*, April 21, May 3, June 6, 1866, April 5, 1867, February 21, April 5, 15, 24, 26, May 6, 31, June 6, 28, August 27, September 18, 24, 1868, April 3, 1869; *New Orleans Bee*, July 12, 1866, April 5, 1867; Eric Arnesen, *Waterfront Workers of New Orleans: Race, Class, and Politics, 1863–1923*, New York, 1991, 40–41, 45–46; Shugg, *Origins of Class Struggle*, 185–88, 191–95, 258, 282–83, 299; Taylor, *Louisiana Reconstructed*, 2, 173, 342.

9. Jacqueline P. Bull, "The General Merchant in the Economic History of the New South," *Journal of Southern History*, 18, 1952, 37–59; Glenn N. Sisk, "Rural Merchandising in the Alabama Black Belt, 1875–1917," *Journal of Farm Economics*, 37, no. 4, November 1955, 705–15; Shugg, *Origins of Class Struggle*, 242, 250.

10. Shugg, *Origins of Class Struggle*, 253; Wayne, *Reshaping of Plantation Society*, 153, 156, 163.

11. Bull, "General Merchant," 40, 41, 52; Sisk, "Rural Merchandising," 705–7; Wayne, *Reshaping of Plantation Society*, 181–83.

12. 46th Congress, 2nd sess., Senate Report no. 693, part 3, 340–55; 45th Congress, 3rd sess., Senate Report no. 855, part 1, 6, 78, 88, 92. Elliott Ashkenazi, *The Business of Jews in Louisiana, 1840–1875*, Tuscaloosa, 1988, 68; William Ivy Hair, *Bourbonism and Agrarian Protest, Louisiana Politics, 1877–1900*, Baton Rouge, 1969, 54, 159; Taylor, *Louisiana Reconstructed*, 400.

13. Ashkenazi, *The Business of Jews*, 68; Bull, "General Merchant," 37–59; Thomas D. Clark, "In the Southern Retail Trade After 1865," *Journal of Economic History*, 33, December 1944, 38–47; Thomas D. Clark, "The Furnishing and Supply System in Southern Agriculture Since 1865," *Journal of Southern History*, 12, 1946, 22–44; Sisk, "Rural Merchandising," 705–15; Glenn N. Sisk, "Town Business in the Alabama Black Belt, 1875–1917," *Mid-America*, 38, January 1956, 47–55.

14. The new Louisiana towns supplied small farmers and planters with dry goods and furnished basic judicial and professional services. Each small town usually had its milliners, dry goods and clothing mer-

chants, jewelers, confectioneries, groceries, drugstores, saloons, butchers, and blacksmiths. They also offered other services such as livery stables, hotels, cotton buyers, cotton warehouses, undertakers, barbers, street vendors, egg peddlers, fat-pine sellers, and native fruit dealers.

15. For example, by 1875 Morgan City, then named Brashear, had a population of 3,000 and about 800 houses, five churches, five schools, a masonic lodge, two fire companies, two newspapers, one social club, one moss factory, one sash factory, four steam sawmills, one icehouse, one customhouse, three drugstores, fifty wholesale and retail stores, fifteen coffee shops, five billiard rooms, and three bakeries. *A History of Morgan City,* Morgan City, 1960, 32.

16. *St. Landry Democrat,* February 9, 1878; *Louisiana Sugar Bowl,* March 24, 1881; *New Orleans Bee,* March 26, 1881.

17. Annual Report of the Board of Metropolitan Police to the General Assembly of Louisiana, 1870, 25, 1871, 41–42, 1872, 36, 1873, 25, 1875, 37; *New Orleans Bee,* April 24, 1874, February 27, 1879; *New Orleans Daily Picayune,* May 30, August 4, 1868, July 23, 1869, April 30, 1870, January 4, June 25, July 8, 1871, January 11, 1874, February 28, 1879, December 3, 1884; *New Orleans Times,* October 14, 1872, October 1, 1876, February 25, March 2, April 7, 29, July 29, August 7, 1879, September 7, November 10, 1880, January 16, 1881; *New Orleans Republican,* October 9, December 18, 1869; *New Orleans Times-Democrat,* February 26, 1884; Joy J. Jackson, *New Orleans in the Gilded Age: Politics and Urban Progress, 1880–1896,* New Orleans, 1969, 232–57.

18. *Le Courier de la Louisiane,* March 11, December 28, 1855, August 16, 1857; *New Orleans Bee,* December 8, 1852, September 16, 1853, December 12, 1855, February 20, 1860; *New Orleans Crescent,* June 14, 1858, May 10, November 8, December 9, 1859, January 10, February 11, March 10, 1860; *New Orleans Daily Picayune,* October 2, 1852, November 15, 1855.

19. Annual Report of the State Attorney General to the General Assembly, 1860, 7, 1861, 11; *New Orleans Bee,* June 2, 1860; Denis C. Rousey, "The New Orleans Police, 1805–1889: A Social History," Ph. D. diss., Cornell University, 1978, 147–48, 155.

20. *New Orleans Daily Picayune,* March 29, 1884; Ferdinand, "Criminal Patterns of Boston," 88–89.

21. The Annual Report of the Superintendent of Police, New Orleans, 1893, 4, 1895, 25, 1896, 33, 1897, 45, 1898, 25.

22. The State Attorney General stated in his 1857 report that information on 95 homicides had been filed in Louisiana for the preceding year; most of them occurred in New Orleans. Annual Report of the State Attorney General to the General Assembly, 1857, 11.

23. 45th Congress, 3rd sess., Senate Report no. 855, ix, 44, 169–93, 198, 204, 225, 229, 231, 236, 263; *Assumption Pioneer,* May 31, 1879; *Natchitoches People's Vindicator,* April 5, 1879; *New Orleans Democrat,* October 22, 1878; *New Orleans Daily Picayune,* April 23, May 6, 1879; *New Orleans Semi-Weekly Louisianian,* April 12, 1879; *New Orleans Times,* May 27, 1879; *Ouachita Telegraph,* January 3, 1879; *Shreveport Times,* November 7, 8, December 29, 1879; *Tensas Gazette,* May 3, 10, June 21, 1879; Hair, *Bourbonism and Agrarian Protest,* 83–106; Morgan D. Peoples, "'Kansas Fever' in North Louisiana," *Louisiana History,* 11, Spring 1970, 125.

24. Included in the study are only the homicide statistics for which the races of the perpetrators have been established.

25. 43rd Congress, 2nd sess., House Report no. 261, 149, 953; 44th Congress, 2nd sess., House Exec. Doc. no. 30, 477; *Shreveport Times,* January 31, 1875.

26. In the killing of whites by whites (79%), blacks by whites (48%), blacks by blacks (89%), and whites by blacks (71%), usually only one assailant was involved during the period 1877–1884.

27. Twenty-six percent of whites who committed homicides in rural areas were involved in more than one case. This percentage rises to 34 percent when only black victims are considered.

28. James G. Dauphine, "The Knights of the White Camelia and the Election of 1868: Louisiana's White Terrorists; a Benighting Legacy," *Louisiana History,* 30, Spring 1989, 173–90; Litwack, *Been in the Storm So Long,* 278–79; Taylor, *Louisiana Reconstructed,* 487; Wetta, "Bulldozing the Scalawags," 43–58.

29. *New Orleans Daily Picayune,* July 28, 1869, March 31, July 12, 1871.

30. The 247 different occupations found in the data set were regrouped for the purpose of the present study into twelve different categories. All people who held local offices such as constable, parish clerk, justice of the peace, or sheriff, were defined as "low professionals." Meanwhile people who held a regional or a state office, or were members of the state legislature were considered as "high officials." The "small professionals" category regrouped all those who were either cashier, clerk, bookkeeper, minister, or teacher. Under the "liberal professionals" are found such occupations as doctor, lawyer, or superintendent. The "small businessmen" category regroups small dealers, small store owners, and peddlers, while the traders, merchants, bankers, brokers, and manufacturers were put in the "businessmen" category. The distinction between "planters" and "farmers" proved the most difficult to make as the census report often interchanged the term in many parishes. The value of the property (more than $10,000) was the basis used to separate planters

from farmers. But in many cases the census reported no value of property. All farm hands and other agricultural workers were entered as "farm laborers." The difference between "skilled workers" and "laborers" was established on the basis of the trade of each person. Finally, students or people at home were classified as "others."

31. *Assumption Pioneer,* January 24, 1880; Redfield, *Homicide, North and South,* 188–89.

32. Nineteen out of twenty murders committed in New Orleans were reported as originating out of unjustified causes, as if murderers acted upon the slightest provocation or on no provocation at all. *New Orleans Times,* October 11, 1875.

33. 39th Congress, 1st sess., House Report no. 30, 153; 41st Congress, 2nd sess., House Misc. Doc. no. 154, part 1, 33, 36, 39, 55, 78, part 2, 117; 43rd Congress, 2nd sess., House Report no. 261, 175, 366–67, 783; 44th Congress, 2nd sess., House Report no. 30, 77, 408; Bellevue, *Bossier Banner,* June 17, 1875; *Louisiana Democrat,* February 1, 1871; *New Orleans Daily Picayune,* December 19, 1871; *New Orleans Times-Democrat,* February 23, 1884; *Richland Beacon News,* June 26, 1875; *Shreveport Southwestern,* September 16, 1868; *Shreveport Times,* February 5, 1884. Homicides resulting from trivial or unspecified causes cannot be dismissed simply as a weakness of this data set. Other studies have found similar patterns and show that, generally speaking, 35 percent of homicides resulted from unspecified causes. Redfield, *Homicide, North and South,* 189; Marvin E. Wolfgang, *Patterns in Criminal Homicide,* Philadelphia, 1958, 191.

34. 44th Congress, 2nd sess., House Exec. Doc. no. 30, 373, 376, 385; 46th Congress, 2nd sess., Senate Report no. 693, part 2, 168; *New Orleans Crescent,* June 8, 1866, April 14, 18, 1868; *New Orleans Southern Star,* September 22, 1865, April 14, 1866; *New Orleans Times,* January 11, 1866; *Shreveport Times,* June 12, July 20, August 27, September 14, November 16, December 25, 1874; Taylor, *Louisiana Reconstructed,* 95, 285.

35. *Shreveport Times,* August 26, 1875.

36. In modern industrial society, one quarter to one half of the homicides are confined to family circles. Daly and Wilson, *Homicide,* 19, 27; Redfield, *Homicide, North and South,* 178–80; J. A. Sharpe, "Domestic Homicide in Early Modern England," *The Historical Journal,* 24, no. 1, 1981, 29–48.

37. *New Orleans Daily Picayune,* February 20, 24, March 8, 1870; *New Orleans Times,* February 17, 1870; Taylor, *Louisiana Reconstructed,* 419.

38. *New Orleans Daily Picayune,* March 2, 1870.

39. *Iberville South,* May 26, 1883.

40. Butterfield, *All God's Children*, 51; Wyatt-Brown, *Southern Honor*, 354, 384.

41. *New Orleans Daily Picayune*, January 31, 1867, June 4, 1878; Butterfield, *All God's Children*, 51–54.

42. *New Orleans Bee*, June 3, 1874; *New Orleans Daily Picayune*, October 2, 1868, June 4, 1878; *Thibodeaux Sentinel*, November 6, 1875; Elmer Noah, "Politics and Reconstruction in Morehouse Parish (1872–1877)," *North Louisiana Historical Association Journal*, 7, no. 1, Fall 1975, 13.

43. *New Orleans Daily Picayune*, July 23, 24, 1869, October 27, 29, 1877; *New Orleans Times*, May 14, 1869, May 5, 1880, February 4, 1881; Daly and Wilson, *Homicide*, 130–31.

44. *Colfax Chronicle*, February 2, 1882; *New Orleans Daily Picayune*, March 3, 1869; *New Orleans Times*, October 29, 1866, April 2, 1873; Redfield, *Homicide, North and South*, 217.

45. *New Orleans Times*, February 25, 1879; St. Landry, *Le courier des Opelousas*, January 14, 1882; Lane, *Violent Death in the City*, 59; Eric H. Monkkonen, "A Disorderly People: Urban Crime in Nineteenth and Twentieth Century," *Journal of American History*, 68, December 1981, 539–59.

46. Annual Report of the Board of Metropolitan Police, 1870, 8, 41; *New Orleans Crescent*, November 5, 1868.

47. Biennial Report of the State Attorney General of Louisiana, 1888–89, New Orleans, 1890, 62–63; *Colfax Chronicle*, February 4, 1882; *Donaldsonville Chief*, November 29, 1879; *Louisiana Sugar Bowl*, March 24, 1881; *New Orleans Bee*, January 11, 1870; *New Orleans Republican*, October 9, 1869; *New Orleans Times*, March 16, 1879; *New Orleans Times-Democrat*, February 27, 1884; *New Orleans Semi-Weekly Louisianian*, October 1, 1871; St. Landry, *Le courier des Opelousas*, July 22, 1875, October 31, 1884; *Assumption Pioneer*, January 24, 1880; *Rapides Democrat*, August 8, 1883; *St. Landry Democrat*, February 9, 1878; *Shreveport Southwestern*, August 8, 1871; *Thibodeaux Sentinel*, May 12, 1877, September 1, 1883; Gilles Vandal, "When Religion Mingled With Commerce: The Controversy Surrounding the Louisiana Sunday Law of 1878," *Mid-America*, 70, October 1988, 141–55.

48. 44th Congress, 2nd sess., House Report no. 30, 165; *Colfax Chronicle*, February 4, 1882; *Donaldsonville Chief*, November 29, 1879, February 19, 1881; *Iberville South*, April 28, 1883; *Le Foyer Creole of St. John the Baptist*, May 23, 1883; *Baton Rouge Louisiana Capitolian*, September 22, 1881; *New Orleans Crescent*, November 15, 1868; *New Orleans Daily Picayune*, February 2, 1876; *New Orleans Republican*, November 24, 1875, March 26, October 23, November 8, 1876; *New Orleans Times-Democrat*, February 23, 1882; *New Orleans Times*, June

26, 1873, February 25, August 18, 1879; St. Landry, *Le courier des Opelousas*, January 14, 1882, October 31, 1884; *Assumption Pioneer*, January 24, May 1, 1880, August 5, 1882; *Richland Beacon News*, September 24, 1881; *Shreveport Southwestern*, August 8, 1871; *Shreveport Times*, March 26, 1878; *Louisiana Sugar Bowl*, May 29, 1880; *Thibodeaux Sentinel*, May 12, 1875, September 1, 1881; Butterfield, *All God's Children*, 53; Jackson, *New Orleans in the Gilded Age*, 234–35.

49. 41st Congress, 2nd sess., House Misc. Doc. no. 154, part 1, 340–41, 355, 474; 43rd Congress, 2nd sess., House Report no. 261, 365, 441, 765, 780–81, 787, 953; 44th Congress, 2nd sess., House Exec. Doc. no. 30, 283. 384; *Bellevue Banner*, July 15, 1871; *Claiborne Guardian*, April 30, 1879; *Iberville South*, April 28, September 28, 1883, September 24, 1881; *Morehouse Clarion*, February 27, 1880; *New Orleans Bee*, January 11, May 1, 1870, May 15, 1874, March 12, 1876, May 14, 1879; *New Orleans Louisianian*, June 7, 1879; *New Orleans Daily Picayune*, January 11, 1866, August 12, September 11, 1868, January 2, April 5, 1871, May 4, June 2, 1871, October 11, 1875, June 20, 1876, May 17, 1877; *New Orleans Republican*, October 9, December 18, 1869, January 12, 1870; *New Orleans Times*, December 19, 1869, November 28, 1870, July 23, 1875, March 7, 1876, February 27, April 6, 13, 1879; *New Orleans Times-Democrat*, February 27, 1884; St. Landry, *Le courier des Opelousas*, October 3, 1868, April 26, 1879, January 14, 1882; *Assumption Pioneer*, January 24, 1880, August 5, 1882; *Franklin Planter's Banner*, December 28, 1867; *Rapides Democrat*, February 23, 1884; *Richland Beacon News*, April 14, 1877; *St. Landry Democrat*, March 8, 1879; *Louisiana Sugar Bowl*, May 27, 1880. See also Butterfield, *All God's Children*, 53; Redfield, *Homicide, North and South*, 188, 193–207.

50. Report of the Attorney General of the State of Louisiana to the General Assembly, New Orleans, 1870, 3–4.

51. Nine out of ten of the murders in the city were directly linked to the carrying of concealed weapons. *New Orleans Bee*, January 11, 1870; *New Orleans Daily Picayune*, May 1, 1879; *New Orleans Republican*, October 9, December 18, 1869; *New Orleans Semi-Weekly Louisianian*, October 1, 1871; *New Orleans Times*, December 19, 1869, February 27, March 16, 1879. See also Lane, *Violent Death in the City*, 61.

52. *New Orleans Bee*, May 1, 14, 1879; *New Orleans Daily Picayune*, May 15, 1877; *New Orleans Semi-Weekly Louisianian*, June 7, 1879 *New Orleans Times*, May 15, 1874, February 27, 1879, November 5, 1879, June 5, 1880.

53. *New Orleans Republican*, January 12, 1869.

54. *Morehouse Clarion*, February 27, 1880.

55. *Baton Rouge Weekly Advocate*, July 7, 1883; *Bellevue Banner*,

November 8, 1883; *Claiborne Guardian,* August 3, 1881; *New Orleans Bee,* April 14, 1874; *New Orleans Republican,* September 1, 1871; *St. Landry Democrat,* July 14, 1883; *Shreveport Times,* April 29, May 30, 1884; Rable, *But There Was No Peace,* 93.

56. *New Orleans Bee,* April 24, 1874; *New Orleans Daily Picayune,* May 8, June 9, November 25, 1868; *New Orleans Republican,* May 1, 1869, September 1, 1871; *New Orleans Times,* September 8, 26, 1880.

57. 40th Congress, 1st sess., Senate Exec. Doc. no. 14, 225; 43rd Congress, 2nd sess., Senate Exec. Doc. no. 17, 7; *New Orleans Times,* January 27, 1875; *New Orleans Daily Picayune,* January 28, 1875; *New Orleans Republican,* December 25, 1874; *Shreveport Times,* June 18, 21, September 21, 1875, December 9, 1883.

58. 43rd Congress, 2nd sess., House Report no. 261, 383; *Shreveport Southwestern,* January 28, 1871.

59. 44th Congress, 2nd sess., House Exec. Doc. no. 30, 373, 376, 385; 46th Congress, 2nd sess., Senate Report no. 693, part 2, 168; *New Orleans Crescent,* April 14, 1868; *Shreveport Times,* June 12, July 20, August 27, September 14, November 16, December 25, 1874; Taylor, *Louisiana Reconstructed,* 285.

60. *New Orleans Bee,* February 11, 1870, April 30, 1880; *New Orleans Daily Picayune,* February 25, April 15, 23, July 21, 1868, June 30, 1869, January 15, November 3, 1870, December 3, 1884; *New Orleans Republican,* May 22, 1867.

61. The New Orleans police force varied between 250 and 300 men during the 1850s. Its numbers rose to more than 700 in 1869 and remained above 500 for most of the Reconstruction period. *New Orleans Bee,* December 12, 1855; *New Orleans Crescent,* April 27, 1854; *New Orleans Daily Picayune,* December 26, 1856; Annual Report of the Board of Metropolitan Police, 1870, 6, 1871, 7, 1872, 5, 1873, 7, 1874, 9, 1875, 8; Rousey, "The New Orleans Police," 131–38, 218–31.

62. Capt F. A. Osbourn to Lt. L. O. Parker, Plaquemines, August 10, 1867, letters received, 1867–1870, Civil Affairs, Fifth Military District, box no. 4, book 60, War Department, National Archives.

63. 41st Congress, 2nd sess., House Misc. Doc. no. 154, part 2, 77; *Louisiana Sugar Bowl,* August 14, October 2, 1873; *Natchitoches People's Vindicator,* December 4, 1875; *Richland Beacon News,* June 26, 1875.

64. 44th Congress, 2nd sess., House Exec. Doc. no. 30, 157, 178, 180–81, 224–25, 250–52, 296–304, 381, 389, 402; 43rd Congress, 2nd sess., House Report no. 261, 617; *St. James, Le Louisianais,* December 11, 1869; *New Orleans Daily Picayune,* October 29, 1875; *New Orleans Republican,* April 1, 1870; *Rapides Gazette,* April 12, 1873; Amos L.

Armstrong, *Sabine Parish Louisiana, Land of Green Gold,* Shreveport, 1958, 207.

65. *Lafayette Advertiser,* August 8, 1874; see also *Richland Beacon News,* August 27, 1881.

66. 44th Congress, 2nd sess., House Exec. Doc. no. 30, 266, 402; Frederick W. and Lillian Herron Williamson, *Northeast Louisiana: A Narrative of the Ouachita River Valley and the Concordia Country,* Monroe, 1939, 170.

67. 39th Congress, 2nd sess., Senate Exec. Doc. no. 6, 86; 43rd Congress, 2nd sess., House Report no. 261, 439, 440; 44th Congress, 2nd sess., House Exec. Doc. no. 30, 176, 205, 239, 272, 307, 311, 363, 399, 431; 44th Congress, 2nd sess., House Report no. 156, part 1, 106, part 2, 45–47; *Baton Rouge Weekly Advocate,* November 18, 1882; *Colfax Chronicle,* December 4, 1880; *Lafayette Advertiser,* May 20, 1882; *Natchitoches Semi-Weekly Times,* October 9, 1869; *New Orleans Bee,* May 23, 1874, August 1, 1878; *New Orleans Daily Picayune,* October 20, 24, 1869, August 21, September 27, December 11, 1878, December 31, 1879; *New Orleans Times,* December 31, 1879, January 8, 1880; *Ouachita Telegraph,* May 19, 1883; *Assumption Pioneer,* December 14, 1878; *Rapides Democrat,* February 28, 1877; *Richland Beacon News,* June 20, 1874, March 24, 1877, September 3, 1881; *St. Tammany Farmer,* January 3, 1880; *Shreveport Times,* January 31, 1875, May 15, 1883, April 3, 29, October 23, 24, 31, 1884; *Thibodeaux Sentinel,* April 14, 1877; Rable, *But There Was No Peace,* 98.

68. *New Orleans Tribune,* December 8, 1866, July 7, 18, November 12, 1867; Charles Nordhoff, *The Cotton States in the Spring and Summer of 1875,* New York, 1876, 44; Dauphine, "Knights of the White Camelia," 183; Taylor, *Louisiana Reconstructed,* 177.

69. 42nd Congress, 2nd sess., House Report no. 211, 295; *New Orleans Times,* November 16, 1870; Otis Singletary, *Negro Militia and Reconstruction,* Austin, 1957, 13–15, 24, 67, 80; Taylor, *Louisiana Reconstructed,* 177.

70. 39th Congress, 1st sess., House Report no. 30, 142; *Bellevue Banner,* July 9, 1870; *Jefferson State Register,* July 23, 1870; *New Orleans Bee,* October 24, 1865; *New Orleans Crescent,* July 17, 1870; *New Orleans Daily Picayune,* October 21, 1865, July 8, 19, 1870; *New Orleans Republican,* August 2, 1870; *New Orleans Times,* July 17, 1870; *Shreveport Southwestern,* July 25, 1866, January 30, 1867, June 29, 1870; Singletary, *Negro Militia,* 13–15, 67, 114, 117; Taylor, *Louisiana Reconstructed,* 177; Tunnell, *Crucible Reconstruction,* 161.

71. 42nd Congress, 2nd sess., House Report no. 211, 295; 43rd Congress, 2nd sess., House Report no. 261, 171; *New Orleans Times,*

November 16, 1870; Singletary, *Negro Militia,* 13–15, 24, 67, 80; Taylor, *Louisiana Reconstructed,* 177.

72. *New Orleans Daily Picayune* and *New Orleans Times,* March to June 1867, October to November 1867, September and October 1874, and January 1875.

73. W. H. Emory to W. T. Sherman, January 8, 1873, serial no. 1962, Gulf Department, War Department, RG 393, National Archives; 43rd Congress, 2nd sess., Senate Exec. Doc. nos. 13, 17; 44th Congress, 2nd sess., House Exec. Doc. no. 30, contain hundreds of letters on the influence of the army on violence.

74. Gilles Vandal, *The New Orleans Riot of 1866: The Anatomy of a Tragedy,* Lafayette, La., 1983, 171–93.

75. *New Orleans Times,* July 24, 1874; *New Orleans Tribune,* November 12, 1867; Joseph G. Dawson, *Army Generals and Reconstruction, Louisiana, 1862–1877,* Baton Rouge, 1982, 3–4, 95; Foner, *Reconstruction,* 550; Taylor, *Louisiana Reconstructed,* 94, 138–39.

76. *New Orleans Daily Picayune,* June 22, 1876; *New Orleans Semi-Weekly Louisianian,* January 30, 1875; *New Orleans Bulletin,* January 29, 1875; *New Orleans Times,* January 15, 1869, January 27, 1875; Dauphine, "Knights of the White Camelia," 185; Dawson, *Army Generals,* 81, 87, 92, 103.

77. Capt. Alex. Bailey to A. A. General, September 27, 1866, Gulf Department, War Department, RG 393, National Archives; *New Orleans Daily Picayune,* June 22, 1876; *New Orleans Semi-Weekly Louisianian,* January 30, 1875; *New Orleans Bulletin,* January 29, 1875; *New Orleans Times,* January 15, 1869, January 27, 1875; Dauphine, "Knights of the White Camelia," 185; Dawson, *Army Generals,* 81, 87, 92, 103; J. E. Sefton, *The United States Army and Reconstruction,* Baton Rouge, 1967, 207–8; Taylor, *Louisiana Reconstructed,* 94.

Chapter 2: Homicides in Rural Areas

1. *Donaldsonville Chief,* March 27, 1875; *Jefferson State Register,* July 23, 1870; 41st Congress, 2nd sess., House Misc. Doc. no. 154, part 2, 36, 161; 43rd Congress, 2nd sess., House Report no. 261, 64, 379, 787; 44th Congress, 2nd sess., House Exec. Doc. no. 30, 362; 44th Congress, 2nd sess., House Report no. 156, part 1, 123.

2. Redfield, *Homicide, North and South,* 9–11.

3. William B. Bankston and H. David Allen, "Rural Social Areas and Patterns of Homicide: An Analysis of Lethal Violence in Louisiana," *Rural Sociology,* 45, 1980, 226; H. David Allen and William B. Bankston, "Another Look at the Southern Culture of Violence Hypothesis: The Case

of Louisiana," *Southern Studies,* 20, Spring 1981, 55–66; Daly and Wilson, *Homicide,* 277; Nisbett and Cohen, *Culture of Honor,* 14; George Rudé, "English Rural and Urban Disturbances on the Eve of the First Reform Bill, 1830–31," *Past and Present,* 37, July 1967, 87–102; I. A. Thompson, "A Map of Crime in Sixteenth-Century Spain," *Economic History Review,* 21, August 1968, 244–67; Vandal, "Bloody Caddo," 373–88.

4. Bankston and Allen, "Rural Social Areas and Patterns of Homicide," 226; Gilles Vandal, "The Policy of Violence in Caddo Parish, 1865–1884," *Louisiana History,* 32, Spring 1991, 159–82.

5. Lane, *Violent Death in the City,* 55; Monkkonen, "Systematic Criminal Justice History," 452; Zehr, "The Modernization of Crimes," 85–86.

6. A murder committed in a village of 5,000 people had a different social impact than 20 murders committed in a city of 100,000, although the rates were the same.

7. Alvin L. Bertrand, *The Many Louisianas: Rural Social Areas and Cultural Islands,* Baton Rouge, 1955, 5–44; Allen and Bankston, "The Case of Louisiana," 55–66; Bankston and Allen, "Rural Social Areas and Patterns of Homicide," 223–37; Charles E. Lively and Cecil L. Gregory, "The Sociocultural Area As A Field For Research," *Rural Sociology,* 1953, 21–31.

8. Allen and Bankston, "The Case of Louisiana," 55–66; Lawrence E. Estaville, "The Louisiana French in 1900," *Journal of Historical Geography,* 14, January 1988, 342–59; Lewis W. Newton, "Creoles and Anglo-Americans in Old Louisiana: A Study in Cultural Conflicts," *Southwestern Social Science Quarterly,* 14, 1933, 31–48; Taylor, *Louisiana Reconstructed,* 159; Vandal, "When Religion Mingled With Commerce," 141–55.

9. Wrotnoski divided Louisiana into what he called the Florida parishes, the Alluvial parishes, the Western and Southern parishes, and the Northwestern parishes. Samuel A. Lockett, *Louisiana As It Is; A Geographical and Topographical Description of the State,* Reprint, Baton Rouge, 1969, 5.

10. Lockett's six geographical regions were the Good Uplands, the Pine Hills, the Bluff Lands, the Prairies, the Alluvial, and the Coastal Marsh. Lockett, *Louisiana As It Is,* xvi, 43–58.

11. According to Hilgard, Louisiana was composed of the following regions: North of the Red River, South of the Red River, Tide Water parishes, Bluff region, Attakapas region, Long Leaf Pine region, and the Oak Lands. Eugene W. Hilgard, *Report on Cotton Production of the State of Louisiana,* Washington, 1884, 1–72.

12. In 1955, Bertrand described Louisiana as having the ten following rural social areas: Red River Delta, North Louisiana Uplands, Mississippi

Delta, North Central Cutover, West Central Cutover, Southwest Rice Farming, South Central Mixed Farming, Sugar Bowl, Florida Parishes, New Orleans. Bertrand, *The Many Louisianas,* 5–44.

13. We pay particular attention to the percentage of blacks in each parish. Consequently, parishes were grouped in a particular region only when they had approximately the same percentage of blacks among their population. The cultural, ethnic, and economic characteristics of each region were defined from the extensive parochial and regional comments made by contemporary observers that toured rural Louisiana during the second half of the nineteenth century. Walter Pritchard, ed., "A Tourist's Description of Louisiana in 1860," *Louisiana Historical Quarterly,* 21, 1938, 1110–213; Daniel Dennett, *Louisiana As It Is,* New Orleans, 1876; Lockett, *Louisiana As It Is;* Bertrand, *The Many Louisianas,* 5–44; Estaville, "The Louisiana French in 1900," 342–59.

14. Many portions of northwestern Louisiana were still basically a frontier area whose parishes were located between 350 to 500 miles from New Orleans. Northwestern Louisiana was furthermore composed of numerous lakes, bayous, and swamps, which made large portions of the parish territory practically impenetrable. These geographical characteristics enabled rogues of all kinds to commit homicides and other crimes with impunity, since they could either take refuge within the region or make their escape to Texas. 39th Congress, 2nd sess., Senate Exec. Doc. no. 6, 87; 41st Congress, 2nd sess., House Misc. Doc. no. 154, part 1, 36, 71, part 2, 132; 43rd Congress, 2nd sess., House Report no. 261, 448; *Shreveport Southwestern,* March 10, 1869; *Shreveport Times,* August 27, 1874; 44th Congress, 2nd sess., House Exec. Doc. no. 30, 383; Hilgard, *Report on Cotton Production,* 3–6, 49, 67–70; Lockett, *Louisiana As It Is,* 58–59.

15. During Reconstruction two of those parishes, Caddo and Bossier, with a respective population of 21,784 and 12,714 in 1870, each had about as many killed as the city of New Orleans, which had a population close to 200,000 inhabitants. These rates would appear almost incredible to twentieth-century eyes used to rates below 10.0 per 100,000 individuals.

16. 39th Congress, 2nd sess., Senate Exec. Doc. no. 6, 87; 41st Congress, 2nd sess., House Misc. Doc. no. 154, part 1, 36, part 2, 132; 43rd Congress, 2nd sess., House Report no. 261, 448; *Shreveport Southwestern,* March 10, 1869; *Shreveport Times,* August 27, 1874.

17. Butterfield, *All God's Children,* 9; Grimsted, *American Mobbing,* 86; McWhiney, *Cracker Culture,* 149–55; Nisbett and Cohen, *Culture of Honor,* 7–10.

18. Hilgard, *Report on Cotton Production,* 3–6, 49, 67–69; Lockett, *Louisiana As It Is,* 60.

19. Vandal, "The Policy of Violence," 159–82; Vandal, "Bloody Caddo," 373–88.

20. 43rd Congress, 1st sess., House report no. 30, 160; Vandal, "Bloody Caddo," 377; Texas was the only other Southern state that suffered from a similar situation. Cantrell, "Racial Violence," 333–55.

21. 39th Congress, 1st sess., House Report no. 30, 142; *New Orleans Bee,* October 24, 1865; *New Orleans Daily Picayune,* October 21, 1865; *Shreveport Southwestern,* July 25, 1866, July 30, 1867.

22. 44th Congress, 2nd sess., House Exec. Doc. No. 30, 194, 280, 383, 388; 43rd Congress, 2nd sess., House Report no. 261, 361, 367; 43rd Congress, 2nd sess., Senate Exec. Doc. No. 17, 4–6; *New Orleans Times,* January 27, 1875; *Shreveport Times,* July 20, 1874.

23. Wetta, "Bulldozing the Scalawags," 52, 55, 57; Vandal, "The Policy of Violence," 159–82.

24. Otis A. Singletary, "The Election of 1878 in Louisiana," *Louisiana Historical Quarterly,* 40, January 1957, 53; Vandal, "The Policy of Violence," 159–82; Vandal, "Albert H. Leonard's Road from the White League to the Republican Party: A Political Enigma," *Louisiana History,* 36, Winter 1995, 55–74.

25. Hilgard, *Report on Cotton Production,* 3–6, 61, 65; see also Luther Sandell, *The Free State of Sabine and Western Louisiana,* Many, 1982; John T. Cupit, *A Brief History of Vernon Parish, Louisiana,* Rosepine, La., 1963.

26. Armstrong, *Sabine Parish Louisiana,* 207.

27. Hilgard, *Report on Cotton Production,* 3–6, 60; Lockett, *Louisiana As It Is,* 80–82; Donald J. Millett, "The Lumber Industry of 'Imperial' Calcasieu: 1865–1900," *Louisiana History,* 7, Winter 1966, 51–69; Donald J. Millett, "Some Aspects of Agricultural Retardation in Southwest Louisiana, 1865–1900," *Louisiana History,* 11, Winter 1970, 37–67.

28. Hilgard, *Report on Cotton Production,* 3–6, 60; Lawrence E. Estaville Jr., "Changeless Cajuns: Nineteenth-Century Reality and Myth," *Louisiana History,* 28, 1987, 117–40; Donald J. Millett, "Cattle and Cattlemen of Southwest Louisiana, 1860–1900," *Louisiana History,* 28, no. 3, Summer 1987, 324–25.

29. Millett, "The Lumber Industry," 51–69; Millett, "Some Aspects of Agricultural Retardation," 37–67.

30. 43rd Congress, 2nd sess., House Report no. 261, 617; *Abbeville Meridional,* April 6, 1878, March 13, 1880, February 10, 1884; *Lafayette Advertiser,* June 2, September 18, 1869, July 12, 1873; *Louisiana Sugar Bowl,* February 2, 1871, March 13, May 13, July 3, August 7, 14, September 4, October 7, 1873, April 8, 1875, May 11, 16, 1876, December 12, 1878; *New Orleans Daily Picayune,* November 19, 1869, May

29, 1870, January 20, 1872; *New Orleans Times-Democrat,* November 12, 1883; Carl A. Brasseaux, *Acadian to Cajun, Transformation of a People, 1803–1877,* Jackson, Miss., 1992, 55.

31. Lafayette, *Louisiana Cotton Boll,* October 1, 1873; *Louisiana Sugar Bowl,* September 4, 11, 1873; *New Orleans Daily Picayune,* September 14, 1873; *New Orleans Republican,* September 16, November 16, 1873, August 19, 1876; St. Landry, *Le courier des Opelousas,* November 14, 1873; *Richland Beacon News,* September 20, October 1, 1873; *Thibodeaux Sentinel,* October 4, 1873; Millet, "Cattle and Cattlemen," 324–25; Taylor, *Louisiana Reconstructed,* 420.

32. *New Orleans Republican,* September 16, November 16, 1873; St. Landry, *Le courier des Opelousas,* November 14, 1873.

33. *Abbeville Meridional,* July 5, 1879; *Louisiana Sugar Bowl,* August 17, 1876; *New Orleans Republican,* August 19, 1876; St. Landry, *Le courier des Opelousas,* November 14, 1873.

34. Millett, "The Lumber Industry," 56–57.

35. Lockett, *Louisiana As It Is,* 44, 46, 61, 68.

36. 44th Congress, 2nd sess., House Exec. Doc. no. 30, 266; *Carroll Record,* June 13, 1868; *Colfax Chronicle,* May 3, 1879, October 9, 1880; *Donaldsonville Chief,* May 22, 1875; *New Orleans Daily Picayune,* August 1, 1869, December 17, 1870.

37. Hilgard, *Report on Cotton Production,* 3–6, 48; Lockett, *Louisiana As It Is,* 71–75.

38. 43rd Congress, 2nd sess., House Report no. 261, 584; John Cromie to Governor Henry C. Warmoth, May 2, May 5, 1870, letters sent, Warmoth Papers, Archives of Tulane University; A. W. Ragan to Com. McFarlen, Sept. 5, 1866, Winn parish, no. 1756, box 16, BFRAL; *New Orleans Republican,* May 8, June 5, 1870.

39. Hilgard, *Report on Cotton Production,* 3–6, 45–47; Lockett, *Louisiana As It Is,* 63–64; see also Williamson and Williamson, *Northeast Louisiana,* 170.

40. 39th Congress, 2nd sess., Senate Exec. Doc. no. 6, 86; 43rd Congress, 2nd sess., House Report no. 261, 361; 44th Congress, 2nd sess., House Exec. Doc. no. 30, 280, 355; Governor H. C. Warmoth to General Emory, micro 4501, box 4, October 26, 1869, Gulf Department, War Department; Petition of Isaac Crawford and Others to H. C. Warmoth, micro 4501, box 2, September 68, Gulf Department, War Department; *New Orleans Daily Picayune,* August 8, 1868; Dauphine, "Knights of the White Camelia," 182–83; Rable, *But There Was No Peace,* 16–32; Taylor, *Louisiana Reconstructed,* 61, 93.

41. 44th Congress, 2nd sess., House Exec. Doc. no. 30, 178, 224–25, 296, 157, 180–81, 250–52, 381, 296–304, 399; 43rd Congress, 2nd sess., House Report no. 261, 617; *New Orleans Republican,* April 1, 1870; Williamson and Williamson, *Northeast Louisiana,* 170.

42. 41st Congress, 2nd sess., House Misc. Doc. No. 154, part 1, 328–29, 335–37; Trelease, *White Terror,* 128; Dauphine, "Knights of the White Camelia," 182–83.

43. Hilgard, *Report on Cotton Production,* 3–6, 47; Williamson and Williamson, *Northeast Louisiana,* 170.

44. Dauphine, "Knights of the White Camelia," 183.

45. Dauphine, "Knights of the White Camelia," 185; Trelease, *White Terror,* 64.

46. 45th Congress, 3rd sess., Senate Report no. 855, 169–70, 194, 210, 230–31; *New Orleans Democrat,* October 17, 18, 1878; Hair, *Bourbonism and Agrarian Protest,* 178–79; Marguerite T. Leach, "The Aftermath of Reconstruction in Louisiana," *Louisiana Historical Quarterly,* 32, July 1949, 651–54; Singletary, "The Election of 1878," 52.

47. Hilgard, *Report on Cotton Production,* 3–6, 59.

48. 44th Congress, 2nd sess., House Exec. Doc. no. 30, 231–32; *New Orleans Daily Picayune,* July 8, 1869; William Henry Perrin, ed., *Southwest Louisiana Biographical and Historical Memoirs,* New Orleans, 1891, part 2, 25–26; Scraps from newspapers, "Destroying the Guillory," September 1873, U.S. Marshall, correspondence of the attorney general, National Archives, RG 60, Washington, D.C.

49. Perrin, *Southwest Louisiana,* part 2, 25–26.

50. Delatte, "The St. Landry Riot," 41–49; Dauphine, "Knights of the White Camelia," 184; Dawson, *Army Generals,* 86–88.

51. St. Landry, *Le journal des Opelousas,* May 29, 1874.

52. James H. Dormon, "Aspects of Acadian Plantation Life in the Mid-nineteenth Century: A Microcosmic View," *Louisiana History,* 16, Fall 1975, 361–70.

53. Hilgard, *Report on Cotton Production,* 3–6, 51–53; John A. Heitmann, "Responding to the Competition: The Louisiana Sugar Planters' Association, The Tariff, and the Formation of the Louisiana Sugar Exchange, 1877–1885," *Southern Studies,* 25, Winter 1986, 315–40; Charles P. Roland, "Difficulties of Civil War Sugar Planting in Louisiana," *Louisiana Historical Quarterly,* 38, October 1955, 40–62.

54. Gilles Vandal, "Politics and Violence in Bourbon Louisiana: The Loreauville Riot of 1884 as a Case Study," *Louisiana History,* 30, Winter 1989, 23–42.

55. *New Orleans Daily Picayune,* August 27, 1884; *Donaldsonville Chief,* July 3, 1880; *Assumption Pioneer,* August 5, 1882; *Iberville South,* March 10, 1883.

56. Hilgard, *Report on Cotton Production,* 3–6, 56–58; Lockett, *Louisiana As It Is,* 89–91.

57. Dawson, *Army Generals,* 226–27.

58. 44th Congress, 2nd sess., House Misc. Doc. no. 34, part 1, 16, 26, 28, 35, 56, 60, 61, 75, 77, 87, 98, 115, 179, 192, 199, 268, 334,

369; Journal of the House of Representatives of the State of Louisiana, New Orleans 1874, 110–11; *Bellevue Banner,* January 17, 1874; *New Orleans Bulletin,* October 15, 1875; *New Orleans Daily Picayune,* January 17, 1874, December 29, 1875; *New Orleans Times,* October 15, 16, 1875; Floyd M. Clay, "Economic Survival of the Plantation System within the Feliciana Parishes," M. A. thesis, Louisiana State University, 1962, 135; Rable, *But There Was No Peace,* 178–79; Taylor, *Louisiana Reconstructed,* 422–24.

59. Hilgard, *Report on Cotton Production,* 3–6, 63–65.

60. *St. Tammany Farmer,* January 3, 1880. The Amite lynching attracted the state's attention because it occurred in 1879, the year that saw both the adoption of a new constitution and a mass black exodus to Kansas. In response to these developments, state authorities and local newspapers launched an antiviolence campaign in an attempt to convince blacks that they would feel at home in Louisiana. The Amite lynching was a powerful reminder to blacks that violence remained a tool in the hands of whites.

61. Hilgard, *Report on Cotton Production,* 3–6, 34; Lockett, *Louisiana As It Is,* 117–20.

62. Dawson, *Army Generals,* 88, 92, 100.

63. P. H. Sheridan to W. W. Belknap, telegram of January 10, 1875, Sheridan Papers, Library of Congress; 43rd Congress, 2nd sess., Senate Exec. Doc. no.. 13, 29–31; Reports on the Bossier, St. Bernard, and St. Landry Riots, serial 4501, box 1, Gulf Department, War Department, RG 393, National Archives; See also 41st Congress, 2nd sess., House Misc. Doc. no. 154, 411–501; Taylor, *Louisiana Reconstructed,* 164–73.

64. *Baton Rouge Tri-Weekly Advocate,* January 27, 1871; *Franklin Planter's Banner,* December 7, 1870; *New Orleans Times,* November 16, 1870.

65. 44th Congress, 2nd sess., House Exec. Doc. no. 30, 306; W. P. Kellogg to Major General N. W. Emory, April 18, 1873, letters received, serial 1869, Gulf Department, War Department, RG 393; *New Orleans Bee,* April 13, May 4, 1873; *New Orleans Daily Picayune,* April 16, 29, 30, 1873; *New Orleans Republican,* April 9, 29, May 4, 7, 8, 9, 13, 16, 1873; *New Orleans Times,* January 6, 1873; Sefton, *United States Army and Reconstruction,* 239; Taylor, *Louisiana Reconstructed,* 245, 268–73, 279–80.

66. *New Orleans Daily Picayune,* September 25, October 28, December 13, 1874; *New Orleans Times,* September 5, 6, 1874.

67. *New Orleans Bee,* September 8, 1875, January 21, 22, 1876; *New Orleans Daily Picayune,* September 19, 21, 22, 24, October 12, 14, 15, 20, December 26, 1875, January 16, 21, 22, March 25–28, May 15, 16,

June 20, 21, 22, 26, October 21, 25, 29, 30, 1876; *New Orleans Times,* January 28, October 12, 15, 16, 1875.

68. *New Orleans Times,* July 17, 1870; Dauphine, "Knights of the White Camelia," 183–85.

Chapter 3: A Most Troubled State

1. 41st Congress, 2nd sess., House Misc. Doc. no. 154, part 1, 125–32; Trelease, *White Terror,* 130; Tunnell, *Crucible Reconstruction,* 155–56.

2. G. David Garson and Gail O'Brien, "Collective Violence in Reconstruction South," in *Violence in America, Historical & Comparative Perspectives,* edited by Hugh Davis Graham and Ted Robert Gurr, Beverly Hills, 1979, 243–60. For other societies see John Bohstedt and Dale E. Williams, "The Diffusion of Riots: The Patterns of 1766, 1795 and 1801 in Devonshire," *Journal of Interdisciplinary History,* 19, Summer 1988, 1–24; Grimsted, *American Mobbing;* Charles Tilly, "Collective Violence in European Cultures," in *Violence in America,* 83–118; David Snyder and Charles Tilly, "Hardship and Collective Violence in France, 1830 to 1960," *American Sociological Review,* 48, October 1972, 520–32; John Stevenson, *Popular Disturbances in England, 1700–1870,* London, 1979; Eric Van Young, "Agrarian Rebellion and Defense Community: Meaning and Collective Violence in Late Colonial and Independence Era Mexico," *Journal of Social History,* 27, Winter 1993, 245–69.

3. *Acts of Louisiana,* Act no. 164 of 1868, 218–25, Act no. 100 of 1870, 145–61, Acts no. 7 and 41 of 1873, 46–47, 80–81; *New Orleans Daily Picayune,* January 15, February 1, 20, 1870; *New Orleans Commercial Bulletin,* January 19, 1870; *New Orleans Republican,* February 16, August 27, 29, 1874.

4. Vincent E. McHale and Jeffrey Bergner, "Collective and Individual Violence: Berlin and Vienna, 1875–1913," *Criminal Justice History,* 2, 1981, 31–61; Garson and O'Brien, "Collective Violence in Reconstruction South," 243–60; Stewart E. Tolnay and E. M. Beck, *A Festival of Violence: An Analysis of Southern Lynchings, 1882–1930,* Urbana, 1992, 4–5; Shapiro, *White Violence and Black Response,* 5–21.

5. This comparison between individual and collective homicidal behavior was undertaken by Professors McHale and Bergner in their study of Berlin and Vienna. McHale and Bergner, "Collective and Individual Violence," 31–61.

6. A. J. Cole, "The Moral Economy of the Crowd: Some Twentieth-Century Food Riotings," *Journal of British Studies,* 17, Fall 1978, 157–76; McHale and Bergner, "Collective and Individual Violence,"

31–61; Garson and O'Brien, "Collective Violence in Reconstruction South," 243–60; Snyder and Tilly, "Hardship and Collective Violence in France," 520–32; Tilly, "Collective Violence in European Perspective," 83–118.

7. Charles Tilly, *From Mobilization to Revolution*, Reading, Mass., 1978, 177.

8. Stevenson, *Popular Disturbances*, 5–11.

9. Eric J. Hobsbawm, *Primitive Rebels, Studies in Archaic Forms of Social Movement in the Nineteenth and Twentieth Centuries*, New York, 1963; George Rudé, *The Crowd in History: A Study of Popular Disturbances in France and England 1730–1848*, New York, 1964; Edward P. Thompson, "The Moral Economy of the English Crowd in the Eighteenth Century," *Past And Present*, 50, 1971, 73–136.

10. Stevenson, *Popular Disturbances*, 12–14; Louise A. Tilly and Charles Tilly, eds, *Class Conflict and Collective Action*, Beverly Hills, 1981, 48; McHale and Bergner, "Collective and Individual Violence," 31–61; Garson and O'Brien, "Collective Violence in Reconstruction South," 243–60; Snyder and Tilly, "Hardship and Collective Violence in France," 520–32; John Bohstedt, *Riots and Community Politics in England and Wales 1790–1810*, Cambridge, 1983.

11. For example, the Bossier riot of 1868 included not only the disturbances at the Shady Grove plantation, but also the following incidents: on October 1, a band of some 75 whites from Shreveport on its way to the scene of the Bossier riot met a group of nine blacks who were taken to the bank of the Red River and shot after being told to swim for their lives; on the same night, thirty blacks were taken from around Shreveport, marched to the bank of the Red River, tied together with ropes and shot in the back; a few days later, seven blacks were chained in an old abandoned building which was then burned to the ground. 41st Congress, 2nd sess., House Misc. Doc., no. 154, part 1, 126; 44th Congress, 2nd sess., House Exec. Doc., no. 30, 293, 391; 43rd Congress, 2nd sess., House Report no. 261, 379; T. F. Monroe to J. M. Lee, A. A. Inspector General, October 12, 1868, letters sent and report, box 1, micro 4501, BFRAL; Supplemental Report, 265; Trelease, *White Terror*, 130; Tunnell, *Crucible Reconstruction*, 155–56.

12. Edna Bonacich, "A Theory of Ethnic Antagonism: The Split Labor Market," *American Sociological Review*, 37, 1972, 547–49; Tolnay and Beck, *A Festival of Violence*, 24–25, 45, 59.

13. The owners of the *Caucasian,* George Stafford, Robert P. Hunter, and W. F. Blackman, who were staunch defenders of white supremacy in Natchitoches parish, were at the same time, on matters directly related to agriculture, strongly in favor of diversifying crops. In this sense they broke away with the plantation system and the planter class who wanted to

maintain as much as possible the old system. Howard K. Beale, "On Re-writing Reconstruction History," *American Historical Review*, 45, July 1940, 807–27; Tolnay and Beck, *A Festival of Violence*, 24–25, 69–75; William E. Highsmith, "Louisiana Landholding During War and Recon-struction," *Louisiana Historical Quarterly*, 38, January 1955, 43.

14. Lt. M. F. Daugherty to Capt. A. F. Hayden, March 31, 1866, let-ters sent, BFRAL; *New Orleans Times*, March 27, 1866; Dawson, *Army Generals*, 81; Taylor, *Louisiana Reconstructed*, 93–94.

15. *Attakapas Register*, May 18, 1878; *Baton Rouge Tri-Weekly Ad-vocate*, September 24, 1866; *Bellevue Banner*, April 8, 1880; *Louisiana Sugar Bowl*, March 21, 24, 1881; *New Orleans Bee*, March 26, 1881; *New Orleans Daily Picayune*, July 21, 1871; *St. Landry Democrat*, Feb-ruary 9, 1878.

16. 43rd Congress, 2nd sess., House Report no. 261, 584; John Cro-mie to Governor Henry C. Warmoth, May 2, 5, 1870, letters sent, War-moth Papers, Archives of Tulane University; A. W. Ragan to Com. McFarlen, Sept. 5, 1866, Winn parish, no. 1756, box 16, BFRAL; *New Orleans Republican*, May 8, June 5, 1870.

17. 44th Congress, 2nd sess., House Exec. Doc. no. 30, 157, 178, 180–81, 224–25, 231–32, 250–52, 296–304, 381, 399, 401–2; 43rd Congress, 2nd sess., House Report no. 261, 584; John Cromie to Gover-nor Henry C. Warmoth, May 2, 5, 1870, letters sent, Warmoth Papers; A. W. Ragan to Com. McFarlen, September 5, 1866, Winn parish, no. 1756, box 16, BFRAL; Governor H. C. Warmoth to General Emory, micro 4501, box 4, October 26, 1869, Gulf Department, War Depart-ment; Petition of Isaac Crawford and others to H. C. Warmoth, micro 4501, box 2, September 68, Gulf Department, War Department; *New Orleans Daily Picayune*, August 8, 1868; *New Orleans Republican*, April 1, May 8, June 5, 1870, September 16, 1873; Brasseaux, *Acadian to Ca-jun*, 127.

18. District Attorney Wm. H. Wise to Wm. P. Kellogg, July 16, 1875, William P. Kellogg Papers, Louisiana State University Archives; *Donald-sonville Chief*, May 29, 1875; St. Landry, *Le journal des Opelousas*, June 8, 1882; *New Orleans Semi-Weekly Louisianian*, June 15, 1882; Gilles Vandal, "Property Offenses, Social Tension and Racial Antagonism in Post–Civil War Rural Louisiana," *Journal of Social History*, 31, Septem-ber 1997, 127–53.

19. 39th Congress, 1st sess., House Report no. 30, 156, 280; 39th Congress, 2nd sess., Senate Exec. Doc. no. 6, 86–87; 41st Congress, 2nd sess., House Misc. Doc. no. 154, part 1, 338, 342, part 2, 132; *New Orleans Republican*, December 25, 1874; *New Orleans Daily Picayune*, August 8, 11, 12, 1868; Brasseaux, *Acadian to Cajun*, 124–25; Dawson, *Army Generals*, 29, 33–35; Taylor, *Louisiana Reconstructed*, 62–63, 68,

91–92, 317. A similar situation prevailed in Texas as shown in Cantrell, "Racial Violence," 333–55, and Crouch, "A Spirit of Lawlessness," 226.

20. *Franklin Planter's Banner,* December 28, 1867; St. Landry, *Le journal des Opeloulas,* January 4, 1868.

21. St. Landry, *Le courier des Opelousas,* December 28, 1867; *New Orleans Times,* December 21, 1867.

22. *New Orleans Daily Picayune,* September 3, 1868

23. *Ouachita Telegraph,* September 21, 1872.

24. *Donaldsonville Chief,* June 27, 1874.

25. Capt. F. A. Osbourn to Lt. L. O. Parker, Plaquemines, August 10, 1867, letters received, 1867–1870, box no. 4, book 60, Civil Affairs, Fifth Military District, War Department, National Archives.

26. *Bellevue Banner,* August 29, September 5, 12, 1868; St. Landry, *Le courier des Opelousas,* September 12, 1868.

27. 39th Congress, 2nd sess., Senate Exec. Doc. no. 6, 86.

28. *New Orleans Bulletin,* September 26, 1874.

29. General Hatch Report, published in Supplemental Report, 21, 257; 45th Congress, 3rd sess., Senate Report, no. 855, 11–12; *New Orleans Daily Picayune,* August 8, 1868.

30. 43rd Congress, 2nd sess., House Report no. 261, 366; *Natchitoches People's Vindicator,* July 25, 1874.

31. 43rd Congress, 2nd sess., House Report no. 261, 149; *Donaldsonville Chief,* June 25, 1881; *Baton Rouge Louisiana Capitolian,* August 23, 1881; St. James, *Le Louisianais,* December 11, 1869; *Louisiana Sugar Bowl,* July 3, September 4, 1873; *New Orleans Daily Picayune,* July 20, 21, 1868; *New Orleans Bee,* March 7, 1872; *Shreveport Times,* July 23, 1874, January 31, 1875; *Thibodeaux Sentinel,* September 1, 1883.

32. *Donaldsonville Chief,* June 25, 1881.

33. *Morehouse Clarion,* April 9, 1880.

34. *Baton Rouge Louisiana Capitolian,* August 23, 1881.

35. James Smallwood, "Perpetuation of Caste: Black Agricultural Workers in Reconstruction Texas," *Mid-America,* 61, January 1979, 5–23; Roger L. Ransom and Richard Sutch, "The Ex-slave in the Post-Bellum South: A Study of the Economic Impact of Racism in a Market Environment," *Journal of Economic History,* 33, March 1973, 137.

36. *Colfax Chronicle,* March 3, 10, 1878. For other similar incidents see *New Orleans Daily Picayune,* October 8, 1868, May 3, 1873; *Thibodeaux Sentinel,* March 24, 1880.

37. *New Orleans Daily Picyaune,* February 24, December 8, 1870; St. Charles, *L'Avant-Coureur,* September 16, 1871.

38. St. Charles, *L'Avant-Coureur,* September 16, 1871.

39. *New Orleans Daily Picyaune,* February 24, 1870.

40. *Baton Rouge Tri-Weekly Advocate,* June 23, 1871; *Donaldsonville Chief,* August 28, 1875; *New Orleans Bee,* May 19, 1877; *New Orleans Daily Picayune,* August 24, September 1, 1875, May 17, 22, 1877; *Ouachita Telegraph,* April 8, 1882, March 5, 1883; *Shreveport Times,* September 2, 1875, November 6, 7, 1880; *Shreveport Southwestern,* September 16, 1869; Millet, "The Lumber Industry," 55–57, 64.

41. *New Orleans Daily Picyaune,* September 1, 1875.

42. *Donaldsonville Chief,* August 28, 1875; *New Orleans Daily Picayune,* August 24, 1875.

43. Arnesen, *Waterfront Workers of New Orleans,* 83–89; Blassingame, *Black New Orleans,* 59–74; Taylor, *Louisiana Reconstructed,* 384–88.

44. Arnesen, *Waterfront Workers of New Orleans,* 21–23, 30, 39, 53–66.

45. *New Orleans Times,* December 22–24, 1865, October 18, 20, 1872, February 21, March 10, 17, May 6, 7, 1874, September 28, 1879, January 13, March 25, November 25, 1880, May 14, 1881; *New Orleans Bee,* October 16, 1873; *New Orleans Daily Picayune,* May 16, 1867, April 16, July 11, 1868, August 11, 27, October 7, 1869, October 13, 30, 31, 1873, May 6, June 25, 1874, February 5, 1875, November 23, December 1, 16, 1876; *New Orleans Bulletin,* April 3, 7, 1874, January 31, 1875.

46. *New Orleans Daily Picayune,* December 3, 1877, June 4, 1878, March 7, 1878, February 4, April 8, 13, October 7, November 24, 1884; *New Orleans Times-Democrat,* February 9, 10, June 30, July 9, 18, 1882, January 18, 1883, February 4, 5, 8, November 4, December 28, 29, 30, 1884; *New Orleans Times,* September 3, 7, 10, 22, 1880; *New Orleans Republican,* December 1, 1870; June 25, 1872; *New Orleans Bee,* June 24, 1872; *Iberville South,* November 11, 1880.

47. 43rd Congress, 2nd sess., House Report no. 261, 361; 44th Congress, 2nd sess., House Exec. Doc. no. 30, 280; Rable, *But There Was No Peace,* 16–32; Taylor, *Louisiana Reconstructed,* 61; Tolnay and Beck, *A Festival of Violence,* 166–201.

48. 41st Congress, 1st sess. House Misc. Doc. no. 12, 12–14; 41st Congress, 2nd sess., House Misc. Doc. no. 154, 64, 66, 69; 41st Congress, 1st sess., House Misc. Doc. no. 16, 5, 7, 9; J. F. White to Capt. L. H. Warren, May 20, 1868, micro 1027, vol. 24, 507, BFRAL; Oscar A. Rice to Capt. Wm. Sterling, Vermilionville, May 10, 1868, micro 1027, vol. 23, 1001, BFRAL; A. N. Murtagh to Capt. L. H. Warren, May 20, 1868, Abbeville, micro 1027, vol. 23, 434, BFRAL; James White to L. H. Warren, Vidalia, July 30, 1868, micro 1027, vol. 24, 788, BFRAL; Geo. Brunning to Hon. Charles Teller, Mayor of Carrolton, March 1868, letters sent, micro 1540, vol. 237, 30, BFRAL; Monthly Report, September

1867, vol. 287, BFRAL; Henderson to Sterling, September 23, 1867, letters sent, vol. 482, 133, BFRAL; Allie B. Webb, "Organization and Activities of the Knights of White Camelia in Louisiana, 1867–1869," *The Proceedings of the Louisiana Academy of Sciences,* 17, March 1954, 110–18; Dauphine. "Knights of the White Camelia," 173–90.

49. Supplemental Report, v.

50. Supplemental Report, v; Dauphine, "Knights of the White Camelia," 175.

51. Taylor, *Louisiana Reconstructed,* 164–73; Trelease, *White Terror,* 127–36.

52. 43rd Congress, 2nd sess., House Report no. 261, 5, 246, 410, 415, 477; Tolnay and Beck, *A Festival of Violence,* 5–6.

53. 43rd Congress, 2nd sess., House Report no. 261, 613, 786; Lafayette, *Louisiana Cotton Boll,* July 8, 1874.

54. Major W. F. Blackman and George W. Stafford, prominent White Leaguers from Natchitoches parish, launched a white supremacist newspaper called the *Caucasian* in the Spring of 1874. They then followed the lead of the *Shreveport Times* in advocating the murders of Republican candidates during the 1874 election. 43rd Congress, 2nd sess., House Report no. 261, 91, 361, 367; 44th Congress, 2nd sess., House Exec. Doc. no. 30, 194, 280, 383, 388; *Shreveport Times,* June 12, July 9, 20, 29, August 27, September 14, 1874; see also 43rd Congress, 2nd Sess, Senate Exec. Doc. no. 13, 32–33; Senate Exec. Doc. no. 17, 4–6; Nordhoff, *The Cotton States in the Spring and Summer of 1875,* 42; Wetta, "Bulldozing the Scalawags," 56.

55. Senate Exec. Doc. no. 17, 5, 50, 53; 43rd Congress, 2nd sess., House Report no. 261, 146–55, 175, 189, 230–36, 783, 953; 44th Congress, 2nd sess., House Misc. Doc. No. 30, 193, 382, 415; *New Orleans Daily Picayune,* August 21, 1874, January 28, 1875; *New Orleans Bee,* January 20, 1875; *New Orleans Republican,* August 9, 18, 20, December 25, 1874; *Shreveport Times,* July 19, 1874, January 21, 1875; Tunnell, *Crucible Reconstruction,* 203–4; Taylor, *Louisiana Reconstructed,* 299.

56. *Shreveport Times,* November 14, 16, December 25, 1874; see also 44th Congress, 2nd sess., House Exec. Doc. no. 30, 161, 209, 373, 376, 381, 385; 46th Congress, 2nd sess., Senate Report no. 693, part 11, 168; Senate Report no. 855, part 1, 21; General P. Sheridan to Secretary of War W. W. Belknap, January 10, 1875, in Senate Exec. Doc. no. 13, 31; 43rd Congress, 2nd sess., House Report no. 261, 395, 429; Taylor, *Louisiana Reconstructed,* 271, 290; Tunnell, *Crucible Reconstruction,* 199.

57. 43rd Congress, 2nd sess., House Report no. 261, 189, 333–37, 607, 613–15; Senate Exec. Doc. no. 17, 53; 46th Congress, 2nd sess., Senate Report no. 693, 172–73, 182; *Louisiana Sugar Bowl,* July 19, 29, 1874; *New Orleans Bee,* January 20, 1875; *New Orleans Daily Pica-*

yune, October 20, 29, 1874, January 28, 1875; *New Orleans Times,* January 27, 1875; *Shreveport Times,* January 18, 19, 21, 1875; Taylor, *Louisiana Reconstructed,* 274–75, 283.

58. Dauphine, "Knights of the White Camelia," 180–81; T. B. Tunnell Jr., "The Negro, The Republican Party, and the Election of 1876 in Louisiana," *Louisiana History,* 7, Spring 1966, 112–13; Hair, *Bourbonism and Agrarian Protest,* 4–5; Singletary, "White Supremacy," 29–52; Taylor, *Louisiana Reconstructed,* 484–85.

59. 44th Congress, 2nd sess., House Report no. 156, part 1, 42; *New Orleans Daily Picayune,* June 22, 1876.

60. Vandal, "The Policy of Violence," 179.

61. 45th Congress, 3rd sess., Senate Report, no. 855, ix; *Shreveport Times,* November 7, 8, December 29, 1879.

62. 45th Congress, 3rd sess., Senate Report, no. 855, ix, 44; *Ouachita Telegraph,* January 3, 1879; *Shreveport Times,* November 7, 8, December 29, 1878; Hair, *Bourbonism and Agrarian Protest,* 78; Vandal, "The Policy of Violence," 179–81.

63. 45th Congress, 3rd sess., Senate Report no. 855, part 1, 11–12; *Shreveport Daily Standard,* November 3, 7, 1878; *Shreveport Times,* October 19, November 3, 1878, March 19, 1879; *Ouachita Telegraph,* January 3, 1879; Hair, *Bourbonism and Agrarian Protest,* 76–78; Vandal, "The Policy of Violence," 179.

64. Forth-fifth Congress, 3rd sess., Senate Report no. 855, v-x, 44; *Bellevue Banner,* September 26, 1878; *Natchitoches People's Vindicator,* September 28, October 12, 1878; *New Orleans Bee,* October 22, 25, 1878; *New Orleans Daily Picayune,* October 17, 18, 22, 1878; *Ouachita Telegraph,* October 11, 1878, January 3, 1879; *Shreveport Times,* November 7, 8, December 29, 1878, January 15, 1879; Hair, *Bourbonism and Agrarian Protest,* 77–78; Vandal, "The Policy of Violence," 179–81.

65. Dauphine, "Knights of the White Camelia," 173–90; Litwack, *Been in the Storm So Long,* 278–79; Wetta, "Bulldozing the Scalawags," 43–58.

66. 41st Congress, House Misc. Doc. no. 154, part 2, 443; 44th Congress, 2nd sess., House Exec. Doc. no. 30, 170, 264, 459, 478; Delatte, "The St. Landry Riot," 47.

67. Dauphine, "Knights of the White Camelia," 175; Tolnay and Beck, *A Festival of Violence,* 171–72.

68. 43rd Congress, 2nd sess., House Report no. 261, 134–35, 146–49, 241, 282–83, 362–64, 391, 584, 617; Wetta, "Bulldozing the Scalawags," 54–55.

69. 41st Congress, 2nd sess., House Misc. Doc. No. 154, xviii, 132–42; 44th Congress, 2nd sess., House Exec. Doc. no. 30, 165, 206, 254, 262–67, 270, 367; *New Orleans Republican,* May 20, 1869; *New*

Orleans Times, October 15, 1875; *Franklin Planter's Banner,* May 26, 1869; Tunnell, *Crucible Reconstruction,* 154.

70. 43rd Congress, 2nd Sess, House Report no. 261, 169; 44th Congress, 2nd Sess, House Exec. Doc. no. 30, 394, 434, 442, 443, 490, 494, 506, 542, 546; Brasseaux, *Acadian to Cajun,* 130.

71. 44th Congress, 2nd sess., House Exec. Doc. no. 30, 170–71, 178, 179, 180, 184, 185, 187, 267; *New Orleans Daily Picayune,* August 8, 1868; *New Orleans Republican,* August 9, 18, 1874.

Chapter 4: *Toward a Reign of Terror*

1. *Donaldsonville Chief,* September 6, 1877.

2. H. Jon Rosenbaum and Peter C. Sedeiberg, "Vigilantism: An Analysis of Established Violence," in *Vigilante Politics,* ed. Rosenbaum and Sedeiberg, Philadelphia, 1976, 17.

3. Richard M. Brown, *Strain of Violence, Historical Studies of American Violence and Vigilantism,* New York, 1975, 114–17, 154; Butterfield, *All God's Children,* 55–56; Robert P. Ingalls, "Lynching and Establishment Violence in Tampa, 1858–1935," *Journal of Southern History,* 53, no. 4, November 1987, 614–16; Michael Pfeifer, "Lynching and Criminal Justice in South Louisiana, 1878–1930," *Louisiana History,* 40, no. 2, Spring 1999, 155–77; H. Jon Rosenbaum and Peter C. Sedeiberg, "Vigilantism: An Analysis of Established Violence" in *Vigilante Politics,* edited by Rosenbaum and Sedeiberg, Philadelphia, 1976, 17.

4. David J. Bodenhamer, "Law and Disorder on the Early Frontier: Marion County, Indiana, 1823–1850," *Western Historical Quarterly,* 10, July 1979, 323–36; W. Fitzbugh Brundage, *Lynching in the New South, Georgia and Virginia, 1880–1930,* Urbana, Ill., 1993; William C. Culberson, *Vigilantism: Political History of Private Power in America,* New York, 1990; Philip J. Ethington, "Vigilantes and the Police: The Creation of a Professional Police Bureaucracy in San Francisco, 1847–1900," *Journal of Social History,* 21, Winter 1987, 197–227; William F. Holmes, "Whitecapping in Mississippi: Agrarian Violence in the Populist Area," *Mid-America,* 55, April 1973, 134–48; David A. Johnson, "Vigilance and the Law: The Moral Authority of Popular Justice in the Far West," *American Quarterly,* 33, Winter 1981, 558–86; Paul Lack, "Slavery and Vigilantism in Austin, Texas, 1840–1860," *Southwestern Historical Quarterly,* 85, no. 1, July 1981, 1–20; James R. McGovern, *Anatomy of a Lynching, The Killing of Claude Neal,* Baton Rouge, 1982; Roger D. McGrath, *Gunfighters, Highwaymen & Vigilantes, Violence on the Frontier,* Berkeley, 1984; Patrick B. Nolan, *Vigilantes On the Middle Border, A Study of Self-Appointed Law Enforcement of the Upper Mississippi*

from 1840 to 1880, New York, 1987; Robin Wiegman, "The Anatomy of Lynching," *Journal of Historical Sexuality,* 3, January 1993, 445–67; George C. Wright, *Racial Violence in Kentucky, 1865–1940: Lynchings, Mob Rule and 'Legal Lynching,'* Baton Rouge, 1990.

5. Ingalls, "Lynching and Establishment Violence in Tampa," 613; McGovern, *Anatomy of a Lynching,* 3; Rable, *But There Was No Peace,* 98.

6. Jay Corzine, James Creech, and Lin Corzine, "Black Concentration and Lynchings in the South: Testing Blalock's Power-Threat Hypothesis," *Social Forces,* 61, March 1983, 776–96; Jay Corzine, Lin Huff-Corzine, and James C. Creech, "The Tenant Labor Market and Lynching in the South: A Test of Split Labor Market Theory," *Sociological Inquiry,* 58, Summer 1988, 261–78; Charles David Phillips, "Exploring Relations Among Forms of Social Control: The Lynching and Execution of Blacks in North Carolina, 1889–1918," *Law & Society Review,* 21, 1987, 362–73; John S. Reed, "Percent Black and Lynching: A Test of Blalock's Theory," *Social Forces,* 50, March 1972, 356–60; Stewart E. Tolnay, E. M. Beck, and James L. Massey, "Black Lynchings: The Power Threat Hypothesis Revisited," *Social Forces,* 67, March 1989, 605–27; Tolnay and Beck, *A Festival of Violence.*

7. Several sociologists have studied the pattern of lynching in Louisiana during the 1890s. See R. P. Bagozzi, "Populism and Lynching in Louisiana: Comment on Inverarity," *American Sociological Review,* 42, 1977, 355–58; James M. Inverarity, "Populism and Lynching in Louisiana, 1889–1896: A Test of Erickson's Theory of the Relationship Between Boundary Crises and Repressive Justice," *American Sociological Review,* 41, April 1976, 262–80; Whity Pope and Charles Ragan, "Mechanical Solidarity, Repressive Justice and Lynching in Louisiana," *American Sociological Review,* 42, April 1977, 363–70; Ibra M. Wasserman, "Southern Violence and the Political Process: Comment on Inverarity," *American Sociological Review,* 42, 1977, 359–62. Moreover, Professor Wright, *Racial Violence in Kentucky,* is the only systematic study of post–Civil War lynching in a particular state in the South. See also Tolnay and Beck, *A Festival of Violence,* 53.

8. Brown, *Strain of Violence,* 97, 150; James E. Cutler, *Lynch-Law: An Investigation into the History of Lynching in the United States,* New York, 1906, 135; Johnson, "Vigilance and the Law," 561.

9. Brown, *Strain of Violence,* 95–96; Johnson, "Vigilance and the Law," 564–69; Rable, *But There Was No Peace,* 98; Peter Sederberg, "The Phenomonology of Vigilantism in Contemporary America: An Interpretation," *Terrorism: An International Journal,* 1, 1978, 287–303.

10. Several authors have defined lynching as the expression of "popular justice." Samuel Walker, *Popular Justice: A History of American Crim-*

inal Justice, New York, 1980; Tolnay and Beck, *A Festival of Violence,* 86–118.

11. Brown, *Strain of Violence,* 95–96; Nolan, *Vigilantes On the Middle Border,* 22, 29.

12. *Baton Rouge Tri-Weekly Advocate,* June 1, 1868; *Baton Rouge Tri-Weekly Capitolian,* August 11, 1881; *Morehouse Clarion,* August 12, 1881; *Louisiana Sugar Bowl,* June 6, 1876; Nolan, *Vigilantes On the Middle Border,* 2.

13. In 1906, James Cutler came up with a definition that has since been widely accepted: "A lynching may be defined as an illegal and summary execution at the hands of a mob, or a number of persons, who have in some degree the public opinion of the community behind them." Professor Brown adopted a similar yet more limited definition of lynching: "The practice or custom by which persons are punished for real or alleged crimes without due process of law." Brown, *Strain of Violence,* 21; Cutler, *Lynch-Law,* 276; Johnson, "Vigilance and the Law," 564; Nolan, *Vigilantes On the Middle Border,* 2–3.

14. Professor Wright adopted a similar conservative approach in his investigation of lynching choosing not to count as lynchings murders and other incidents in which blacks were apparently in a position to defend themselves. However, all cases defined as "instant vigilantism" by Professor Brown were considered as lynching for the purpose of the present study. Brown, *Strain of Violence,* 103; Wright, *Racial Violence in Kentucky,* 70–71.

15. *Lafayette Advertiser,* June 21, 1873; *New Orleans Bulletin,* October 22, 1875; *Richland Beacon News,* October 11, 1873; Wyatt-Brown, *Southern Honor,* 401–2, 453.

16. Professor Wright in his examination of lynching in Kentucky reached similar results. Furthermore, we find it important to differentiate the number of people lynched from the number of lynching incidents. Cutler, *Lynch-Law,* 160; Wright, *Racial Violence in Kentucky,* 71.

17. Professor Inverarity who studies lynching in Louisiana during the years 1889–1896 has obtained an annual average of 12. The annual average of the post–Civil war period, a much more troubled and violent period, was 16 as shown by this study's data. Inverarity, "Populism and Lynching in Louisiana," 263.

18. Cutler, *Lynch-Law,* 132, 218.

19. St. Landry, *Le courier des Opelousas,* July 18, 1874; Taylor, *Louisiana Reconstructed,* 267, 284–85; Williamson, *Crucible of Race,* 117; Wyatt-Brown, *Southern Honor,* 104, 349, 454.

20. My investigation unveils only 5 incidents of lynching in which 8 blacks were killed during the 1850s. Indeed whites had been responsible for the plantation's disciplinary measures serving regularly on patrols. Under the parish law, all whites above twenty-one years old were required

in rural areas to serve on patrols to maintain the plantation discipline. The patrol's job was to apprehend and summarily punish all fugitives or runaway slaves found roaming in the countryside without a pass from their master. During the 1850s Louisiana regulations concerning patrols were reinforced. Professor David Grimsted reports for the years 1828–1861 for the whole South the killing of 414 slaves by lynching mobs. These lynchings were concentrated in 35 different incidents that took place during panic time about slave insurrection. Grimsted, *American Mobbing*, 135–36. U. B. Phillips, Revised Statutes of Louisiana, New Orleans, 1856, 49–65; Minutes of the Police Jurors, Ascension parish, January 1853, Caddo Parish, June 1861, Lafayette Parish, September 1860, September 1861.

21. Brown, *Strain of Violence*, 151; Cutler, *Lynch-Law*, 135, 198, 205.

22. These percentages are comparable to the one for the 1890s. To be correctly understood, these percentages must be put in relation with the fact that lynching was essentially a rural phenomenon and that blacks formed more than 60 percent of the population in rural Louisiana. Inverarity, "Populism and Lynching in Louisiana," 262–80; Brown, *Strain of Violence*, 21; Williamson, *Crucible of Race*, 185; Woodward, *Origins of the New South*, 350–51; Wright, *Racial Violence in Kentucky*, 71.

23. Tolnay and Beck, *A Festival of Violence*, 31.

24. The percentage of integrated mobs found in the data is comparable to the one for the period of 1882 to 1930. Tolnay and Beck, *A Festival of Violence*, 93.

25. 43rd Congress, 2nd sess., House Report, no. 261, 617; Lafayette, *Cotton Boll*, October 1, 1873; St. James, *Le Louisianais*, December 11, 1869; see also *Morehouse Clarion*, September 10, 1880; *Natchitoches People's Vindicator*, May 19, 26, 1877; *New Orleans Daily Picayune*, April 8, 1877; Hair, *Bourbonism and Agrarian Protest*, 15; Wright, *Racial Violence in Kentucky*, 102.

26. 43rd Congress, 2nd sess., House Report no. 261, 192, 439.

27. 43rd Congress, 2nd sess., House Report no. 261, 617; *Louisiana Sugar Bowl*, May 11, 1876.

28. A recent study on Georgia and Virginia shows the importance of economic particularity and distribution of agricultural labor on the geographical distribution of lynchings. Brundage, *Lynching in the New South;* Tolnay and Beck, *A Festival of Violence*, 119.

29. Jay Corzine et. al., "Black Concentration and Lynchings in the South," 788; Inverarity, "Populism and Lynching in Louisiana," 268–69; Reed, "Percent Black and Lynching," 356–60; Tolnay et al., "Black Lynchings," 605–27; Tolnay and Beck, *A Festival of Violence*, 38–39, 55–85.

30. The data for this study confirms Cutler's view that there was no

distinct correlation between the distribution of lynching and the percentage of blacks in the population. Indeed, the Bayou, Eastern Bluff Land, Mississippi Delta, and the Sugar Bowl areas had large black populations with lower rates of lynchings, while the Southwestern Frontier, North Central Hill, and Florida Parishes areas had small black populations and higher rates of lynchings. Cutler, *Lynch-Law*, 186, 187, 190; Tolnay and Beck, *A Festival of Violence*, 36–37. For different conclusions see Brown, *Strain of Violence*, 214; Wright, *Racial Violence in Kentucky*, 71–72.

31. Cutler, *Lynch-Law*, 191.

32. 44th Congress, 2nd sess., House Exec. Doc. no. 30, 546; *Abbeville Meridional*, July 5, 1879; *Louisiana Sugar Bowl*, July 20, 1874; Taylor, *Louisiana Reconstructed*, 284.

33. John Cromie to Governor H. C. Warmoth, May 2, 5, 1870, Warmoth Papers; *New Orleans Republican*, May 8, June 5, 1870.

34. Lafayette, *Louisiana Cotton Ball*, October 1, 1873; *New Orleans Daily Picayune*, September 14, 1873; *New Orleans Republican*, September 16, November 16, 1873; St. Landry, *Le courier des Opelousas*, November 14, 1873; *Richland Beacon News*, October 1, 1873; *Louisiana Sugar Bowl*, September 11, 1873; *Thibodeaux Sentinel*, October 4, 1873; Brown, *Strain of Violence*, 164; Taylor, *Louisiana Reconstructed*, 420.

35. Tolnay and Beck, *A Festival of Violence*, 7–10, 19.

36. Professor David Grimsted argues that sadism was already a major phenomenon in Southern lynchings before the Civil War. Grimsted, *American Mobbing*, 103–106. Brown, *Strain of Violence*, 216; Hair, *Bourbonism and Agrarian Protest*, 187–89; Shapiro, *White Violence and Black Response*, 31; Taylor, *Louisiana Reconstructed*, 420; Williamson, *Crucible of Race*, 117, 187–88.

37. 44th Congress, 2nd sess., House Exec. Doc. no. 30, 169, 209, 250, 251, 255, 257, 272, 424, 426, 437, 442, 460, 461, 476, 478, 488, 498, 510, 514, 542; *New Orleans Republican*, January 29, 1869; Tolnay and Beck, *A Festival of Violence*, 23; Wyatt-Brown, *Southern Honor*, 454.

38. 44th Congress, 2nd sess., House Exec. Doc. no. 30, 461, 467, 488.

39. Supplemental Report, 256.

40. 44th Congress, 2nd sess., House Exec. Doc. no. 30, 169, 209, 250, 251, 255, 257, 272, 342, 424, 426, 437, 442, 460, 461, 467, 476, 477, 478, 488, 498, 510, 514, 542; *New Orleans Republican*, January 29, 1869.

41. General P. H. Sheridan to Secretary of War, W. W. Belnap, January 10, 1875, 43rd Congress, 2nd sess., Senate Exec. Doc. no. 13, 31; 43rd Congress, 2nd sess., House Report no. 261, 387, 395, 429; 44th Congress, 2nd sess., House Exec. Doc. no. 30, 180, 381; 43rd Congress, 2nd sess., Senate Exec. Doc., no. 17, 13; Rable, *But There Was No Peace*,

135; Taylor, *Louisiana Reconstructed,* 271, 290; Tunnell, *Crucible Reconstruction,* 199.

42. 43rd Congress, 2nd sess., House Report no. 261, 362–64, 391.

43. Tolnay and Beck, *A Festival of Violence,* 64.

44. *Abbeville Meridional,* August 20, 1881; *Baton Rouge Weekly Advocate,* July 7, 1883; *Morehouse Clairon,* September 2, 1881; *New Orleans Daily Picayune,* September 19, 1881; *New Orleans Times,* January 8, 1880; *Richland Beacon News,* October 1, 1881; *St. Tammany Farmer,* January 3, 1880; *Louisiana Sugar Bowl,* October 8, 1881; Brown, *Strain of Violence,* 218; Hair, *Bourbonism and Agrarian Protest,* 187, 189; Shapiro, *White Violence and Black Response,* 31; Wyatt-Brown, *Southern Honor,* 437, 454.

45. 39th Congress, 2nd sess., Senate Exec. Doc. no. 6, 86; 43rd Congress, 2nd sess., House Report no. 261, 439, 440; 44th Congress, 2nd sess., House Exec. Doc. no. 30, 176, 363, 399, 431; *Baton Rouge Weekly Advocate,* November 18, 1882; *Colfax Chronicle,* December 4, 1880; *Lafayette Advertiser,* May 20, 1882; *Natchitoches Semi-Weekly Times,* October 9, 1869; *Ouachita Telegraph,* May 19, 1883; *Assumption Pioneer,* December 14, 1878; *Rapides Democrat,* February 28, 1877; *Richland Beacon News,* June 20, 1874, March 24, 1877, September 3, 1881; *St. Tammany Farmer,* January 3, 1880; *Shreveport Times,* January 31, 1875, May 15, 1883, April 3, 29, October 23, 24, 31, 1884; *Thibodeaux Sentinel,* April 14, 1877.

46. *New Orleans Daily Picayune,* September 27, 1878.

47. *Abbeville Meridional,* April 6, 1878, March 13, 1880, February 10, 1884; *Bellevue Banner,* February 16, 1867; *Carroll Record,* March 6, 1869; *Iberville South,* May 21, 1881; *Lafayette Advertiser,* August 30, 1873; *Le Foyer Creole of St. John the Baptist,* April 26, 1882, May 23, 1883; *Louisiana Democrat,* November 8, 1882; *New Orleans Bulletin,* January 18, 1876; *Shreveport Times,* April 25, 1879; *Louisiana Sugar Bowl,* February 2, 1871, August 29, 1872, August 14, 1873, May 11, 1876, December 12, 1878; Brown, *Strain of Violence,* 106–7, 124.

48. *New Orleans Bulletin,* May 15, 20, 1874; *New Orleans Daily Picayune,* April 27, 1876, July 23, August 3, 10, 1881, January 27, March 16, 1882; *New Orleans Times,* August 15, 1880, July 20, 21, 1881. Joy Jackson, "Crime and the Conscience of a City," *Louisiana History,* 9, no. 3, Summer 1968, 234.

49. *Baton Rouge Tri-Weekly Advocate,* June 1, 1868.

50. *New Orleans Bulletin,* October 15, 1875; *New Orleans Times,* October 15, 1875. See also *New Orleans Daily Picayune,* January 17, 1874; *Colfax Chronicle,* September 18, December 10, 1880; *St. Tammany Farmer,* December 21, 1878; *Richland Beacon News,* September 18, 1878; Rable, *But There Was No Peace,* 178–79.

51. These were cases of people clearly killed by lynch mobs that I could not link to any "terrorist" organization such as the Knights of the White Camelia.

52. Professor Wright reaches a similar percentage (29%) of murders and attempted murders as causes for lynching in Kentucky. Wright, *Racial Violence in Kentucky,* 96.

53. Tolnay and Beck, *A Festival of Violence,* 114.

54. Professor David Grimsted demonstrates clearly how mob violence was already used before the Civil War in the South as a means to intimidate moderate whites and to enforce white men's rule. Grimsted, *American Mobbing,* 124. 44th Congress, 2nd sess., House Exec. Doc. no. 30, 498, 501; *New Orleans Bulletin,* May 14, 1874; *New Orleans Republican,* February 5, 1869; Brown, *Strain of Violence,* 214.

55. Tolnay and Beck, *A Festival of Violence,* 63.

56. 44th Congress, 2nd sess., House Exec. Doc. no. 30, 373, 376, 385; 46th Congress, 2nd sess., Senate Report no. 693, part 11, 168; *New Orleans Crescent,* April 14, 1868; *Shreveport Times,* June 12, July 20, August 27, September 14, November 16, December 25, 1874; Taylor, *Louisiana Reconstructed,* 285; see also Butterfield, *All God's Children,* 39–40; Tolnay and Beck, *A Festival of Violence,* 66–68.

57. 44th Congress, 2nd sess., House Exec. Doc. no. 30, 519; *New Orleans Semi-Weekly Louisianian,* June 15, 1872; St. Landry, *Le journal des Opelousas,* June 8, 1872.

58. 44th Congress, 2nd sess., House Exec. Doc. no. 30, 459.

59. 44th Congress, 2nd sess., House Exec. Doc. no. 30, 408; 43rd Congress, 2nd sess., House Report no. 261, 343.

60. *New Orleans Bee,* April 14, 1874; see also *Bellevue Banner,* November 8, 1883; *Claiborne Guardian,* August 3, 1881; *St. Landry Democrat,* July 14, 1883; *Shreveport Times,* April 29, May 30, 1884; *Baton Rouge Weekly Advocate,* July 7, 1883.

61. Tolnay and Beck, *A Festival of Violence,* 18, 87–88.

62. 43rd Congress, 2nd sess., House Report no. 261, 196; *Baton Rouge Weekly Advocate,* July 7, 1883; *Claiborne Guardian,* August 3, 1881; St. Landry, *Le courier des Opelousas,* August 6, 1870; *New Orleans Republican,* December 25, 1874, December 24, 1875; *Richland Beacon News,* October 6, 1877, September 3, 1881; *Shreveport Times,* February 27, 1872, June 12, October 27, 29, 1874, January 31, June 18, 21, September 21, December 24, 1875, September 28, 1877, March 28, 1879, December 9, 23, 1883, February 5, May 30, October 23, November 27, 1884; Ayers, *Vengeance and Justice,* 243; Brown, *Strain of Violence,* 70–71, 112–13, 115, 116, 123; Nolan, *Vigilantes On the Middle Border,* 8–9, 11; Rable, *But There Was No Peace,* 98.

63. 41st Congress, 2nd sess., House Misc. Doc. no. 154, 340–41, 355, 374; 43rd Congress, 2nd sess., House Report no. 261, 365, 441, 765, 780–81, 787, 953; 44th Congress, 2nd sess., House Exec. Doc. no. 30, 70, 283, 384; *Baton Rouge Tri-Weekly Advocate,* January 10, 1866; St. Landry, *Courier des Opelousas,* October 3, 1868; *Louisiana Democrat,* November 2, 1868; *Natchitoches People's Vindicator,* August 15, 1874; *Ouachita Telegraph,* September 21, 1872; *Richland Beacon News,* June 20, 1874; *Shreveport Times,* June 30, July 12, 19, 29, 1874, January 31, 1875, November 7, 8, 13, December 29, 1878; Dan T. Carter, "The Anatomy of Fear: The Christmas Day Insurrection Scare of 1865," *Journal of Southern History,* 42, August 1976, 345–64; Rable, *But There Was No Peace,* 71, 76, 84, 127, 131, 134–35, 178–79.

64. *New Orleans Daily Picayune,* June 30, 1876.

65. Forth-fifth Congress, 3rd sess., Senate Report No. 855, vi–ix; *New Orleans Democrat,* July 7, 1878; *Shreveport Times,* October 16, 29, November 3, 7, 8, December 29, 1878; *Shreveport Daily Standard,* July 30, September 23, October 15, 29, 1878; Hair, *Bourbonism and Agrarian Protest,* 78–84.

66. *Ouachita Telegraph,* October 18, 1878.

67. *Baton Rouge Weekly Advocate,* September 23, 1881; *Bellevue Banner,* November 8, 1883; *Donaldsonville Chief,* September 8, 1877; *Natchitoches People's Vindicator,* December 5, 1875, May 5, 1877, August 10, 1878; St. Landry, *Le courier des Opelousas,* August 6, 1870; St. Landry, *Le journal des Opelousas,* October 28, 1871; *Richland Beacon News,* February 7, 1880, February 5, 1881; *St. Landry Democrat,* April 27, 1878; *Thibodeaux Sentinel,* November 6, 1875; *Shreveport Times,* June 12, 1874, April 3, October 23, 24, 31, 1884; Cutler, *Lynch-Law,* 153.

68. Ida B. Wells-Barnett, *On Lynchings: Southern Horrors; A Red Record & Mob Rule in New Orleans,* Reprint, New York, 1969, 8–10; Shapiro, *White Violence and Black Response,* 38; Williamson, *Crucible of Race,* 117.

69. 44th Congress, 2nd sess., House Exec. Doc. No. 30, 437; *Louisiana Sugar Bowl,* June 6, 1876; Shapiro, *White Violence and Black Response,* 37.

70. Tolnay and Beck, *A Festival of Violence,* 88–89.

71. *Claiborne Guardian,* August 3, 1881; *Thibodeaux Sentinel,* April 14, 1877; *St. Tammany Farmer,* July 1, 1882, February 23, 1884; *Shreveport Times,* July 17, 1883, February 5, October 23, 1884; Williamson, *Crucible of Race,* 117; Wright, *Racial Violence in Kentucky,* 77.

72. *Shreveport Times,* July 17, 1883, February 5, October 23, 1884; Ayers, *Vengeance and Justice,* 243, 246–47, 252; McGovern, *Anatomy*

of a Lynching, 7–8; Rable, *But There Was No Peace*, 97–98; Shapiro, *White Violence and Black Response*, 30, 51; Wright, *Racial Violence in Kentucky*, 76–77.

73. *Donaldsonville Chief*, November 29, 1879; *New Orleans Bulletin*, October 22, 1875; *New Orleans Daily Picayune*, August 2, 1878, December 31, 1879; *New Orleans Times*, December 31, 1879; *Richland Beacon News*, October 11, 1873; *St. Tammany Farmer*, January 3, 1880; *Shreveport Times*, October 23, 31, 1884; Rable, *But There Was No Peace*, 99; Wright, *Racial Violence in Kentucky*, 64–65.

74. *Shreveport Times*, October 24, 31, November 1, 1884.

75. *Donaldsonville Chief*, June 16, 1877; *Richland Beacon News*, March 24, 1877.

76. *St. Tammany Farmer*, July 1, 1882.

77. Brown, *Strain of Violence*, 120–21; Johnson, "Vigilance and the Law," 559; Millet, "Cattle and Cattlemen," 324–25.

78. *New Orleans Republican*, September 16, November 16, 1873; St. Landry, *Le courier des Opelousas*, November 14, 1873; Millett, "Cattle and Cattlemen," 324–25; Shugg, *Origins of Class Struggle*, 61–62.

79. 43rd Congress, 2nd sess., House Report, no. 261, 439; *Monroe Bulletin*, March 19, 1884; *Richland Beacon News*, October 13, 1877; *Shreveport Times*, June 18, 21, 1875, March 28, 1879, December 23, 1883, April 3, 1884; *Thibodeaux Sentinel*, April 14, 1877; Brown, *Strain of Violence*, 126–27, 160.

80. Professor Grimsted shows how the tolerance of violence by the Southern people was part of the Southern culture of violence. Grimsted, *American Mobbing*, 85–88. 41st Congress, 2nd sess., House Misc. Doc. no. 154, 36; *Monroe Bulletin*, March 19, 1884; *New Orleans Republican*, August 2, 1870, December 25, 1874; *Shreveport Times*, May 8, 1875; Ayers, *Vengeance and Justice*, 245, 249; Brown, *Strain of Violence*, 146–47, 161; Cutler, *Lynch-Law*, 152; McGovern, *Anatomy of a Lynching*, 5; Rable, *But There Was No Peace*, 70, 98; Shapiro, *White Violence and Black Response*, 31; Tolnay and Beck, *A Festival of Violence*, 25–28; Wright, *Racial Violence in Kentucky*, 91–96, 102–3.

Chapter 5: Homicides in a Gender Perspective

1. *New Orleans Daily Picayune*, April 13, 1870.

2. Martha Hodes, "The Sexualization of Reconstruction Politics: White Women and Black Men in the South After the Civil War," *Journal of Historical Sexuality*, 3, January 1993, 402–17; Suzanne Lebsock, "Radical Reconstruction and Property Rights of Southern Women," *Journal of Southern History*, May 1977, 195–216; Stephanie McCurry, "The

Politics of Yeoman Household in South Carolina," in *A Family Venture: Men and Women on the Southern Frontier,* edited by Joan E. Cashin, New York, 1991; Charles E. Rosenberg, "Sexuality, Class, and Role in 19th-Century America," *American Quarterly,* 25, 1973, 131–53.

3. Freda Adler, *Sisters in Crime: The Rise of the New Female Criminal,* New York, 1975; Barbara Brenzel, "Domestication as Reform: A Study of the Socialization of Wayward Girls, 1856–1905," *Harvard Educational Review,* 50, May 1980, 196–213; Nicole Gonthier, "Délinquantes ou victimes, les femmes dans la soiété lyonnaise au XVe siècle," *Revue Historique,* 1984, 24–46; Eric A. Johnson, "Women as Victims and Criminals: Female Homicide and Criminality in Imperial Germany, 1873–1914," *Criminal Justice History,* 6, 1985, 151–75; Els Kloek, "Criminality and Gender in Leiden's Confessieboeken, 1678–1794," *Criminal Justice History,* 11, 1990, 1–29; André Lachance, "Women and Crime in Canada in the Early Eighteenth Century, 1712–1759," in *Crime and Criminal Justice in Europe and Canada,* edited by Louis A. Knafla, Waterloo, 1981, 157–78; Carol Smart, *Women, Crime and Criminology: A Feminist Critique,* London, 1976; Claudine Schweber, "Women and Federal Crime in the Early Twentieth Century," *The Law and American Society: New Historical Perspectives and Resources,* Washington, 1978; Wolfgang and Ferracuti, *The Subculture of Violence,* 258–59.

4. J. M. Beattie, "The Criminality of Women in Eighteenth-Century England," *Journal of Social History,* 8, 1975, 82; Daly and Wilson, *Homicide,* 137–61, 169; Malcom Feeley, "The Decline of Women in the Criminal Process: A Comparative History," *American Justice History,* 15, 1994, 274; Barbara Hanawalt, "The Female Felon in Fourteenth-Century England," *Viator,* 5, 1974, 257; V. Verkko, "Static and Dynamic 'Laws' of Sex and Homicides" in *Studies in Homicides,* edited by M. E. Wolfgang, New York, 1967, 36–44.

5. This is also in line with the findings of recent studies bearing on other regions or periods. Beattie, "The Criminality of Women," 82; Hanawalt, "The Female Felon," 257; Johnson, "Women as Victims and Criminals," 151–75; Kloek, "Criminality and Gender," 1–29; Wolfgang and Ferracuti, *The Subculture of Violence,* 258–59.

6. Johnson, "Women as Victims and Criminals," 151–52; Smart, *Women, Crime and Criminology,* 14; Susan M. Socolow, "Women and Crime in Buenos Aires, 1757–1797," *Latin American Studies,* 12, 1980, 43.

7. 44th Congress, 2nd sess., House Exec. Doc. no. 30, 170, 264, 459, 478; *Opelouas Journal,* October 28, 1871. A similar case had occurred in 1868 in Bossier parish. 44th Congress, 2nd sess., House Exec. Doc. no. 30, 205.

8. Dell Upton, ed., *Madaline, Love and Survival in Antebellum New*

Orleans, The Private Writings of a Kept Woman, Athens, Ga., 1996, 26–27.

9. Daly and Wilson develop their sociological gender analysis from a biological framework by which they argue that males played a greater role in society because biological competition is greater between males than females. Daly and Wilson, *Homicide*, 137–40.

10. Nisbett and Cohen, *Culture of Honor*, 27; Annie Firor Scott, *The Southern Lady, From Pedestal to Politics, 1830–1930*, Chicago, 1970, 26, 35, 37, 42; Wyatt-Brown, *Southern Honor*, 228–30; Williamson, *Crucible of Race*, 25. Not all women accepted the norms imposed by the Southern culture of honor and the Victorian morality. But they almost always paid a high price for violating these norms. Upton, *Madaline*, 9, 24–27.

11. *New Orleans Daily Picayune*, June 24, July 28, November 6, 1868; Ayers, *Vengeance and Justice*, 266; Scott, *The Southern Lady*, 26, 35, 37, 42; Upton, *Madaline*, 12–13; Wyatt-Brown, *Southern Honor*, 227, 450.

12. Claudia Goldin, "Female Labor Force Participation: The Origins of Black and White Difference, 1870–1880," *Journal of Economic History*, 37, March 1977, 91–96; Herbert Gutman, *The Black Family in Slavery and Freedom, 1750–1925*, New York, 1976, 167–68; Litwack, *Been in the Storm So Long*, 243–44; Foner, *Reconstruction*, 85–87.

13. 41st Congress, 2nd sess., House Misc. Doc. no. 154, 443; 44th Congress, 2nd sess., House Exec. Doc. no. 30, 189, 260, 460, 478, 542.

14. *New Orleans Bee*, February 20, 1873.

15. 44th Congress, 2nd sess., House Exec. Doc. no. 30, 167, 177, 179, 210, 423, 434, 435, 446, 447, 461, 500, 542, 543.

16. 44th Congress, 2nd sess., House Exec. Doc. no. 30, 177, 179, 435; *Rapides Gazette*, April 12, 1873.

17. Forth-fourth Congress, 2nd sess., House Exec. Doc. no. 30, 167, 423, 442.

18. 44th Congress, 2nd sess., House Exec. Doc., no. 30, 167, 177, 179, 210, 325, 418, 421–23, 425–26, 435, 442, 444–47, 461, 498, 501.

19. 44th Congress, 2nd sess., House Exec. Doc. no. 30, 167, 210, 423, 434, 446, 447, 500, 543.

20. *New Orleans Daily Picayune*, November 14, 1871; *New Orleans Times-Democrat*, February, 23, 1884; *Shreveport Times*, February, 5, 1884.

21. Vandal, "When Religion Mingled With Commerce," 145; see also Wyatt-Brown, *Southern Honor*, 273, 278–79.

22. In modern industrial society, a third to one half of the homicides occur within family circles. Seven percent of the killings that occurred in

Texas in 1969 were perpetrated by wives against their husbands. Johnson, "Women as Victims and Criminals," 161–62; Wyatt-Brown, *Southern Honor*, 381–82; see also Redfield, *Homicide, North and South*, 178–80.

23. Wyatt-Brown, *Southern Honor*, 381–83.

24. Nesbitt and Cohen, *Culture of Honor*, 65–66.

25. Scott, *The Southern Lady*, 58–59; Wyatt-Brown, *Southern Honor*, 231, 283; David Peterson, "Wife-beating: An American Tradition," *Journal of Interdisciplinary History*, 23, Summer 1992, 97–118; E. Pleck, "Wife-beating in Nineteenth Century America," *Victimology*, 4, 1979, 60–74.

26. 43rd Congress, 2nd sess., House Report no. 261, 539, 555, 639, 645; 44th Congress, 2nd sess., House Exec. Doc. no. 30, 421, 425, 451, 452, 453, 454, 522; *Donaldsonville Chief*, March 8, 1884; *Iberville South*, August 11, 1883; St. James, *Le Louisianais*, October 12, 1872; *Louisiana Sugar Bowl*, March 14, April 3, 1873; *New Orleans Bee*, July 2, 1870; *New Orleans Daily Picayune*, August 6, 1869, December 15, 1870, November 14, 1871, January 25, 1875, April 6, 1876, August 30, 1884; *New Orleans Times-Democrat*, February 23, 1884; St. Landry, *Le journal des Opelousas*, April 25, 1868; *Shreveport Southwestern*, September 23, 1868; *Shreveport Times*, January 31, 1875, February 5, 1884; Redfield, *Homicide, North and South*, 178, 180.

27. 43rd Congress, 2nd sess., House Report no. 261, 539, 555, 639, 645; *Louisiana Sugar Bowl*, February 20, 1873, April 3, 1877; *New Orleans Daily Picayune*, November 14, 1871; *New Orleans Times-Democrat*, February 23, 1884; St. Landry, *Le journal des Opelousas*, April 25, 1868; *Shreveport Times*, February 5, 1884; *Thibodeaux Sentinel*, May 12, 1877; Redfield, *Homicide, North and South*, 178, 180.

28. Scott, *The Southern Lady*, 54–55; Upton, *Madaline*, 24–25.

29. *New Orleans Daily Picayune*, June 24, July 11, October 2, November 4, 1868, May 27, 1870; *New Orleans Republican*, September 10, 15, 1871; *New Orleans Times*, March 26, 1866; *New Orleans Southern Star*, January 17, 1866.

30. *New Orleans Daily Picayune*, January 13, 1869.

31. Supplemental Report, 256.

32. *New Orleans Daily Picayune*, September 23, 1868.

33. 44th Congress, 2nd sess., House Exec. Doc. no. 30, 167, 210, 423, 434, 446, 447, 500, 543; Litwack, *Been in the Storm So Long*, 265–66, 277; Scott, *The Southern Lady*, 53; Upton, *Madaline*, 19.

34. *New Orleans Daily Picayune*, September 26, 1871.

35. 44th Congress, 2nd sess., House Exec. Doc. no. 30, 325, 404; *Louisiana Sugar Bowl*, May 28, 1874; *Richland Beacon News*, August 27, 1881.

36. 44th Congress, 2nd sess., House Exec., Doc., No. 30, 273; 43rd Congress, 2nd sess., House Report no. 261, 515; *Louisiana Sugar Bowl,* June 6, 1876; St. James, *Le Louisianais,* June 10, 1871.

37. Newspapers scraps on "Destroying the Guillory," U.S. Marshall Report, Attorney General Correspondence for Louisiana, September 1873, RG 60, National Archives, Washington, D.C.

38. Studies show the difficulty encountered by law enforcement officers during unstable periods. W. R. Jones, "Violence, Criminality, and Culture Disjunction on the Anglo-Irish Frontier: The Example of Armagh, 1350–1550," *Criminal Justice History,* 2, 1981, 29–47; Mark D. Szuchman, "Disorder and Social Control in Buenos Aires, 1810–1860," *Journal of Interdisciplinary History,* 17, Summer 1984, 83–110.

39. Prisons and Asylums, Report of the Commissioners to the City Council, 1882, 4–5; Annual Report of the Board of Control of the Louisiana State Penitentiary for 1866, 60, for 1867, 111; Proceedings of City Council of New Orleans, July 15, 1870, 247, February 14, 1871, 232; *New Orleans Daily Picayune,* November 7, 1867, October 2, 1869, December 22, 1871, March 24, June 16, 1872, July 16, 1874; *New Orleans Republican,* February 13, 15, 1874; *New Orleans Southern Star,* April 4, 1866; *New Orleans Times,* April 4, 1866, October 2, 1872; Ayers, *Vengeance and Justice,* 63.

40. Hanawalt, "The Female Felon," 123.

41. Annual Report of the Board of Metropolitan Police for 1870, 24, for 1871, 42, for 1872, 36, for 1873, 25, for 1874, 33, and for 1875, 37.

42. We have not included infanticide in the data set for the methodological reasons stated in the introduction. However it is important to deal with this problem as it is most revealing about homicidal behavior, particularly where women are concerned.

43. Peter Hoffer and N. E. Hull, *Murdering Mothers: Infanticide in England and New England, 1558–1803,* New York 1981; Roger Lane, *Roots of Violence in Black Philadelphia, 1860–1900,* Cambridge, Mass., 1986, 135; Lane, *Violent Death in the City,* 91; R. W. Malcolmson, "Infanticide in Eighteenth Century" in *Crime in England, 1550–1800,* edited by J. S. Cockburn, Princeton, 1977, 187–209; James C. Mohr, *Abortion in America, The Origins and Evolution of a National Policy, 1800–1900,* New York, 1978, 77–85; Keith Wrightson, "Infanticide in European History," *Criminal Justice History,* 3, 1982, 1–21; Wyatt-Brown, *Southern Honor,* 381.

44. Police authorities reported an average of three women per year arrested for infanticide during Reconstruction. *New Orleans Daily Picayune,* November 5, 1868, January 4, June 25, 1871, September 9, 1874, August 10, 1875, July 10, August 8, September 6, 1879; *New Orleans*

Times, August 8, September 6, 1879. Annual Report of the Board of the Metropolitan Police to the General Assembly of Louisiana for 1870, 24, for 1871, 42, for 1872, 36, for 1873, 25, for 1874, 33, and for 1875, 37.

45. *Baton Rouge Tri-Weekly Advocate,* June 23, 1871.

46. *New Orleans Daily Picayune,* August 10, 1875.

47. Annual Report of the Board of the Metropolitan Police to the General Assembly of Louisiana for 1870, 24, for 1871, 42, for 1872, 36, for 1873, 25, for 1874, 33, and for 1875, 37.

48. *New Orleans Daily Picayune,* August 7, 10, 1875.

49. Verkko, "Static and Dynamic 'Laws'" 36–44. See also Beattie, "The Criminality of Women," 82; Hanawalt, "The Female Felon," 257; Wolfgang, *Patterns in Criminal Homicides,* 61–64.

50. *Donaldsonville Chief,* March 8, 1884; St. James, *Le Louisianais,* October 12, 1872.

Chapter 6: Economic Conflict and Homicide

1. *Louisiana Sugar Bowl,* February 25, 1875; *New Orleans Daily Picayune,* February 20, 1875; *New Orleans Bulletin,* February 20, 1875.

2. Two groups of French-speaking people had come to Louisiana bringing with them two different sets of cultural baggage. While French settlers, who became known as Creoles, concentrated mainly in New Orleans, the second group were descendants of the 5,000 Acadians who settled the areas of the Atchaflaya river basin, the southwest coastal region, the Lafourche Bayou, and the Opelousas prairies during the late eighteenth century. Brasseaux, *Acadian to Cajun,* 75, 87.

3. *Baton Rouge Weekly Gazette & Comet,* April 13, 1856; Bertrand, *The Many Louisianas,* 20–21; Brasseaux, *Acadian to Cajun,* 75, 87; Glenn R. Conrad, ed. *The Cajuns: Essays on their Culture and History,* Lafayette, La., 1978, 1–20, 115–28; James H. Dormon, *The People Called Cajuns: An Introduction to an Ethnohistory,* Lafayette, La., 1983; Estaville, "Changeless Cajuns," 117–40.

4. *St. Landry Democrat,* October 21, 1882; *Thibodeaux Sentinel,* September 1, 1883.

5. Tolnay and Beck, *A Festival of Violence,* 119–65.

6. Forth-fourth Congress, 2nd sess., House Exec. Doc. no. 30, 383; Lockett, *Louisiana As It Is,* 58–59. The parishes of Lafourche, Terrebonne, and Assumption, areas with numerous bayous and swamps, were particularly troubled by bands of robbers. *Assumption Pioneer,* July 26, December 6, 1879, September 25, 1880; *Iberville Sentinel,* August 14, September 18, 1869, November 11, 18, 1872; *Lafayette Advertiser,*

August 21, 1869; *Louisiana Sugar Bowl,* August 29, 1872, November 13, 1873; *New Orleans Times-Democrat,* November 12, 1883; St. Landry, *Le courier des Opelousas,* February 4, 1871.

7. *Abbeville Meridional,* September 10, 1884; *Baton Rouge Advocate-Comet,* December 13, 1866; *Baton Rouge Tri-Weekly Gazette & Comet,* April 3, 1866, December 5, 1867; *Baton Rouge Tri-Weekly Advocate,* February 6, 1866; *Donaldsonville Chief,* August 22, 1874, May 22, 1880; *Lafayette Advertiser,* June 12, 1869; *Le Foyer Créole of St. John the Baptist,* April 26, 1882; St. James, *Le Louisianais,* June 11, July 15, 1871, August 14, December 4, 1875; *Louisiana Sugar Bowl,* February 2, 1871, August 7, 14, 1873, April 23, 1874, April 8, 1875; *New Orleans Daily Picayune,* December 8, 1868, October 20, 1869, September 9, 1871; St. Landry, *Le courier des Opelousas,* February 4, 1871; *Assumption Pioneer,* December 6, 1879, September 25, 1880; *Iberville Sentinel,* August 14, 1869; Taylor, *Louisiana Reconstructed,* 91, 322.

8. *Donaldsonville Chief,* September 8, 1877; *Lafayette Advertiser,* June 2, September 18, 1869, July 12, 1873; *Louisiana Sugar Bowl,* May 13, 1873; *New Orleans Daily Picayune,* September 3, 1868, November 19, 1869, May 29, 1870; *New Orleans Republican,* June 5, 1870.

9. *Iberville South,* May 21, 1881; *Le Foyer Créole de St. Jean de Baptiste,* April 26, 1882, May 23, 1883, October 22, 1884; St. James, *Le Louisianais,* June 11, July 15, 1871, August 14, Dec. 4, 1875; *Louisiana Sugar Bowl,* February 2, 1871, August 29, 1872, August 14, 1873, May 11, 1876, December 12, 1878; *New Orleans Bulletin,* May 14, 1874, January 18, 1876; *New Orleans Daily Picayune,* October 20, 1869, August 24, 1870.

10. 44th Congress, 2nd sess., House Misc. Doc. no. 34, 169, 178, 179, 295; 43rd Congress, 2nd sess., House Report no. 261, 375; *Baton Rouge Tri-Weekly Advocate,* December 6, 1867, June 9, 1869, May 9, 1870; *Baton Rouge Tri-Weekly Advocate,* December 9, 1866; *Baton Rouge Tri-Weekly Gazette & Comet,* April 3, 1866, February 21, December 5, 1867; *Louisiana Sugar Bowl,* August 12, 1872; *New Orleans Daily Picayune,* September 12, November 25, 1869; St. Landry, *Le courier des Opelousas,* November 14, 1873; St. Landry, *Le journal des Opelousas,* August 12, 1871; Brasseaux, *Acadian to Cajun,* 75; Taylor, *Louisiana Reconstructed,* 422–23.

11. *New Orleans Daily Picayune,* September 3, 1868.

12. H. Henderson to Captain W. Sterling, September 23, 1867, micro 1027, vol. 482, 133, BFRAL; *New Orleans Times,* August 9, 1868.

13. Oscar A. Rice to Captain W. Sterling, Vermilionville, May 10, 1868, micro 1027, vol. 23, 1001, BFRAL; A. N. Murtagh to Capt. L. H. Warren, May 20, 1868, Abbeville, micro 1027, vol. 23, 434, BFRAL; 41st

Congress, 1st sess., House Misc. Doc. no. 16, 5, 7, 9; 41st Congress, 1st sess., House Misc. Doc. no. 12, 12–14; 41st Congress, 2nd sess., House Misc. Doc., no. 154, 64, 66, 69; Trelease, *White Terror,* 128.

14. Supplemental Report, v; 41st Congress, 2nd sess., House Misc. Doc. No. 154, 476–77, 495–96; Delatte, "The St. Landry Riot," 41–49; Dauphine, "Knights of the White Camelia," 173–90.

15. 44th Congress, 2nd sess., House Exec. Doc. No. 30, 179; Oscar A. Rice to Major B. F. Hutchins, Vermilionville, September 30, 1868, micro 1027, vol. 23, 1138, BFRAL; R. W. Mullen to B. F. Hutchins, Franklin, October 21, 1868, micro 1027, vol. 23, 797, BFRAL; M. Violet to L. H. Warren, Opelousas, September 21, 1868, micro 1027, vol. 23, 1693, BFRAL; *Franklin Planter's Banner,* September 5, October 17, 1868; *New Orleans Daily Picayune,* October 19, 20, 27, 1868; *New Orleans Republican,* October 20, 1868; *New Orleans Times,* October 20, 1868; Dauphine, "Knights of the White Camelia," 173–90; Trelease, *White Terror,* 128–29.

16. 44th Congress, 2nd sess., House Exec. Doc. No. 30, 236–37; Wetta, "Bulldozing the Scalawags," 53.

17. 43rd Congress, 2nd sess., House Report No. 261, 640; 44th Congress, 2nd sess., House Exec. Doc. No. 30, 317.

18. 43rd Congress, 2nd sess., House Report No. 261, 246; 43rd Congress, 2nd sess., Senate Exec. Doc. No. 13, 1–33; 43rd Congress, 2nd sess., Senate Exec. Doc. No. 17, 1–75; 44th Congress, 2nd sess., House Exec. Doc. No. 30, 249–71; St. James, *Le Louisianais,* May 10, 24, 31, 1873; *New Orleans Bee,* May 7, 9, 17, 27, 1873; *New Orleans Republican,* April 13, 1873; *Louisiana Sugar Bowl,* May 8, 1873.

19. 44th Congress, 2nd sess., House Exec. Doc. No. 30, 174–75, 222, 408; *Louisiana Sugar Bowl,* September 17, 1874; Henry Lewis Griffin, *The Attakapas County, A History of Lafayette Parish,* Gretna, La., 1974, 65–71.

20. 43rd Congress, 2nd sess., House Report No. 261, 343, 791–92; 44th Congress, 2nd sess., House Exec. Doc. No. 30, 364, 408, 546; *New Orleans Times,* January 29, 1875; Griffin, *The Attakapas County,* 65–71.

21. *Baton Rouge Capitolan Advocate,* July 25, August 23, 1884; *New Orleans Daily Picayune,* August 12, 18, 1884; St. Landry, *Le courier des Opelousas,* August 9, 1884; St. Landry, *Le journal des Opelousas,* August 9, 1884; Vandal, "Politics and Violence in Bourbon Louisiana: The Loreauville Riot of 1884 as a Case Study," *Louisiana History,* 30, no. 1, Winter 1989, 37–38.

22. *Baton Rouge Weekly Advocate,* November 8, 1884; *Baton Rouge Capitolian Advocate,* July 25, August 23, 1884; *Baton Rouge Weekly Truth,* November 7, 1884; *New Orleans Daily Picayune,* August 12, 18, November 3, 1884; *St. Landry Democrat,* November 8, 1884; St. Landry,

Le courier des Opelousas, August 9, 1884; St. Landry, *Le journal des Opelousas,* August 9, 1884; Vandal, "The Loreauville Riot," 37–38.

23. State Legislature Report of 1868, xviii, 132–42; 44th Congress, 2nd sess., House Exec. Doc. No. 30, 206; 44th Congress, 2nd sess., House Misc. Doc. no. 34, part 3, 100; *New Orleans Republican,* May 20, 1869; *Franklin Planter's Banner,* May 26, 1869; *Rapides Gazette,* April 12, 1873.

24. *Louisiana Democrat,* September 21, 1871; *New Orleans Times,* April 27, 1874; St. Landry, *Le journal des Opelousas,* February 18, 1871; *Rapides Gazette,* January 13, 1872; *Tensas Gazette,* March 11, 1882; Hingsmith, "Some Aspects of Reconstruction," 470–77.

25. *New Orleans Times,* July 4, 1871; *Thibodeaux Sentinel,* November 29, 1873; Taylor, *Louisiana Reconstructed,* 364–65.

26. Millett, "Some Aspects of Agricultural Retardation," 37–61; Taylor, *Louisiana Reconstructed,* 364–65.

27. *Baton Rouge Capitolian Advocate,* August 2, 1884. For the annual prices of sugar see *New Orleans Daily Picayune,* September 1, 1873, September 1, 1874, September 1, 1876; *New Orleans Bee,* June 15, 1879; Jeffrey Gould, "The Strike of 1887: Louisiana Sugar War," *Southern Exposure,* 12, November-December 1984, 47; Taylor, *Louisiana Reconstructed,* 376.

28. *Donaldsonville Chief,* February 7, 1880; *Louisiana Sugar Bowl,* June 1, 15, 1866, March 16, 1882; Heitman, "Louisiana Sugar Planters' Association," 315–37; Millet, "Some Aspects of Agricultural Retardation," 53; Taylor, *Louisiana Reconstructed,* 360–61.

29. *Baton Rouge Capitolian Advocate,* August 2, 1884; *Baton Rouge Weekly Truth,* November 8, 11, 1882, June 22, 1883; *New Orleans Daily Picayune,* September 1, 1876, December 30, 1883; *New Orleans Times-Democrat,* January 13, August 15, 1884.

30. *Baton Rouge Weekly Truth,* November 8, 1882; *St. Landry Democrat,* March 22, 1884; *New Orleans Times-Democrat,* August 19, 1884; *New Orleans Daily Picayune,* December 30, 1883, July 25, 1884; *Shreveport Times,* January 19, 1884.

31. *Baton Rouge Weekly Truth,* January 11, 18, 1884.

32. *Baton Rouge Tri-Weekly Gazette & Comet,* June 30, 1860.

33. *Baton Rouge Weekly Advocate,* October 14, 1881; *Morehouse Clarion,* April 9, 1880, January 29, 1881; *Natchitoches People's Vindicator,* March 19, 1881; *New Orleans Times,* July 4, 1871; *Thibodeaux Sentinel,* November 29, 1873. Tolnay and Beck, *A Festival of Violence,* 119–65.

34. *Baton Rouge Weekly Advocate,* October 14, 1881; *Morehouse Clarion,* April 9, 1880, January 29, 1881; *Natchitoches People's Vindica-*

tor, March 19, 1881; *New Orleans Times,* July 4, 1871; *Assumption Pioneer,* May 31, 1879; *Thibodeaux Sentinel,* November 29, 1873; Smallwood, "Perpetuation of Caste," 6–7.

35. *Assumption Pioneer,* May 31, 1879, June 2, 1883; *Baton Rouge Capitolian Advocate,* August 2, 1884; *Franklin Planter's Banner,* November 9, 1870; *Natchitoches People's Vindicator,* February 5, 1881; *Louisiana Sugar Bowl,* February 3, 1876, March 9, 1876; *New Orleans Daily Picayune,* October 24, 1869; *Thibodeaux Sentinel,* July 31, 1880, January 28, 1882; Millett, "Some Aspects of Agricultural Retardation," 37–61; Taylor, *Louisiana Reconstructed,* 364–67.

36. *Iberville South,* February 4, 1871; *New Orleans Daily Picayune,* January 7, 26, 1866, January 20, February 4, 8, 23, 1871.

37. *Baton Rouge Weekly Advocate,* October 14, 1881; *Iberville South,* February 4, 1871; *Morehouse Clarion,* April 9, 1880; *Natchitoches People's Vindicator,* March 19, 1881; *Louisiana Sugar Bowl,* March 17, 1883; *New Orleans Daily Picayune,* January 7, 26, 1866, February 4, 23, 1871.

38. *Baton Rouge Weekly Advocate,* October 14, 1881; *Louisiana Sugar Bowl,* January 6, 1876; *New Orleans Semi-Weekly Louisianian,* January 21, 1882; *New Orleans Republican,* November 21, 1869; *Assumption Pioneer,* June 2, 1883.

39. *Donaldsonville Chief,* January 5, 1878.

40. Experienced sugar laborers who mastered the lucrative skill of cutting the cane at the inch bottom were particularly in demand in southern Louisiana as they could make the difference between a profit or a loss for the planters. Pfeifer, "Lynching and Criminal Justice," 158. *Baton Rouge Capitolian Advocate,* December 20, 1881; *Claiborne Guardian,* December 28, 1881; *New Orleans Daily Picayune,* February 24, 1870; *New Orleans Times,* December 21, 1881.

41. *Assumption Pioneer,* June 2, 1883; *New Orleans Semi-Weekly Louisianian,* January 21, 1882; *New Orleans Republican,* November 21, 1869.

42. *Baton Rouge Weekly Truth,* January 26, 1883; *Carroll Watchman,* August 12, 1875; *Franklin Planter's Banner,* November 9, December 7, 1870; *Natchitoches Semi-Weekly Times,* March 30, 1867; *New Orleans Republican,* November 21, 1869; *New Orleans Daily Picayune,* January, 7, 26, 1866; *Rapides Democrat,* December 8, 1880; *Thibodeaux Sentinel,* November 16, 1872; Taylor, *Louisiana Reconstructed,* 388–91.

43. *Baton Rouge Weekly Advocate,* October 14, 1881; *Natchitoches People's Vindicator,* March 19, 1881; *Morehouse Clarion,* April 9, 1880; *Louisiana Sugar Bowl,* March 2, 1876.

44. *Donaldsonville Chief,* October 20, 1877.

45. N. W. Morris to B. J. Hutchins, November 10, 1868, Houma, letters sent, vol. 295, 85–89, BFRAL; *Thibodeaux Sentinel,* October 19, 1867; Taylor, *Louisiana Reconstructed,* 332.

46. *Franklin Planter's Banner,* November 9, 1870; *Thibodeaux Sentinel,* November 16, 1872.

47. Taylor, *Louisiana Reconstructed,* 369.

48. 44th Congress, 2nd sess., House Misc. Doc. No. 34, part 3, 49–50; Journal of the House of Representatives of the State of Louisiana, New Orleans, 1874, 62; *Donaldsonville Chief,* October 20, 1877; *Louisiana Sugar Bowl,* January 15, 22, 1874; *New Orleans Bee,* January, 15, 17, 1874; *New Orleans Daily Picayune,* January 10, 16, 20, 1874; *New Orleans Republican,* January 20, 1874; *New Orleans Times,* January 15, 17, 18, 1874; St. Landry, *Le journal des Opelousas,* January 23, 1874; St. Landry, *Le courier des Opelousas,* January 23, 1874; *Thibodeaux Sentinel,* January 24, 1874; Gould, "The Strike of 1887," 46; Taylor, *Louisiana Reconstructed,* 318, 385–86.

49. A substantial number of blacks in St. John the Baptist parish refused to sign new contracts and to leave their cabins while they attempted to prevent planters from hiring replacement workers. Eventually they were persuaded to accept the new contract. Journal of the House of Representatives of the State of Louisiana, New Orleans, 1874, 62; *Louisiana Sugar Bowl,* January 15, 22, 1874; *New Orleans Bee,* January, 15, 17, 1874; *New Orleans Daily Picayune,* January 10, 16, 17, 20, 1874; *New Orleans Republican,* January 20, 1874; *New Orleans Times,* January 15, 17, 18, 1874; St. Landry, *Le courier des Opelousas,* January 23, 1874; *Thibodeaux Sentinel,* January 24, 1874; Gould, "The Strike of 1887," 46.

50. *Donaldsonville Chief,* January 5, 1878; *Lafayette Advertiser,* April 5, 1879; *Monroe Bulletin,* April 7, 1880; *New Orleans Daily Picayune,* January 20, 1880; Gould, "The Strike of 1887," 48.

51. *Abbeville Meridional,* April 3, 10, 1880; *Assumption Pioneer,* March 13, 1880; *Donaldsonville Chief,* March 27, May 1, 8, 1880; St. James, *Le Louisianais,* April 17, May 1, 1880; *New Orleans Bee,* May 15, 1880; *New Orleans Daily Picayune,* March 20, 1880; *New Orleans Times,* March 27, April 1, 2, May 15, 16, 1880; *Rapides Democrat,* May 19, 1880; *Louisiana Sugar Bowl,* April 28, 1880; *Thibodeaux Sentinel,* March 24, 27, 1880; Bernard A. Cook and James R. Watson, *Louisiana Labor: From Slavery To "Right-to-Work,"* New York, 1985, 58; Hair, *Bourbonism and Agrarian Protest,* 175.

52. *Abbeville Meridional,* April 3, 10, 1880; *Donaldsonville Chief,* March 27, May 22, 1880; *New Orleans Daily Picayune,* March 20, 1880; *New Orleans Times,* March 27, April 1, 2, 1880; *Thibodeaux Sentinel,* March 24, 27 1880; Hair, *Bourbonism and Agrarian Protest,* 172.

53. *Abbeville Meridional,* April 3, 10, 1880; *New Orleans Bee,* April

8, 1880; St. James, *Le Lousianais de St-Jacques*, April 17, May 1, 1880; Hair, *Bourbonism and Agrarian Protest*, 172.

54. *Iberville South*, August 9, 1884; *New Orleans Daily Picayune*, April 19, 1881; *New Orleans Times-Democrat*, August 15, 1884; Cook and Watson, *Louisiana Labor*, 58; Hair, *Bourbonism and Agrarian Protest*, 175.

55. William Ivy Hair, "Black Protest and White Power," *Many Pasts: Readings in American Social History*, vol. 2, Englewood Cliffs, N.J., 1973, 33–35.

56. In January 1874 blacks in New Iberia planned to strike under the direction of representative Henry Demas. Meanwhile, two radical leaders, C. B. Darrall and J. Hale Sypher, were organizing a labor union among the blacks in the Teche. *Donaldsonville Chief*, August 28, 1875; *New Orleans Daily Picayune*, August 24, September 1, 1875; *Shreveport Times*, September 2, 1875; *Thibodeaux Sentinel*, April 24, 1880; Hair, "Black Protest and White Power," 32.

57. *Baton Rouge Tri-Weekly Advocate*, June 23, 1871; *Donaldsonville Chief*, August 28, 1875; *New Orleans Bee*, May 19, 1877; *New Orleans Daily Picayune*, August 24, September 1, 1875, May 17, 22, 1877; *Ouachita Telegraph*, April 8, 1882, March 5, 1883; *Shreveport Times*, September 2, 1875, November 6, 7, 1880; *Shreveport Southwestern*, September 16, 1869.

58. Ransom and Sutch, "The Ex-slave in the Post-Bellum South," 137–38; Smallwood, "Perpetuation of Caste," 5–7; Tolnay and Beck, *A Festival of Violence*, 119–65.

59. *Colfax Chronicle*, March 3, 10, 1878; *New Orleans Daily Picayune*, October 8, 1868, May 3, 1873; *Thibodeaux Sentinel*, March 24, 1880; Shugg, *Origins of Class struggle*, 252.

60. *Baton Rouge Capitolian Advocate*, August 2, 1884; *Donaldsonville Chief*, July 19, 1884; *New Orleans Daily Picayune*, March 13, 1884; *Shreveport Times*, January 19, 1884; Hair, *Bourbonism and Agrarian Protest*, 75–76; Shugg, *Origins of Class Struggle*, 152–57; Taylor, *Louisiana Reconstructed*, 360.

61. 45th Congress, 3rd sess., Senate Report No. 855, xxi.

Chapter 7: Black Violence in Post–Civil War Rural Louisiana

1. *Franklin Planter's Banner*, December 12, 1871. See also an article from the same newspaper on September 8, 1871.

2. The quality and quantity of recent literature on the black experience is outstanding. See Blassingame, *Black New Orleans*; Boles and Nolen, eds., *Interpreting Southern History*, 162–307; Barbara J. Fields,

Slavery and Freedom on the Middle Ground, Maryland During the Nineteenth Century, New Haven, 1985; Gerald D. Jaynes, *Branches Without Roots, Genesis of the Black Working Class in the American South, 1862–1882,* New York, 1986; Litwack, *Been in the Storm So Long;* Rabinowitz, *Race Relations in the Urban South;* Tunnell, *Crucible Reconstruction;* Wayne, *Reshaping of Plantation Society.*

3. Huff-Corzine et al., "Southern Exposure," 1906–24; Harold Garfinkel, "Research Notes on Inter and Intra-Racial Homicides," *Social Forces,* 27, 1949, 469–81; Lane, *Roots of Violence in Black Philadelphia,* 131–43; Messner, "Regional and Racial Effects on the Urban Homicide Rates," 1000–1002; Thomas F. Pettigrew and Rosalind B. Spier, "The Ecological Structure of Negro Homicides," *American Journal of Sociology,* 67, no. 6, Spring 1962, 621–29; Porterfield, "Indices of Suicides and Homicides," 488; Robert J. Sampson, "Urban Black Violence: The Effect of Male Joblessness and Family Disruption," *American Journal of Sociology,* 93, no. 2, September 1987, 348–82; Yangsock Shin, Davor Jedlicko, and Everett S. Lee, "Homicide Among Blacks," *Phylon,* 38, 1977, 398–407; Schultz, "Why Negroes Carry Weapons," 476–83; Robert Staples, "White Racism, Black Crime and American Justice: An Application of the Colonial Model to Explain Crime and Race," *Phylon,* 36, 1975, 14–22; Williams, "Economic Sources of Homicide," 283–89; Marvin E. Wolfgang, *Crime and Race: Conception and Misconceptions,* New York, 1964, 31; Wolfgang and Ferracuti, *The Subculture of Violence,* 263–64.

4. Sampson, "Urban Black Violence," 349.

5. 43rd Congress, 2nd sess., House Report no. 261, 539, 555, 639, 645; see also *Bellevue Banner,* July 19, 1870; *Jefferson State Register,* July 23, 1870; *Louisiana Democrat,* February 23, 1875; *New Orleans Crescent,* July 17, 1870; *New Orleans Daily Picayune,* October 20, 1874, January 16, February 6, 16, 1875; *New Orleans Times,* June 30, July 12, 19, 29, 1874, January 11, 31, 1875; *Shreveport Times,* January 31, 1875, November 7, 8, 13, December 29, 1878.

6. Ayers, *Vengeance and Justice,* 227; Redfield, *Homicide, North and South,* 13, 171–75; Taylor, *Louisiana Reconstructed,* 421.

7. *Jefferson State Register,* October 15, 1870.

8. On May 26, 1866 the *Bellevue Banner* asserted that following the war "the crime that is daily committed the country over, is appalling. We scarcely read our own exchange, that is not filled with accounts of revolting acts that we deem unfit to place before our readers" and concluded that "the negroes in the South monopolize the criminal calendar." See also *Baton Rouge Tri-Weekly Advocate,* September 24, 1866; *Shreveport Times,* January 24, 1875; *Franklin Planter's Banner,* December 12, 1871; *Louisiana Sugar Bowl,* November 24, 1874, April 3, 1877; *Thibodeaux Sentinel,* May 12, 1877.

9. 43rd Congress, 2nd sess., House Report No. 261, 9–10; *Bellevue Banner,* May 26, 1866; *Louisiana Democrat,* February 23, 1875; St. Landry, *Le courier des Opelousas,* July 22, 1875; *Assumption Pioneer,* January 24, 1880; *Shreveport Times,* January 24, 1875; *Louisiana Sugar Bowl,* April 3, August 21, 1873, November 24, 1874, April 3, 1877; *Thibodeaux Sentinel,* May 12, 1877.

10. 43rd Congress, 2nd sess., House Report no. 261, 439, 617; *Attakapas Register,* May 18, 1878; *Baton Rouge Tri-Weekly Advocate,* September 24, 1866; *Baton Rouge Weekly Advocate,* January 4, 1881; *Baton Rouge Weekly Truth,* December 9, 1882; *Bellevue Banner,* April 8, 1880; *Donaldsonville Chief,* November 18, 1879; *Iberville South,* October 19, 1878; *Baton Rouge Louisiana Capitolian,* September, 22, 1881; St. James, *Le Louisianais,* December 11, 1869; *Natchitoches People's Vindicator,* July 25, 1874; *New Orleans Daily Picayune,* September 22, 1874; *New Orleans Times,* February 25, 1879; St. Landry, *Le courier des Opelousas,* July 22, 1875; *Assumption Pioneer,* June 28, 1879, January 24, 1880; *Richland Beacon News,* September 24, 1881; *St. Landry Democrat,* February 9, 1878; *Shreveport Southwestern,* November 30, 1870, August 8, 1871; *Louisiana Sugar Bowl,* January 10, April 3, 1873, March 24, 1881; *Thibodeaux Sentinel,* May 12, 1877, September 1, 1883.

11. *Louisiana Democrat,* May 10, 1870; *New Orleans Commercial Bulletin,* September 11, 1869; *Franklin Planter's Banner,* September 8, 1869, March 1, 1871.

12. *Shreveport Daily Standard,* June 19, 1880.

13. *Assumption Pioneer,* August 5, 1882; see also *Donaldsonville Chief,* July 3, 1880.

14. *Iberville South,* April 28, 1883.

15. *Bellevue Banner,* May 26, 1866; *Louisiana Democrat,* November 2, 1868, May 10, 1871; *New Orleans Daily Picayune,* January 25, February 6, 1875; *New Orleans Times,* January 11, 1875; St. Landry, *Le courier des Opelousas,* July 22, 1875; *Ouachita Telegraph,* April 15, 1871, April 15, 1879; *Assumption Pioneer,* August 5, 1882; *Franklin Planter's Banner,* September 8, 1871; *Shreveport Daily Standard,* June 19, 1880; *Louisiana Sugar Bowl,* August 21, 1873, November 24, 1874, April 3, 1877; *Thibodeaux Sentinel,* May 12, 1877.

16. *New Orleans Daily Picayune,* January 25, February 6, 1875.

17. *Louisiana Democrat,* February 23, 1875.

18. C. Vann Woodward acknowledged in 1951 that "the record of violence should not be hastily attributed to the negro, for whites killed much more often, in proportion to their number, than did negroes. Race violence there was, undoubtedly, but it was only a part of the general relation of Southern violence and can be understood best against that background." Eric Foner reached a similar conclusion: "And after emanci-

pation, freedmen proved far less prone than whites to commit violent acts, either within their own community or against outsiders." Foner, *Reconstruction*, 436; Woodward, *Origins of the New South*, 159–60.

19. Taylor, *Louisiana Reconstructed*, 91, 421; Williamson, *Crucible of Race*, 58.

20. *Iberville South*, November 11, 1882.

21. The overall percentages are extrapolated from the total number in the table with the "unknown" removed.

22. 43rd Congress, 2nd sess., House Report no. 261, 149, 953; 44th Congress, 2nd sess., House Exec. Doc. no. 30, 477; *Shreveport Times*, January 31, 1875.

23. James W. Blackwell, "Ethnic Inequality and the Rates of Homicides," *Social Forces*, 69, September 1990, 53–70; Blau and Blau, "The Cost of Inequality," 126–27; Parker, "Poverty, Subculture of Violence," 985; Ramage, "Homicide in the Southern States," 214–15.

24. Ramage confirms that situation for the 1890s. Ramage, "Homicide in the Southern States," 216.

25. *Iberville South*, April 28, 1883; *Louisiana Democrat*, February 9, 1880; *Natchitoches People's Vindicators*, August 22, 1874; *Louisiana Sugar Bowl*, November 24, 1870.

26. The annual rates for the years 1865 to 1876 and 1877 to 1884 have been respectively calculated on the basis of the rural population for both blacks and whites as reported in the Federal Census Report of 1870 and 1880.

27. Vandal, "Property Offenses," 127–53. See also Ayers, *Vengeance and Justice*, 176–77.

28. This is also in line with the findings of recent studies bearing on other regions or periods. Beattie, "The Criminality of Women," 82; Hanawalt, "The Female Felon," 257; Wolfgang and Ferracuti, *The Subculture of Violence*, 258–59.

29. *New Orleans Daily Picayune*, January 25, 1875.

30. *Assumption Pioneer*, January 24, 1880; Redfield, *Homicide, North and South*, 188–89.

31. *New Orleans Daily Picayune*, December 19, 1871; *New Orleans Times-Democrat*, February 23, 1884; *Shreveport Times*, February 5, 1884. Homicides resulting from trivial or unspecified causes cannot be dismissed simply as a weakness of this data set. Other studies have found similar patterns and show that, generally speaking, 35 percent of homicides resulted from trivial or unspecified causes. Redfield, *Homicide, North and South*, 189; Wolfgang, *Patterns in Criminal Homicide*, 191.

32. Hackney, "Southern Violence," 921–22.

33. Ayers, *Vengeance and Justice*, 231–33, 344–45; Butterfield, *All God's Children*, 86.

34. Butterfield, *All God's Children*, 47, 53, 84–85.

35. *Iberville South*, April 28, 1883; *Louisiana Democrat*, February 9, 1880; *Natchitoches People's Vindicator*, August 22, 1874; *Louisiana Sugar Bowl*, November 24, 1870; *New Orleans Semi-Weekly Louisianan*, June 11, 1881.

36. 43rd Congress, 2nd sess., House Report no. 261, 539, 555, 639, 645; *Donaldsonville Chief*, March 8, 1884; St. James, *Le Louisianais*, October 12, 1872; *New Orleans Daily Picayune*, November 14, 1871, August 30, 1884; *New Orleans Times-Democrat*, February 23, 1884; St. Landry, *Le journal des Opelousas*, April 25, 1868; *Shreveport Southwestern*, September 23, 1868; *Shreveport Times*, January 31, 1875, February 5, 1884.

37. St. Landry, *Le courier des Opelousas*, July 22, 1875; Butterfield, *All God's Children*, 53.

38. *Iberville South*, October 19, 1878; St. Landry, *Le courier des Opelousas*, July 22, 1875; *Natchitoches People's Vindicator*, July 25, 1874; *Thibodeaux Sentinel*, May 12, 1872, September 1, 1883; *Richland Beacon News*, September 24, 1881.

39. Biennial Report of the State Attorney General of Louisiana, 1888–89, New Orleans, 1890, 62–63; *Colfax Chronicle*, February 4, 1882; *Donaldsonville Chief*, November 29, 1879; St. Landry, *Le courier des Opelousas*, July 22, 1875, October 31, 1884; *Assumption Pioneer*, January 24, 1880; *Rapides Democrat*, August 8, 1883; *St. Landry Democrat*, February 9, 1878; *Louisiana Sugar Bowl*, March 24, 1881; *Shreveport Southwestern*, August 8, 1871; *Thibodeaux Sentinel*, May 12, 1877, September 1, 1883. See also Gilles Vandal, "When Religion Mingled With Commerce," 141–55.

40. *New Orleans Daily Picayune*, February 2, 1876

41. 44th Congress, 2nd sess., House Report no. 30, 165; *Colfax Chronicle*, February 4, 1882; *Donaldsonville Chief*, November 29, 1879, February 19, 1881; *Iberville South*, April 28, 1883; *Le Foyer Creole de St-Jean Baptiste*, May 23, 1883; *Baton Rouge Louisiana Capitolian*, September 22, 1881; *New Orleans Crescent*, November 15, 1868; *New Orleans Daily Picayune*, February 2, 1876; *New Orleans Republican*, November 24, 1875, March 26, October 23, November 8, 1876; *New Orleans Times-Democrat*, February 23, 1882; *New Orleans Times*, June 26, 1873, February 25, August 18, 1879; St. Landry, *Le courier des Opelousas*, January 14, 1882, October 31, 1884; *Assumption Pioneer*, January 24, May 1, 1880, August 5, 1882; *Richland Beacon News*, September 24, 1881; *Shreveport Southwestern*, August 8, 1871; *Shreveport Times*, March 26, 1878; *Louisiana Sugar Bowl*, May 29, 1880; *Thibodeaux Sentinel*, May 12, 1875, September 1, 1881. Butterfield, *All God's Children*, 53; Jackson, *New Orleans in the Gilded Age*, 234–35.

42. 41st Congress, 2nd sess., House Misc. Doc. no. 154, part 1, 340–41, 355, 474; 43rd Congress, 2nd sess., House Report no. 261, 365, 441, 765, 780–81, 787, 953; 44th Congress, 2nd sess., House Exec. Doc. no. 30, 283, 384; *Bellevue Banner,* July 15, 1871; *Claiborne Guardian,* April 30, 1879; *Iberville South,* April 28, September 28, 1883, September 24, 1881; *Morehouse Clairon,* February 27, 1880; *New Orleans Bee,* January 11, May 1, 1870, May 15, 1874, March 12, 1876, May 14, 1879; *New Orleans Semi-Weekly Louisianian,* June 7, 1879; *New Orleans Daily Picayune,* January 11, 1866, August 12, September 11, 1868, January 2, April 5, 1871, May 4, June 2, 1871, October 11, 1875, June 20, 1876, May 17, 1877; *New Orleans Republican,* October 9, December 18, 1869, January 12, 1870; *New Orleans Times,* December 19, 1869, November 28, 1870, July 23, 1875, March 7, 1876, February 27, April 6, 13, 1879; *New Orleans Times-Democrat,* February 27, 1884; St. Landry, *Le courier des Opelousas,* October 3, 1868, April 26, 1879, January 14, 1882; *Assumption Pioneer,* January 24, 1880, August 5, 1882; *Rapides Democrat,* February 23, 1884; *Richland Beacon News,* April 14, 1877; *St. Landry Democrat,* March 8, 1879; *St. Mary Planter's Banner,* December 28, 1867; *Louisiana Sugar Bowl,* May 27, 1880. See also Redfield, *Homicide, North and South,* 188, 193–207.

43. *Colfax Chronicle,* February 2, 1882; *New Orleans Times,* October 29, 1866, April 2, 1873. See also Ramage, "Homicide in the Southern States," 215; Redfield, *Homicide, North and South,* 217; Vandal, "Property Offences," 133.

Chapter 8: The Black Response to White Violence

1. 43rd Congress, 2nd sess., House Report no. 261, 366; *Natchitoches People's Vindicator,* July 25, 1874.

2. Several historians such as Foner, *Reconstruction,* Litwack, *Been in the Storm So Long,* and Williamson, *Crucible of Race,* have partly dealt with the black reaction to white violence for the Reconstruction period. But Professors Shapiro and Norris are the only ones to address the issue directly. Marjorie M. Norris, "An Early Instance of Nonviolence: The Louisville Demonstrations of 1870–1871," *Journal of Southern History,* 32, November 1966, 487–504; Shapiro, *White Violence and Black Response;* Herbert Shapiro, "Afro-American Responses to Race Violence During Reconstruction," *Science and Society,* Summer 1972, 158–70.

3. *New Orleans Semi-Weekly Louisianian,* September 12, 1874; Franklin, *Reconstruction After the Civil War,* 86.

4. Blassingame, *Black New Orleans,* 10–11; William P. Connor, "Reconstruction Rebels: The New Orleans Tribune in Post–War Louisi-

ana," *Louisiana History*, 21, no. 2, Spring 1980, 159–81; David C. Rankin, "The Impact of the Civil War on the Free Colored Community of New Orleans," *Perspectives in American History*, 1977–78, 379–415; David C. Rankin, "The Origins of Black Leadership in New Orleans During Reconstruction," *Journal of Southern History*, 40, August 1974, 417–40; Tunnell, *Crucible Reconstruction;* Gilles Vandal, "Black Utopia in Early Reconstructed New Orleans: The People's Bakery as a Case-Study," *Louisiana History*, 38, Summer 1997, 437–52.

5. *New Orleans Tribune*, January 11, 13, 14, 15, 1865; Charles Vincent, *Black Legislators in Louisiana During Reconstruction,* Baton Rouge, 1976, 31–34.

6. Articles 13, 93, 135 of 1868 Constitution; Tunnell, *Crucible Reconstruction,* 119.

7. *New Orleans Tribune*, February 18, 1869; St. Landry, *Le courier des Opelousas,* May 9, 1868; *Shreveport Southwestern,* March 28, 1868; Taylor, *Louisiana Reconstructed,* 95, 98–99, 117, 121.

8. *New Orleans Tribune*, February 18, 1869; St. Landry, *Le courier des Opelousas,* May 9, 1868; *Shreveport Southwestern,* March 28, 1868; Foner, *Reconstruction,* 370, 539; Roger A. Fisher, *Segregation Struggle in Louisiana, 1862–1877,* Urbana, 1974, 66–68; Taylor, *Louisiana Reconstructed,* 209–11; Vincent, *Black Legislators,* 93–97.

9. Acts of Louisiana, 1869, 37; Act 84 of 1873, 156–57; John Ray, Revised Laws and Statutes of Louisiana, vol. 1, New Orleans, 1870, 287–88; Foner, *Reconstruction,* 370, 539; Fisher, *Segregation Struggle,* 66–68; Taylor, *Louisiana Reconstructed,* 209–11; Vincent, *Black Legislators,* 93–97.

10. 43rd Congress, 2nd sess., House Report no. 261, 181; *Louisiana Democrat,* November 5, 1873; *Marksville Weekly Register,* March 21, 31, 1869; *Franklin Planter's Banner,* March 27, 1872; Foner, *Reconstruction,* 370, 539; Fisher, *Segregation Struggle,* 66–68; Taylor, *Louisiana Reconstructed,* 209–11; Vincent, *Black Legislators,* 93–97.

11. 43rd Congress, 2nd sess., House Report *no. 261,* 620–21; *New Orleans Bee,* June 14, 1872; *New Orleans Daily Picayune,* August 13, 1871, February 25, 1872, March 26, 1873; *New Orleans Times,* April 15, June 15, 1872; Taylor, *Louisiana Reconstructed,* 279.

12. *New Orleans Bee,* August 13, 1878.

13. *New Orleans Daily Picayune,* February 13, 1884.

14. 44th Congress, 2nd sess., House Exec. Doc. No. 30, 172, 206, 271, 367; State Legislative Report of 1868, xviii, 132–42; *New Orleans Republican,* May 20, 1869; *Franklin Planter's Banner,* May 26, 1869.

15. 43rd Congress, 2nd sess., House Report no. 261, 388–89, 395–96; 44th Congress, 2nd sess., House Exec. Doc. No. 30, 165, 254, 262–67; 44th Congress, 2nd sess., House Misc. Doc. no. 34, part 3, 100;

45th Congress, 3rd sess., Senate Report no. 855, 132–40; *Rapides Gazette*, April 12, 1873; Tunnell, *Crucible Reconstruction,* 154.

16. *New Orleans Daily Picayune,* June 30, 1876.

17. *Thibodeaux Sentinel,* June 15, 1867; *New Orleans Daily Picayune,* October 1, 1873; *Natchitoches People's Vindicator,* July 25, 1875.

18. *Donaldsonville Chief,* June 27, 1874; *Franklin Planter's Banner,* December 28, 1867; St. Landry, *Le journal des Opeloulas,* January 4, 1868; *Ouachita Telegraph,* September 21, 1872.

19. 43rd Congress, 2nd sess., House Report no. 261, 149; St. James, *Le Louisianais,* December 11, 1869; *Louisiana Sugar Bowl,* July 3, September 4, 1873; *Shreveport Times,* July 23, 1874, January 31, 1875.

20. M. Violet to Lt.-Col. L. H. Warren, Opelousas, September 21, 1868, micro 1027, vol. 23, 1693, BFRAL; James DeGrey to Mayor Hughes, Jackson, August 15, 1867, BFRAL, micro 1546, vol. 246, 80. St. Landry, *Le courier des Opelousas,* January 14, October 3, 1868; *Franklin Planter's Banner,* December 28, 1867; *New Orleans Daily Picayune,* September 7, 11, 1868; *Baton Rouge Tri-Weekly Advocate,* January 10, 1866.

21. *Assumption Pioneer,* January 24, 1880, August 5, 1882; *Louisiana Sugar Bowl,* May 27, 1880.

22. James DeGrey to Mayor Hughes, Jackson, August 15, 1867, micro 1546, vol. 246, 80, BFRAL; R. W. Mullen to Capt. S. H. Warren, parish of St. Mary, April 10, 1868, micro 1598, vol. 276, 68, BFRAL; Lt. James Hugh to Lt. J. M. Lee, Amite City, September 30, 1867, micro 1027, vol. 14, BFRAL.

23. R. W. Mullen to Wm. H. Sterling, parish of St. Mary, May 10, 1868, BFRAL, micro 1598, vol. 276; Thomas F. Moore to L. O. Parker, August 20, 1867, Shreveport, BFRAL, micro 1027, vol. 18; Lt. Webster to Capt. Wm. H. Sterling, April 30, 1868, April report, micro 1027, vol. 24, 455, BFRAL; A. Finch to L. O. Parker, Bayou Sara, July 27, 1867, micro 1027, vol. 23, BFRAL; Lt. James Hough to Lt. J. M. Lee, September 30, 1867, Amity City, micro 1027, vol. 16, BFRAL; *New Orleans Daily Picayune,* September 7, 11, 1868; *Franklin Planter's Banner,* December, 28, 1867; *Baton Rouge Tri-Weekly Advocate,* January 10, 1866.

24. Lt. J. M. Keller to Capt. M. H. Sterling, September 11, 1868, micro 1598, vol. 275, 65–66, BFRAL.

25. Congressional reports, the correspondence of the Freedmen's Bureau, and local newspapers reported countless rumors of bands of armed blacks in a state of revolt. Dawson, *Army Generals,* 65, 145; Taylor, *Louisiana Reconstructed,* 89, 168, 169, 267–70, 288–89; Trelease, *White Terror,* 130; Tunnell, *Crucible Reconstruction,* 153–57.

26. 43rd Congress, 2nd sess., House Report no. 261, 410–13, 474–75; 44th Congress, 2nd sess., House Report no. 156, part 1, 42; *St.*

Landry Democrat, November 8, 1884; Vandal, "Loreauville Riot," 37–38.

27. *New Orleans Daily Picayune,* June 1, 1870.

28. 44th Congress, 2nd sess., House Exec. Doc. no. 30, 254–55; 44th Congress, 2nd sess., House Misc. Doc. no. 34, part 1, 5; *Baton Rouge Tri-Weekly Advocate,* May 27, 1868; *Colfax Chronicle,* December 11, 1880; *Lafayette Advertiser,* September 18, 1869; *Louisiana Sugar Bowl,* August 14, 1873; *New Orleans Daily Picayune,* June 1, 1870; *Ouachita Telegraph,* February 21, 1879; *Assumption Pioneer,* July 26, 1879, April 9, 1881; *Richland Beacon News,* April 14, 1877; *Shreveport Times,* October 31, 1884; *West Baton Rouge Sugar Planter,* December 22, 1866; Smith, "Arson as Protest," 527–64; Taylor, *Louisiana Reconstructed,* 423.

29. 44th Congress, 2nd sess., House Exec. Doc. no. 30, 159, 272, 325, 402–3, 408, 505; 44th Congress, 2nd sess., House Misc. Doc. no. 34, part 1, 16, 26, 21, 353, 363; *Donaldsonville Chief,* March 20, 1880; *Louisiana Sugar Bowl,* August 27, 1874; *Richland Beacon News,* March 24, 1877.

30. 43rd Congress, 2nd sess., House Report no. 261, 366; *New Orleans Semi-Weekly Louisianian,* April 9, 1871, June 29, 1872; *Baton Rouge Tri-Weekly Advocate,* September 25, 1868; Tolnay and Beck, *A Festival of Violence,* 209–11.

31. Governor Warmoth wrote to President Johnson that 150 people had been killed between mid-June and August 1, 1868, throughout the state. A similar situation prevailed during the summer of 1874. *New Orleans Daily Picayune,* August 8, 1868; *New Orleans Republican,* August 9, 18, 1874; Tunnell, *Crucible Reconstruction,* 154.

32. The election law was subsequently revised in 1870 and in 1873. Louisiana Laws, Acts of 1868, 65–70, Act no. 164, 218–25; 1870, Act no. 100, 145–61; 1873, Act no. 7, 46–47, and Act no. 41, 80–81; *New Orleans Daily Picayune,* January 15, February 1, 20, 1870; *New Orleans Commercial Bulletin,* January 19, 1870; *New Orleans Republican,* February 16, August 27, 1874; Taylor, *Louisiana Reconstructed,* 180–81.

33. Acts of Louisiana, 1870 extra sess., 94–96; Taylor, *Louisiana Reconstructed,* 238. In many instances sheriffs and other local officials were the accomplices of perpetrators of violence. 44th Congress, 2nd sess., House Report no. 156, part 1, 106, part 2, 45–47; 39th Congress, 2nd sess., Senate Exec. Doc. no. 6, 86; 43rd Congress, 2nd sess., House Report no. 261, 439, 440; 44th Congress, 2nd sess., House Exec. Doc. no. 30, 176, 307, 363, 399, 431; Supplemental Report, 235; *Shreveport Times,* January 31, 1875; *Natchitoches Semi-Weekly Times,* October 9, 1869; *New Orleans Bee,* May 23, 1874; *New Orleans Daily Picayune,* October 20, 24, 1869, September 27, 1878; Rable, *But There Was No Peace,* 98; Tunnell, *Crucible Reconstruction,* 157–61.

34. 43rd Congress, 2nd sess., House Report no. 261, 346; *Louisiana Democrat,* February 1, 1871; *Louisiana Sugar Bowl,* October 2, 1873.

35. 39th Congress, 2nd sess., Senate Exec. Doc., no. 6, 85–86; 39th Congress, 1st sess., House Report no. 30, 153; 41st Congress, 2nd sess., House Misc. Doc. no. 154, part 1, 33, 36, 39, 55, 78, part 2, 117; 43rd Congress, 2nd sess., House Report no. 261, 175, 366–67, 783; 44th Congress, 2nd sess., House Report no. 30, 77, 408; *Shreveport Southwestern,* September 16, 1868; *Bellevue Banner,* June 17, 1875; *Louisiana Democrat,* February 1, 1871; Taylor, *Louisiana Reconstructed,* 421.

36. 43rd Congress, 2nd sess., House Report no. 261, 366–67; 43rd Congress, 2nd sess., Senate Exec. Doc. no. 13, 4.

37. 42nd Congress, 2nd sess., House Report no. 211, 295; *New Orleans Times,* November 16, 1870; Singletary, *Negro Militia,* 13–15, 24, 67, 80; Taylor, *Louisiana Reconstructed,* 177.

38. The very presence of an armed black annoyed and scared the whole white community as whites saw the "demoralizing effects" that black soldiers had on freedmen. 39th Congress, 1st sess., House Report no. 30, 142; John L. Ludeling to Henry C. Warmoth, September 7, 1870, Warmoth Papers; *Bellevue Banner,* July 9, 1870; *Jefferson State Register,* July 23, 1870; *New Orleans Crescent,* July 17, 1870; *New Orleans Daily Picayune,* October 21, 1865, July 8, 19, 1870; *New Orleans Republican,* August 2, 1870; *New Orleans Times,* July 17, 1870; *Shreveport Southwestern,* July 25, 1866, January 30, 1867, June 29, 1870; Singletary, *Negro Militia,* 13–15, 67, 114, 117; Taylor, *Louisiana Reconstructed,* 177; Tunnell, *Crucible Reconstruction,* 161.

39. 42nd Congress, 2nd sess., House Report no. 211, 295; *New Orleans Times,* November 16, 1870; Singletary, *Negro Militia,* 13–15, 24, 67, 80; Taylor, *Louisiana Reconstructed,* 177.

40. R. W. Mullen to B. F. Hutchins, Franklin, October 21, 1868, micro 1027, vol. 23, 797, BFRAL; letter to General Sherman, New Orleans, October 20, 1868, micro 4482, vol. 205, 135, War Department, Fifth Military District; St. Landry, *Le courier des Opelousas,* December 28, 1867; *New Orleans Times,* December 21, 1867; *New Orleans Daily Picayune,* October 19, 20, 1868; J. Thomas May, "The Freedmen's Bureau at the Local Level: A Study of a Louisiana Agent," *Louisiana History,* 9, Winter 1968, 5–19.

41. 39th Congress, 1st sess., House Exec. Doc. no. 30, 70; *New Orleans Bee,* October 19, 21, 1865; *New Orleans Times,* October 21, 1865; Foner, *Reconstruction,* 157, 190; W. S. McFeely, *Yankee Stepfather, General O. O. Howard and the Freedmen,* New Haven, 1968, 173–79; Howard A. White, *The Freedmen's Bureau in Louisiana,* Baton Rouge, 1970, 19–24.

42. Lt. M. F. Daugherty to Capt. A. F. Hayden, March 31, 1866,

BFRAL; *New Orleans Times,* March 27, 1866; Dawson, *Army Generals,* 81; May, "The Freedmen's Bureau at the Local level," 5–19; Taylor, *Louisiana Reconstructed,* 93–94.

43. *New Orleans Daily Picayune,* June 22, 1876; *New Orleans Semi-Weekly Louisianian,* January 30, 1875; *New Orleans Bulletin,* January 29, 1875; *New Orleans Times,* January 15, 1869, January 27, 1875; Dauphine, "Knights of the White Camelia," 184–85; Dawson, *Army Generals,* 81, 87, 92, 103.

44. *New Orleans Daily Picayune,* March 28, April 14, May 4, 1867; *New Orleans Times,* January 31, August 17, November 19, 1867; *New Orleans Tribune,* May 1–10, 1867; Dawson, *Army Generals,* 90–93; Roger A. Fisher, "A Pioneer Protest: The New Orleans Street Car Controversy of 1867," *Journal of Negro History,* 53, July 1968, 219–33; Taylor, *Louisiana Reconstructed,* 114–55.

45. Dawson, *Army Generals,* 90–92; Sefton, *United States Army and Reconstruction,* 213–35; Taylor, *Louisiana Reconstructed,* 114–55.

46. *New Orleans Times,* July 24, 1874; *New Orleans Tribune,* November 12, 1867; Dawson, *Army Generals,* 3–4, 95; Foner, *Reconstruction,* 550; Taylor, *Louisiana Reconstructed,* 94, 138–39.

47. *New Orleans Daily Picayune,* June 22, 1876; *New Orleans Semi-Weekly Louisianian,* January 30, 1875; *New Orleans Bulletin,* January 29, 1875; *New Orleans Times,* January 15, 1869, January 27, 1875; Dauphine, "Knights of the White Camelia," 185; Dawson, *Army Generals,* 81, 87, 92, 103.

48. Data show that no less than seventeen blacks were killed for testifying against whites. 41st Congress, 2nd sess., House Misc. Doc. no. 154, 476–77, 495; 44th Congress, 2nd sess., House Misc. Doc. no. 30, 168, 532; Dauphine, "Knights of the White Camelia," 178; Taylor, *Louisiana Reconstructed,* 313; Trelease, *White Terror,* 103–5.

49. 43rd Congress, 2nd sess., Senate Exec. Doc. no. 13, 8, 17; 42nd Congress, 2nd sess., House Exec. Doc. No. 209, 268.

50. 41st Congress, 2nd sess., House Misc. Doc. no. 154, part 2, 516–20; 43rd Congress, 2nd sess., House Report no. 261, 201; *Claiborne Guardian,* February 26, 1879; *Franklin Planter's Banner,* December 7, 1870; *Baton Rouge Tri-Weekly Gazette & Comet,* January 27, 1871; *New Orleans Semi-Weekly Louisianian,* March 30, 1871; *New Orleans Bulletin,* March 28, 1876; *Shreveport Times,* March 19, 1879; Taylor, *Louisiana Reconstructed,* 272–73, 488; Dawson, *Army Generals,* 50, 152, 156.

51. *New Orleans Bee,* June 3, 1874; Dawson, *Army Generals,* 50, 152, 156; Taylor, *Louisiana Reconstructed,* 272–73, 488.

52. Gillette, *Retreat From Reconstruction,* 302–3.

53. *New Orleans Bee,* August 13, 1878.

54. *New Orleans Daily Picayune,* February 25, 1872.

55. *Baton Rouge Tri-Weekly Advocate,* September 25, 1868.

56. 43rd Congress, 2nd sess., House Report no. 261, 249, 259; *New Orleans Daily Picayune,* July 16, 1873; Taylor, *Louisiana Reconstructed,* 278–79; Harry T. Williams, "The Louisiana Unification Movement of 1873," *Journal of Southern History,* 11, August 1945, 349–69.

57. 43rd Congress, 2nd sess., House Report no. 261, 649–50; *New Orleans Daily Picayune,* October 14, 25, November 11, 1874; Taylor, *Louisiana Reconstructed,* 301.

58. 44th Congress, 2nd sess., Senate Report no. 701, part 1, 2325; 43rd Congress, 2nd sess., House Report no. 261, 473, 620, 648–50; *New Orleans Times,* September 27, October 13, 1874; *New Orleans Daily Picayune,* October 13, 18, 1874.

59. 43rd Congress, 2nd sess., House Report no. 261, 620–21; 44th Congress, 2nd sess., Senate Report no. 701, part 1, xxxiii, 2325.

60. 43rd Congress, 2nd sess., House Report no. 261, 907–8; *New Orleans Daily Picayune,* November 11, 12, 1874.

61. Foner, *Reconstruction,* 554–55; James T. Otten, "The Wheeler Adjustment in Louisiana: National Republicans Begin to Reappraise Their Reconstruction Policy," *Louisiana History,* 13, Fall 1972, 349–67; Taylor, *Louisiana Reconstructed,* 306–7; for a recent analysis of the Wheeler Compromise see my article on Albert Leonard, "Albert H. Leonard's Road from the White League," 55–76.

62. *New Orleans Bee,* February 15, 1876; *New Orleans Bulletin,* September 24, 1875; *New Orleans Crescent,* April 15, 1868; *New Orleans Daily Picayune,* October 16, 1873, August 23, 1876.

63. 45th Congress, 3rd sess., Senate Report no. 855, 225, 229, 231; *Baton Rouge Capitolian Advocate,* August 23, 1884; *Donaldsonville Chief,* April 5, 1884; *Thibodeaux Sentinel,* March 8, 1884.

64. 45th Congress, 3rd sess., Senate Report, no. 855, 169–93, 204, 225, 229, 231, 236, 263.

65. 41st Congress, 2nd sess., House Misc. Doc. no. 154, part 1, appendix xxvi, part 2, 521; Trelease, *White Terror,* 135; Henry C. Warmoth, *War, Politics and Reconstruction,* New York, 1930, 78–79; Dauphine, "Knights of the White Camelia," 175, 177.

66. House Report no. 261 of 1875 contains hundreds of pages citing intimidation of blacks during the 1874 election. See 43rd Congress, 2nd sess., House Report no. 261, 14, 148, 165, 168, 183, 310, 322, 333–37, 346, 365, 373, 613–15, 753, 783, 786, 789, 793; *Natchitoches People's Vindicator,* December 9, 1874; *Louisiana Sugar Bowl,* August 13, 1874; *New Orleans Daily Picayune,* October 20, December 27, 1874; *New Orleans Times,* January 29, 1875; *Shreveport Times,* January 14, 19, 29, 1875; Taylor, *Louisiana Reconstructed,* 284–85.

67. St. Landry, *Le journal des Opelousas,* May 29, 1874.

68. Leach, "The Aftermath of Reconstruction in Louisiana," 637; Taylor, *Louisiana Reconstructed,* 174.

69. Forty-first Congress, 2nd sess., House Misc. Doc. no. 154, part 1, 323; 44th Congress, 2nd sess., Senate Report no. 701, 647–48, 721; *Ouachita Telegraph,* October 28, 1876; Vincent, *Black Legislators,* 217.

70. 44th Congress, 2nd sess., House Report no. 156, part 2, 6; 41st Congress, 2nd sess., House Misc. Doc. no. 154, part 1, 323; 44th Congress, 2nd sess., Senate Report no. 701, 27, 647–48, 721, 787–88, 856; *Ouachita Telegraph,* October 28, 1876; Gillette, *Retreat From Reconstruction,* 311; Tunnell, "The Negro, the Republican Party," 107, 114; Taylor, *Louisiana Reconstructed,* 489; Vincent, *Black Legislators,* 217.

71. Lafayette, *Louisiana Cotton Boll,* July 19, 1876; *Louisiana Sugar Bowl,* February 10, 1876.

72. *Louisiana Sugar Bowl,* March 27, 1879.

73. *Tensas Gazette,* November 11, 1882.

74. *Iberville South,* October, 18, 25, 1884; Vandal, "Loreauville Riot," 37–38.

75. Still, these 135 black Democrats represent only a small fraction, with 5.8 percent, of the 2,283 black leaders on whom we collected information.

76. 43rd Congress, 2nd sess., House Report no. 261, 148, 175, 189, 953; 44th Congress, 2nd sess., House Exec. Doc. no. 30, 193, 415; 43rd Congress, 2nd sess., Senate Exc. Doc. no. 17, 7, 50, 53; *New Orleans Daily Picayune,* August 21, 1874, January 28, 1875; *New Orleans Bee,* January 20, 1875; *New Orleans Republican,* August 9, 18, December 25, 1874.

77. J. F. White to Capt. L. H. Warren, May 20, 1868, micro 1027, vol. 24, 507, BFRAL; 43rd Congress, 2nd sess., House Report no. 261, 146–55, 175, 230–36; *New Orleans Daily Picayune,* December 29, 1875; Clay, "Economic Survival," 135; Taylor, *Louisiana Reconstructed,* 424. A similar situation prevailed in Texas. Smallwood, "Perpetuation of Caste," 8.

78. Taylor, *Louisiana Reconstructed,* 424.

79. 45th Congress, 3rd sess., Senate Report no. 855, lx, 44, 169–93, 198, 204, 225, 229, 231, 236, 263; *Assumption Pioneer,* May 31, 1879; *Carroll Conservative,* February 1, 1879; *Natchitoches People's Vindicator,* April 5, 1879; *Louisiana Sugar Bowl,* April 24, 1879; *New Orleans Democrat,* October 22, 1878; *New Orleans Daily Picayune,* March 17, 27, April 16, 23, May 6, June 2, 1879; *New Orleans Semi-Weekly Louisianian,* April 12, 1879; *Ouachita Telegraph,* January 3, 1879; *New Orleans Times,* May 25, 27, 28, 1879; *Shreveport Times,* November 7, 8, December 29, 1879; *Tensas Gazette,* April 12, 1879; Hair, *Bourbonism and Agrarian Protest,* 78; Peoples, "Kansas Fever," 125.

80. *New Orleans Daily Picayune,* March 27, May 3, 1879; see also

New Orleans Times, March 25, 1879; *Louisiana Sugar Bowl,* July 3, 1879.

81. *New Orleans Daily Picayune,* June 2, 1879; *New Orleans Times,* November 12, 1879; *Assumption Pioneer,* May 31, 1879.

82. *Assumption Pioneer,* December 20, 1879; *New Orleans Daily Picayune,* May 6, 1879; *Thibodeaux Sentinel,* July 5, 1879; *St. Landry Democrat,* July 5, 1879.

83. Forty-fifth Congress, 3rd sess., Senate Report no. 855, 132–40; 46th Congress, 2nd sess., House Report no. 693, part 2, 101–88; Tunnell, *Crucible Reconstruction,* 154; Peoples, "Kansas Fever," 122, 129–30.

84. *Baton Rouge Weekly Advocate,* April 25, 1879; *New Orleans Daily Picayune,* April 18, 19, 20, 1879; *New Orleans Times,* April 18, 1879; Hair, *Bourbonism and Agrarian Protest,* 93; Peoples, "Kansas Fever," 132.

85. 46th Congress, 2nd sess., House Report no. 693 (3 parts); *Shreveport Daily Standard,* February 20, 1880; Hair, *Bourbonism and Agrarian Protest,* 93.

86. *Donaldsonville Chief,* February 7, 1880; *New Orleans Times,* April 20, 22, 1879; *Tensas Gazette,* May 3, 10, June 21, 1879.

87. *Donaldsonville Chief,* February 7, 1880; *New Orleans Daily Picayune,* March 27, 1879.

88. *Baton Rouge Louisiana Capitolian,* March 13, 1880; *Donaldsonville Chief,* February 7, March 20, 1880; *Louisiana Sugar Bowl,* January 10, 1880; *New Orleans Daily Picayune,* January 20, 1880; St. John the Baptist, *Le Meschaceebe,* January 24, 1880; *Natchitoches People's Vindicator,* August 27, 1881, November 20, 1880: *St. Tammany Farmer,* January 3, 1880.

Aftermath

1. William Ivy Hair, *Carnival of Fury, Robert Charles and the New Orleans Riot of 1900,* Baton Rouge, 1976, 1–3, 117–36, 157–82, 184–85, 188; Williamson, *Crucible of Race,* 202–7; Woodward, *Origins of the New South,* 351.

2. Hair, *Carnival of Fury,* 1–3, 148.

3. Dethloff and Jones, "Race Relations in Louisiana," 141–59; Germaine A. Reed, "Race Legislation in Louisiana, 1864–1920," *Louisiana History,* 6, Fall 1965, 379–92; Dale A. Somers, "Black and White in New Orleans: A Study in Urban Race Relations, 1865–1900," *Journal of Southern History,* February 1974, 19–42.

4. Hair, *Bourbonism and Agrarian Protest,* 113–16; Vandal, "Loreauville Riot," 28–30.

5. Hair, *Bourbonism and Agrarian Protest*, 99; Allie B. Webb-Windham, "A History of Negro Voting in Louisiana, 1877–1906," Ph.D. diss., Louisiana State University, 1962, 111–15.

6. *Louisiana Laws*, Act 58 of 1877, 96; 45th Congress, 3rd sess., Senate Report no. 855, part 1, 13; William A. Seay and John S. Young, Louisiana Statutes & Laws, The Revised Statutes of the State of Louisiana from the Organization of the Territory to the Year 1884 Inclusive, Baton Rouge, 1886, 206–7.

7. Louisiana Laws, Act 101 of 1882, 152; William A. Seay and John S. Young, The Revised Statutes of the State of Louisiana from the Organization of the Territory to the Year 1884 Inclusive, Baton Rouge, 1886, 205; *Rapides Democrat*, August 30, 1882; *St. Landry Democrat*, September 2, 1882, August 4, 1884; Hair, *Bourbonism and Agrarian Protest*, 61, 118–19; Vandal, "Loreauville Riot," 30; Webb-Windham, "History of Negro Voting," 134–40.

8. Hair, *Bourbonism and Agrarian Protest*, 113–16; Webb-Windham, "History of Negro Voting," 192.

9. Inverarity, "Populism and Lynching in Louisiana," 266; Vandal, "Bloody Caddo," 378–79.

10. Bourbons resorted to fraud by stuffing ballot boxes. Blacks who were dead or who had left for Kansas were still on voting lists ten years later. As a consequence the Democratic party was able to carry many parishes with huge, if fraudulent, majorities. Hair, *Bourbonism and Agrarian Protest*, 113–15; Vandal, "Loreauville Riot," 30; Webb-Windham, "History of Negro Voting," 192.

11. Tolnay and Beck, *A Festival of Violence*, 173–76.

12. Hair, *Bourbonism and Agrarian Protest*, 228–30, 237–38; Inverarity, "Populism and Lynching in Louisiana," 266; Webb-Windham, "History of Negro Voting," 194–204; Woodward, *Origins of the New South*, 261, 277.

13. Hair, *Bourbonism and Agrarian Protest*, 261; Webb-Windham, "History of Negro Voting," 220–26; Woodward, *Origins of the New South*, 288.

14. Hair, *Bourbonism and Agrarian Protest*, 262; Woodward, *Origins of the New South*, 288.

15. Hair, *Bourbonism and Agrarian Protest*, 264; Inverarity, "Populism and Lynching in Louisiana," 266; Woodward, *Origins of the New South*, 288.

16. Richard L. Watson, "From Populism Through the New Deal," in *Interpreting Southern History*, edited by John B. Boles and Evelyn Thomas Nolen, Baton Rouge, 1987, 325–26; Hair, *Bourbonism and Agrarian Protest*, 276–78.

17. Hair, *Bourbonism and Agrarian Protest*, 273; I. A. Newby, *Jim*

Crow's Defense, Anti-Negro Thought in America, 1900–1930, Baton Rouge, 1965, 145–53; Webb-Windham, "History of Negro Voting," 230; Woodward, *Origins of the New South,* 322, 348–49.

18. Butterfield, *All God's Children,* 49; Hair, *Bourbonism and Agrarian Protest,* 276–78; Tolnay and Beck, *A Festival of Violence,* 182; Watson, "From Populism Through the New Deal," 326; Webb-Windham, "History of Negro Voting," 234–36; Woodward, *Origins of the New South,* 342–43.

19. Harold D. Woodman, "Economic Reconstruction and the New South," in *Interpreting Southern History,* 260; Tolnay and Beck, *A Festival of Violence,* 180–81.

20. Gould, "The Strike of 1887," 48; Hair, *Bourbonism and Agrarian Protest,* 276–78; Inverarity, "Populism and Lynching in Louisiana," 266–67.

21. Arnesen, *Waterfront Workers of New Orleans,* 91–98; Cook and Watson, *Louisiana Labor,* 68–74; Brian Gary Ettinger, "John Fitzpatrick and the Limits of Working-class Politics in New Orleans, 1892–1896," *Louisiana History,* 26, Fall 1985, 343, 353; Roger Wallace Shugg, "The New Orleans General Strike of 1892," *Louisiana Historical Quarterly,* 21, 1938, 547–60; Jackson, *New Orleans in the Gilded Age,* 226.

22. Arnesen, *Waterfront Workers of New Orleans,* 114; Cook and Watson, *Louisiana Labor,* 71; Bernard A. Cook, "The Typographical Union and the New Orleans General Strike of 1892," *Louisiana History,* 34, Fall 1983, 379; Jackson, *New Orleans in the Gilded Age,* 228; Shugg, "The General Strike of 1892," 547–55.

23. Arnesen, *Waterfront Workers of New Orleans,* 115; Cook, "The Typographical Union," 379; Cook and Watson, *Louisiana Labor,* 71–72; Jackson, *New Orleans in the Gilded Age,* 228; Shugg, "The General Strike of 1892," 551–52.

24. Arnesen, *Waterfront Workers of New Orleans,* 76–77, 116; Cook and Watson, *Louisiana Labor,* 70; Ettinger, "John Fitzpatrick," 347–49; Jackson, *New Orleans in the Gilded Age,* 37–38, 227; Shugg, "The General Strike of 1892," 551–52.

25. Arnesen, *Waterfront Workers of New Orleans,* 116–17; Cook, "The Typographical Union," 380; Cook and Watson, *Louisiana Labor,* 73–75; Jackson, *New Orleans in the Gilded Age,* 229; Shugg, "The General Strike of 1892," 558.

26. Arnesen, *Waterfront Workers of New Orleans,* 118–23; Cook and Watson, *Louisiana Labor,* 81–82; Ettinger, "John Fitzpatrick," 361; Woodward, *Origins of the New South,* 267.

27. Philip S. Foner, *History of the Labor Movement in the United States,* vol. 2, New York, 1977, 161; Cook and Watson, *Louisiana Labor,* 57–60; Hair, *Bourbonism and Agrarian Protest,* 181–85.

28. Cook and Watson, *Louisiana Labor,* 58; Gould, "The Strike of 1887," 49–50.

29. Cook and Watson, *Louisiana Labor*, 59; Gould, "The Strike of 1887," 50; Hair, *Bourbonism and Agrarian Protest*, 177–78.

30. Gould, "The Strike of 1887," 51–52.

31. Foner, *History of the Labor Movement*, 161; Cook and Watson, *Louisiana Labor*, 57–60; Gould, "The Strike of 1887," 52–53; Hair, *Bourbonism and Agrarian Protest*, 181–85.

32. Shapiro, *White Violence and Black Response*, 27.

33. Arnesen, *Waterfront Workers of New Orleans*, 90; Gould, "The Strike of 1887," 53; Cook and Watson, *Louisiana Labor*, 59.

34. Cook and Watson, *Louisiana Labor*, 60; Gould, "The Strike of 1887," 55; Foner, *History of the Labor Movement*, 161; Hair, *Bourbonism and Agrarian Protest*, 185.

35. Bonacich, "A Theory of Ethnic Antagonism," 553; Jay R. Mandle, *The Roots of Black Poverty, The Southern Plantation Economy After the Civil War*, Durham, 1978, 45–51; Carole Marks, "Split Labor Markets and Black-White Relations, 1865–1920," *Phylon*, 62, Winter 1981, 293–308; Pfeifer, "Lynching and Criminal Justice," 158; Stewart E. Tolnay and E. M. Beck, "Black Flight: Lethal Violence and the Great Migration, 1900–1930," *Social Science History*, 14, no. 3, Fall 1990, 352; Woodman, "Economic Reconstruction and the New South," 266.

36. Hair, *Bourbonism and Agrarian Protest*, 189. A similar campaign was conducted by white planters in other Southern states during the 1890s. Butterfield, *All God's Children*, 56–57; Tolnay and Beck, *A Festival of Violence*, 24–26, 151.

37. Hyde, *Pistols and Politics*, 209.

38. William F. Holmes, "Whitecapping in Mississippi," 134–48; William F. Holmes, "Whitecapping: Agrarian Violence in Mississippi, 1902–1906," *Journal of Southern History*, 35, 1969, 165–85; Hyde, *Pistols and Politics*, 208–11; Tolnay and Beck, "Black Flight," 363.

39. Tolnay and Beck, "Black Flight," 363–64.

40. Shapiro, *White Violence and Black Response*, 117.

41. Butterfield, *All God's Children*, 45, 49–51; Ellwood, "Has Crime Increased in the United States Since 1880," 382–83; Hair, *Bourbonism and Agrarian Protest*, 112–13, 186; Hair, *Carnival of Fury*, 82–85; Jackson, *New Orleans in the Gilded Age*, 232–57; Hyde, *Pistols and Politics*, 199–201; Ramage, "Homicide in the Southern States," 211–15, 223.

42. Ramage, "Homicide in the Southern States," 213–14.

43. Hyde, *Pistols and Politics*, 227–62.

44. Brown, "Southern Violence," 231, 245–48; Nisbett and Cohen, *Culture of Honor*, 2; Ramage, "Homicide in the Southern States," 215–16, 225, 231.

45. Hair, *Carnival of Fury*, 82; Ramage, "Homicide in the Southern States," 212–32; Williamson, *Crucible of Race*, 58; Woodward, *Origins of the New South*, 159–60.

46. Butterfield, *All God's Children*, 58; Ramage, "Homicide in the Southern States," 215–16.

47. Shapiro, *White Violence and Black Response*, 126; Woodward, *Origins of the New South*, 352.

48. Lane, *Roots of Violence in Black Philadelphia*, 165; Ramage, "Homicide in the Southern States," 214, 219.

49. Hair, *Bourbonism and Agrarian Protest*, 187; Hyde, *Pistols and Politics*, 203–6.

50. Louisiana Laws, Act 11 of 1882, 9; Report of the Louisiana Attorney General, 1888–89, 72.

51. Between 1882 and 1903, 285 cases of lynching were recorded in Louisiana. Jackson, *New Orleans in the Gilded Age*, 244; Walter White, *Rope and Faggot: A Biography of Judge Lynch*, New York, 1929, 255.

52. Ettinger, "John Fitzpatrick," 345; Jackson, *New Orleans in the Gilded Age*, 247–53.

53. Hair, *Bourbonism and Agrarian Protest*, 187–90; Ramage, "Homicide in the Southern States," 219.

54. Butterfield, *All God's Children*, 57; Hair, *Carnival of Fury*, 50–51; Tolnay and Beck, *A Festival of Violence*, 170–72. Pfeifer, "Lynching and Criminal Justice," 155–58, particularly examines the close link between lynching and enforcement of criminal justice in Louisiana during the 1880s and 1890s.

55. Citation taken from Charles David Phillips, "Exploring Relations Among Forms of Social Control," 365.

56. Williamson, *Crucible of Race*, 186.

57. Inverarity, "Populism and Lynching in Louisiana," 269, 274; Tolnay and Beck, *A Festival of Violence*, 156.

58. Ramage, "Homicide in the Southern States," 219; Shapiro, *White Violence and Black Response*, 31; Tolnay and Beck, *A Festival of Violence*, 21.

59. Dan T. Carter, "From Segregation to Integration," *Interpreting Southern History*, 411.

60. Tolnay and Beck, *A Festival of Violence*, 170.

61. Shapiro, *White Violence and Black Response*, 64–73, 75, 97–103, 104–10, 113.

62. Tolnay and Beck, "Black Flight," 356.

63. During the first decade of the twentieth century, 170,000 blacks left the South for Northern cities. The number grew to 450,000 during the second decade to 750,000 during the 1920s. By 1960 some four million blacks had left the South to emigrate either to cities located either in the North, the Midwest, or the Pacific states. If more than 90 percent of black people lived until 1910 in Southern rural communities, a majority of them lived by 1960 outside of the South. John H. Bracey, August Meir,

and Elliott Rudwick, *The Rise of the Ghetto,* Belmont, Calif., 1971, 3–4, 41–43, 49–51; Carter, "From Segregation to Integration," 414; Allan H. Spear, *Black Chicago, The Making of a Negro Ghetto, 1890–1920,* Chicago, 1967, 129–38; Tolnay and Beck, "Black Flight," 348, 354, 356–57, 359, 362.

64. Nisbett and Cohen, *Culture of Honor,* 13, 37–39; Daly and Wilson, *Homicide,* 126–27.

65. Although they formed only 11 percent of the population, blacks committed a large proportion of the homicides that occurred in the United States during the last century. What is more striking is the fact that the percentage of homicides committed by blacks had been steadily on the increase between 1930 and 1970, rising from 34 percent in 1933 to 40 percent in 1940, 46 percent in 1950, 57 percent in 1960, and 62 percent in 1969. Sampson, "Urban Black Violence," 349; Leonard D. Savitz, "Black Crime," in *Comparative Studies of Blacks and Whites in the United States,* edited by Kent S. Miller and Ralph N. Dreger, New York, 1973, 476–77. Shapiro, *White Violence and Black Response,* 222–23.

66. Social scientists illustrate how blacks born in the South who had recently moved to the Northern cities, regularly carried weapons as a sign of toughness and masculinity. Moreover, blacks did not hesitate to use their weapons in response to feeling insulted or for any other trivial reason. They were perpetuating, in the process, the Southern culture of honor that they had integrated. Baron and Straus, "Cultural and Economic Sources of Homicide," 377–78; Butterfield, *All God's Children,* 8; Lane, *Roots of Violence in Black Philadelphia,* 166; Schultz, "Why Negroes Carry Weapons," 478, 479, 481

67. Spear, *Black Chicago,* 21–23, 26, 34–35, 201–22.

68. Land et al., "Structural Covariates of Homicide Rates," 925.

69. Butterfield, *All God's Children,* 206–7; Lane, *Roots of Violence in Black Philadelphia,* 170, 173; Parker, "Poverty, Subculture of Violence," 999, 1001; Baron and Straus, "Cultural and Economic Sources of Homicide," 373.

Bibliography

Primary Sources

Manuscript Collections

National Archives

Correspondence of the Attorney General of the United States, RG 60
Correspondence and Documents, Bureau of Freedmen, Refugees and Abandoned Lands, RG 105
Correspondence and Documents, Gulf Department, Civil Affairs, 1867–1870, RG 393
Census of Population, Nominal Reports, Louisiana 1870–1880, RG 29

Library of Congress

P. H. Sheridan Papers
Federal Census Report of Louisiana, 1860, 1870, 1880

Tulane University, Archives

Henry C. Warmoth Papers
Benjamin F. Flanders Papers

Louisiana State University, Archives

Francis T. Nicholls Letter Book
William P. Kellogg Papers
Minutes of the Police Jurors, Ascension Parish, 1850–85
Minutes of the Police Jurors, Caddo Parish, 1850–85
Minutes of the Police Jurors, Lafayette Parish, 1850–85

Official Reports and Documents

Federal

39th Congress, 1st Session, House Report no. 30
39th Congress, 1st Session, Senate Executive Document no. 2

39th Congress, 2nd Session, House Report no. 16
39th Congress, 2nd Session, House Executive Document no. 68
39th Congress, 2nd Session, Senate Executive Document no. 6
40th Congress, 1st Session, Senate Executive Document no. 14
40th Congress, 2nd Session, House Executive Document no. 209
40th Congress, 2nd Session, Senate Executive Document no. 53
40th Congress, 3rd Session, Senate Executive Document no. 15
41st Congress, 1st Session, House Report no. 27
41st Congress, 1st Session, House Miscellaneous Document no. 12
41st Congress, 1st Session, House Miscellaneous Document no. 13
41st Congress, 1st Session, House Miscellaneous Document no. 16
41st Congress, 2nd Session, House Miscellaneous Document no. 152
41st Congress, 2nd Session, House Miscellaneous Document no. 154
41st Congress, 2nd Session, House Executive Document no. 142
41st Congress, 2nd Session, House Executive Document no. 209
41st Congress, 2nd Session, House Executive Document no. 268
42nd Congress, 2nd Session, House Report no. 92
42nd Congress, 3rd Session, House Executive Document no. 91
42nd Congress, 2nd Session, House Miscellaneous Document no. 104
42nd Congress, 2nd Session, House Miscellaneous Document no. 211
42nd Congress, 2nd Session, Senate Report no. 41
42nd Congress, 3rd Session, Senate Report no. 417
42nd Congress, 3rd Session, Senate Report no. 457
42nd Congress, 3rd Session, Senate Executive Document no. 47
43rd Congress, 1st Session, House Report no. 597
43rd Congress, 1st Session, House Report no. 732
43rd Congress, 2nd Session, House Report no. 101
43rd Congress, 2nd Session, House Report no. 261
43rd Congress, 2nd Session, Senate Executive Document no. 13
43rd Congress, 2nd Session, Senate Executive Document no. 17
43rd Congress, 2nd Session, Senate Miscellaneous Document no. 45
43rd Congress, 2nd Session, Senate Miscellaneous Document no. 46
43rd Congress, 2nd Session, Senate Report no. 626
44th Congress, 1st Session, House Report no. 442
44th Congress, 1st Session, House Report no. 816
44th Congress, 2nd Session, House Report no. 30
44th Congress, 2nd Session, House Report no. 44
44th Congress, 2nd Session, House Report no. 100
44th Congress, 2nd Session, House Report no. 156
44th Congress, 2nd Session, House Miscellaneous Document no. 34
(Three Parts)
44th Congress, 2nd Session, Senate Executive Document no. 2

44th Congress, 2nd Session, Senate Report no. 701 (Four Parts)

45th Congress, 3rd Session, House Report no. 140

45th Congress, 2nd Session, House Miscellaneous Document no. 52

45th Congress, 3rd Session, House Miscellaneous Document no. 31 (Three Parts)

45th Congress, 3rd Session, Senate Report no. 855 (Three Parts)

46th Congress, 2nd Session, Senate Report no. 693

Louisiana

Acts of Louisiana, 1863–85

Annual Report of the Board of the Louisiana State Penitentiary to the General Assembly, New Orleans, 1865–79

Annual Report of the State Attorney General to the General Assembly, New Orleans, 1857, 1867–78, 1881, 1883

Annual Report of the Board of Metropolitan Police to the General Assembly of Louisiana, New Orleans, 1868–75

Journal of the House of Representatives of the State of Louisiana, New Orleans, 1874

Biennial Report of the State Attorney General of Louisiana, 1888–89, New Orleans, 1890

Phillips, U. B. Revised Statutes of Louisiana, New Orleans, 1856

Ray, John. Revised Laws and Statutes of the State of Louisiana, vols. 1–2, New Orleans, 1870

Report of the Joint Committee of the General Assembly of Louisiana on the Conduct of the Late Election and on the Condition of Peace and Order in the State, New Orleans, 1868

Seay, William A., and John S. Young. The Revised Statutes of the State of Louisiana from the Organization of the Territory to the Year 1884 Inclusive, Baton Rouge, 1886

Supplemental Report of the Joint Committee of the General Assembly of Louisiana on the Conduct of the Late Election and the Condition of Peace and Order in the State, New Orleans, 1869

Report of the General Assembly of Louisiana on the Conduct of the Election of April 17, and 18, 1868, and the Condition of Peace and Order in the State, New Orleans, 1868

New Orleans Public Library, City Archives

The Annual Report of the Superintendent of Police, New Orleans, 1893–98

Prisons and Asylums, Report of the Commissioners to the City Council, New Orleans, 1882

Proceedings of City Council of New Orleans, New Orleans, 1865–75

Louisiana Newspapers

Alexandria, *Caucasian*, 1874–75
Alexandria, *Louisiana Democrat*, 1865–84
Alexandria, *Rapides Gazette*, 1871–73, 1876–78
Amite Democrat, 1876
Amite Independent, 1874–75
Assumption Pioneer, 1865–84
Baton Rouge Advocate-Comet, 1866
Baton Rouge Capitolian Advocate, 1884
Baton Rouge Louisiana Capitolian, 1879–84
Baton Rouge Tri-Weekly Advocate, 1865–71
Baton Rouge Tri-Weekly Capitolian, 1881–83
Baton Rouge Weekly Advocate, 1869–72, 1878–84
Baton Rouge Weekly Truth, 1882–84
Baton Rouge Tri-Weekly Gazette & Comet, 1865–68
Bossier, *Bellevue Banner*, 1866–84
Carroll Conservative, 1879
Carroll Record, 1868–69
Carroll Republican, 1873–76
Carroll Watchman, 1875
Claiborne Guardian, 1879–81
Colfax Chronicle, 1876–84
Franklin Planter's Banner, 1867–72
Iberville Sentinel, 1869
Iberville South, 1865–69, 1871, 1876–84
Jefferson State Register, 1872–74
Lafayette Advertiser, 1869–70, 1873–74, 1877–78, 1882
Lafayette, *Louisiana Cotton Boll*, 1873–77
Le Courier de la Louisiane, 1855, 1857
Madison Times, 1884
Marksville Weekly Register, 1868–69
Monroe Bulletin, 1880, 1882–84
Morehouse Clarion, 1879–81
Morgan City, *Attakapas Register*, 1876–78
Natchitoches Semi-Weekly Times, 1866–67
Natchitoches People's Vindicator, 1874–81
New Orleans Bee, 1852–84
New Orleans Bulletin, 1874–76
New Orleans Black Republican, 1865
New Orleans Crescent, 1852–69
New Orleans Commercial Bulletin, 1865–71
New Orleans Daily Picayune, 1852–84
New Orleans Democrat, 1876–81

New Orleans Louisianian, 1871–82
New Orleans Republican, 1867–76
New Orleans Semi-Weekly Louisianian, 1871–82
New Orleans Times, 1865–81
New Orleans Times-Democrat, 1881–84
New Orleans Tribune, 1864–67, 1869
New Iberia, *Louisiana Sugar Bowl,* 1870–81
New Iberia Southern Star, 1865–66
Ouachita Telegraph, 1871–83
Pointe Coupée Democrat, 1884
Rapides Democrat, 1877–83
Richland Beacon News, 1872–82
St. Charles, *L'Avant-Coureur,* 1866–69, 1871–72
St. James, *Le Louisianais,* 1871–76, 1881
St. James Sentinel, 1873–75
St. John the Baptist, *Le Foyer Créole,* 1865–84
St. John the Baptist, *Le Meschaceebe,* 1865–81
St. Landry Democrat, 1877–84
St. Landry, *Le courier des Opelousas,* 1865–84
St. Landry, *Le journal des Opelousas,* 1868–78
St. Mary, *Brashear News,* 1875
St. Tammany Farmer, 1878–84
Shreveport Daily Standard, 1878–81
Shreveport Southwestern, 1865–71
Shreveport Times, 1871–77, 1879–84
Tangipahoa Democrat, 1874
Tensas Gazette, 1872–74, 1879–84
Vermilion, *Abbeville Meridional,* 1877–81
West Baton Rouge Sugar Planter, 1866–70

Published Accounts, Articles, and Documents

Cable, George W., and George E. Waring. *History and Present Conditions of New Orleans.* Washington, 1981, 213–95.
Dennett, Daniel. *Louisiana As It Is.* New Orleans, 1876.
Ellwood, Charles A. "Has Crime Increased in the United States Since 1880." *Journal of Criminal Law and Criminology and Police Science,* 1, 1910–11, 382–83.
Hilgard, Eugene W. *Report on Cotton Production of the State of Louisiana.* Washington, 1884.
Lockett, Samuel A. *Louisiana As It Is; A Geographical and Topographical Description of the State.* 1873. Reprint, Baton Rouge, 1969.
Nordhoff, Charles. *The Cotton States in the Spring and Summer of 1875.* New York, 1876.

Ramage, B. J. "Homicide in the Southern States," *The Sewanee Review,* 4, 1895–1896, 211–25.

Redfield, Horace V. *Homicide, North and South.* Philadelphia, 1880.

Warmoth, Henry C. *War, Politics and Reconstruction: Stormy Days in Louisiana.* New York, 1930.

Wells-Barnett, Ida B. *On Lynchings: Southern Horrors; A Red Record & Mob Rule in New Orleans.* 1895. Reprint, New York, 1969.

———. *County-Parish Boundaries in Louisiana.* W.P.A., New Orleans, 1939.

Biographical Accounts and Dictionaries

Biographical and Historical Memoirs of Louisiana. Chicago, 1892.

Booth, Andrew B. *Record of Louisiana Confederate Soldiers and Louisiana Confederate Commands,* 3 vols., Baton Rouge, 1920.

Conrad, Glenn R. *Dictionary of Louisiana Biography,* 2 vols., Lafayette, 1988.

Fortier, Alcee, ed. *Louisiana, Comprising Sketches of Parishes, Towns, Events, Institutions, and Persons, Arranged in Cyclopedic Form,* 3 vols., Atlanta, 1914.

Goodspeed, *Biographical and Historical Memoirs of Northwest Louisiana.* Chicago, 1890.

Livingston, John. *United States Law Register.* New York, 1852, 1854, 1859, 1866, 1868.

Meynier, A., Jr., ed. *Louisiana Biographies.* New Orleans, 1882.

Perkins, A. E., ed. *Who's Who in Colored Louisiana.* New Orleans, 1930.

Perrin, William Henry, ed. *Southwest Louisiana Biographical and Historical Memoirs.* New Orleans, 1891.

Tunnell, Ted, ed. *Carpetbagger from Vermont, The Autobiography of Marshall Harvey Twitchell.* Baton Rouge, 1989.

Whitaker, John S. *Sketches of Life and Character in Louisiana.* New Orleans, 1847.

Secondary Sources

Books

Adler, Freda. *Sisters in Crime: The Rise of the New Female Criminal.* New York, 1975.

Armstrong, Amos L. *Sabine Parish Louisiana, Land of Green Gold.* Shreveport, 1958.

Arnesen, Eric. *Waterfront Workers of New Orleans: Race, Class, and Politics, 1863–1923.* New York, 1991.

Ashkenazi, Elliott. *The Business of Jews in Louisiana, 1840–1875.* Tuscaloosa, 1988.

Ayers, Edward L. *Vengeance and Justice: Crime and Punishment in the Nineteenth-Century American South.* New York, 1984.

Benning, R. C., and O. J. Schroeder. *Homicides in an Urban Community.* Springfield, Ill., 1960.

Bertrand, Alvin L. *The Many Louisianas: Rural Social Areas and Cultural Islands.* Baton Rouge, 1955.

Blassingame, John W. *Black New Orleans, 1860–1880.* Chicago, 1973.

Bohstedt, John. *Riots and Community Politics in England and Wales 1790–1810.* Cambridge, 1983.

Boles, John B., and Evelyn T. Nolen, eds. *Interpreting Southern History, Historiographical Essays in Honor of Sanford W. Higgenbotham.* Baton Rouge, 1987.

Bracey, John H., August Meir, and Elliott Rudwick. *The Rise of the Ghetto.* Belmont, Calif., 1971.

Brasseaux, Carl A. *Acadian to Cajun, Transformation of a People, 1803–1877.* Jackson, Miss., 1992.

Brearly, Henry C. *Homicide in the United States.* Chapel Hill, 1932.

Brown, Richard M. *Strain of Violence, Historical Studies of American Violence and Vigilantism,* New York, 1975.

Bruce, Dickson D., Jr. *Violence and Culture in the Antebellum South.* Austin, 1979.

Brundage, W. Fitzhugh. *Lynching in the New South. Georgia and Virginia, 1880–1930.* Urbana, Ill., 1993.

Butterfield, Fox. *All God's Children: The Bosket Family and the American Tradition.* New York, 1995.

Carter, Hodding, ed. *The Past as Prelude, New Orleans, 1718–1968.* New Orleans, 1969.

Cash, Wilbur. *The Mind of the South.* New York, 1941.

Cashin, Joan E., ed. *A Family Venture: Men and Women on the Southern Frontier.* New York, 1991.

Cockburn, J. S., ed. *Crime in England, 1550–1800.* Princeton, 1977.

Conrad, Glenn R., ed. *The Cajuns: Essays on their Culture and History.* Lafayette, La., 1978.

Cook, Bernard A., and James R. Watson. *Louisiana Labor: From Slavery To "Right-to-Work."* New York, 1985.

Culberson, William C. *Vigilantism: Political History of Private Power in America.* New York, 1990.

Cutler, James E. *Lynch-Law: An Investigation into the History of Lynching in the United States.* New York, 1906.

Daly, Martin, and Margo Wilson. *Homicide.* New York, 1988.

Davis, David Brion. *From Homicide to Slavery, Studies in American Culture.* Oxford, 1986.

Dawson, Joseph G. *Army Generals and Reconstruction, Louisiana, 1862–1877.* Baton Rouge, 1982.

Dormon, James H. *The People Called Cajuns: An Introduction to an Ethnohistory.* Lafayette, La., 1983.

DuBois, W. E. B. *Black Reconstruction.* New York, 1962.

Fields, Barbara J. *Slavery and Freedom on the Middle Ground, Maryland During the Nineteenth Century.* New Haven, 1985.

Fisher, Roger A. *Segregation Struggle in Louisiana, 1862–1877.* Urbana, 1974.

Foner, Eric. *Reconstruction: America's Unfinished Revolution, 1863–1877.* New York, 1988.

Franklin, John Hope. *Reconstruction After the Civil War.* Chicago, 1961.

———. *The Militant South, 1800–1861.* New York, 1964.

Fraser, Walter J., and Winfred B. Moore Jr., eds. *The Southern Enigma: Essays on Race, Class, and Folk Culture.* Westport, Conn., 1983.

Gillette, William. *Retreat From Reconstruction, 1869–1879.* Baton Rouge, 1979.

Graham, Hugh Davis, and Ted Robert Gurr, eds. *Violence in America, Historical & Comparative Perspectives.* Beverly Hills, 1979.

Griffin, Henry Lewis. *The Attakapas County, A History of Lafayette Parish.* Gretna, La., 1974.

Grimsted, David, *American Mobbing, 1828–1861, Toward the Civil War,* New York, 1998.

Gutman, Herbert. *The Black Family in Slavery and Freedom, 1750–1925.* New York, 1976.

Hair, William Ivy. *Bourbonism and Agrarian Protest, Louisiana Politics, 1877–1900.* Baton Rouge, 1969.

———. *Carnival of Fury, Robert Charles and the New Orleans Riot of 1900.* Baton Rouge, 1976.

Henry, Andrew F., and James F. Short Jr. *Suicide and Homicide: Some Economic, Sociological and Psychological Aspects of Aggression.* New York, 1964.

Hindus, Michael S. *Prison and Plantation: Crime, Justice, and Authority in Massachusetts and South Carolina, 1767–1878.* Chapel Hill, 1980.

Hobsbawm, Eric J. *Primitive Rebels, Studies in Archaic Forms of Social Movement in the Nineteenth and Twentieth Centuries.* New York, 1963.

Hoffer, Peter, and N. E. Hull. *Murdering Mothers: Infanticide in England and New England, 1558–1803.* New York, 1981.

Hoffman, Frederic. *The Homicide Problem.* Newark, 1925.

Hyde, Samuel C., Jr. *Pistols and Politics, The Dilemma of Democracy in Louisiana's Florida Parishes, 1810–1899.* Baton Rouge, 1996.

Jackson, Joy J. *New Orleans in the Gilded Age: Politics and Urban Progress, 1880–1896.* New Orleans, 1969.

Jaynes, Gerald D. *Branches Without Roots, Genesis of the Black Working Class in the American South, 1862–1882.* New York, 1986.

Jones, David J. V. *Crime in Nineteenth-Century Wales.* Cardiff, 1992.

Kennedy, Stetson. *After Appomattox: How the South Won the War.* Gainesville, 1995.

Knafla, Louis A., ed. *Crime and Criminal Justice in Europe and Canada.* Waterloo, 1981.

Lane, Roger. *Violent Death in the City: Suicide, Accident & Murders in Nineteenth-Century Philadelphia.* Cambridge, Mass., 1979.

———. *Roots of Violence in Black Philadelphia, 1860–1900.* Cambridge, Mass., 1986.

Litwack, Leon F. *Been in the Storm So Long: The Aftermath of Slavery.* New York, 1979.

Lonn, Ella. *Reconstruction in Louisiana After 1868.* New York, 1918.

Macdonald, Robert R., John R. Kemp, and Edward F. Haas, eds. *Louisiana's Black Heritage.* New Orleans, 1979.

Mandle, Jay R. *The Roots of Black Poverty, The Southern Plantation Economy After the Civil War.* Durham, 1978.

McFeely, W. S. *Yankee Stepfather, General O. O. Howard and the Freedmen.* New Haven, 1968.

McGovern, James R. *Anatomy of a Lynching, The Killing of Claude Neal.* Baton Rouge, 1982.

McGrath, Roger D. *Gunfighters, Highwaymen & Vigilantes, Violence on the Frontier.* Berkeley, 1984.

McWhiney, Grady. *Cracker Culture, Celtic Ways in the Old South.* Tuscaloosa, 1988.

Miller, Kent S., and Ralph N. Dreger, eds. *Comparative Studies of Blacks and Whites in the United States.* New York, 1973.

Mohr, James C. *Abortion in America, The Origins and Evolution of a National Policy, 1800–1900.* New York, 1978.

Newby, I. A. *Jim Crow's Defense, Anti-Negro Thought in America, 1900–1930.* Baton Rouge, 1965.

Nisbett, Richard E., and Dov Cohen. *Culture of Honor: The Psychology of Violence in the South.* Boulder, Colo., 1996.

Nolan, Patrick B. *Vigilantes On the Middle Border, A Study of Self-Appointed Law Enforcement of the Upper Mississippi from 1840 to 1880.* New York, 1987.

Perman, Michael. *The Road to Redemption: Southern Politics, 1869–1879.* Chapel Hill, 1984.

Rable, George C. *But There Was No Peace: The Role of Violence in the Politics of Reconstruction*. Athens, Ga., 1984.

Rabinowitz, Howard N. *Race Relations in the Urban South, 1865–1890*. Urbana, 1980.

———. *Race, Ethnicity and Urbanization, Selected Essays*. Columbia, 1994.

Rosenbaum, H. Jon, and Peter C. Sedeiberg, eds. *Vigilante Politics*. Philadelphia, 1976.

Rudé, George. *The Crowd in History: A Study of Popular Disturbances in France and England 1730–1848*. New York, 1964.

Scott, Annie Firor. *The Southern Lady, From Pedestal to Politics, 1830–1930*. Chicago, 1970.

Sefton, J. E. *The United States Army and Reconstruction*. Baton Rouge, 1967.

Shapiro, Herbert. *White Violence and Black Response, From Reconstruction to Montgomery*. Amherst, 1988.

Shugg, Roger W. *Origins of Class Struggle in Louisiana, A Social History of White Farmers and Laborers During Slavery and After, 1840–1875*. Baton Rouge, 1969.

Sinclair, Harold. *The Port of New Orleans*. New York, 1942.

Singletary, Otis. *Negro Militia and Reconstruction*. Austin, 1957.

Slotkin, Richard. *Regeneration Through Violence, The Mythology of the American Frontier, 1600–1860*. Middleton, Conn., 1973.

Smart, Carol. *Women, Crime and Criminology: A Feminist Critique*, London, 1976.

Spear, Allan H. *Black Chicago, The Making of a Negro Ghetto, 1890–1920*. Chicago, 1967.

Stevenson, John. *Popular Disturbances in England, 1700–1870*. London, 1979.

Summers, Mark W. *The Era of Good Stealings*. Oxford, 1993.

Taylor, Joe Gray. *Louisiana Reconstructed, 1863–1877*. Baton Rouge, 1974.

Tilly, Charles. *From Mobilization to Revolution*. Reading, Mass., 1978.

Tilly, Louise A., and Charles Tilly, eds. *Class Conflict and Collective Action*. Beverly Hills, 1981.

Tolnay, Stewart E., and E. M. Beck. *A Festival of Violence: An Analysis of Southern Lynchings, 1882–1930*. Urbana, 1992.

Trelease, Allen W. *White Terror: The Ku Klux Klan Conspiracy and Southern Reconstruction*. New York, 1971.

Tunnell, Ted. *Crucible Reconstruction, War, Radicalism and Race in Louisiana, 1862–1877*. Baton Rouge, 1984.

Upton, Dell, ed. *Madaline, Love and Survival in Antebellum New Orleans, The Private Writings of a Kept Woman*. Athens, Ga., 1996.

Vandal, Gilles. *The New Orleans Riot of 1866: The Anatomy of a Tragedy.* Lafayette, La., 1983.

Vincent, Charles. *Black Legislators in Louisiana During Reconstruction.* Baton Rouge, 1976.

Wade, Wynn Craig. *The Fiery Cross: The Ku Klux Klan in America.* New York, 1987.

Walker, Samuel. *Popular Justice: A History of American Criminal Justice.* New York, 1980.

Wayne, Michael. *The Reshaping of Plantation Society, The Natchez District, 1860–1880.* Baton Rouge, 1983.

White, Howard A. *The Freedmen's Bureau in Louisiana.* Baton Rouge, 1970.

White, Walter. *Rope and Faggot: A Biography of Judge Lynch.* New York, 1929.

Wiener, Jonathan. *Social Origins of the New South, Alabama, 1860–1865.* Baton Rouge, 1978.

Williams, Jack Kinney. *Vogues in Villainy, Crime and Retribution in Antebellum South Carolina.* Charleston, 1959.

Williamson, Frederick W., and Lillian Herron Williamson. *Northeast Louisiana: A Narrative of the Ouachita River Valley and the Concordia Country.* Monroe, 1939.

Williamson, Joel. *The Crucible of Race: Black-White Relations in the American South Since Emancipation.* New York, 1984.

Wolfgang, Marvin E. *Crime and Race: Conception and Misconceptions.* New York, 1964.

———. *Patterns in Criminal Homicide.* Philadelphia, 1958.

Wolfgang, Marvin, and Franco Ferracuti. *The Subculture of Violence, Toward an Integrating Theory of Criminality.* New York, 1967.

Wolfgang, M. E., ed. *Studies in Homicides.* New York, 1967.

Wood, Forrest G. *Black Scare: The Racist Response to Emancipation and Reconstruction.* Berkeley, 1968.

Wright, George C. *Racial Violence in Kentucky, 1865–1940: Lynchings, Mob Rule and 'Legal Lynching.'* Baton Rouge, 1990.

Wrigley, E. A., ed., *Nineteenth-Century Society: Essays in the Use of Quantitative Methods For the Study of Social Data.* Cambridge, 1972.

Wyatt-Brown, Bertram. *Southern Honor, Ethics & Behavior in the Old South.* New York, 1982.

Zehr, Howard. *Crime and the Development of Modern Society: Patterns of Criminality in Nineteenth-Century Germany and France.* London, 1976.

———. *A History of Morgan City.* Morgan City, 1960.

Articles

Allen, H. David, and William B. Bankston. "Another Look at the Southern Culture of Violence Hypothesis: The Case of Louisiana." *Southern Studies*, 20, Spring 1981, 55–66.

Baenziger, Ann Patton. "The Texas State Police During Reconstruction: A Reexamination." *Southwestern Historical Quarterly*, 72, April 1969, 470–91.

Bagozzi, R. P. "Populism and Lynching in Louisiana: Comment on Inverarity." *American Sociological Review*, 42, 1977, 355–58.

Bankston, William B., and H. David Allen. "Rural Social Areas and Patterns of Homicide: An Analysis of Lethal Violence in Louisiana." *Rural Sociology*, 45, 1980, 223–37.

Baron, Larry, and Murray A. Straus. "Cultural and Economic Sources of Homicide in the United States." *Sociological Quarterly*, 29, no. 3, 1988, 371–90.

Beale, Howard K. "On Rewriting Reconstruction History." *American Historical Review*, 45, July 1940, 807–27.

Beattie, J. M. "The Patterns of Crime in England, 1660–1800." *Past and Present*, 62, February 1974, 47–95.

———. "The Criminality of Women in Eighteenth-Century England." *Journal of Social History*, 8, 1975, 80–116.

Black, Donald J. "Production of Crime Rates." *American Sociological Review*, 35, August 1970, 733–47.

Blackwell, James W. "Ethnic Inequality and the Rates of Homicides." *Social Forces*, 69, September 1990, 53–70.

Blau, Judith R., and Peter M. Blau. "The Cost of Inequality: Metropolitan Structure and Violent Crimes." *American Sociological Review*, 47, 1982, 114–29.

Bodenhamer, David J. "Law and Disorder on the Early Frontier: Marion County, Indiana, 1823–1850." *Western Historical Quarterly*, 10, July 1979, 323–36.

Bohstedt, John, and Dale E. Williams. "The Diffusion of Riots: The Patterns of 1766, 1795 and 1801 in Devonshire." *Journal of Interdisciplinary History*, 19, Summer 1988, 1–24.

Bonacich, Edna. "A Theory of Ethnic Antagonism: The Split Labor Market." *American Sociological Review*, 37, 1972, 547–59.

Brenzel, Barbara. "Domestication as Reform: A Study of the Socialization of Wayward Girls, 1856–1905." *Harvard Educational Review*, 50, May 1980, 196–213.

Brown, Richard Maxwell. "Southern Violence–Regional Problem or National Nemesis?: Legal Attitudes Toward Southern Homicide in Historical Perspective." *Vanderbilt Law Review*, 32, 1979, 219–33.

Bull, Jacqueline P. "The General Merchant in the Economic History of the New South." *Journal of Southern History,* 18, 1952, 37–59.

Bullock, Henry Allen. "Urban Homicides in Theory and Fact." *Journal of Criminal Law, Criminology and Police Science,* 45, 1955, 565–75.

Cantrell, Gregg. "Racial Violence and Reconstruction Policy in Texas, 1867–1868." *Southwestern Historical Quarterly,* January 1990, 333–55.

Cardwell, Guy H. "The Duel in the Old South: Crux of a Concept." *South Atlantic Quarterly,* 66, Winter 1967, 50–69.

Carpenter, John A. "Atrocities in the Reconstruction Period." *Journal of Negro History,* 47, October 1962, 234–47.

Chenault, William W., and Robert C. Reinders. "The Northern-born Community of New Orleans." *Journal of American History,* 51, September 1964, 232–47.

Clark, Thomas D. "In the Southern Retail Trade After 1865." *Journal of Economic History,* 33, December 1944, 38–47.

———. "The Furnishing and Supply System in Southern Agriculture Since 1865." *Journal of Southern History,* 12, 1946, 22–44.

Cockburn, J. S. "Patterns of Violence in English Society: Homicide in Kent 1560–1985." *Past & Present,* 130, February 1991, 70–106.

Cohen, David, and Eric A. Johnson. "French Criminality: Urban-Rural Differences in the Nineteenth Century." *Journal of Interdisciplinary History,* 13, no. 3, Winter 1982, 477–501.

Cole, A. J. "The Moral Economy of the Crowd: Some Twentieth-Century Food Riotings." *Journal of British Studies,* 17, Fall 1978, 157–76.

Connor, William P. "Reconstruction Rebels: The New Orleans Tribune in Post-War Louisiana." *Louisiana History,* 21, no. 2, Spring 1980, 159–81.

Conway, Allan. "New Orleans as a Port of Immigration, 1820–1860." *Louisiana Studies,* 1, Fall 1962, 1–17.

Cook, Bernard A. "The Typographical Union and the New Orleans General Strike of 1892." *Louisiana History,* 34, Fall 1983, 377–88.

Corzine, Jay, James Creech, and Lin Corzine. "Black Concentration and Lynchings in the South: Testing Blalock's Power-Threat Hypothesis." *Social Forces,* 61, March 1983, 774–96.

Corzine, Jay, Lin Huff-Corzine, and James C. Creech. "The Tenant Labor Market and Lynching in the South: A Test of Split Labor Market Theory." *Sociological Inquiry,* 58, Summer 1988, 261–78.

Crouch, Barry A. "A Spirit of Lawlessness: White Violence; Texas Blacks, 1865–1868." *Journal of Social History,* 18, Winter 1984, 217–32.

Dauphine, James G. "The Knights of the White Camellia and the Election of 1868: Louisiana's White Terrorists; a Benighting Legacy." *Louisiana History,* 30, Spring 1989, 173–90.

Delatte, Carolyn E. "The St. Landry Riot: A Forgotten Incident of Reconstruction Violence." *Louisiana History,* 17, Winter 1976, 41–49.

Dethloff, Henry C., and Robert R. Jones. "Race Relations in Louisiana, 1877–1898." *Louisiana History,* 9, Fall 1968, 301–23.

Estaville, Lawrence E. "The Louisiana French in 1900." *Journal of Historical Geography,* 14, January 1988, 342–59.

Estaville, Lawrence E., Jr. "Changeless Cajuns: Nineteenth-Century Reality and Myth." *Louisiana History,* 28, 1987, 117–40.

Ettinger, Brian Gary. "John Fitzpatrick and the Limits of Working-class Politics in New Orleans, 1892–1896." *Louisiana History,* 26, Fall 1985, 341–67.

Ethington, Philip J. "Vigilantes and the Police: The Creation of a Professional Police Bureaucracy in San Francisco, 1847–1900." *Journal of Social History,* 21, Winter 1987, 197–227.

Feeley, Malcom. "The Decline of Women in the Criminal Process: A Comparative History." *American Justice History,* 15, 1994, 235–74.

Ferdinand, Theodore W. "The Criminal Patterns of Boston Since 1849." *American Journal of Sociology,* 73, July 1967, 84–99.

Fisher, Roger A. "A Pioneer Protest: The New Orleans Street Car Controversy of 1867." *Journal of Negro History,* 53, July 1968, 219–33.

Garfinkel, Harold. "Research Notes on Inter and Intra-Racial Homicides." *Social Forces,* 27, 1949, 469–81.

Gastill, Raymond P. "Homicides and a Regional Culture of Violence." *American Sociological Review,* 36, 1971, 412–27.

Goldin, Claudia. "Female Labor Force Participation: The Origins of Black and White Difference, 1870–1880." *Journal of Economic History,* 37, March 1977, 91–96.

Gonthier, Nicole. "Délinquantes ou victimes, les femmes dans la soiété lyonnaise au Xve siècle." *Revue Historique,* 1984, 24–46.

Gould, Jeffrey. "The Strike of 1887: Louisiana Sugar War." *Southern Exposure,* 12, November-December 1984, 45–55.

Graff, Harvey J. "Crime and Punishment in the Nineteenth Century: A New Look at the Criminal." *Journal of Interdisciplinary History,* 7, Winter 1977, 477–91.

———. "A Reply." *Journal of Interdisciplinary History,* 9, Winter 1979, 465–71.

Granada, Ray. "Violence: An Instrument of Policy in Reconstruction Alabama." *Alabama Historical Quarterly,* 30, Fall-Winter 1968, 191–202.

Hackney, Sheldon. "Southern Violence." *American Historical Review,* 74, February 1969, 906–25.

Hanawalt, Barbara. "The Female Felon in Fourteenth-Century England." *Viator,* 5, 1974, 253–68.

Harr, John L. "Law and Lawlessness in the Lower Mississippi Valley,

1815–1860." *Northeast Missouri State College Studies,* 19, June 1955, 51–70.

Harris, W. Stuart. "Rowdyism, Public Drunkenness, and Bloody Encounters in Early Perry County." *Alabama Review,* 33, no. 1, January 1980, 15–24.

Heitmann, John A. "Responding to the Competition: The Louisiana Sugar Planters' Association, The Tariff, and the Formation of the Louisiana Sugar Exchange, 1877–1885." *Southern Studies,* 25, Winter 1986, 315–40.

Hennessey, Melinda M. "Race and Violence in Reconstruction New Orleans: The 1868 Riot." *Louisiana History,* 20 Winter, 1979, 77–92.

———. "Political Terrorism in the Black Belt: The Eutaw Riot." *Alabama Review,* 33, January 1980, 112–25.

Highsmith, William E. "Louisiana Landholding During War and Reconstruction." *Louisiana Historical Quarterly,* 38, January 1955, 39–55.

Hodes, Martha. "The Sexualization of Reconstruction Politics: White Women and Black Men in the South After the Civil War." *Journal of Historical Sexuality,* 3, January 1993, 402–17.

Holmes, William F. "Whitecapping in Mississippi: Agrarian Violence in the Populist Area." *Mid-America,* 55, April 1973, 134–48.

———. "Whitecapping: Agrarian Violence in Mississippi, 1902–1906." *Journal of Southern History,* 35, 1969, 165–85.

Huff-Corzine, Lin, Jay Corzine, and David C. Moore. "Southern Exposure: Deciphering the South's Influence on Homicide Rates." *Social Forces,* 64, June 1986, 1906–24.

Ingalls, Robert P. "Lynching and Establishment Violence in Tampa, 1858–1935." *Journal of Social History,* 53, no. 4, November 1987, 613–44.

Inverarity, James M. "Populism and Lynching in Louisiana, 1889–1896: A Test of Erickson's Theory of the Relationship Between Boundary Crises and Repressive Justice." *American Sociological Review,* 41, April 1976, 262–80.

Jackson, Joy. "Crime and the Conscience of a City." *Louisiana History,* 9, no. 3, Summer 1968, 229–44.

Johnson, David A. "Vigilance and the Law: The Moral Authority of Popular Justice in the Far West." *American Quarterly,* 33, Winter 1981, 558–86.

Johnson, Eric A. "Cities Don't Cause Crime: Urban-Rural Differences in Late Nineteenth and Early Twentieth-Century German Criminality." *Social Science History,* 16, Spring 1992, 129–76.

———. "Women as Victims and Criminals: Female Homicide and Criminality in Imperial Germany, 1873–1914." *Criminal Justice History,* 6, 1985, 151–75.

Jones, W. R. "Violence, Criminality, and Culture Disjunction on the

Anglo-Irish Frontier: The Example of Armagh, 1350–1550." *Criminal Justice History*, 2, 1981, 29–47.

Kilpatrick, J. J. "Murder in the Deep South." *Survey Graphic*, 32, October 1943, 395–97.

Kloek, Els. "Criminality and Gender in Leiden's Confessieboeken, 1678–1794." *Criminal Justice History*, 11, 1990, 1–29.

Lack, Paul. "Slavery and Vigilantism in Austin, Texas, 1840–1860." *Southwestern Historical Quarterly*, 85, no. 1, July 1981, 1–20.

Land, Kenneth C., Patricia L. McCall, and Laurence E. Cohen. "Structural Covariates of Homicide Rates: Are There any Invariances across Time and Regional Space?" *American Journal of Sociology*, 95, January 1990, 922–63.

Lane, Roger. "Crime and Criminal Statistics in Nineteenth-Century Massachusetts." *Journal of Social History*, Winter 1968, 156–63.

Leach, Marguerite T. "The Aftermath of Reconstruction in Louisiana." *Louisiana Historical Quarterly*, July 1949, 631–716.

Lebsock, Suzanne. "Radical Reconstruction and Property Rights of Southern Women." *Journal of Southern History*, May 1977, 195–216.

Lively, Charles E., and Cecil L. Gregory. "The Sociocultural Area As A Field For Research." *Rural Sociology*, 1953, 21–31.

Loftin, Colin, and Robert H. Hill. "Regional Subculture and Homicides: An Examination of the Gastill-Hackney Thesis." *American Sociological Review*, 39, October 1974, 714–24.

Lottier, Stuart. "Distribution of Criminal Offences in Sectional Regions." *Journal of Criminal Law*, 29, May-June 1938, 329–44.

Maltz, Michael D. "Crime Statistics: A Historical Perspective." *Crime and Delinquency*, January 1977, 32–40.

Marks, Carole. "Split Labor Markets and Black-White Relations, 1865–1920." *Phylon*, 62, Winter 1981, 293–308.

May, J. Thomas. "The Freedmen's Bureau at the Local Level: A Study of a Louisiana Agent." *Louisiana History*, 9, Winter 1968, 5–19.

McHale, Vincent E., and Jeffrey Bergner. "Collective and Individual Violence: Berlin and Vienna, 1875–1913." *Criminal Justice History*, 2, 1981, 31–61.

Messner, Steven F. "Regional and Racial Effects on the Urban Homicide Rates: The Subculture of Violence Revisited." *American Journal of Sociology*, 88, 1983, 997–1007.

Millett, Donald J. "The Lumber Industry of 'Imperial' Calcasieu: 1865–1900." *Louisiana History*, 7, Winter 1966, 51–69.

———. "Some Aspects of Agricultural Retardation in Southwest Louisiana, 1865–1900." *Louisiana History*, 11, Winter 1970, 37–67.

———. "Cattle and Cattlemen of Southwest Louisiana, 1860–1900." *Louisiana History*, 28, no. 3, Summer 1987, 311–29.

Monkkonen, Eric H. "The Organized Response to Crime in Nineteenth and Twentieth Century America." *Journal of Interdisciplinary History,* 14, Summer 1983, 113–28.

———. "A Disorderly People: Urban Crime in Nineteenth and Twentieth Century." *Journal of American History,* 68, December 1981, 539–59.

———. "Systematic Criminal Justice History: Some Suggestions." *Journal of Interdisciplinary History,* 9, Winter 1979, 451–64.

———. "New York City Homicides: A Research Note." *Social Science History,* 19, Summer 1995, 201–14.

Newton, Lewis W. "Creoles and Anglo-Americans in Old Louisiana: A Study in Cultural Conflicts." *Southwestern Social Science Quarterly,* 14, 1933, 31–48.

Noah, Elmer. "Politics and Reconstruction in Morehouse Parish (1872–1877)." *North Louisiana Historical Association Journal,* 7, no. 1, Fall 1975, 12–19.

Norris, Marjorie M. "An Early Instance of Nonviolence: The Louisville Demonstrations of 1870–1871." *Journal of Southern History,* 32, November 1966, 487–504.

Nye, Robert A. "Crime in Modern Societies: Some Research Strategies For Historians." *Journal of Social History,* 11, Summer 1978, 491–507.

Otten, James T. "The Wheeler Adjustment in Louisiana: National Republicans Begin to Reappraise Their Reconstruction Policy." *Louisiana History,* 13, Fall 1972, 349–67.

Parker, Robert Nash. "Poverty, Subculture of Violence, and Type of Homicide." *Social Forces,* 67, June 1989, 983–1007.

Peek, Ralph L. "Lawlessness in Florida, 1868–1871." *Florida Historical Quarterly,* 40, October 1961, 164–85.

Peoples, Morgan D. "'Kansas Fever' in North Louisiana." *Louisiana History,* 11, Spring 1970, 121–35.

Perrot, Michel. "Délinquences et systèmes pénitentiaires en France au XIXe siècle." *Annales, Économie, Société, Civilisations,* Janvier-Fevrier 1975, 67–91.

Peterson, David. "Wife-beating: An American Tradition." *Journal of Interdisciplinary History,* 23, Summer 1992, 97–118.

Pettigrew, Thomas F., and Rosalind B. Spier. "The Ecological Structure of Negro Homicides." *American Journal of Sociology,* 67, no. 6, Spring 1962, 621–29.

Pfeifer, Michael. "Lynching and Criminal Justice in South Louisiana, 1878–1930." *Louisiana History,* 40, no. 2, Spring 1999, 155–77.

Phillips, Charles David. "Exploring Relations Among Forms of Social Control: The Lynching and Execution of Blacks in North Carolina, 1889–1918." *Law & Society Review,* 21, 1987, 362–73.

Pleck, E. "Wife-beating in Nineteenth-Century America." *Victimology*, 4, 1979, 60–74.

Pope, Whity, and Charles Ragan. "Mechanical Solidarity, Repressive Justice and Lynching in Louisiana." *American Sociological Review*, 42, April 1977, 363–70.

Porterfield, Austin L. "Indices of Suicides and Homicides by States and Cities: Some Southern–Non-Southern Constitutions with Implications for Research." *American Sociological Review*, 14, 1949, 481–92.

Radelet, Michael L., and Glenn L. Pierce. "Race and Prosecutorial Discretion in Homicide Cases." *Law & Society Review*, 19, 1985, 587–621.

Rankin, David C. "The Impact of the Civil War on the Free Colored Community of New Orleans." *Perspectives in American History*, 1977–78, 379–415.

———. "The Origins of Black Leadership in New Orleans During Reconstruction." *Journal of Southern History*, 40, August 1974, 417–40.

Ransom, Roger L., and Richard Sutch. "The Ex-slave in the Post-Bellum South: A Study of the Economic Impact of Racism in a Market Environment." *Journal of Economic History*, 33, March 1973, 131–48.

Reed, Germaine A. "Race Legislation in Louisiana, 1864–1920." *Louisiana History*, 6, Fall 1965, 379–92.

Reed, John S. "To Live—And Die—In Dixie: A Contribution to the Study of Southern Violence." *Political Science Quarterly*, 86, September 1971, 429–43.

———. "Percent Black and Lynching: A Test of Blalock's Theory." *Social Forces*, 50, March 1972, 356–60.

Robinson, Armstead L. "Beyond the Realm of Social Consensus: New Meanings of Reconstruction for American History." *Journal of American History*, 78, September 1981, 276–97.

Roland, Charles P. "Difficulties of Civil War Sugar Planting in Louisiana." *Louisiana Historical Quarterly*, 38, October 1955, 40–62.

Rosenberg, Charles E. "Sexuality, Class, and Role in 19th-Century America." *American Quarterly*, 25, 1973, 131–53.

Rudé, George. "English Rural and Urban Disturbances on the Eve of the First Reform Bill, 1830–31." *Past and Present*, 37, July 1967, 87–102.

Sampson, Robert J. "Urban Black Violence: The Effect of Male Joblessness and Family Disruption." *American Journal of Sociology*, 93, no. 2, September 1987, 348–82.

Schultz, Leroy C. "Why Negroes Carry Weapons." *Journal of Criminal Law: Criminology and Police Science*, 53, December 1962, 476–83.

Sederberg, Peter. "The Phenomonology of Vigilantism in Contemporary America: An Interpretation." *Terrorism: An International Journal*, 1, 1978, 287–303.

Shannon, Lyle. "The Spatial Distribution of Criminal Offences by States." *Journal of Criminal Law*, 45, September-October 1954, 264–73.

Sharpe, J. A. "Domestic Homicide in Early Modern England." *The Historical Journal*, 24, no. 1, 1981, 29–48.

Shapiro, Herbert. "The Ku Klux Klan During Reconstruction: The South Carolina Episode." *Journal of Negro History*, 49, January 1964, 35–55.

———. "Afro-American Responses to Race Violence During Reconstruction." *Science and Society*, Summer 1972, 158–70.

Shin, Yangsock, Davor Jedlicko, and Everett S. Lee. "Homicide Among Blacks." *Phylon*, 38, 1977, 398–407.

Shugg, Roger Wallace. "The New Orleans General Strike of 1892." *Louisiana Historical Quarterly*, 21, 1938, 547–60.

Singletary, Otis A. "The Election of 1878 in Louisiana." *Louisiana Historical Quarterly*, 40, January 1957, 46–53.

Sisk, Glenn N. "Rural Merchandising in the Alabama Black Belt, 1875–1917." *Journal of Farm Economics*, 37, no. 4, November 1955, 705–15.

———. "Town Business in the Alabama Black Belt, 1875–1917." *Mid-America*, 38, January 1956, 47–55.

Sloan, John Z. "The Ku Klux Klan and the Alabama Election of 1872." *Alabama Review*, 18, April 1965, 113–24.

Smallwood, James. "Perpetuation of Caste: Black Agricultural Workers in Reconstruction Texas." *Mid-America*, 61, January 1979, 5–23.

Smith, Albert C. "'Southern Violence' Reconsidered: Arson as Protest in Black Belt Georgia, 1865–1910." *Journal of Southern History*, 51, November 1985, 526–64.

Snyder, David, and Charles Tilly. "Hardship and Collective Violence in France, 1830 to 1960." *American Sociological Review*, 48, October 1972, 520–32.

Somers, Dale A. "Black and White in New Orleans: A Study in Urban Race Relations, 1865–1900." *Journal of Southern History*, February 1974, 19–42.

Spierenburg, Pieter. "Faces of Violence: Homicide Trends and Cultural Meanings: Amsterdam, 1431–1816." *Journal of Social History*, 27, Summer 1994, 701–16.

Staples, Robert. "White Racism, Black Crime and American Justice: An Application of the Colonial Model to Explain Crime and Race." *Phylon*, 36, 1975, 14–22.

Szuchman, Mark D. "Disorder and Social Control in Buenos Aires, 1810–1860." *Journal of Interdisciplinary History*, 17, Summer 1984, 83–110.

Thompson, Edward P. "The Moral Economy of the English Crowd in the Eighteenth Century." *Past and Present*, 50, 1971, 73–136.

Thompson, I. A. "A Map of Crime in Sixteenth-Century Spain." *Economic History Review*, 21, August 1968, 244–67.

Tolnay, Stewart E., and E. M. Beck. "Black Flight: Lethal Violence and the Great Migration, 1900–1930." *Social Science History,* 14, no. 3, Fall 1990, 347–70.

Tolnay, Stewart E., E. M. Beck, and James L. Massey. "Black Lynchings: The Power Threat Hypothesis Revisited." *Social Forces,* 67, March 1989, 605–27.

Tregle, Joseph G. "Early New Orleans Society: A Reappraisal." *Journal of Southern Society,* 18, February 1952, 21–36.

Tunnell, T. B., Jr. "The Negro, The Republican Party, and the Election of 1876 in Louisiana." *Louisiana History,* 7, Spring 1966, 112–13.

Vandal, Gilles. "Politics and Violence in Bourbon Louisiana: The Loreauville Riot of 1884 as a Case Study." *Louisiana History* 30, no. 1, Winter 1989, 23–42.

———. "When Religion Mingled With Commerce: The Controversy Surrounding the Louisiana Sunday Law of 1878." *Mid-America,* 70, October 1988, 141–55.

———. "The Policy of Violence in Caddo Parish, 1865–1884." *Louisiana History,* 32, Spring 1991, 159–82.

———. "'Bloody Caddo': White Violence Against Blacks in a Louisiana Parish, 1865–1876." *Journal of Social History,* 25, December 1991, 373–88.

———. "Black Violence in Post–Civil War Louisiana." *Journal of Interdisciplinary History,* 25, Summer 1994, 45–64.

———. "Albert H. Leonard's Road from the White League to the Republican Party: A Political Enigma." *Louisiana History,* 36, Winter 1995, 55–74.

———. "Black Utopia In Early Reconstructed New Orleans: The People's Bakery as a Case-Study." *Louisiana History,* 38, Summer 1997, 437–52.

———. "Property Offenses, Social Tension and Racial Antagonism in Post–Civil War Rural Louisiana." *Journal of Social History,* 31, September 1997, 127–53.

Walker, Samuel. "Counting Cops and Crime." *Review of American History,* 10, June 1982, 212–17.

Wasserman, Ibra M. "Southern Violence and the Political Process: Comment on Inverarity." *American Sociological Review,* 42, 1977, 359–62.

Webb, Allie B. "Organization and Activities of the Knights of White Camellia in Louisiana, 1867–1869." *The Proceedings of the Louisiana Academy of Sciences,* 17, March 1954, 110–18.

Wetta, Frank J. "'Bulldozing the Scalawags': Some Examples of the Persecution of Southern White Republicans in Louisiana During Reconstruction." *Louisiana History,* 21, Winter 1980, 43–58.

Wiegman, Robin. "The Anatomy of Lynching." *Journal of Historical Sexuality,* 3, January 1993, 445–67.

Williams, Harry T. "The Louisiana Unification Movement of 1873." *Journal of Southern History,* 11, August 1945, 349–69.

Williams, Kirk R. "Economic Sources of Homicide: Reestimating the Effects of Poverty and Inequality." *American Sociological Review,* 49, April 1985, 283–89.

Wrightson, Keith. "Infanticide in European History." *Criminal Justice History,* 3, 1982, 1–21.

Young, Eric Van. "Agrarian Rebellion and Defense Community: Meaning and Collective Violence in Late Colonial and Independence Era Mexico." *Journal of Social History,* 27, Winter 1993, 245–69.

———. "Islands in the Storm: Quiet Cities and Violent Countryside in the Mexican Independence Era." *Past and Present,* 118, 1988, 130–55.

Zehr, Howard. "The Modernization of Crimes in Germany and France, 1830–1919." *Journal of Social History,* 8, 1975, 117–41.

Dissertations and Theses

Clay, Floyd M. "Economic Survival of the Plantation System within the Feliciana Parishes." M.A. thesis, Louisiana State University, 1962.

Pearce, Arthur R. "The Rise and Decline of Labor in New Orleans." M.A. thesis, Tulane University, 1938.

Rousey, Denis C. "The New Orleans Police, 1805–1889: A Social History." Ph.D. diss., Cornell University, 1978.

Singletary, Otis A. "The Reassertion of White Supremacy in Louisiana." M.A. thesis, Louisiana State University, 1949.

Snyder, Perry A. "Shreveport During the Civil War and Reconstruction." Ph.D. diss., Florida State University, 1979.

Uzee, Philip D. "Republican Politics in Louisiana, 1877–1900." Ph.D. diss., Louisiana State University, 1950.

Webb, Allie B. "Methods and Mechanisms Used To Restore White Supremacy in Louisiana." M.A. thesis, Louisiana State University, 1948.

Webb-Windham, Allie B. "A History of Negro Voting in Louisiana, 1877–1906." Ph.D. diss., Louisiana State University, 1962.

Index

The History of Crime and Criminal Justice Series
David R. Johnson and Jeffrey S. Adler, Series Editors

The series explores the history of crime and criminality, violence, criminal justice, and legal systems without restrictions as to chronological scope, geographical focus, or methodological approach.

Controlling Vice: Regulating Brothel Prostitution in St. Paul, 1865–1883
Joel Best

Murder in America: A History
Roger Lane

Violent Death in the City: Suicide, Accident, and Murder in Nineteenth-Century Philadelphia, 2nd Edition
Roger Lane

Race, Labor, and Punishment in the New South
Martha A. Myers

Men and Violence: Gender, Honor, and Rituals in Modern Europe and America
Edited by Pieter Spierenburg